THE GEOPOLITICAL ECONOMY OF FOOTBALL

This book examines the new geopolitical economy of football, exploring the intersection of money, politics, and power in the world's most popular sport.

Against a background of international conflict and the emergence of powerful new state actors in world sport, the book considers how football investments and events have become instruments of soft power and industrial development, and how football plays an increasingly significant role in global politics and international relations. Featuring the work of leading researchers from around the world, and case studies from five continents, the book examines key contemporary issues such as the Gulf States' interests in European soccer and debates around 'sportwashing' and human rights, the global politics of artificial intelligence (AI) in football, and football's complex relationship with migration and identity in Africa and Latin America. It considers the seismic impact of Russia's invasion of Ukraine on the geopolitics of football; on the shifting landscape of the governance of football in Europe; the rise of Major League Soccer and the 'Messi effect', and how the development of China and India into global economic superpowers is reflected in their vision for their domestic football leagues. The book also considers the importance of Fédération Internationale de Football Association (FIFA) and their commercial partners and stakeholders as geopolitical actors on the world stage.

This is a fascinating read for anybody with an interest in sport, political economy, international politics, globalisation, or development.

Simon Chadwick is a Professor of Sport and Geopolitical Economy. Over the last three decades, he has worked extensively with some of the most prominent people and organisations in world football, including clubs, governing bodies, tournament organisers, and sponsors.

Paul Widdop is Reader at Manchester Metropolitan University, UK. His research explores social and economic networks around the consumption and production of sport. He has published widely in the areas of sport and culture including articles in the *Journal of Consumer Culture, Cultural Sociology, Cultural Trends, Electoral Studies,* and the *Journal of Political Marketing.* Widdop serves on the editorial board of several academic journals and is co-founder of the Football Collective, a learned society of academics researching impacts of football on society.

Michael M. Goldman is Professor with the Sport Management Program at the University of San Francisco, USA, while also working with the Gordon Institute of Business Science in South Africa. He works with students, managers, and clients to enhance their abilities to acquire, grow, and retain profitable customers and fans.

THE GEOPOLITICAL ECONOMY OF FOOTBALL

Where Power Meets Politics and Business

Edited by Simon Chadwick, Paul Widdop and Michael M. Goldman

LONDON AND NEW YORK

Designed cover image: Ahmad on Unsplash

First published 2025
by Routledge
4 Park Square, Milton Park, Abingdon, Oxon OX14 4RN

and by Routledge
605 Third Avenue, New York, NY 10158

Routledge is an imprint of the Taylor & Francis Group, an informa business

© 2025 selection and editorial matter, Simon Chadwick, Paul Widdop and
Michael M. Goldman; individual chapters, the contributors

The right of Simon Chadwick, Paul Widdop and Michael M. Goldman to be
identified as the authors of the editorial material, and of the authors for their
individual chapters, has been asserted in accordance with sections 77 and 78 of
the Copyright, Designs and Patents Act 1988.

British Library Cataloguing-in-Publication Data
A catalogue record for this book is available from the British Library

ISBN: 978-1-032-75369-0 (hbk)
ISBN: 978-1-032-75364-5 (pbk)
ISBN: 978-1-003-47367-1 (ebk)

DOI: 10.4324/9781003473671

Typeset in Optima
by KnowledgeWorks Global Ltd.

CONTENTS

LIST OF CONTRIBUTORS

Timur Absalyamov is an independent researcher, who holds a MSc in Economics and a MA in Sports Ethics and Integrity. Timur's fields of expertise include Russian football, funding mechanisms of football clubs, geopolitics of sport, sport as social and cultural phenomenon, and issues of fandom.

Gerard A. Akindes is Sport Management Researcher and Consultant at Northwestern University, Qatar and New York University, USA.

Sergey Altukhov is Professor and Director of the Institute of Sports Management and Law in the Higher School of Law and Administration of the HSE University, Russia. He is the Academics Director of the International Sport Management Master programme at this university. His main research interests deal with good governance in sport and geopolitics in sport. He is a Visiting Professor at the Russian International Olympic University, a member of the Council for Professional Qualifications in Sports, a member of the Expert Council for Physical Culture, Sports and Tourism of the Russian Parliament.

Michael Anagnostou is an academic working for Loughborough University, UK. Michael had a professional industry career over 23 years in sports management which comprised senior positions in organisations such as FIFA, UEFA, Nottingham Forest F.C., Athens 2004 Olympic Games Organising Committee, Super League-Greece, European Leagues Association, and ARIS Thessaloniki F.C.

Georgios A. Antonopoulos is Professor of criminology at Northumbria University, UK. His research interests include 'organised crime', illegal markets, illicit finances, and corruption. He is the editor-in-chief of *Trends in Organised Crime*.

Veronica Astashkina is a sports lawyer, researcher, and The-All Russian State University of Justice law graduate with an analytical mind, and keen interest in successful sports business management strategies.

Raymond Boyle is Professor of Communications (Theatre, Film & Television Studies) at the University of Glasgow, UK.

Laura Bradshaw is an early career researcher in the Institute for Sport Business at Loughborough University London, UK. Laura previously worked in professional football, as well as the London 2012 Olympic and Paralympic Games. Her research interests focus on understanding the high-performance environment in professional sport and its impact on and off the field of play, particularly in the areas of sport innovation, athlete management, performance innovation, and strategic sport management.

Martin Carlsson-Wall is Professor and Director of the Center for Sports and Business at the Stockholm School of Economics, Sweden. His research focuses on how sport organisations can be seen as hybrid organisations in coping with institutional complexity and passionate interests.

Andy Carmichael works on disaster risk reduction projects for the University of Central Lancashire, UK, publishing on a range of subjects relating to environmental activity. A former sports turf lecturer, he has undertaken research in areas such as sustainability in cricket, engagement in climate transitions, and pro-environmental practices for community football clubs.

Vitas Carosella is a freelance writer who has covered sports, politics, and climate for a variety of outlets. He has a master's in International Relations from Institut Barcelona d'Estudis Internacionals and published his thesis on the use of football as a soft power tool in the Gulf. He also has a background in football coaching and covers everything about the game from its history and culture to the business and political sides of the sport.

Samir Ceric is a C-level executive in a number of tech and financial institutions, former Senior Executive in finance, telecom and aviation industries; former Chairman of football club; investor and serial entrepreneur with 20+ years of experience in Asia, Western Europe and the Balkans region; a judge, mentor, philanthropist, board member, public speaker (including London Business School TEDx), alumni member of George Soros Foundation, The Open Society, guest lecturer, and mental health campaigner focused on blockchain technology and innovation in the fields of sport, finance, investment and creative industry, aiming to create more transparency and openings in these industries for high-level investments. He's been labelled as one of the 'UK's Most Powerful People in Art & Fashion' by the Times Magazine and 'London's Top Tastemaker' by Time Out London.

Kristian Coates Ulrichsen is the Fellow for the Middle East at Rice University's Baker Institute for Public Policy, USA. His research spans the history, political and international political economy, and international relations of the Gulf States and their changing position within the global order.

Leon Davis is Senior Lecturer in Marketing and Events Management in the Department of Finance, Performance and Marketing in the Teesside University International Business School at Teesside University, UK. Leon's research interests cover several fields across sports and events including fandom, consumer culture, marketing, user experience (UX), and accessibility provisions. Leon is a Senior Fellow of the Higher Education Academy (SFHEA) and a member of the Chartered Institute for Marketing (CIM).

Kai Demott is Assistant Professor at Concordia University in Montreal, Canada. His research projects mainly focus on interdisciplinary accounting research using qualitative methods and adopting the perspective of accounting as social and institutional practice.

Yoav Dubinsky is Instructor of Sports Business in the Lundquist College of Business at the University of Oregon, USA. His research focuses on sports, nation branding, and public diplomacy, especially in the contexts of international sports, the Olympic Movement, the USA and Israel. He has been involved with the International Olympic Academy as a lecturer, coordinator, and student, using sports as a tool for inclusion in diverse international environments, and was also a visiting research scholar at the University of Southern California Center for Public Diplomacy, USA.

Nick Flowers is a dual-qualified attorney in South Africa and New York, and Associate Attorney at Javelin Sports Consulting. He holds Commerce and Law degrees from the University of the Witwatersrand, South Africa. Specialising in sports law with an LLM from the University of Miami, USA, he's a Vice President at Gridiron South Africa, actively shaping American football's growth nationwide.

Thomas Ross Griffin focuses on the connections between sport and culture, particularly national identity, in the Arabian Gulf. His work on sport in the region, includes amongst others, the legacies of Qatar 2022, national identity performance in the Qatar MNT, and work on road cycling in Qatar.

İlknur Hacısoftaoğlu works in the Department of Sport Management at Istanbul Bilgi University, Turkey. Hacısoftaoğlu has publications in the field of gender, migration, and sports and continues her works in the fields of women, masculinity, migration, and spectatorship in sports.

Richard Haynes is Professor of Communications, Media and Culture at the University of Stirling, UK.

Ren Huitao is Professor in sport management, mainly focused on sport governance and China. Ren also serves as the Deputy Director of the Social Science Development Research Center of Quanzhou Normal University, China, and Researcher in the Institute for Olympic & Global Sport Governance Studies at Wenzhou University, China.

Rahşan İnal is Lecturer at the Faculty of Economics and Administrative Sciences at EBYU, Erzincan, Turkey. Her research interests are in political sociology, social class, migration studies, and sociology of sport. She was a postdoctoral visitor at the School of Sport, Exercise and Health Sciences, Loughborough University, UK.

Olivier Jarosz has over ten years of experience in research and development activities in the European Club Association (ECA), where he was also the Head of Club Affairs and Club Management Programme Director. Having visited over 200 football clubs globally, Olivier is a leading international voice on football management.

Robert Kaspar is Assistant Professor for sports management at the Seeburg Castle University (SCU), Austria. Before, he served as a special events coordinator with the Special Olympics World Winter Games 2017 and in various sports mega events such as the Salzburg bid for the 2010 Olympic Winter Games. In the Netherlands he has been lecturing about football tournaments and leagues.

Vitaly Kazakov is RANNÍS Postdoctoral Fellow at University of Iceland.

Abhishek Khajuria is a PhD candidate at the Centre for European Studies in the School of International Studies in Jawaharlal Nehru University, New Delhi, India. His research interests include sports and politics, the geopolitical economy of sport, sports and nationalism and national identity, European politics, electoral politics, and Indian foreign policy. Presently, he is looking at the role football has played in the Catalan and Basque nationalisms for his PhD thesis.

Ioannis Konstantopoulos is the CEO of The Sports Footprint, a sustainability consultancy focusing on the world of sports and external researcher for the

University of Lausanne, Switzerland. He has been working with numerous clients on sustainability programmes and has also developed several educational courses in sport and sustainability.

Konstantin Kornakov is a club football expert with an analytical mind, a systematic approach to solving football's strategic challenges, and a keen interest in knowledge sharing and multidisciplinary methods, with a combined experience of more than two decades in the football industry in club operational and advisory roles.

Lindsay Sarah Krasnoff is a historian, writer, speaker, and consultant who helps industry professionals be more effective communicators across the global sports arena by drawing on her deep expertise in global sports, communications, and diplomacy.

Daniel Lugner is Doctorate Student at WHU – Otto Beisheim School of Management in Germany. Daniel is interested in the future of sports organisations and ecosystems in a digital and dynamically evolving world.

Argyro Elisavet Manoli is Associate Professor of Marketing and Management in the University of Bergamo, Italy. Her research falls under the themes of marketing communications and integrity in the context of sport and has been published extensively in highly esteemed journals, books, and policy reports.

Sanchit Mehra is a passionate sports enthusiast and management professional. He seamlessly integrates his love for sports with his writing. Drawing from grassroots involvement and high-level sports management, he offers a multifaceted perspective. Through analysis and advocacy, he aims to bring positive change to the dynamic realm of sports.

Steve Menary is Journalist and regular contributor to Play the Game, Josimar and World Soccer magazine. He was part of the team that won a 2023 IJ4EU Impact award for their investigation into football, data, and illegal betting. Steve is a CIES Research scholar and lectured at the universities of East London, Solent and Winchester.

Adam Metelski is a former professional basketball player with experience in the USA and Europe. He has graduated from five universities in economics, psychology, and sociology and is currently Assistant Professor at the Poznań University of Economics and Business, Poland, researching various topics including sport economy and athlete dual careers.

Mark Middling is Assistant Professor of Accounting at Northumbria University, UK. He researches accounting, accountability, and governance in football and completed his doctorate in 2022 entitled 'Accounting for Supporters'. Mark has made many media appearances commenting on football finance and governance matters.

Jacqueline Mueller is Sport Management Lecturer & Leadership Consultant at Loughborough University London, UK.

Stuart Murray is Associate Professor in International Relations and Diplomacy at Bond University, Australia, a Global Fellow at the Academy of Sport at The University of Edinburgh, UK, an Honorary Member of the Centre for Sports Law, Policy, and Diplomacy at the University of Rijeka, Croatia, and an Adjunct Research Fellow at Griffith University, Australia. A globally respected editor, writer, speaker, and expert on International Relations, Diplomacy and Sports Diplomacy, he regularly advises governments, international institutions, and non-state actors on a broad range of matters relating to diplomacy, international affairs, and sport.

Alessio Norrito is Lecturer in Sociology and Management of Sport. He is an expert in the field of sport for development and peace, with a particular interest on cross-cultural interactions and forced migration. He holds a PhD from Loughborough University, UK, and was the managing editor for the *Journal of Sport for Development*.

Christina Philippou is Associate Professor in Accounting and Sport Finance at the University of Portsmouth, UK. Her research focuses on finance, governance, ethics, and corruption in sport. It has been used by the UK government to support reforms in football governance, and she has been on government advisory panels on both men's and women's football.

Daniel Plumley is Principal Lecturer in Sport Finance in the Department of Finance, Accounting and Business Systems in the Sheffield Business School at Sheffield Hallam University, UK. His research interests include performance measurement, governance and regulation and competitive balance, all under the broader research area of the economics and finance of professional team sports. He is an active researcher, delivering funded projects for ESRC and regularly consults with the industry on sport finance matters. He is also a Chartered Global Management Accountant (CGMA).

Gavin Price is the UK/Europe Director at global consulting agency Sports Diplomacy Alliance, an expert on sports diplomacy in small nations and football diplomacy, an Honorary Member of the Centre for Sports Law, Policy and Diplomacy at the University of Rijeka, Croatia and co-author of the British Council's research report: Towards a Welsh sports diplomacy strategy. An established writer and speaker, he has delivered publications, podcasts, and lectures on topics as wide-ranging as Australian and Asian Football Diplomacy, Athlete Activism and sports diplomacy policy and practice in major nations. He is co-director and curator of the 2023 Australia-UK sports diplomacy dialogue series and the first-ever World Congress on sports diplomacy (Basque Country, 2023).

J. Simon Rofe is a world leading expert in Sports Diplomacy and Reader/Associate Professor of International Politics at the University of Leeds, UK. He is a Senior Research Fellow and Assistant Programme Director for the MA Leadership in Sports at the Institute for Sport Humanities, and Visiting Professor at the Centre of Sports Law, Sports Policies and Sports Diplomacy of the University of Rijeka, Faculty of Law, Croatia. He is currently expert member of the United Kingdom's Sports Diplomacy Working Group.

Sascha L. Schmidt is Professor, Chair Holder and Director of the Center for Sports and Management (CSM) at WHU – Otto Beisheim School of Management in Germany with the Future of Sports being his key research area. He is also Lecturer at the Massachusetts Institute of Technology (MIT) Sports Entrepreneurship Bootcamp as well as a member of the 'Digital Initiative' at Harvard Business School in Boston, USA.

Mathias Schubert is Senior Researcher in Sports Management and Sports Governance at the Institute of Sport Science at Johannes Gutenberg University Mainz, Germany. He was Visiting Scholar at University of Technology Sydney (Australia) and at Molde University College (Norway). His main research interests lie in ethical issues in sports management.

Chris Toronyi is full-time PhD candidate in the Institute of Sport Business at Loughborough University London, UK. His research focuses on the intersection of nation branding, diplomacy, sport, club ownership, and supporters.

Jorge Tovar is Associate Professor at Universidad de Los Andes, Colombia, and Visiting Professor at the University of Wisconsin–Madison, USA. He was previously a Visiting Scholar at Stanford University, USA. His research includes various sports-related publications, including journal articles, book chapters, and books.

Shane Wafer is a leading sports lawyer in South Africa, trusted by major entities like SuperSport, CAF, and SAIDS, as well as national federations and athletes. As Managing Partner at Javelin Sports Consulting, he oversees the practice and serves clients directly. Shane is also an accredited AFSA Arbitrator specialising in sports dispute resolution, advising top rugby teams' disciplinary committees and serving on national federations' boards.

Ma Yang is Associate Professor in sport, soccer, and governance. He received his doctorate from the University of Bayreuth and currently works at the Institute for Olympic & Global Sport Governance Studies of Wenzhou University, China.

Daniel Ziesche is academic staff member in the English Department and Chair of Anglophone Area Studies at Chemnitz University of Technology, Germany.

1

INTRODUCTION TO THE GEOPOLITICAL ECONOMY OF FOOTBALL

Simon Chadwick, Paul Widdop, and Michael M. Goldman

At the end of the 21st century's first quarter, the world seems to be more turbulent and complex than ever before. This is an era of giga changes that are impacting upon every aspect of contemporary life. Globalism, digitalisation, and climate concerns are converging in ways that are fundamentally changing why and how decisions are made, and who is involved in making them.

Nowhere is this more evident than in football: globalisation means that the majority of a club's fans may no longer be local people or that owners of the same club could be private equity investors from the United States or an oil rich nation from the Persian Gulf; digitalisation nowadays means that we are consuming football in very different ways compared to even just ten years ago, whilst small clubs in lower leagues have become a focus for Hollywood superstars and global media corporations; climate change means that the scheduling and staging of football tournaments faces profound challenges, at the same time as airline sponsors continue to be a lucrative source of revenues in football.

As such, football in the 21st century and the environment in which it operates have outpaced the way in which many people conceive of and think about the sport. These giga changes have induced a pivot from the Global North to the Global South, which in turn has given rise to the growth of multipolarism – whereby new centres of power are emerging that challenge the football's long-standing hegemony. One illustration of this are the numbers of former European professional footballers who bemoan the influence on football of countries from the Global South, having played lucrative careers themselves in powerful leagues in the Global North consisting of clubs that wielded economic power.

DOI: 10.4324/9781003473671-1

Central to such polemic are notions of power, a game in which private equity investors, nation states, media corporations, governing bodies, commercial partners, clubs, players, and many more are engaged. Given the turbulent, dynamic global environment to which football is exposed across the world, this raises numerous questions, including: from where is power derived, who holds power and how do they use it, for whose benefit is power deployed, and how are those who hold power governed?

For anyone with even the most rudimentary understanding of football, these questions will be familiar ones, indeed they drive to the heart of the sport's biggest and most pressing issues. This book addresses such matters, thus serving as an important call to readers to think beyond media headlines and fan hysteria. We believe that what unites the likes of loss-making football clubs, shirt sponsors seeking a return on their investments, leagues that may feel they are losing ground to their rivals or media giants, is their need to understand the geopolitical economy.

And we do not simply mean being aware of giga trends and multipolarism, but also how the changing nature of our changing world intersects with and is shaped by geography, politics, and economics. The human geography of the United States is one factor that dictated the signing of Argentinian player Lionel Messi by Inter Miami of the Major League Soccer (MLS). Politically, the British government's deployment of the Premier League as an instrument of global soft power is more than two decades old, whilst the role that FC Barcelona plays in drawing tourists to the Spanish city is an ongoing example of successful economic impact. In the Middle East, major developments are taking place – both within football and across life more generally – impacting hoe sport is consumed and positioned in these societies. At the same time, we are witnessing some incredible changes in women's football that are seeing it elevated to a prominent new position.

In this book – alongside its companion volume – Continental Perspectives of Football's Geopolitical Economy (Chadwick et al., 2023), it is our contention that football's global complexities and sensitivities need to be explained in a more detailed and coherent way. We do not seek to achieve this by being abstract or esoteric, we want this book to address the realities of football at the end of the 21st century's first quarter, in an accessible, relevant, and meaningful way. In particular, we would like readers to think about how geography, politics, and economics intersect with the giga changes of globalism, digitalisation, and environmentalism to shape decision-making.

As such, we structure it in the following way, to reflect the major trends, changing geographies, themes, and issues with which football is dealing with:

- Global issues
- Women's football

- Ownership and investment
- The FIFA World Cup and tournament football
- Business, society, and culture

Reference

Chadwick, S., Widdop, P. and Goldman, M. (2023). *Continental Perspectives on the Geopolitical Economy of Football*. Oxford: Routledge, Taylor & Francis Group.

PART I
Global Issues

2

THE GEOPOLITICAL ECONOMY OF FOOTBALL

Dense Networks, Complex Decisions

Simon Chadwick and Paul Widdop

Following a severe escalation in conflict and violence involving Israel and Palestine in late 2023, many people publicly expressed their support for one country or the other. Among them were numerous football players, including Tottenham Hotspur's Israeli international Manor Solomon, whilst Bayern Munich's Moroccan international Noussair Mazraoui wished Palestinians "victory" in an Instagram post. The German club appeared unhappy with the player's position, which contrasted sharply with its own, official stance on the conflict. In a Twitter posting, Bayern emphasised that, "There is no justification for the killings and brutal violence against the civilian population. We are worried about our friends in Israel and hope for peaceful coexistence of all people in [sic] Middle East."

The German club's dissatisfaction with Mazraoui allied to its support of Israel was interesting, as for several years previously Bayern Munich had been engaged in a shirt sponsorship deal with Hamad International Airport in Doha. The Qatari state-owned facility paid around US$100 million to the club between 2018 and 2023 for the deal. When it was originally signed, Qatar was already highly active in Palestine, notably Gaza. Some observers were concerned about the country's relationship with Hamas, which perpetrated the October 2023 attacks on Israeli civilians. At the time, Bayern officials nevertheless appeared unperturbed by Qatari links to a group that some have designated as a terrorist organisation (and despite Hamas having an office in Doha during the sponsorship). Yet even the Israeli government has acknowledged for some time that Qatar has played a crucial moderating role in Palestine. As Qatar signed its deal with Bayern, it was also helping broker a truce between Hamas and Israel amid rising Palestinian protests on the eastern border of the Gaza Strip.

DOI: 10.4324/9781003473671-3

For a period before the 2023 troubles, Bayern Munich fans had protested about associations with Qatar, though not because of links to Hamas or Palestine. Rather, concerns were repeatedly expressed about the Gulf nation's treatment of migrant workers and about LGBTQ+ rights. Some fans held banners during matches that read, "For money, we wash everything clean." Prior to this, at the German club's annual general meeting in 2021, a fractious confrontation with the board of directors resulted in fans chanting "we are Bayern, and you are not." In 2023, the club decided not to continue in its relationship with Hamad International Airport, a decision claimed as a victory for its fans. Ironically, back in 2006, Bayern Munich played a friendly match in Tehran and was accused of showing support for then Iranian president Mahmoud Ahmadinejad, who had called for the destruction of Israel. At the time, club officials claimed, "[Bayern is] playing for the people, not for the regime." Former Munich shirt sponsor Qatar has long had a cooperative and cordial relationship with Iran, borne of their shared gas field interests.

This series of episodes is not intended to single-out, diminish, or disparage any single player, club, country, or issue; rather, it illustrates the nature and characteristics of football's geopolitical economy. Furthermore, it serves to highlight the sensitivities of leading and managing in 21st-century football. Without exception, this is surely the most difficult period in the sport's modern history, which has significant implications for those working in, following, or observing it. Whether strategically or operationally, those employed in football are faced with difficult decisions that, almost inevitably, result in difficult choices needing to be made and the consequences of these decisions having to be managed and evaluated.

As the above shows, football today is embedded in a dense network of interconnected nodes and relationships, which bring with them complexity and sensitivity but also contradiction and, possibly, accusations of hypocrisy. For instance, a club that actively supports the LGBTIQA+ community may sign a sponsorship deal with a state entity from a country in which the suppression of this community's rights is practised. In many cases, networks are both global and local in nature, necessitating that organisations involved in the sport must constantly reconcile competing demands. La Liga is a Spanish league comprising teams from Spain and has, over many decades, established a schedule of games that has become normalised – many matches are played on a Saturday evening. However, the globalisation of football means that many Spanish teams' fans are distributed across the world, in places such as China. In the likes of Beijing and Shanghai, it is the middle of the night and people are asleep when Saturday night matches played in Spain. La Liga has therefore taken the decision to kick-off some games during Saturday lunchtime local time – when early evening television audiences are at their peak in China. There was some disquiet in Spain about this, though the tensions between local and global are a feature of both interconnected networks and football in the 21st century.

Football's networks are also characterised by resource issues, most notably pertaining to oil and gas but also to issues of capital and its flow around these networks. Investments in the sport made by countries such as Saudi Arabia, Qatar, and Abu Dhabi illustrate how profoundly natural resources are shaping both the sport and the networks of which it is comprised. Qatar's staging of the 2022 FIFA men's World Cup, the Saudi Arabian Public Investment Fund's acquisition of Premier League club Newcastle United, and Abu Dhabi owned City Football Group's global franchise network are examples of how these natural resource rich nations have not only embedded themselves in football networks but also are fundamentally re-shaping the sport. We see their influence in everything from its governing bodies and governance to club ownership and commercial relationships. This is driven by a multitude of factors, including their over dependence on oil and gas revenues hence the need for industrial diversification and a desire to manage their images and reputation (which some label soft power projection whilst others call it sport washing). Yet it is not only state actors that are impacting football non-state actors are also inducing significant changes to network configuration. Over the last decade, there has been a marked increase in private equity flows into the sector, permeating club acquisitions and equity sales of governing bodies' commercial activities. These non-state actors may have somewhat different motives and expected outcomes to state actors, but their impact is no less significant and has, indeed, resulted in football now having a much stronger financial, commercial, and industrial basis. American private equity investors have led the way in this regard, often with leading industry figures or celebrities serving as figureheads for the likes of club investment.

This is perhaps most potently embodied at Wrexham, an underachieving football club located in a small Welsh town. In 2021, Hollywood film stars Ryan Reynolds and Rob McElhenney acquired the club, since when a process of "Disneyfication" has taken place that has resulted in the club having its own Disney+ series, "Welcome to Wrexham." The role that broadcasting initially played, latterly given impetus by digitalisation and speculation about the metaverse, has had a profound effect on football's network. For instance, during a diplomatic feud involving Qatar and Saudi Arabia (which lasted from 2017 to 2021), state actors from the latter were accused of pirating football content from the former's beIN Sports, a state-owned broadcasting service. This led to the World Trade Organisation investigating the case which, in turn, initially became an obstacle to the Saudi Arabian Public Investment Fund's acquisition of Newcastle. As the feud dissipated, the Saudi bid subsequently passed the English Premier League's Owners and Directors Test, and more recently there have even been rumours of a Saudi Arabian investor taking an equity stake in beIN Sports. Once more, the digital networks of football are not just a matter of state actors, they are also the domain of non-state actors as well. Sensing profitable returns from a mature industry there is a growing number of instances where their investments are evident – the potential acquisition of a stake in Italy's Serie A media rights business being one case of this.

Viewing football as a global network consisting of nodes and interconnections raises all manner of questions and issues. Though globalisation, resource endowment, and digitalisation form the context within which networks were, and continue to be, established it is facets of geopolitical economy that shape the engagement of state and non-state actors with and in them. Though inextricably linked, for the purposes of illustration, it is helpful to deconstruct the notion of geopolitical economy as being at the confluence of geography, politics, and economics.

Geography as an influence upon football is somewhat undervalued (and certainly merits more detailed analysis), though it plays a fundamental role in determining the nature of networks, the nodes of which they consist, and the type of interconnections there are between members. Physical geography – oil and gas reserves and over dependence upon them – is one reason why Saudi Arabia has been heavily investing in the sport. Similarly, over the last two decades China has actively engaged in stadium diplomacy in Africa. In return for building stadiums (either free-of-charge or funded by soft loans), government in Beijing has secured preferential access to the natural resources needed for the country to sustain its economic growth. Human geography also pays a role: only ten per cent of Qatar's population is native Qatari hence football serves as means through which to promote a coherent national identity; as an outcome of both colonialism and globalisation, player naturalisation has become an increasingly challenging issue; and religious divisions, such as those between Scotland's Celtic and Rangers, have long been a feature of football.

The British government's routine deployment of the country's football assets as channel through which to globally project soft power is evidence of the role that politics plays in football. So too was FIFA president Gianni Infantino's 2022 pre-World Cup speech in which he attempted to reconcile, albeit rather clumsily, the disparate demands of countries in the Global North and Global South, as the world pivots from one to the other. Appearances by Brazilian international Neymar alongside an electioneering president Jair Bolsanaro in 2022 and French president Emmanuel Macron with his arm around Kylian Mbappé are testament to the power of politics' network influence. The last two examples are neither accidental nor incidental, in terms of policy, strategy, and even markets, political factors are pivotal in shaping football's networks. For nearly two decades, Russian state-owned energy corporation Gazprom invested in a series of football sponsorship deals (for instance, it secured the right to appear on German club Schalke 04's shirts in 2007), which were an attempt to "Putinise" football. In this case, the shirt deal was deployed as part of moves to distract key audiences from the Kremlin's moves to induce a European dependence upon Russian gas supplies (the consequences of which became clearly apparent in the aftermath of Ukraine's invasion in 2022). Policy and strategy moves are not always malign, though they are commonly a matter of power and control, and of influence.

England's Premier League makes an annual contribution to the British economy of up to £7.6bn billion and is responsible for sustaining 100,000 jobs. Football's networks demonstrably consist of economic dimensions, which is further illustrated by a swathe of state-owned airline sponsors, most notably from the Gulf region. Through deals with clubs such as Spain's Real Madrid and Italy's AC Milan, Emirates Airline has established itself as one of the world's leading carriers. In turn, this has contributed both to Dubai airport becoming a significant global transit hub and to the country becoming a major tourism destination. Non-state economic contributions through football are just as significant and are often enabled through free-market ideology and business operating environments where innovation and investment are prompted by light touch regulatory interventions (reflecting the economic embeddedness of all networks). Lionel Messi's move to Major League Soccer's Inter Miami may have, at one level, given the world's best footballer a chance to extend his career though he has been handsomely remunerated for moving to the club. Among the organisations that have financially underwritten the Argentinian's transfer are the likes of Apple and Adidas; the former now streams the series "Messi Meets America," whilst the latter is benefiting from record shirt sales for Major League Soccer (MLS) club.

As the above serves to highlight, the networks of football's geopolitical economy are dense, sometimes characterised by direct relationships though at other times connections may be indirect, less powerful, and with fewer consequences. The challenge for athletes, sport organisations, and other industry stakeholders is therefore one of understanding these networks and navigating through them. Leaders, managers, and decision-makers need to have sharp sense of cause-and-effect, which must be allied to techniques of geopolitical risk assessment but also to ways of predicting the future (including scenario planning). Who could have imagined that in the mid-2000s, when Germany and Russia agreed to construct a gas pipeline in Baltic Sea (known as Nord Steam 1), there would later be serious consequences for football? But that is exactly what happened; when Russia invaded Ukraine in 2022, European football's governing body the Union of European Football Associations (UEFA) terminated its Gazprom sponsorship deal and moved staging of its Champions League final away from the Gazprom-owned stadium in Saint Petersburg in Russia. It is important to note that the stadium is normally home to the Gazprom-owned club team Zenit. In 21st-century football, everything is connected which brings complexities and challenges which, even 20 years ago, the sport did not face.

References

Chadwick, S. (2022). From utilitarianism and neoclassical sport management to a new geopolitical economy of sport. *European Sport Management Quarterly, 22*(5), 685–704.

Chadwick, S., Widdop, P., Anagnostopoulos, C. and Parnell, D., Eds. (2022). *The Business of the FIFA World Cup*. Abingdon: Routledge.

Chadwick, S., Widdop, P. and Goldman, M. M., Eds. (2023). *The Geopolitical Economy of Sport: Power, Politics, Money, and the State*. Oxfordshire: Taylor & Francis.

3

WILL AI TURN THE FOOTBALL WORLD UPSIDE DOWN?

Sascha L. Schmidt and Daniel Lugner

The potential applications of artificial intelligence (AI) appear to be vast and are poised, sooner or later, to revolutionize every sector of our lives. Some predict it will be the next 'general-purpose technology,' with a similar impact to that of the combustion engine in the 20th century, whereas others worry about job losses and diminished human control (Brynjolfsson and McAfee, 2017). In recent years, few technologies have sparked as much debate as AI. The advent of ChatGPT in November 2022 and the subsequent widespread adoption of generative AI added new dimensions to these discussions (Candelon et al., 2023). At its essence, generative AI involves systems trained on expansive data sets, enabling them to generate new, creative, and dynamic outputs (Steelberg, 2023). The capabilities of Large Language Models (LLMs) in tasks such as writing articles, composing music, creating artwork, and simulating human conversations are expected to transform businesses and society at large (Edelman and Abraham, 2023). Generative AI, with its almost limitless applications, is projected to contribute up to 4.4 trillion dollars in economic value by enhancing productivity and enabling new business models (McKinsey and Company, 2023). Although it is difficult to foresee how these transformational changes are going to unravel in detail in the future, the mainstream adoption of LLM applications by hundreds of millions of users shows that generative AI is here to stay (Paris, 2023).

In professional football, AI holds immense potential in almost every aspect. It promises to elevate athletes' performance through innovative coaching and tactical insights, identify exceptional talents, and forge deeper connections with increasingly diverse fan groups (Chmait and Westerbeek, 2021; Schmidt and Stoneham, 2024). However, realizing these benefits is challenging. Historically, digital innovations in professional football have often fallen short of

DOI: 10.4324/9781003473671-4

their potential. A key barrier is the substantial investment required for techno-logical solutions and skilled personnel. Despite their high visibility and large fan bases, most football clubs operate with relatively modest revenues. The disparity in financial resources is significant, as seen in the German Bundes-liga in 2022, where annual revenues ranged from over 625 million euros for Bayern Munich to just 26 million euros for SV Darmstadt 98, with an average of 190 million euros across the league (Deutsche Fußball Liga, 2023). Conse-quently, investment budgets are notoriously tight for most clubs, and only a few top-tier organizations could harness the full benefits of new technologies such as AI.

Another development in global football is further widening these financial disparities and has garnered high attention among fans and club representa-tives in recent years. International investors, aiming to claim a share of foot-ball's lucrative market, have been pouring vast sums of money into the sport. High-profile acquisitions, such as Chelsea FC's takeover by US investors Todd Boehly and Clearlake Capital in 2022 for over three billion US dollar, and Newcastle United's acquisition by the Saudi Arabia owned Public Investment Fund (PIF) in 2021 for 400 million US dollar, exemplify this trend (Chel-sea, 2022; Hellier, 2021). These investments, aimed at enhancing squads and technological infrastructure, are set to deepen the competitive divide within club football.

Moreover, these capital inflows are not only reshaping Europe's elite clubs but also boosting emerging domestic leagues in the US and Kingdom of Saudi Arabia (KSA), intensifying their activities to challenge the continental hegem-ony. The US-based Major League Soccer (MLS) made headlines by luring Li-onel Messi to Miami FC in 2023 and by strategically collaborating with tech giant Apple to grow its entertainment product (Apple, 2022; ESPN, 2023). In KSA, PIF has invested billions to bring star players such as Cristiano Ronaldo and Neymar to its Saudi Pro League (SPL), taking a majority ownership stake in four of the country's leading clubs. This move is part of the government's strategy to grow the game of football domestically and increase its influence in the sport globally (Panja and Al Omran, 2023). Already, these developments are showing effects by increasing local stadium attendances (Schreyer and Singleton, 2023) and disrupt football on a global scale, leading to skyrocket-ing transfer fees and draining talent from established leagues (Woodyatt et al., 2023). Bringing AI into the picture could further accelerate these changes. Both the US and KSA are not just nurturing ambitious football leagues but are also at the forefront of technological advancements, including AI. Silicon Valley, home to leading tech firms like OpenAI, Microsoft, and Nvidia, posi-tions the US as the global AI innovation leader. Concurrently, KSA is making significant strides by constructing substantial supercomputer clusters and de-veloping LLMs tailored for Arabic speakers (Murgia et al., 2023). If AI fulfills its potential in football, these structural and technological advantages could significantly boost the competitiveness of MLS and SPL clubs, potentially triggering a seismic shift in global football.

Who AI ultimately makes winners and losers in professional football is complex. Assessing how generative AI might impact the industry is crucial for understanding the dynamics at play. In the following, we will provide an overview of generative AI's transformative potential and explore its implications for professional football across three critical application areas: (1) field match analysis, (2) scouting and player development, and (3) fan experiences.

The Transformative Potential of Generative Artificial Intelligence

Generative AI marks a paradigm shift in AI's interaction with humans and its output capabilities – moving from mere analysis to creative generation. Unlike 'traditional' AI, primarily used for analyzing large volumes of structured data to detect patterns, make predictions, and offer recommendations, generative AI transcends these limits. It can generate novel content, ranging from text and images to videos and audio (Noy and Zhang, 2023). This capability allows AI not only to automate routine, codifiable tasks but also to venture into realms of creative work (Eapen et al., 2023). AI is now positioned to automate up to 26 percent of tasks in sectors like arts, design, entertainment, media, and sports (Briggs and Kodnani, 2023). Moreover, the inherent creativity of generative AI models may empower organizations to forge entirely new business models, breaching into domains previously considered exclusive to human ingenuity. In creativity assessments, models like GPT-4 have already demonstrated near-human capabilities (Haase et al., 2023; Koivisto and Grassini, 2023).

The recent evolution of generative AI has been marked by rapid developments, with frequent introductions of new models and applications. A trend toward integrating features and new data sources is expected to further enhance capabilities. Multimodal models, such as GPT-4, merge different generative abilities (text, image, audio, video) with computer vision and text-to-speech features. This integration facilitates more realistic machine interactions, simulating real-life scenarios and enabling comprehensive end-to-end use cases (Wadhwani, 2023). Furthermore, the integration of standalone LLMs with private and real-time public data will provide models with richer contexts, enhancing their ability to respond to queries and perform tasks (Suleyman and Bhaskar, 2023). The imminent incorporation of LLMs in mainstream applications such as Microsoft Office is set to revolutionize day-to-day tasks like email composition, presentation creation, and market research (Burtsev et al., 2023). With these advancements, the concept of nearly autonomous AI agents is no longer a distant possibility. Soon, AI could independently interact and engage with its digital environment, guided by goals predefined by humans. This development, although still in its nascent stages, is being hinted at through applications like OpenAI's GPT function, which enables the creation of task-specific bots (Mollick, 2023). The progression could automate complete workflows fundamentally altering operational dynamics also in football.

Application Field: Match Analysis and Coaching

The integration of generative AI into football match analysis and coaching heralds a new era of strategic refinement and competitive edge. Pioneering clubs like FC Midtjylland have already successfully employed data-based strategies on a large scale in the past. To be able to compete as a smaller club with limited financial resources, they based game preparation and tactics mostly on objective performance metrics (Jones, 2020). In the everlasting arms race in professional football to find a secret weapon to gain a competitive advantage, this data-driven approach inspired wide replication (Torgler, 2024). Obviously extensive data collection forms the basis for these types of strategy. Equipped with modern camera tracking systems as well as sensor-based systems, football clubs are gathering vast amounts of data during practice and games. This data has become the main currency to fuel AI and machine learning systems to enable data-driven decisions, improve athletes' performance, and find a competitive edge on the pitch (Chase, 2024).

The adoption of generative AI can elevate these approaches to new heights. In the future LLMs could be fine-tuned to the specific use cases of a club based on performance data and medical data collected for each player. Acting as an assistant coach, AI models can provide real-time tactical insights for in-game coaching decisions and assist in crafting effective strategies for upcoming games (Chase, 2024). In the future, digital twins of two teams could be used to simulate various match scenarios in 'what if' scenarios, helping coaches to choose optimal lineups and game tactics against specific opponents (Hsieh et al., 2019). On an individual player level, AI coaches could become a personalized companion and support in game preparation by providing automated reports on tactics and video analysis on potential game situations (Siegel and Morris, 2024). In this scenario, the role of human coaches in game preparation would change significantly. They would act more like supervisors of AI agents and could allocate more time to tasks where human involvement and expertise is non-negotiable such as pregame one-on-one talks.

Application Field: Scouting and Player Development

In the area of scouting and player development, AI's potential to identify and nurture the next generation of football talent is enormous. Data-based approaches challenge traditional scouting methods in sports by going beyond problematic result-based talent identification and adopting a more strategic view on player development (Brouwers et al., 2012). Examples, such as German Bundesliga club TSG Hoffenheim, involving the collection and analysis of comprehensive data on young players, represent the initial steps toward a more systematic and data-driven process for scouting and player development (Zhu et al., 2015). To find the perfect match for a team, evaluation criteria do not just include athletic abilities on the pitch but also personal attributes, injury history, and nutritional habits of players (Schmidt, 2024). However, due to the recent onset of systematic data collection for youth players and the complexities involved in a player's development, AI is yet to fully realize its predictive capabilities. As more historical data becomes available on successful players, new machine learning models will constantly improve in identifying hidden potential of young athletes (Chase, 2024).

Moreover, the future of scouting is poised for a significant transformation with the advent of generative AI-driven platforms and agents. We are already witnessing the emergence of interactive scouting platforms, akin to ChatGPT, offering personalized reports and insights based on prompts. These platforms can process specific queries, such as identifying a technically skilled right back who aligns with a team's playing style and budget constraints (Carey, 2023). Envisioning a step further, an AI agent scout could continuously monitor global game footage, proactively seeking interaction with human scouts when a potential match is found. Based on feedback, the agent would learn and refine its search parameters, making the scouting process more dynamic and interactive. In developing top talents, generative AI-based coaching tools hold high potential, too. First applications are already capable of crafting individualized training and nutrition plans, tailored to each athlete's unique data profile (Achauer, 2023). In the future, these tools may serve as a one-on-one support system, offering personalized guidance and supplementing traditional coaching methods.

However, it is important to acknowledge the inherent limitations of AI in this field. While it can provide probabilities and predictions regarding player development, AI cannot account for unforeseen events like injuries or personal crises that might impact a player's career trajectory. Ultimately, rather than replacing earlier decision-making methods, these advancements will simply enhance them, complementing the insights of human scouts and coaches (Torgler, 2024).

Application Field: Fan Experiences

In the dynamic world of sports entertainment, where football clubs compete not only with each other but also against giants like Netflix and Disney Plus for fan attention, generative AI is emerging as a transformative force in creating hyper-personalized fan experiences. It revolutionizes how fans interact with their sport, offering bespoke content that resonates with individual preferences and enhances overall engagement with leagues and clubs. At the forefront of this revolution is the application of generative AI in creating automated content pieces for social media or other channels, tailored to cater to specific fan segments (Kottke, 2023; Schmidt et al., 2023a). For instance, North American Bundesliga fans might receive personalized highlight clips featuring players like Giovanni Reyna or Alphonso Davies automatically in the future. In sports broadcasting, advancements in computer vision already allow TV presenters to explore locations and trajectories, providing meaningful real-time statistics for viewers (Thomas et al., 2017). AI-generated commentary, exemplified by IBM's initiatives at tennis events like Wimbledon and the Augusta Masters in 2023, represents a next step in engaging audiences with personalized experiences (IBM, 2023). This technology offers the potential for real-time, multilingual commentary, breaking language barriers and catering to unique preferences of fans worldwide. Such innovation enhances the viewing experience, making football broadcasts more inclusive and appealing to a broader audience.

The emergence of AI personas, like the digital versions of sports stars Tom Brady and Naomi Osaka created by Meta in 2023, marks a new era in fan interaction (Meta, 2023). These AI-driven entities offer fans the chance to engage in unique conversations, gain insights, and experience an unprecedented level of connection with their sports heroes. When integrated with developments in virtual reality and text-to-speech technology, these AI personas can lead to highly immersive interactions in digital worlds, offering fans novel ways to connect with their favorite players and teams. Looking to the future, the integration of AI agents in fan experiences promises even more personalized interactions. Through an AI persona that acts as a personal host for sports content, fans receive personalized sports news, immersive virtual reality experiences, and interactive game simulations tailored to their individual needs. Such developments point to a future where fan experiences are not only about watching a match and following a club on social media but engaging in a fully immersive, interactive journey into the heart of football.

Conclusion

As we have explored in the three main application areas, generative AI, and particularly the emergence of AI agents, could fundamentally transform how football is played and managed on and off the pitch. However, the key question remains: when will the influence of AI play a significant role in football, and who will be the winners and losers?

In the short term, technological limitations of current LLMs could limit applications and need to be overcome to achieve widespread adoption. Even cutting-edge models like GPT-4 exhibit significant rates of generating plausible but inaccurate content, which compromises their reliability (Dell'Acqua et al., 2023). Additionally, these models, developed from extensive historical data, often replicate existing biases in human-generated texts, necessitating careful management (Chase, 2024). In the entertainment sphere, the need for stringent guidelines on copyright and data security, brought into sharp focus by the Writers Guild of America strike in 2023, cannot be understated (Koblin and Barnes, 2023). Solutions to these challenges will undoubtedly emerge over time, but exactly when this will be remains uncertain for the time being.

Identifying the long-term winners and losers of this technological shift is also not straightforward. As outlined, emerging international leagues such as the MLS and SPL will have an advantage of strategic backing of investors and are in a good position to take a first-mover position in utilizing AI models and building up necessary infrastructure. Besides the financial resources to invest heavily in AI, these leagues will also benefit from the entertainment-centric culture in the US and Saudi Arabia. This aspect sets them apart from the traditional fan cultures prevalent in many European countries, where technological innovations altering existing fan experiences need to be addressed with care to avoid fan backlash. As such, AI could become a pivotal tool for these upcoming leagues to captivate fan attention worldwide, potentially reshaping the global hierarchy in football. On the other hand, harnessing the benefits of future advancements in generative AI will highly depend on the integration of club-specific data and information into frontier models. Consequently, the availability of well-structured databases going back several years could become a more significant factor than sheer financial power and expertise. Clubs with established tech-based strategies, like Manchester City focused on digital fan experience in the metaverse, or TSG Hoffenheim with their data-driven sporting approach, could also be leading the way in embracing new forms of AI (Schmidt et al., 2023). On top, it is even unclear if financial funds will be at all a deciding factor for leveraging generative AI to its full potential in the future. The technology could also result in leveling the playing field. Frontier models like GPT-4 are universally accessible and leverage natural language interfaces, which lessen the demand for specialized data-science expertise. Generative AI could democratize access to cutting-edge technology and offer smaller clubs a chance to apply the latest AI applications (Perri, 2023). This could enable competition with top clubs on an equal technological basis, promoting outcome uncertainty, which is so incremental to the attractiveness of sports events (Schreyer et al., 2016, 2017, 2018a, b).

Ultimately, the transformation of football through generative AI seems inevitable but is difficult to predict. Clubs and leagues that are agile in recognizing and responding to new opportunities will likely gain a competitive edge, independent of financial power. In contrast, those overlooking the potential of generative AI may find themselves at a disadvantage in the long term. The key to success lies in a willingness to experiment and learn rapidly. Nonetheless, it is crucial to acknowledge that success in football will always remain a blend of art and science. Experts agree that advanced technology is essential to form and run a competitive team. However, competitive advantage only emerges when the scientific backbone offers a fruitful ground for artistic ingenuity (Beiderbeck et al., 2022). While technology will greatly improve various aspects of the sport, it is ultimately the human elements – both on and off the pitch – that remain crucial to winning championships and the hearts of fans around the world.

References

Achauer, H. (2023). Your next fitness coach could be a robot. *The New York Times*. Available at: https://www.nytimes.com/2023/04/26/well/move/ai-fitness-trainer-coach.html [Accessed 22 December 2023].

Apple (2022). Apple and Major League Soccer announce MLS season pass launches February 1, 2023. Available at: https://www.apple.com/newsroom/2022/11/apple-and-major-league-soccer-announce-mls-season-pass-launches-february-1-2023/ [Accessed 22 December 2023].

Beiderbeck, D., Evans, N., Frevel, N. and Schmidt, S. L. (2022). The impact of technology on the future of football – A global Delphi study. *Technological Forecasting & Social Change*, 187(2023), 122186.

Briggs, J. and Kodnani, D. (2023). *The Potentially Large Effects of Artificial Intelligence on Economic Growth*. Goldman Sachs. Available at: https://www.gspublishing.com/content/research/en/reports/2023/03/27/d64e052b-0f6e-45d7-967b-d7be35fabd16.html [Accessed 22 December 2023].

Brouwers, J., De Boscher, V. and Sotiriadou, P. (2012). An examination of the importance of performances in youth and junior competition as an indicator of later success in tennis. *Sport Management Review*, 15(4), 461–475.

Brynjolfsson, E. and McAfee, A. (2017). The business of artificial intelligence. *Harvard Business Review*, 7, 3–11.

Burtsev, M., Candelon, F., Jha, G., Sack, D., Zhukov, L. and Martínez, D. Z. (2023). *GPT Was only the Beginning—Autonomous Agents Are Coming*. Boston Consulting Group. Available at: https://www.bcg.com/publications/2023/gpt-was-only-the-beginning-autonomous-agents-are-coming [Accessed 22 December 2023].

Candelon, F., Gupta, A., Krayer, L. and Zhukov, L. (2023). *The CEO's Guide to the Generative AI Revolution*. Boston Consulting Group. Available at: https://www.bcg.com/publications/2023/ceo-guide-to-ai-revolution [Accessed 22 December 2023].

Carey, M. (2023). 'Will Harry Kane be a good signing for Bayern?': The rise of generative AI in football scouting. *The Athletic*. Available at: https://theathletic.com/4765545/2023/08/24/the-rise-of-generative-ai-in-football-scouting/ [Accessed 22 December 2023].

Chase, C. (2024). The data revolution: cloud computing, artificial intelligence, and machine learning in the future of sports. In S. L. Schmidt (Ed.), *21st Century Sports: How Technologies Will Change Sports in the Digital Age* (2nd ed.) (pp. 191–207). Cham: Springer.

Chelsea, F. C. (2022). Club statement. Available at: https://www.chelseafc.com/en/news/article/club-statement1 [Accessed 22 December 2023].

Chmait, N. and Westerbeek, H. (2021). Artificial intelligence and machine learning in sport research: an introduction for non-data scientists. *Frontiers in Sports Active Living*, 3, 682287.

Dell'Acqua, F., McFowland, E., Mollick, E. R., Lifshitz-Assaf, H., Kellogg, K., Rajendran, S., Krayer, L., Candelon, F. and Lakhani, K. R. (2023). Navigating the jagged technological frontier: field experimental evidence of the effects of AI on knowledge worker productivity and quality. Harvard Business School Technology & Operations Management Unit Working Paper No. 24-013. Available at: https://papers.ssrn.com/sol3/papers.cfm?abstract_id=4573321.

Deutsche Fußball Liga (2023). Finanzkennzahlen der Proficlubs. Available at: https://www.dfl.de/de/hintergrund/lizenzierungsverfahren/finanzkennzahlen-der-proficlubs/ [Accessed 22 December 2023].

Eapen, T., Finkenstadt, D., Folk, J. and Venkataswamy, L. (2023, July–August). How generative AI can augment human creativity. *Harvard Business Review*. Available at: https://hbr.org/2023/07/how-generative-ai-can-augment-human-creativity [Accessed 22 December 2023].

Edelman, D. C. and Abraham, M. (2023). Generative AI will change your business. Here's how to adapt. *Harvard Business Review*. Available at: https://hbr.org/2023/04/generative-ai-will-change-your-business-heres-how-to-adapt [Accessed 22 December 2023].

ESPN (2023). Messi's impact on Inter Miami, MLS in 2023 and beyond. Available at: https://www.espn.com/soccer/story/_/id/38704303/messi-impact-inter-miami-mls-2023-beyond [Accessed 22 December 2023].

Haase, J., Hanel, P. H. P. and Gronau, N. (2023). Creativity enhancement methods for adults: a meta-analysis. *Psychology of Aesthetics, Creativity, and the Arts*. https://doi.org/10.1037/aca0000557.

Hellier, D. (2021). *Saudi Wealth Fund Weighs Buying Another Top Football Club in Europe. Bloomberg*. Available at: https://www.bloomberg.com/news/articles/2023-07-13/saudi-wealth-fund-weighs-buying-another-top-football-club-in-europe [Accessed 22 December 2023].

Hsieh, H.-Y., Chen, C.-Y., Wang, Y.-S. and Chuang, J. H. (2019). BasketballGAN: generating basketball play simulation through sketching. In Proceedings of the 27th ACM International Conference on Multimedia (MM'19), 21–25 October 2019, Nice, France.

IBM (2023). What the Masters app can teach us about large language models. *IBM Blog*. Available at: https://www.ibm.com/blog/masters-tournament-ai-commentary/ [Accessed 22 December 2023].

Jones, S. (2020). The world's most innovative club? The secrets behind Liverpool's Champions League opponents Midtjylland. *Goal.com*. Available at: https://www.goal.com/en/news/the-worlds-most-innovative-club-the-secrets-behind-liverpools-champions-league-opponents-midtjylland/1g6flveievyep1lywgw1c3g7d9 [Accessed 22 December 2023].

Koblin, J. and Barnes, B. (2023). What's the latest on the writers' strike? *The New York Times*. Available at: https://www.nytimes.com/article/wga-writers-strike-hollywood.html [Accessed 22 December 2023].

Koivisto, M. and Grassini, S. (2023). Best humans still outperform artificial intelligence in a creative divergent thinking task. *Scientific Reports, 13*, 13601 (2023). https://doi.org/10.1038/s41598-023-40858-3.

Kottke, M., (2023). Digital support for fan experience: How artificial intelligence can help the sports industry. Available at: https://sportfive.com/beyond-the-match/insights/artificial-intelligence-digital-support-for-fan-experience [Accessed 22 December 2023].

McKinsey & Company (2023). The economic potential of generative AI: The next productivity frontier. Available at: https://www.mckinsey.com/capabilities/mckinsey-digital/our-insights/the-economic-potential-of-generative-ai-the-next-productivity-frontier#introduction [Accessed 22 December 2023].

Meta (2023). Introducing new AI experiences across our family of apps and devices. Available at: https://about.fb.com/news/2023/09/introducing-ai-powered-assistants-characters-and-creative-tools/ [Accessed 22 December 2023].

Mollick, E. (2023). Almost an agent: What GPTs can do. One useful thing. Available at: https://www.oneusefulthing.org/p/almost-an-agent-what-gpts-can-do [Accessed 22 December 2023].

Murgia, M., England, A., Liu, Q., Olcott, E. and Al-Atrush, S. (2023). Saudi Arabia and UAE race to buy Nvidia chips to power AI ambitions. *Financial Times*. Available at: https://www.ft.com/content/c93d2a76-16f3-4585-af61-86667c5090ba [Accessed 22 December 2023].

Noy, S. and Zhang, W. (2023). Experimental evidence on the productivity effects of generative artificial intelligence. *Science*, *381*(6654), 187–192. https://doi.org/10.1126/science.adh2586.

Panja, T. and Al Omran, A. (2023). Saudi Soccer League creates huge fund to sign global stars. *The New York Times*. Available at: https://www.nytimes.com./2023/06/02/sports/soccer/saudi-soccer-messi-benzema-ronaldo.html [Accessed 22 December 2023].

Paris, M. (2023). ChatGPT hits 100 million users, Google invests in AI bot and Chat-GPT goes viral. *Forbes*. Available at: https://www.forbes.com/sites/martineparis/2023/02/03/chatgpt-hits-100-million-microsoft-unleashes-ai-bots-and-catgpt-goes-viral/ [Accessed 22 December 2023].

Perri, L. (2023). Generative AI can democratize access to knowledge and skills. *Gartner*. Available at: https://www.gartner.com/en/articles/generative-ai-can-democratize-access-to-knowledge-and-skills [Accessed 22 December 2023].

Schmidt, S. L. (2024). How technologies impact sports in the digital age. In S. L. Schmidt (Ed.), *21st Century Sports: How Technologies Will Change Sports in the Digital Age* (2nd ed.) (pp. 3–16). Cham: Springer.

Schmidt, S. L., Geissler, D. and Schreyer, D. (2023a). Top-tier sports product and its production in 2030. *CSM Research Reports*. Düsseldorf: WHU – Otto Beisheim School of Management.

Schmidt, S. L. and Stoneham, K. (2024). Beyond 2030: what sports will look like for athletes, consumers and managers. In S. L. Schmidt (Ed.), *21st Century Sports: How Technologies Will Change Sports in the Digital Age* (2nd ed.) (pp. 367–376). Cham: Springer.

Schmidt, S. L., von der Gracht, H., Beiderbeck, D. and Heidemann, G. (2023b). AI, blockchain and immersive technologies: metaversal business models of professional football clubs in 2030. *CSM Research Reports*. Düsseldorf: WHU – Otto Beisheim School of Management.

Schreyer, D., Schmidt, S. L. and Torgler, B. (2016). Against all odds? Exploring the role of game outcome uncertainty in season ticket holders' stadium attendance demand. *Journal of Economic Psychology*, *56*, 192–217.

Schreyer, D., Schmidt, S. L. and Torgler, B. (2017). Game outcome uncertainty and the demand for international football games: evidence from the German TV market. *Journal of Media Economics*, *30*(1), 31–45.

Schreyer, D., Schmidt, S. L. and Torgler, B. (2018a). Game outcome uncertainty in the English Premier League: Do German fans care? *Journal of Sports Economics*, *19*(5), 625–644.

Schreyer, D., Schmidt, S. L. and Torgler, B. (2018b). Game outcome uncertainty and television audience demand: new evidence from German football. *German Economic Review*, *19*(2), 140–161.

Schreyer, D. and Singleton, C. (2024). Cristiano of Arabia: Did Ronaldo increase Saudi Pro League attendances?. *Contemporary Economic Policy*. 1–11. Available at: https://doi.org/10.1111/coep.12661.

Siegel, J. and Morris, D. (2024). Robotics, automation, and the future of sports. In S. L. Schmidt (Ed.), *21st Century Sports: How Technologies Will Change Sports in the Digital Age* (2nd ed.) (pp. 67–85). Cham: Springer.

Steelberg, R. (2023). Generative AI: A critical new team player for the sports industry. *Forbes*. Available at: https://www.forbes.com/sites/forbestechcouncil/2023/09/28/

generative-ai-a-critical-new-team-player-for-the-sports-industry/ [Accessed 22 December 2023].

Suleyman, M. and Bhaskar, M. (2023). *The Coming Wave. Technology, Power, and the Twenty-First Century's Greatest Dilemma*. New York: Random House USA Inc.

Thomas, G., Gade, R., Moeslund, T. B., Carr, P. and Hilton, A. (2017). Computer vision for sports: current applications and research topics. *Computer Vision and Image Understanding, 159*, 3–18.

Torgler, B. (2024). Big data, artificial intelligence, and quantum computing in sports. In S. L. Schmidt (Ed.), *21st Century Sports: How Technologies Will Change Sports in the Digital Age* (2nd ed.) (pp. 169–190). Cham: Springer.

Wadhwani, R. (2023). A dive into multimodal generative AI. *Spiceworks*. Available at: https://www.spiceworks.com/tech/artificial-intelligence/articles/multimodal-generative-ai-adoption/ [Accessed 22 December 2023].

Woodyatt, A., Shveda, K. and Cubero, A. (2023). Saudi Arabia is trying to disrupt soccer's world order. The reasons why might surprise you. *CNN*. Available at: https://edition.cnn.com/2023/09/20/sport/saudi-arabia-soccer-spl-bin-salman-intl-spt-cmd-dg/index.html [Accessed 22 December 2023].

Zhu, F., Lakhani, K. R., Schmidt, S. L. and Herman, K. (2015). TSG Hoffenheim: football in the age of analytics. *Harvard Business School Case* 616–010. (Revised May 2017).

4

FOOTBALL FANS

Complacent Cheerleaders Representing Nation States?

Chris Toronyi and Jacqueline Mueller

Introduction

On 7 October 2021, the 300-million-pound takeover of Newcastle United Football Club took place, years in the making for the Kingdom of Saudi Arabia (KSA) and its investment arm, the Public Investment Fund (PIF). Whereas immediate reactions to the takeover by the United Kingdom (UK) Foreign Office were largely positive, reactions by Newcastle United supporters can only be described as conflicted (Brown, 2021). To provide more context, the additional investment in the region was perceived as great news for the UK by local Members of Parliament as well as the UK foreign Office (Crafton, 2023). The once neglected city of Newcastle, who has suffered from high unemployment and record child poverty (Butler, 2020), would now have a partner in KSA to return prosperity back to the city of Newcastle and the region of Northumberland.

Moreover, a change in club ownership was wished for by most Newcastle United supporters given that the previous owner, Mike Ashley, became increasingly unpopular in the later years of his 14-year tenure. Supporters voiced their dissatisfaction through the "anybody but Ashley" chant emphasizing they would prefer anyone else as their owner. When the sale was finally completed, supporters celebrated with the #cans hashtag on Twitter, posting pictures, toasting the new KSA ownership (Waugh, 2020). However, when the long-desired takeover finally occurred, some supporters started to question their own ethical values and expressed their fear of being complicit in the KSA attempts of altering perceptions of Saudi Arabia as a nation.

Newcastle United supporters found themselves in the middle of one of the pressing sport and political debates of our time, when and at what

DOI: 10.4324/9781003473671-5

cost can foreign investment in sport and other forms of entertainment be accepted? On the one side, a substantial influx of funds would likely bring more glory on the pitch as well as local investments off the pitch, optimistically reproducing Abu Dhabi's takeover of Manchester City (Crafton, 2023).

Specifically, the owners from the KSA promised investment in the squad and training facilities, as well an upgrade to St. James Park and surrounding area where Newcastle United plays their home matches, and even investment in the Newcastle United women's team. Whereas, on the other side, accepting investments from foreign states in the global South continues to manifest the relationship between sport and politics at the local and international level. In other words, to what extent should sport and other forms of entertainment be scrutinized for engaging in the re-branding attempts of foreign nations, under the premise that foreign investment will significantly increase their chances for success?

This conceptual book chapter does not claim to provide an ultimate solution but will offer a starting point for future research, by shedding light on some of the theoretical underpinnings of this ethical debate, namely *nation branding* and its *stakeholders*, on the one hand, and *soft power* and *sport diplomacy*, on the other. Before delving deeper into the Newcastle United and KSA nation branding relationship, key terms and theoretical underpinnings will be introduced to ensure conceptual clarity.

Nation Branding Kick-off

Anholt (2007) defines nation branding as a perception competition between countries displayed through exports, governance, tourism, investment, and culture. Kaneva (2011) views nation branding as the reconstruction and reimagination of a nation's identity through marketing and branding principles. Nation brands must solidify an identity to differentiate and communicate global relevance in an interconnected society (Eugenio-Vela et al., 2020; Kaneva, 2011). Put simply, identity creation and image management are the key elements in the nation branding process (Dinnie, 2022).

It is important to note that the act of nation branding alone does not automatically lead to a change in perceptions of a nation's international image. Stakeholders' engagement and involvement with the nation branding process instead largely defines its success (Andersson and Ekman, 2009; Dinnie, 2022). Or to put it in the words of Fan (2010), the creation of an image through nation branding requires continuous evaluations. As such, focusing on key stakeholders and understanding their active and passive involvement in the nation branding process depict an intriguing and underexplored line of inquiry.

Nation Branding Stakeholders

Many definitions of stakeholder exist in the nation branding literature. Freeman and McVea (2001) define stakeholders as any group or individual who shapes and affects a brand's goals. Haddaway et al. (2017) add that a stakeholder possesses the power to amplify and affect the brand image implementation, and Kavaratzis (2012) notes stakeholders' power to co-create the nation's image. Stakeholders define meaning through activity and participation in contrast to passive stakeholder groups who require guidance and consultation.

Participating stakeholders add credibility and attractiveness to the (nation) brand (Andersson and Ekman, 2009) and, thereby knowingly or not, take on the role of brand ambassadors of the nation (Simmons, 2009). More precisely, brand ambassadors amplify the state's branding objectives through action and inaction (Dinnie, 2022), providing authenticity as well as credibility, acting as a narrator of the nation brand (Andersson and Ekman, 2009).

That is, the ambassadors of the nation brand provide the key to creating a very public brand identity and delivering brand value. This relationship between the brand and the ambassador and the process itself forms brand equity, the perceived trust, and credibility of the brand on the global stage (Berry, 2000). It's this positive brand equity that's pushed out into the world that has been created and shaped by the brand ambassador, delivering, and amplifying varying degrees of awareness, relevance, and credibility (Dinnie, 2022).

Applying the theoretical concepts of nation branding and its stakeholders to the practical example of Newcastle United, we argue that supporters should be placed at the heart of this discussion, given that they can be regarded the most important stakeholder in football (Asada et al., 2020; Jaeger, 2021; McDonald et al., 2013; Yiapanas et al., 2022). Football supporters represent more than consumerism and their loyalty and passion (Parker and Stuart, 1997) make them an important driver in the evolution of the club's brand (García and Welford, 2015).

Mullin et al. (2000) discussed sport supporters' deep connection and involvement in the brand, stating supporters are the gatekeeper and fabric of the club, as they influence behavior and shape branding narratives around the club (Funk and James, 2004; Gladden and Funk, 2001). As Senaux (2008) stated, football supporters are the definitive stakeholder, given their power and legitimacy in and around the football club. By exploring the nation branding process through the eyes of Newcastle United supporters we are posing a perhaps provocative question: do supporters understand their complicity in cheerleading the branding and normalization of the state, and if so to which extent?

Soft Power and Sport Diplomacy

Having introduced the first two theoretical concepts underpinning the discussion, namely nation branding and supporters as the key stakeholder in football, the focus is now shifted to soft power and sport diplomacy. As argued by Brannagan and Giulianotti (2018) an important distinction between nation branding and soft power must be made as nation branding is an amplification of an image and soft power is the act of influencing the image and creating relationships. In this context, sport diplomacy can be regarded the strategy that brings soft power characteristics to live. An introduction to the concepts of soft power and sport diplomacy is offered in the subsequent section and their link with the chosen example of KSA's purchase of Newcastle United emphasized.

Soft Power

American political scientist, Joseph Nye, created the concept of soft power in response to America's perceived declining hard power concepts, namely military and economic power (Nye, 1990). In contrast to hard power, soft power refers to the means of a nation to influence others "by attraction and persuasion rather than just coercion and payment" (Nye, 2004, p. 256). Dubinsky (2023) adds, "soft power does not rely on military force or on sanctions, but on the possibility to shape the preferences of others through attractions and seductions" (p. 46).

The idea of soft power can be summarized as the motivation of a nation to construct a favorable image that creates trust and discourse between different nations (Plavsak, 2002). Once, a favorable image has been created, true power, expressed through the replication or acceptance of cultural norms, social ideologies, and policies, can be achieved (Nye, 2008). This allows foreign nation's cultural norms and ideologies to become normalized and establishes the existence of a trusted relationship between nations.

Applying the concept of soft power to the chosen example, it can be inferred that the KSA intentionally or not utilizes soft power to increase the acceptance of their cultural norms on a global stage, as well as re-positioning themselves as an attractive and influential nation (Nye, 2008). However, to what extent the KSA's efforts in using soft power have been successful in persuading supporters to perceive their nation in a positive light is yet to be determined.

Similar to nation branding, the final judge of success is the stakeholders, or more precisely the Newcastle United supporter as well as the local community in Newcastle. These stakeholders not only accept or reject the projected and communicated image of the KSA but also determine the acceptance of the foreign nation's ownership of Newcastle United in general.

Sport Diplomacy

Despite it only becoming a hot and highly debated topic in the last few years, the use of sport to support diplomacy initiatives is nothing new and can be traced back as far as the Olympics in Ancient Greece (Miller, 2006). Sport diplomacy can be defined as the act of using sport as a diplomatic tool to enhance a nation's global relevance, as well as facilitating the dissemination of a nation's social and cultural norms across the globe (Grix and Lee, 2013; Krzyzaniak, 2018).

Moreover, sport diplomacy nations can facilitate the creation of global connections and relationships as sport allows countries to introduce cultures and customs to one another (Murray and Pigman, 2014), that is, effective sport diplomacy can significantly affect and shape a country's global image and credibility and can support domestic as well as foreign policy goals of the nation (Dubinsky, 2023). Put differently, sport diplomacy can influence the nation's international and domestic image, as well as support public diplomacy goals (Murray and Pigman, 2014). The more recent involvement of previously underrepresented nations saw new regions entering the nation branding through sport diplomacy arena, thereby adding new cultural and political perspectives to the ever-evolving web of the global market (Chadwick, 2022; Dubinsky, 2023).

Today, especially smaller nation states in places like the Middle East are heavily investing in sport diplomacy through the hosting of mega-sporting events (e.g., Men's and Women's FIFA World Cups, Winter and Summer Olympic Games), global and regional sponsorship deals, and football club ownership (Brannagan and Giulianotti, 2015; Krzyzaniak, 2018). Football club ownership arguably depicts the most popular sport diplomacy strategy in this context (Braun et al., 2013; Chadwick et al., 2022). Some of the most public and prevailing football club ownerships are situated in the Middle East, specifically the state of Qatar's ownership of Paris St. Germain in 2011 (sole ownership attained in 2012), the United Arab Emirates acquisition of Manchester City Football Club in 2008, and the subject of this discussion, the KSA's purchase of Newcastle United in 2021 (Brannagan and Giulianotti, 2015, 2018; Chadwick et al., 2022; Haut et al., 2017; Krzyzaniak, 2018).

More precisely, for the chosen example it can be argued that the KSA utilizes sport diplomacy at the global and regional level as a nation branding tool to support the creation of soft power characteristics: credibility and relevance (Dinnie, 2022; Kemp et al., 2012). The subsequent awarding in hosting sporting events ranging from the Women's Tennis Association Final, to big money boxing events, to Esports World Cup to the Spanish Super Cup and the mega-event, the 2034 Men's Football World Cup, illustrate the growing acceptance of The Kingdom's soft power.

The discussion to this point has centered on the key theoretical underpinnings of the nation branding and sport diplomacy debate. We now delve deeper into the position of supporters at Newcastle United and their role in the KSA nation branding process. The importance of a positive and engaging relationship between the new ownership and the Newcastle United supporters, the cheerleaders of the club on and off the pitch, will be of key interest in the following sections.

The Complacent Cheerleader

Newcastle United played its first home game under the new ownership against Tottenham in October of 2021, a date that, in hindsight, could be regarded as the introduction to the complacent Newcastle United nation branding cheerleader. What on the surface appeared to be a global showcase of how supporters welcomed foreign ownership and normalized the KSA's role at Newcastle United is indeed not as simple as that. The negative media headlines and narratives that once followed the KSA seemed an afterthought at the game, all one had to do was pick up a paper or watch the highlights to understand the, perhaps temporary, acceptance of the Newcastle United ownership (Brown, 2021).

Even though the new ownership originally put out a club statement requesting supporters to "refrain from wearing traditional Arabic clothing or Middle East-inspired head coverings at matches if they would not ordinarily wear such attire", multiple supporters dressed in the traditional Middle Easter thobe and headdress, the Arabic keffiyeh. A display that could be deemed "culturally inappropriate", on the one hand, but can also be interpreted as a welcome gesture and sign of appreciation of the new ownership, on the other (Brown, 2021).

Revising its original statement, the club made a point of communicating to supporters that cultural and religious norms are welcome through dress, acknowledging the diversity in the local community. They went on to state that supporters who wished to wear "appropriate culturally inspired clothing" were welcome to do so and emphasized the act of dressing up was not offensive to the ownership group.

This acceptance of the supporters' behavior exemplifies the evolved but maybe still somewhat conflicted position between the KSA and the Newcastle United supporters. The embrace of the new ownership, represented through the dress in traditional cloth, could be defined as effective relationship marketing between the club owners and the supporters. However, in this instance we would argue it is even more than this, embracing the KSA traditional clothing symbolizes the formation of a bridge between two historically vastly different (political) cultures, that is, supporters as the ambassador, act as promoters and cheerleaders to the new relationship between their local community, the KSA ownership, and the UK government, a prime example for effective nation branding through sport.

Being off to a good start in the nation branding arena, the KSA started to explore in which other and perhaps more "aggressive" ways, they can utilize their ownership of Newcastle United to promote and alter perceptions of them as a nation further. As such, Saudi Arabia tried to find a way to integrate the traditional green color found on the KSA's national team into the historical black and white scheme that Newcastle United is known for on the pitch (Jones, 2023).

The use of color is a more traditional branding techniques, known for its ability to call more attention to a (nation) brand as well as allowing for easy differentiation between brands (Keller, 2020). The first iteration of the green scheme was introduced in the 2022–2023 season, the away kit included a white top with green trim, a combination never worn by Newcastle United, but one that can be found on Saudi's national team. Amnesty International saw this creative execution as a form of "sports-washing" (a non-Western media term according to Skye, 2022), a uniform for Newcastle supporters to indirectly cheerlead the relationship between the state, the club, and the community (MacInnes, 2022).

But it wasn't until the 2023–2024 Premiere League season that the kit was a fully realized billboard and cheerleading outfit for the KSA. The third kit for the season features the non-traditional green and a new front of kit sponsor, *Sela*. Sela is a KSA/PIF-owned experiential event company and replaced the online sports betting firm *Fun88* that previously occupied this position on Newcastle United kits (White, 2023). Additionally, all kits will feature the KSA/PIF-owned digital e-commerce company, *Noon*, who continues as Newcastle United's sleeve sponsor (Williams, 2023).

The new nation branding kit will not only be seen on the players in stadium and during broadcasts, but on supporters at home and away games, normalizing and promoting the legitimacy of ownership and amplifying the KSA/PIF-owned companies. It warrants the question if supporters understand the importance of their role in the nation branding and sport diplomacy process?

The supporter, as noted in this chapter, is not only the key stakeholder at Newcastle United, but at the heart of the nation branding process. Ultimately, the supporter defines and judges the ownership success through consumerism and loyalty and is an integral part in the co-creation of the ownership's brand identity (Dinnie, 2022). This relationship, coupled with the (foreign) investment by the owners, determines the degree of credibility and legitimacy not only in the local Newcastle community but globally (Chadwick, 2022).

Success on the Pitch Essential

Going back to our original question: when and at what cost can foreign investment be accepted, it should not be surprising that delivering the anticipated glory on the pitch is a crucial puzzle piece in the nation branding process. Research has shown that supporters align more closely with the club when successful results occur and disassociate with the club when negativity is produced (Snyder et al., 1986). This phenomenon, traditionally described as basking in reflected glory, on the one hand, and cutting of reflected failure, on the other (Snyder et al., 1986), is amplified in the current case given the additional ethical component.

Consequently, if the KSA does not want to risk losing supporters as their nation brand ambassadors, delivering positive results on the pitch becomes essential. Only by winning, or at the very least demonstrating how the club is successfully moving forward and connecting with community values, will allow the KSA to shape positive attitudes and ensure support and normalization of the ownership at Newcastle United.

Full-time

As has been stated, football fans are the primary stakeholders, the lifeblood of the club, due to their significant influence and involvement within the football club and surrounding community (Senaux, 2008). The supporter is the brand ambassador and billboard to the club, but in the case of KSA and Newcastle United also a complacent nation branding cheerleader. By examining the nation branding process from the perspective of Newcastle United supporters, the discussion raises a potentially contentious point of view: to what degree do supporters recognize their involvement in promoting and normalizing the state's identity and most importantly the state's relevance and credibility, if at all?

References

Andersson, M. and Ekman, P. (2009). Ambassador networks and place branding. *Journal of Place Management and Development*, 2(1), 41–51. https://doi.org/10.1108/17538330910942799

Anholt, S. (2007). *Competitive Identity: The New Brand Management for Nations, Cities and Regions*. London: Palgrave Macmillan.

Asada, A., Yong Jae, K. and Wonseok, J. (2020). Effects of relative size and homogeneity of sports fan community on potential fans' support intentions. *Journal of Sport Management*, 34(2), 103–119. https://doi.org/10.1123/jsm.2019-0055

Berry, L. L. (2000). Cultivating service brand equity. *Journal of the Academy of Marketing Science*, 28(1), 128–137. https://doi.org/10.1177/0092070300281012

Brannagan, P. M. and Giulianotti, R. (2015). Soft power and soft disempowerment: Qatar, global sport and football's 2022 World Cup finals. *Leisure Studies*, 34(6), 703–719. https://doi.org/10.1080/02614367.2014.964291

Brannagan, P. M. and Giulianotti, R. (2018). The soft power–soft disempowerment nexus: the case of Qatar. *International Affairs*, *94*(5), 1139–1157. https://doi.org/10.1093/ia/iiy125

Braun, E., Kavaratzis, M. and Zenker, S. (2013). My city – my brand: the different roles of residents in place branding. *Journal of Place Management and Development*, *6*(1), 18–28. https://doi.org/10.1108/17538331311306087

Brown, M. (2021, October 20). *Newcastle urge fans to avoid 'culturally inappropriate' clothing at games. The Guardian.* https://www.theguardian.com/football/2021/oct/20/newcastle-urge-fans-to-avoid-culturally-inappropriate-clothing-at-games.

Butler, P. (2020). *Child poverty increases in England across the north and Midlands. The Guardian.* https://www.theguardian.com/society/2020/oct/14/child-poverty-increases-in-england-across-the-north-and-midlands.

Chadwick, S. (2022). From utilitarianism and neoclassical sport management to a new geopolitical economy of sport. *European Sport Management Quarterly*, *22*(49), 1–22. https://doi.org/10.1080/16184742.2022.2032251

Chadwick, S., Widdop, P. and Burton, N. (2022). Soft power sports sponsorship – A social network analysis of a new sponsorship form. *Journal of Political Marketing*, *21*(2), 196–217. https://doi.org/10.1080/15377857.2020.1723781

Crafton, A. (2023). *Newcastle's Saudi takeover: New government emails about PIF, Premier League, Staveley and owners.* https://theathletic.com/5077168/2023/11/21/newcastle-saudi-takeover-emails/.

Dinnie, K. (2022). *Nation Branding: Concepts, Issues, Practice* (3rd ed.). Oxford: Routledge. https://doi.org/10.4324/9781003100249

Dubinsky, Y. (2023). *Nation Branding and Sports Diplomacy: Country Image Games in Times of Change.* Cham: Palgrave Macmillan. https://doi.org/10.1007/978-3-031-32550-2

Eugenio-Vela, J. S., Ginesta, X. and Kavaratzis, M. (2020). The critical role of stakeholder engagement in a place branding strategy: a case study of the Empordà brand. *European Planning Studies*, *28*(7), 1393–1412. https://doi.org/10.1080/09654313.2019.1701294

Fan, Y. (2010). Branding the nation: towards a better understanding. *Place Branding and Public Diplomacy*, *6*, 97–103.

Freeman, R. E. E. and McVea, J. (2001). A stakeholder approach to strategic management. *SSRN Electronic Journal.* https://doi.org/10.2139/ssrn.263511

Funk, D. C. and James, J. D. (2004). The fan attitude network (fan) model: exploring attitude formation and change among sport consumers. *Sport Management Review*, *7*(1), 1–26. https://doi.org/10.1016/S1441-3523(04)70043-1

García, B. and Welford, J. (2015). Supporters and football governance, from customers to stakeholders: a literature review and agenda for research. *Sport Management Review*, *18*(4), 517–528. https://doi.org/10.1016/j.smr.2015.08.006

Gladden, J. M. and Funk, D. C. (2001). Understanding brand loyalty in professional sport: examining the link between brand associations and brand loyalty. *International Journal of Sports Marketing and Sponsorship*, *3*(1), 54–81. https://doi.org/10.1108/IJSMS-03-01-2001-B006

Grix, J. and Lee, D. (2013). Soft power, sports mega-events and emerging states: the lure of the politics of attraction. *Global Society*, *27*(4), 521–536. https://doi.org/10.1080/13600826.2013.827632

Haddaway, N. R., Kohl, C., Rebelo da Silva, N., Schiemann, J., Spök, A., Stewart, R., Sweet, J. B. and Wilhelm, R. (2017). A framework for stakeholder engagement during systematic reviews and maps in environmental management. *Environmental Evidence*, *6*(1), 11. https://doi.org/10.1186/s13750-017-0089-8

Haut, J., Grix, J., Brannagan, P. M. and van Hilvoorde, I. (2017). International prestige through 'sporting success': an evaluation of the evidence. *European Journal*

for Sport and Society, *14*(4), 311–326. https://doi.org/10.1080/16138171.2017.
1421502

Jaeger, J. (2021). Football fans and stakeholder theory – a qualitative approach to classifying fans in Germany. *Sport, Business and Management: An International Journal*, *11*(5), 598–619. https://doi.org/10.1108/SBM-11-2020-0127

Jones, J. (2023, June 23). *Newcastle third kit LEAKED with distinct Saudi theme as fans say 'at some point they might realise…'. The US Sun*. https://www.the-sun.com/sport/8440402/newcastle-third-kit-leaked-saudi/amp/

Kaneva, N. (2011). Nation branding: toward an agenda for critical research. *International Journal of Communication*, *5*, 117–141. https://doi.org/10.1057/9781137500991_11

Kavaratzis, M. (2012). From "necessary evil" to necessity: stakeholders' involvement in place branding. *Journal of Place Management and Development*, *5*(1), 7–19. https://doi.org/10.1108/17538331211209013

Keller, L. (2020). *Strategic Brand Management: Building, Measuring, and Managing Brand Equity* (5th ed.). London: Pearson.

Kemp, E., Childers, C. Y. and Williams, K. H. (2012). Place branding: creating self-brand connections and brand advocacy. *Journal of Product & Brand Management*, *21*(7), 508–515. https://doi.org/10.1108/10610421211276259

Krzyzaniak, J. S. (2018). The soft power strategy of soccer sponsorships. *Soccer and Society*, *19*(4), 498–515. https://doi.org/10.1080/14660970.2016.1199426

MacInnes, P. (2022, May 13). *Newcastle kit sharing Saudi colours would be sports-washing, Amnesty says. The Guardian*. https://amp.theguardian.com/football/2022/may/13/newcastle-kit-sharing-saudi-arabia-colours-sportswashing-amnesty

McDonald, H., Karg, A. J. and Vocino, A. (2013). Measuring season ticket holder satisfaction: rationale, scale development and longitudinal validation. *Sport Management Review*, *16*(1), 41–53. https://doi.org/10.1016/j.smr.2012.05.003

Miller, S. G. (2006). *Ancient Greek Athletics*. New Haven: Yale University Press.

Mullin, B., Hardy, S. and Sutton, W. (2000). *Sport Marketing* (2nd ed.). Champaign: Human Kinetics.

Murray, S. and Pigman, G. A. (2014). Mapping the relationship between international sport and diplomacy. *Sport in Society*, *17*(9), 1098–1118. https://doi.org/10.1080/17430437.2013.856616

Nye, J. (1990). *Bound to Lead: The Changing Nature of American Power*. New York: Basic Books.

Nye, J. (2004). Soft power and American foreign policy. *Political Science Quarterly*, *119*(2), 255–270. https://doi.org/10.2307/20202345

Nye, J. S. (2008). Public diplomacy and soft power. *The ANNALS of the American Academy of Political and Social Science*, *616*(1), 94–109. https://doi.org/10.1177/0002716207311699

Parker, K. and Stuart, T. (1997). The West Ham syndrome. *Market Research Society. Journal*, *39*(3), 1–8. https://doi.org/10.1177/147078539703900306

Plavsak, K. (2002). Communicative diplomacy for the 3rd millennium. *Journal of Political Marketing*, *1*(2–3), 109–122. https://doi.org/10.1300/J199v01n02_08

Senaux, B. (2008). A stakeholder approach to football club governance. *International Journal of Sport Management and Marketing*, *4*(1), 4. https://doi.org/10.1504/IJSMM.2008.017655

Simmons, J. A. (2009). "Both sides now": aligning external and internal branding for a socially responsible era. *Marketing Intelligence & Planning*, *27*(5), 681–697. https://doi.org/10.1108/02634500910977890

Snyder, C. R., Lassegard, M. and Ford, C. E. (1986). Distancing after group success and failure: basking in reflected glory and cutting off reflected failure. *Journal of Personality and Social Psychology*, *51*(2), 382–388. https://doi.org/10.1037/0022-3514.51.2.382

Waugh, C. (2020). *#cans – the Newcastle supporters stockpiling hopes and beers.* https://theathletic.com/1782804/2020/04/30/cans-newcastle-takeover/?access_token=13378081&redirected=1

White, M. (2023, June 23). *Is the new Newcastle United away kit the most controversial of the season?* FourFourTwo. https://www.fourfourtwo.com/buying-guide/castore-newcastle-united-away-kit-23-24

Williams, M. (2023, June 7). *Newcastle United extends with sleeve sponsor Noon.* https://www.sportbusiness.com/news/newcastle-united-extends-with-sleeve-sponsor-noon/#:~:text=Premier%20League%20club%20Newcastle%20United,of%20the%202022%2D23%20season

Yiapanas, G., Thrassou, A. and Vrontis, D. (2022). A holistic strategic perspective of football stakeholders. *Journal for International Business and Entrepreneurship Development, 14*(3), 349–377. http://doi.org/10.1504/JIBED.2022.10051858

5

IMAGE LAUNDERING, SPORT WASHING AND GREENWASHING IN AND THROUGH FOOTBALL

Argyro Elisavet Manoli, Ioannis Konstantopoulos, and Georgios A. Antonopoulos

Authors' Biographies

Argyro Elisavet Manoli is an Associate Professor of Marketing and Management in the University of Bergamo, Italy. Her research falls under the themes of marketing communications and integrity in the context of sport and has been published extensively in highly esteemed journals, books and policy reports.

Ioannis Konstantopoulos is the CEO of The Sports Footprint, a sustainability consultancy focusing on the world of sports and external researcher for the University of Lausanne. He has been working with numerous clients on sustainability programmes and has also developed several educational courses in sport and sustainability.

Georgios A. Antonopoulos is professor of criminology at Northumbria University, Newcastle (UK). His research interests include 'organised crime', illegal markets, illicit finances and corruption. He is the editor-in-chief of *Trends in Organised Crime*.

Image laundering, also known as reputation laundering, is a process that involves shaping the public perception in order to restore or improve the reputation of a person, organisation or company that has been affected by negative publicity or in some cases by a scandal (Westland, 2016). Very often public relations professionals work closely even with some of the world's authoritarian regimes and/or with contexts that have been associated with human rights abuses towards improving a country's reputation (see Corporate Europe Observatory, n.d.). The process usually involves a range of strategic actions, such as public relations campaigns, advertising and other forms of messaging, aimed at reshaping the narrative around the entity in question.

DOI: 10.4324/9781003473671-6

Image laundering can be associated with reputation management since it concerns the practice of maintaining or improving the reputation of an individual or an organisation in the eyes of stakeholders. However, while reputation management focuses on proactive measures to create and maintain a positive reputation, image laundering is usually seen as a reaction to negative publicity or a scandal (Westland, 2016).

From a rather cynical viewpoint, image laundering is nothing more than a re-branding exercise. As argued in the seminal work of Keller (2001, 2014), a simple model of brand value consists of components or four levels. While the first level, brand awareness, and the fourth, relationships with the brand, are less relevant in this case, image laundering can be understood through the examination of the other two. Level two refers to the image of the brand, or the perceptions that consumers have of a brand, which are shaped by their experiences, beliefs and feelings about the brand. These perceptions can be divided into two broad categories: the *cognitive* image and the *emotional* image (Keller, 2001, 2014).

The former, the cognitive image, refers to the logical or functional aspects of a brand that consumers associate with it. It includes attributes such as quality, price, technical features and advantages, aspects that are not directly relevant in the case of image laundering. The latter, however, the emotional image, refers to the emotional associations consumers have with a brand. This includes emotions such as excitement, happiness, trust and loyalty. As such, the emotional image is usually linked to the 'personality' and values of a brand and the emotional benefits it offers. In the case of image laundering, this is the aspect that might be viewed as problematic following an unfortunate event or a scandal. That is because the public, existing or prospect consumers might have developed negative associations with a particular entity, be it an individual, an organisation or even a country. Image laundering can then present itself as a re-branding exercise aiming to improve the brand value of said entity, by first improving the brand perceptions it has. By attempting to develop a different and more positive emotional image for the particular brand, image laundering can help improve the overall public perception of an organisation and attempt the make the public 'forget' the previous negative associations.

In the case of a more strategic and long-term image laundering/re-branding exercise, then an organisation can advance towards Keller's (2001, 2014) third level of brand value, the *responses to brand*. Brand responses refer to the way consumers evaluate and feel about a brand based on the previous two levels of brand value, brand recognition and brand image. These responses can be divided into two categories: *judgements* and *emotions* (Fayrene and Lee, 2011). *Judgements* refer to the cognitive evaluations that consumers make of a brand, based on factors such as quality, reliability and value and are once again not relevant to image laundering. *Emotions*, however, can play a pivotal role, since they refer to the emotional reactions consumers have to a brand.

These can be positive or negative and are influenced by their own experiences and perceptions of the brand. For example, a consumer may feel happy or excited when thinking about a particular brand because it reminds them of positive experiences they have had when using its products or because of the association of the brand with other brands that generate these emotions, as in the case of sport. In this way, a brand that is associated with an emotionally intense moment in the eyes of a consumer, such as winning a sport trophy by his/her favourite team or athlete, can generate emotional reactions, thus increasing its value in the eyes of that consumer. In the case of image laundering, this is the ideal response, the one based on a positive emotion, a brand/entity that has developed a negative public perception might want to achieve.

This phenomenon of image laundering, or re-branding, materialises predominantly through two strategies in the world of sport: (a) through the use of sport; or (b) through the use of sustainability or ecology. The process of *image laundering through sport* is a phenomenon that occurs when individuals, organisations or regimes/countries use sporting events or teams to improve their public image (Westland, 2016). This process is often referred to as 'sportwashing'. Although, as we show later this chapter, sportswashing has a long history, the word 'sportswashing' was first used just before the European Games in Baku, Azerbaijan, in 2015, when human rights advocate, Rebecca Vincent, used the term *"in a press release for the 'Sport for Rights' campaign designed to illuminate Azerbaijani dictator Ilham Aliyev's suppressive efforts… to distract from its human rights record with prestigious sponsorship and hosting of events"* (Boykoff, 2022, p. 343). Sportswashing can be done in a number of ways, such as sponsoring a team or an event, making charitable donations or using sports personalities to promote a product or activity. The purpose of the process is to associate the individual, organisation or regime/country with positive attributes such as success, health, openness, inclusion and community involvement, attributes with which sport is already associated. If the sponsored sport entity achieves success, then the potential creation of strong emotions towards the non-sporting entity (individual, organisation or country) is the ideal aim of sportswashing, replacing thus any previous negative associations and emotions.

Sportswashing has a very long history especially in mega-events such as the Olympic Games. Perhaps the best example has been the 1936 Olympic Games in Berlin, which were used by Adolph Hitler to consolidate political support in Germany and promote his white supremacist worldview in his country and internationally; and relatively more recently the 2014 Winter Olympics in Sochi, Russia, which allowed Putin to distract from legal frameworks that openly persecuted members of the LGBTQ+ community (Boykoff and Yasouka, 2014).

Within the context of football, the 1934 World Cup held in Italy was Benito Mussolini's fascist regime 'great global coming out party' designed to show to the rest of the world what the fascist party could achieve (Ronay, 2019). More than 40 years later, the 1978 World Cup was hosted by the military junta of Argentina and coincided with the junta's pursuing of a brutal policy of arrests, torture and disappearances of those who openly opposed the regime (History Extra, 2022). Moreover, the 2018 World Cup was hosted by Russia and for a decade (2012–2022) UEFA Champions League was sponsored by Russian state-owned Gazprom (Greenpeace, 2023).

In addition, internationally important football clubs have been suggested to be parts of sportswashing with one of the earliest best examples, perhaps, being Roman Abramovich's ownership of Chelsea FC for approximately two decades. Many suggest that Abramovich bought the club at Vladimir Putin's command in order for attention to be diverted from human rights issues in Russia (Macdonald, 2023). When Abramovich announced his intention to sell Chelsea FC following the British Government freezing of his assets shortly after the start of the war in Ukraine, he pledged to donate the proceeds of the sale to the victims of the war (Abramovich, 2022). However, sportswashing is not limited only to sport mega-events and individual 'heavyweight' football clubs. For instance, in 2021 Formula 1 season the Azerbaijan Grand Prix was introduced, making the particular country one of the top mentioned countries in English-language articles on 'sportswashing' from 2019 to 2022, following only the 'usual suspects' China, Middle Eastern countries and Russia (Statista, 2023)

On the other hand, *image laundering through sustainability or ecology*, or 'greenwashing', refers to the practice of an individual or organisation making false or exaggerated statements about their efforts for environmental sustainability to create a positive image or gain a competitive advantage (Miller, 2017). Often, this practice is used by sports teams, events and sponsoring companies to attract consumers or fans, who are sensitive to environmental issues and benefit from the positive publicity generated by being perceived as environmentally friendly.

Johnson and Ali (2018), in an attempt to describe the 'light green' approach to environmental sustainability in sports, introduced the concept of 'purposeful ambiguity', which refers to strategically crafting environmental policies and objectives in ways that obscure their implementation, significance and measurement. This intentional lack of clarity allows organisations to define sustainability in a manner favourable to their operations while presenting an external image that pleases stakeholders, contributing to the effectiveness of greenwashing within a light green paradigm. Rio 2016 Summer Olympics offers us several examples of such 'light green approach' and 'greenwashing', examining how environmental initiatives were presented beforehand and implemented in practice. In scrutinising the bid books of the Rio 2016 Olympics, Gaffney (2013) discovered that the term 'environment' and its variants was the second highest occurring term, trailing only behind 'security'.

Additionally, the term 'sustainability' was emphasised, occurring 3 times more frequently than 'education' and 11 times more than 'citizen' in the bid.

In particular, the Rio 2016 bid prominently featured environmental sustainability commitments, such as the cleanup of Guanabara Bay and an ambitious goal to surpass the pledge of planting 24 million trees by the year 2016. These initiatives underscored the bid's dedication to environmental responsibility, shaping its promise to enhance the ecological landscape in the lead-up to the Olympic Games (Boykoff and Mascarenhas, 2016). However, in April 2015, approximately 40 tons of deceased fish appeared under mysterious circumstances at Lagoa Rodrigo de Freitas. Two months earlier, in February 2015, a similar incident happened in Guanabara Bay (Wade, 2015). Despite Rio 2016's commitment to plant 24 million trees by the Olympics and a further pledge of 34 million by the State officials, the 2014 Sustainability Report did not follow up on the tree-planting initiative. By 2015, only 5.5 million trees had been planted, falling significantly short of the promised numbers outlined in the Rio 2016 bid (Boykoff and Mascarenhas, 2016). In the case of football, we recently saw that the Swiss Fairness Commission, the self-regulatory body of the advertising and communications industry, argued that FIFA made false claims about carbon neutrality at Qatar World Cup and advised FIFA from making unsubstantiated claims in future (Revil, 2023).

Beyond the realm of the Olympics and mega-sport events, instances of greenwashing and image laundering are also, apparent in motorsports, revealing a broader pattern of environmental rhetoric that often diverges from genuine sustainability practices. In response to environmental concerns, NASCAR introduced *NASCAR Green*, aiming to mitigate its overall impact through strategic partnerships. In 2011, and in collaboration with Sunoco and American Ethanol, the organisation launched E15, a biofuel designed to reduce emissions by 20% while increasing performance. Additionally, NASCAR claimed to offset carbon emissions through its Clean Air Tree Planting Program, having planted over 400,000 trees in partnership with the Arbor Day Foundation and the Virginia Department of Forestry (Johnson and Ali, 2018).

However, such approaches focus on solving environmental challenges through technological advancements while maintaining economic growth and consumption. They also serve as a great marketing tool building a brand image containing the elements of 'sustainability' and 'innovation', two buzzwords with marketing-branding value and positive connotations. However, when it comes to real environmental impacts, this approach just involves peripheral adjustments, such as developing new forms of biofuel, without attempting to solve fundamental environmental concerns, and without taking into account the complex interactions of flora and fauna within the existing ecosystem concerned.

Similarly, Formula 1 emitted 256,551 tons of CO_2eq, based on their 2019 sustainability report, while 0.7% of those was attributed to the actual racing, with the majority stemming from logistics, including 45% from air, road and sea freight and 27.7% from personnel travel (F1, 2019). In 2019, Formula 1 pledged to achieve a net-zero carbon target by 2030, including the development of 100% sustainable fuel, intended for use in both racing and road cars, presenting a potential transformative impact on global emissions. Moreover, Formula 1 has committed to reducing its own carbon emissions by at least 50% by the year 2030 (Richards, 2023). However, those commitments did not seem to convince some of F1's key sponsors such as Hugo Boss, a fashion brand that has sponsored the McLaren F1 team since the 1970s, which transitioned to Formula E, in an attempt to engage with a younger audience (Næss, 2020).

In conclusion, in relation to 'sportswashing', in particular, countries as well as supranational entities such as the European Union must ensure that activities by PR companies and lobbying associations come under stricter regulation and scrutiny such as a mandatory EU Transparency Register for lobbyists (Corporate Europe Observatory, n.d.), for these companies and associations working with repressive regimes to be identified. However, Fruh et al. (2023) recognise that there is an additional avenue for those of us involved in sports, actively (as sportspeople and coaches), as journalists or as fans/consumers of sports: resistance by exiting the condition of complicity, for example by refusing to participate in the sporting event or consume the spectacle from that event.

In relation to 'greenwashing', as the sports industry is taking its first steps towards sustainability, the absence of credible standards, certifications and clear regulatory frameworks leaves room for deceptive marketing efforts, greenwashing and image laundering. However, public demands for transparent and authentic communication are increasing and emerging sports ventures such as Formula E and SailGP, which have sustainability at their core, are putting pressures to the sports industry, towards positive change and honesty in communication. Moreover, upcoming regional legislation, such as the EU Corporate Sustainability Reporting Directive, is expected to bring additional changes in sustainability reporting and marketing. These collective developments suggest that cases of greenwashing and image laundering in sports are anticipated to be reduced, paving the way for a more responsible and authentic industry. However, as marketing strategies become increasingly sophisticated, and new actors enter the global sports scene, the landscape becomes further complicated. With a lack of global consensus on how sports organisations should communicate their sustainability initiatives, the risk of greenwashing and image laundering remains a challenge. Individuals must maintain a critical mindset when engaging with sports marketing, discerning between genuine sustainability efforts and potential greenwashing. Simultaneously, it is vital for the sports industry to uphold authenticity, recognising that maintaining a sincere commitment to sustainability is not only ethically responsible but also crucial for sustaining popularity among people and connecting with new generations.

References

Abramovich, R. (2022). Statement from Roman Abramovich, *Chelsea FC*, accessed via Statement from Roman Abramovich | News | Official Site | Chelsea Football Club (chelseafc.com).

Boykoff, J. (2022). Towards a theory of sportswashing: mega-events, soft power and political conflict. *Sociology of Sport Journal, 39*, 342–351.

Boykoff, J. and Mascarenhas, G. (2016). The Olympics, sustainability, and greenwashing: the Rio 2016 summer games. *Capitalism, Nature, Socialism, 27*(2), 1–11.

Boykoff, J. and Yasuoka, M. (2014). Media coverage of the 2014 winter Olympics in Sochi, Russia: Putin, politics, and Pussy Riot. *The International Journal of Olympic Studies, 23*, 27–55.

Corporate Europe Observatory (n.d.). *Spin Doctors to the Autocrats: How European PR Firms Whitewash Repressive Regimes*. Brussels: Corporate Europe Observatory.

Fayrene, C. Y. and Lee, G. C. (2011). Customer-based brand equity: a literature review. *Researchers World, 2*(1), 33.

Formula1 (F1) (2019). *Sustainability Strategy*, accessed via https://corp.formula1.com/wp-content/uploads/2021/09/Environmental-sustainability-Corp-website-vFINAL_UPDATED-040821-1.pdf

Fruh, K., Archer, A. and Wojtowicz, J. (2023). Sportswashing: complicity and corruption. *Sport, Ethics and Philosophy, 17*(1), 101–118.

Gaffney, C. (2013). Between discourse and reality: the un-sustainability of mega-event planning. *Sustainability, 5*(9), 3926–3940.

Greenpeace (2023). What is sportswashing and why is it such as big problem? *Greenpeace*, accessed via What is sportswashing and why is it such a big problem? | Greenpeace UK.

History Extra (2022). Sportswashing: a historical perspective on a current trend, accessed via Sportswashing, a History: from Nazi Olympics to Qatar's World Cup | HistoryExtra.

Johnson, J. and Ali, A. E. (2018). Sustainability, greenwashing, and the light green approach to sport environmentalism. In B. P. McCullogh and T. B. Kellison (Eds.), *Routledge Handbook of Sport and the Environment* (pp. 319–329). London: Routledge.

Keller, K. L. (2001). *Building Customer-Based Brand Equity: A Blueprint for Creating Strong Brands*. MSI working paper. Cambridge: Marketing Science Institute.

Keller, K. L. (2014). Consumer brand relationships. *Journal of Brand Management, 21*, 365–365.

Macdonald, E. (2023). The Beautiful Game? The Rise of 'Sportswashing' in Football, *St. Andrews Law Review*, October 4, accessed via https://www.standrewslawreview.com/.

Miller, T. (2017). *Greenwashing Sport*. London: Taylor & Francis.

Næss, H. E. (2020). Corporate greenfluencing: a case study of sponsorship activation in Formula E motorsports. *International Journal of Sports Marketing and Sponsorship, 21*(4), 617–631.

Revil, J. (2023). FIFA made false claims about carbon neutrality at Qatar World Cup, regulator says. *Reuters*, accessed via https://www.reuters.com/sports/soccer/fifa-made-false-claims-about-carbon-neutrality-qatar-world-cup-regulator-2023-06-07/.

Richards, G. (2023). After the flood, storms lie ahead for Formula One in race to hit Carbon Zero, *The Guardian*, May 21.

Ronay, B. (2019). Sportswashing and the tangled web of Europe's biggest clubs, *The Guardian*, February 15.

Statista (2023). Countries mentioned most often in English-language articles on sportswashing from 2019 to 2022, accessed via Countries mentioned the most in sportswashing articles 2022 | Statista.

Wade, S. (2015). Rio Olympic Head Says Venue with Fish Die-Off Will Be Safe. *Associated Press*, April 17.

Westland, N. (2016). Image-laundering by countries through sport. In Transparency International (Ed.), *Global Corruption Report: Sport* (pp. 73–77). Berlin: Transparency International.

6

UNPACKING THE CONCEPT OF SPORTSWASHING IN ELITE MEN'S PROFESSIONAL FOOTBALL IN ENGLAND

Leon Davis and Daniel Plumley

Introduction

As a concept, 'sportswashing' is one of the most recent concepts to abruptly enter the political, media, and popular lexicon, similar to 'social capital' and 'soft power' before it. As a result, in many ways, it is nothing new. Sportswashing is just a rebrand of a concept that has been around for centuries. The term also has geographical resonance, mostly being reserved for use in narrative relating to influence in sport from outside the Western World. One of the highest profile examples of this is the takeover of Newcastle United Football Club by the Saudi Arabian Public Investment Fund (PIF) in 2021. In this chapter, we explore the concept of 'sportswashing' in relation to elite men's professional football in England. In doing so, we put forward an argument of nuance in the concept, further supporting our point that it is nothing new. It is also never just one thing in isolation. To understand the concept of 'sportswashing' and its relevance in elite men's professional football in England, we must also consider the wider landscape of the sport and beyond, including financial incentives, ownership motives, global exposure, and the leveraging opportunity. Any concept of 'sportswashing' is often bigger than the sport itself and we must be aware of the bigger picture story at play. We will return to this later in the chapter, citing examples throughout history to support our case: but first we must attempt to understand the terminology in more detail.

Sportswashing Advancing from Soft Power

As a concept, sportswashing is inextricably linked to 'soft power', a term popularised by Joseph Nye in western circles in the late twentieth century. Nye (1990, 2004, 2021) defined soft power as the ability to achieve goals

DOI: 10.4324/9781003473671-7

through attraction rather than coercion. Soft power is linked to, and bound up with, states' public diplomacy and image management strategies and was originally positioned from a North American (USA) perspective by Nye. Soft power is a popular term within current day international relations (Bonora, 2020; MacDonald, 2020) and has been explored extensively in academia in the twenty-first century.

Scholars have utilised the concept of sportswashing to advance Nye's concept of soft power due to the limitations outlined by the likes of Grix and Brannagan (2016) and Koch (2018) and the multiple re-conceptualisations or understandings of the concept in fields outside of mainstream/traditional politics (see Grix et al., 2015). As highlighted by Skey (2023), sportswashing is a neologism that has begun to appear with increasing regularity in the English-language media over the past few years. The term 'sportswashing' rose to the forefront of sport politics in the mid to late 2010s, primarily due to the rise in nations with questionable human rights records hosting a variety of international sporting events (see Akhundova, 2015; Brannagan and Rookwood, 2016; Delgado, 2016; Koch, 2018; Schausteck et al., 2014). It became a contemporary term in the late 2010s, recognised initially in academia by the likes of Chadwick (2018a, 2018b, 2022), but sportswashing has been used for over a century in modern sporting events (see Rosenberg, 2022) and has also been labelled as a 'new word for an old idea' (Menon, 2019). According to Dubinsky (2023a, p. 157) the use of sport for nation branding and public diplomacy goes 'back to antiquity, not only to the city-states and the athletic competitions in Olympia, in Ancient Greece, but also through the conquests of Alexander the Great'. Boykoff (2022, p. 342), when highlighting the lack of definition of the term in scholarly literature, defined sportswashing as 'a phenomenon whereby political leaders use sports to appear important or legitimate on the world stage while stoking nationalism and deflecting attention from chronic social problems and human-rights woes on the home front'.

Schad (2022) asserted that sportswashing, for world leaders, it is a way to improve their nation's reputation by hosting a prestigious sporting event or financing a popular team. Similar to Sport for Right's element of sportswashing being a 'distraction', Chadwick (2022) believes the concept relies on 'diversion', namely from a variety of human rights issues that may be occurring in said country (also see McGillivray et al., 2022). There have been a number of definitions of the term – and although 'sportswashing' lacks an agreed upon definition, it has become to be a way to criticise typically non-democratic regimes or large corporations for using investment in world-renowned athletes, sports clubs, and sports events to detract from illiberal, non-democratic, and/or exploitative practices in their home countries or businesses (see Ettinger, 2023; Grix et al., 2023). Chadwick (2018a) highlighted the dearth of academic research on sportswashing and that the term has been used to liberally and simplistically by western countries. As the world emerged from the COVID-19 lockdowns of 2020 and 2021, the interest in sportswashing in academia has increased significantly (cf. Boykoff, 2022; Davis et al., 2023; Dubinsky, 2023a, 2023b; Ettinger, 2023; Fruh et al., 2022; Grix et al., 2023; Jephson, 2023; Kearns et al., 2023; Skey, 2023).

Skey (2023) outlined how sportswashing has only been used a pejorative term, much like propaganda, to call into question the activities of those hosting the events, which is in direct contrast to cognate terms, such as soft power or public diplomacy, which are often portrayed as the legitimate actions of states even if they are not viewed as successful. Up until now, it has only been applied to a narrow range of state actors, all of whom are based outside of the Western World. However, we should also question whether or not some of the actors in the Western World have held similar desires to the arguments linked to sportswashing. This links to the nuance in the term and Menon's (2019) label of sportswashing as a 'new word for an old idea'. Is it really that different as a concept and has it only been a strategy deployed in the East? We now turn our attention to English football and a brief history lesson.

English Football and Sportswashing

Although the term (and concept) of sportswashing became vogue when abruptly entering the sporting landscape in the mid-2010s (see Grix et al., 2023; Skey, 2023) the antecedents of the term, as a separate entity to soft power or social capital, can be traced back a little further into the early 2000s, with particular reference to key events in the history of men's football in England. Such events include Roman Abramovich's purchase of Chelsea FC in 2003, the FIFA 2006 World Cup in Germany, and Sheikh Mansour's takeover of Manchester City FC in 2008. When we consider the context of the takeovers at Chelsea (2003) and Manchester City (2008) we arrive at a bigger picture of ownership motives and, ultimately, finance. There has been considerable literature published on the economics and finance of professional team sport and how the professional sport ecosystem continues to hold an allure for investors linked to broadcasting rights contracts, sponsorship opportunities, and the ability to target a global audience (see Plumley and Wilson, 2022). It is beyond the scope of this chapter to examine all of these things in detail: but we must be aware that sport holds significant power for investors for a multitude of reasons. A key word in this debate is 'leverage'. Many actors in the sport investment network are looking for leverage just as much as they are looking for the acquisition. In the context of 'sportswashing' we have already defined some of this leveraging earlier in this chapter linked to human rights issues in certain territories. However, leveraging is not a term exclusive to these territories. All owners of football clubs are looking for some form of leverage and often that leverage is financial. Put simply, despite the morals and ethics involved, it often comes down to money, and who has the most money.

We can see this laid bare in Kearn's et al. (2023) discussion of the investment-based sportswashing methodology. Kearns et al. argued that western powers have utilised a concept similar to sportswashing in the past. We could argue that this is similar to our notion of leverage cited above: the challenge in the early 2020s was that the financial power of these western actors was dwarfed by eastern counterparts. This created a powerful leveraging argument for investors linked to the emotional aspect of football fans. Many fans began to crave state investment in order to see their team compete at the top table. Put simply, they didn't care where the money was coming from, as long as it was more money than the previous owners had. The Glazer family takeover of Manchester United FC in 2005, the Mike Ashley-based takeover of Newcastle United FC in 2007, and, to a lesser extent, Tom Hicks and George Gillett's takeover of Liverpool FC in 2007 set a precedent, which, in essence, made certain fans conclude that to compete at the top of elite club football, state-based ownership was the only option. This was noticeable in the fan reaction to the PIF's takeover of Newcastle United FC in 2021 and the urge for Sheikh Jassim's (Qatar) ultimately failed takeover of Manchester United FC in 2023 (see Jones et al., 2023; Mehta and Gillespie, 2021). However, it must be noted that some supporters' groups were still averse to state-based ownership (see Jackson, 2023).

We cannot ignore the importance of fans in this argument and the power of fan experiences of different takeovers shaping the narrative. Responses are often mixed, adding further nuance to the debate. Whilst Kearns et al.'s (2023) study is admirable, it is framed solely around one club (Manchester City FC). Focusing on a team at the zenith of their powers, when the strategy implemented has fully come to fruition, with Manchester City's men's team winning *The Treble* (UEFA Champions League, Premier League, FA Cup) in 2023 can lead to a skewed opinion of the ethics of the ownership model and any concept of sportswashing. For Kearns et al. (2023), most research (to the time of their publication being released) had focused on one-off event-based sportswashing strategies (such as autocratic states hosting major international sports events) rather than longer term investment-based strategies (such as state actors purchasing sports clubs and teams). However, this shows a lack of consideration of the sports world in the early 2020s, linked to the long-term investment strategies by the likes of the Saudi Arabian PIF into the likes of Newcastle United FC (comparable to the Abu Dhabi [United Arab Emirates] funded Manchester City FC, but at an earlier stage in the process) and men's professional golf (see Chen and Doran, 2022; Davis et al., 2023; Davis and Plumley, 2023; Ettinger, 2023; Jephson, 2023; Taylor et al., 2023).

The Bigger Picture

We close out this chapter by returning to our point of the bigger picture at play. Sportswashing rose to prominence as a concept in the late 2010s, but in many ways, it is merely a term that creates a diversion. As Al-Khalifa and Farello (2021) point out, it is also a legitimisation strategy. If we accept this notion, and ditch the terminology, then geography also becomes irrelevant. The country with which the concept of sportswashing is linked to becomes immaterial. Instead, we should focus on the term of legitimacy and consider the drivers of wealth, money, and finance. It goes above football or sport: it is about something much bigger.

There is no doubt that the term sportswashing has become a popular phrase, but we question its analytical value. The term creates a geopolitical narrative of something that is non-Western and negative. There is also no agreed definition of the term. If we switch from the concept to the strategy it becomes about legitimacy. If we lift our heads up further still, it becomes about the money. Whilst the western media tend to highlight sportswashing as a negative towards the likes of the UAE, Qatar and Saudi Arabia, it is evident that these states do not care what people think of their strategies.

In 2023, the Kingdom of Saudi Arabia Crown Prince, Mohammed bin Salman, said that he does not care about allegations of 'sportswashing' against the kingdom and that he will continue funding sport if it adds to the country's gross domestic product (GDP). Having stated that he has a 1% increase in GDP due to sport (in 2023), Bin Salman said that they are aiming for more in the future, when saying 'Call it whatever you want – we are going to get that 1.5%' (see Sankar, 2023). In the case of Saudi Arabia, they have a goal which is much bigger than football, but football is a good leverage towards the achievement of that goal. In 2023, the PIF invested over £3 billion ($3.6 billion/€3.4 billion) into the Saudi Pro League (SPL), taking over four domestic football clubs – Al-Ahli, Al-Hilal, Al-Ittihad, and Al-Nassr – in the process (see Choukeir and Saba, 2023). The investment in football is linked to a bigger picture for the Kingdom, titled 'Vision 2023'. The wider picture for the vision is GDP.

Conclusion

Whether we like it or not, the horse has bolted. We can continue to debate the concept of sportswashing, but that only serves to further the diversion tactic. It is much bigger, than the concept, and much bigger than sport. Sport is merely leveraging collateral, but a powerful one it must be said. We will continue to see more sports shifting geographically from west to east, just like we have already with football, boxing, Formula 1, golf (men's and women's), and even entertainment brands such as the World Wrestling Entertainment (WWE).

We will also likely see more investment into sport from east to west, typified by the examples cited in this chapter in relation to English football. Due to the economic success of the English Premier League, at elite level in English football, it takes billions to compete. As such, concepts of sportswashing and even legitimacy can go out of the window. To fans, it is mostly about who has the most money and who can implement a strategy to compete at the highest level. Outgoing club owners will continue to sell to the highest bidder and fans of certain clubs are seeing state-based ownership as the best investment. Call it what you will, but it continues to mobilise and is here to stay.

References

Akhundova, Gulnara. (2015). Baku European Games 2015: A fearsome PR machine is using sport to sweep human rights under the carpet. 12 June. Available at: https://www.independent.co.uk/voices/comment/baku-european-games-2015-a-fearsome-pr-machine-is-using-sport-to-sweep-human-rights-under-the-carpet-10314316.html [Accessed 10 October 2023].

Al Khalifa, Hussa K. and Farello, Anna. (2021). The soft power of Arab women's football: changing perceptions and building legitimacy through social media. *International Journal of Sport Policy and Politics*, *13*(2), 241–257.

Bonora, Angela. (2020). Laureus sport for good: KPI framework. *Unpublished speech to the Joint Commonwealth Secretariat and United Nations, Education, Scientific and Cultural Organization Workshop on Sport, Physical Education, Physical Activity and the SDGs.* [Accessed 2 December 2020].

Boykoff, Jules. (2022). Toward a theory of sportswashing: mega-events, soft power, and political conflict. *Sociology of Sport Journal*, *39*(4), 342–351.

Brannagan, Paul M. and Rookwood, Joel. (2016). Sports mega-events, soft power and soft disempowerment: international supporters' perspectives on Qatar's acquisition of the 2022 FIFA World Cup finals. *International Journal of Sport Policy and Politics*, *8*(2), 173–188.

Chadwick, Simon. (2018a). Sports-washing, soft power and scrubbing the stains. Can international sporting events really clean up a country's tarnished image? 24 August. Available at: https://www.policyforum.net/sport-washing-soft-power-and-scrubbing-the-stains/ [Accessed 30 July 2023].

Chadwick, Simon. (2018b). How repressive states and governments use 'sportswashing' to remove stains on their reputation. 25 July. Available at: https://theconversation.com/how-repressive-states-and-governments-use-sportswashing-to-remove-stains-on-their-reputation-100395 [Accessed 1 August 2023].

Chadwick, Simon. (2022). Why the 'Putinisation' of sport must no longer fool the world. March 2. Available at: https://theconversation.com/why-the-putinisation-of-sport-must-no-longer-fool-the-world-178150 [Accessed 1 August 2023].

Chen, Steve and Doran, Karen. (2022). Using sports to "Build It Up" or "Wash It down": how sportswashing give sports a bad name. *Findings in Sport, Hospitality, Entertainment, and Event Management*, *2*(3). https://digitalcommons.memphis.edu/finsheem/vol2/iss1/3.

Choukeir, Jana and Saba, Yousef. (2023). Saudi wealth fund to take control of soccer star Ronaldo's club. 5 June. Available at: https://www.reuters.com/sports/saudi-arabia-revives-sports-clubs-privatisation-plan-2023-06-05/ [Accessed 9 September 2023].

Davis, Leon and Plumley, Daniel. (2023). How men's golf has been shaken by Saudi Arabia's billion-dollar drive for legitimacy. 31 March. Available at: https://

theconversation.com/how-mens-golf-has-been-shaken-by-saudi-arabias-billion-dollar-drive-for-legitimacy-193474 [Accessed 30 July 2023].

Davis, Leon, Plumley, Daniel and Wilson, Rob. (2023). For the love of 'sportswashing'; LIV Golf and Saudi Arabia's push for legitimacy in elite sport. *Managing Sport and Leisure*. http://doi.org/10.1080/23750472.2022.2162953

Delgado, Daniel L. (2016). Opening ceremonies of international sports events: the other face of Chinese soft power. *The International Journal of the History of Sport*, *33*(5), 607–623.

Dubinsky, Yoav. (2023a). Nation branding, public diplomacy, and the dirty business of sportswashing. In *Nation Branding and Sports Diplomacy: Country Image Games in Times of Change* (pp. 157–191). New York: Springer International Publishing.

Dubinsky, Yoav. (2023b). Clashes of cultures at the FIFA World Cup: reflections on soft power, nation building and sportswashing in Qatar 2022. *Place Branding and Public Diplomacy*. https://doi.org/10.1057/s41254-023-00311-8

Ettinger, Aaron. (2023). Saudi Arabia, sports diplomacy and authoritarian capitalism in world politics. *International Journal of Sport Policy and Politics*, *15*(3), 531–547.

Fruh, Kyle, Archer, Alfred, and Wojtowicz, Jake. (2022). Sportswashing: complicity and corruption. *Sport, Ethics and Philosophy*, *17*(3), 1–18.

Grix, Jonathan and Brannagan, Paul M. (2016). Of mechanisms and myths: conceptualising states' "Soft Power" strategies through sports mega-events. *Diplomacy & Statecraft*, *27*(2), 251–272.

Grix, Jonathan, Brannagan, Paul M., and Houlihan, Barrie. (2015). Interrogating states' soft power strategies: a case study of sports mega-events in Brazil and the UK. *Global Society*, *29*(3), 463–479. https://doi.org/10.1080/13600826.2015.1047743

Grix, Jonathan, Dinsmore, Adam, and Brannagan, Paul M. (2023). Unpacking the politics of 'sportswashing': it takes two to tango. *Politics*. https://doi.org/10.1177/02633957231207387

Jackson, Jamie. (2023). Manchester United supporters' group voices concerns over Qatari bid for club. 19 February. Available at: https://www.theguardian.com/football/2023/feb/19/manchester-united-supporters-group-voices-concerns-over-qatari-bid-for-club [Accessed 19 October 2023].

Jephson, Nicholas. (2023). On the intrusion of LIV: brute-force bumps, unexpected unification and the future of professional golf. *International Journal of Sport Policy and Politics*. https://doi.org/10.1080/19406940.2023.2290113

Jones, Ian, Adams, Andrew, and Mayoh, Joanne. (2023). Fan responses to ownership change in the English Premier League: motivated ignorance, social creativity and social competition at Newcastle United F.C. *International Review for the Sociology of Sport*. https://doi.org/10.1177/10126902231179067

Kearns, Colm, Sinclair, Gary, Black, Jack, Doidge, Mark, Fletcher, Thomas, Kilvington, Daniel, Liston, Katie, Lynn, Theo, and Santos, Guto L. (2023). 'Best run club in the world': Manchester City fans and the legitimation of sportswashing? *International Review for the Sociology of Sport*. https://doi.org/10.1177/10126902231210784

Koch, Natalie. (2018). The geopolitics of sport beyond soft power: event ethnography and the 2016 cycling world championships in Qatar. *Sport in Society*, *21*(12), 2010–2031.

MacDonald, Alistair. (2020). *Sources of Soft Power: How Perceptions Determine the Success of Nations*. London: British Council.

McGillivray, David, Koenigstorfer, Joerg, Bocarro, Jason N., and Edwards, Michael B. (2022). The role of advocacy organisations for ethical mega sport events. *Sport Management Review*, *25*(2), 234–253.

Mehta, Amar and Gillespie, Tom. (2021). Saudi-led consortium takeover of Newcastle United approved, Premier League announces. 8 October. Available at: https://news.sky.com/story/saudi-led-takeover-of-newcastle-united-approved-premier-league-announces-12428381 [Accessed 25 September 2023].

Menon, Suresh (2019). Sportswashing, a new word for an old idea. 15 December. Available at: https://sportstar.thehindu.com/columns/lastword-suresh-menon/sportswashing-saudi-arabia-manchester-city-united-psg-champions-league-olympics-f1-boxing-athletics-football/article64863590.ece [Accessed 1 September 2023].

Nye, Joseph S. (1990). Soft power. *Foreign Policy* (80), 153–171.

Nye, Joseph S. (2021). Soft power: the evolution of a concept. *Journal of Political Power*, *14*(1), 196–208.

Nye, Joseph S. (2004). Soft Power: The Means to Success in World Politics. New York: Public Affairs.

Plumley, Daniel and Wilson, Rob. (2022). *The Economics and Finance of Professional Team Sports*. London: Routledge.

Rosenberg, Michael. (2022). Sportswashing Is Everywhere, but It's Not New. 29 December. Available at: https://www.si.com/olympics/2022/12/29/sportswashing-olympics-world-cup-daily-cover [Accessed 18 November 2023].

Sankar, Vimal. (2023). Bin Salman vows to continue doing sportswashing if it increases GDP in Saudi Arabia. 21 September. Available at: https://www.insidethegames.biz/articles/1141008/salman-continues-sportswashing [Accessed 10 October 2023].

Schad, Tom. (2022). LIV Golf shines spotlight on 'sportswashing' – the nascent term for an age-old strategy. Available at: https://eu.usatoday.com/story/sports/golf/2022/06/10/sportswashing-explained-saudis-liv-golf/10003676002/ [Accessed 1 August 2023].

Schausteck de Almeida, Bárbara, Marchi Júnior, Wanderley and Pike, Elizabeth. (2014). The 2016 Olympic and Paralympic games and Brazil's soft power. *Contemporary Social Science*, *9*(2), 271–83.

Skey, Michael. (2023). Sportswashing: media headline or analytic concept? *International Review for the Sociology of Sport*, *58*(5), 749–764.

Taylor, Tom, Burdsey, Daniel, and Jarvis, Nigel. (2023). A critical review on sport and the Arabian Peninsula – the current state of play and future directions. *International Journal of Sport Policy and Politics*, *15*(2), 367–383.

7

ATHLETE ACTIVISM IN GLOBAL FOOTBALL

Taking the Knee

Laura Bradshaw

Introduction

In today's globalised world, the influence of athletes, particularly footballers, extends beyond the pitch. As revered figures in pop culture and symbols of national pride, their voices carry weight, especially when they choose to engage in geopolitical issues. This phenomenon, termed "athlete activation", represents players' proactive stance in the face of social, political, and economic challenges. This chapter examines the evolution, impact, and implications of athlete activation within the context of football's geopolitical economy.

For centuries, athletes have leveraged their prominence in sports and their celebrity to voice political opinions and advocate for change. Yet, in our current era, with the rapid evolution of society and the instantaneous spread of news via diverse media channels, athlete activism appears to be more pronounced than ever before (Crafton, 2021).

This chapter examines the evolution, impact, and implications of athlete activation within the context of football's geopolitical economy. Athlete activism refers to "athletes using their name and brand to make a difference for a cause. Whether political, social, or economical, these causes all aim to improve the world around them" (Berman, 2023). The trend of athlete activism involves athletes using their platform to support various causes, ranging from political to social issues and has grown in today's geopolitical climate, with an expectation for athletes to contribute to social responsibility initiatives. However, when club revenues, sponsorship, and endorsement deals result in balancing the needs of multiple economic stakeholders, athlete activism can create new risks, both reputationally and economically. This chapter highlights the advantages of athlete activism and the risks it poses in the geopolitical economy of football.

DOI: 10.4324/9781003473671-8

Historical Context

Athlete activism has become a crucial part of professional sports, as fans and consumers expect athletes to use their influence for good. The expectation is now about taking action rather than simply raising awareness (Berman, 2023).

Athlete activism as a type of storytelling provides a powerful hook to gain people's interest (Magrath, 2022). Athletes are using storytelling to communicate their feelings and passion about social policies and inequalities or using their sporting platform to show their objection to societal injustice. Almost as long as sport has been played, activists have been within its ranks. The Nika riots of 532AD in Constantinople, which led to many thousands of deaths and half the city being burned down, were instigated by the emperor Justinian's refusal to pardon a pair of rival chariot racers (Ceithernach, 2020). Furthermore, two of the most celebrated examples of sports protest came from 1960s America: in 1966, Muhammad Ali refused to be drafted into the US military (Calamur, 2016); two years later, Tommie Smith and John Carlos gave a Black Power salute on the podium at the 1968 Olympics (Younge, 2012), with the whole world watching.

Historically, athletes have often been discouraged from expressing political sentiments. However, the latter half of the 20th century saw a shift. In the 1970s and 1980s, Brazilian footballer Sócrates used his sport as a vehicle to challenge a military dictatorship and speak out for democracy (Magee, 2022). Players like Sócrates used their status to push for democratic reforms during the military dictatorship. Such instances marked the beginning of footballers' transition from mere entertainers to political influencers.

As money poured into sport in the 1980s and 1990s, along with outsized sponsorship deals and greater scrutiny of off-field activities, athletes tended to become more tight-lipped. The era can be summed up by four words attributed to the basketball legend Michael Jordan around 1990, "Republicans buy sneakers too" (Lewis, 2020). The emphasis on staying in line for the sake of diplomacy and retaining sponsorship deals has since taken a turn in recent years with the rise of social media platforms.

Social Media Amplification

Athlete activism is now an integral aspect of professional sports, with fans and consumers expecting that athletes will use their platform for societal benefit, focusing on action over mere awareness (Berman, 2023). Athletes have embraced storytelling as a tool to emotionally connect with audiences on social and political issues, transforming their sports platform into a stage for social justice (Magrath, 2022).

Historical accounts show that sports and activism have been linked for centuries. The ancient Nika riots, caused by Emperor Justinian's refusal to pardon two chariot racers, led to significant casualties and the burning of half of Constantinople (Ceithernach, 2020). In more recent history, iconic protests include Muhammad Ali's stand against the Vietnam draft (Calamur, 2016) and the Black Power salute by Tommie Smith and John Carlos at the 1968 Olympics, symbolising the fight against racial injustice (Younge, 2012).

By the late 20th century, athletes began to move from being simply entertainers to becoming significant political voices. Sócrates, the Brazilian footballer, notably used his influence to oppose Brazil's military dictatorship and advocate for democracy, signifying a new era where athletes' voices in political discourse became pronounced (Magee, 2022). However, as sports commercialisation peaked in the 1980s and 1990s with substantial sponsorship deals, athletes often remained silent on contentious issues, encapsulated by Michael Jordan's alleged comment suggesting a reluctance to jeopardise commercial interests (Lewis, 2020). This cautious approach persisted until the advent of social media, which has recently empowered athletes to voice their opinions more freely and visibly, signalling a renewed phase of active and open athlete activism. It raises an important question: why do footballers use their status or fame and air their views through social platforms?

Over recent years, there has been an uptick in social protests by footballers. However, none have resonated as deeply or stirred the national sentiment as much as kneeling during the national anthem (Smith, 2019). Players taking the knee for human rights and racial equality were inspired by the Black Lives Matter (BLM) movement and in response to the killing of George Floyd (Dobson and McVeigh, 2020). Footballers worldwide began taking a knee before kick-off to protest racial injustice and in solidarity with the BLM movement (Dobson and McVeigh, 2020). This act drew both widespread support but also familiar backlash that footballers should "stick to sport", igniting discussions about race, colonial histories, and the role of athletes in political protests and echoing protests against racial injustice.

Beyond football, athletes like National Basketball Association (NBA) all-star LeBron James and Tennis player Naomi Osaka faced criticism for their political stances, illustrating the increasing involvement of sports figures in advocacy (Guardian, 2018; Sky Sports, 2019). Colin Kaepernick's kneeling protest against racial injustice notably cost him his National Football League (NFL) career, highlighting the potential personal cost of such activism. Conversely, footballer Mohamed Salah's popularity in Egypt has made him a symbol of unity and hope, transcending sport amid political unrest (Saleh, 2018). Charity initiatives by footballers like Didier Drogba (Common Goal, 2020; Goodyer, 2017; Guiberteau, 2020) and Marcus Rashford have had tangible societal impacts, with Rashford's efforts leading to a UK government policy reversal on child food poverty.

The concept of cultural diplomacy is evident in sports, with North and South Korean athletes marching together at the Olympics (Marcus, 2018) and historical examples like the "Christmas Truce" football match of World War

I (IWM, 2023). Current events, such as the 2022 FIFA World Cup in Qatar, demonstrate football's role in global image-building despite controversies (Reuters, 2022; Sands and Hudson, 2022).

The rise of social media has amplified athlete activism, with platforms like Twitter and Instagram enabling direct influence over public opinion and policy. This was highlighted by Marcus Rashford's use of social media to combat child food poverty, which exemplifies this new era of digital activism, where athletes command significant global influence and can shape societal change beyond the sports arena.

Economic Dimensions of Athlete Activation

Athlete activation is a multifaceted concept within the sports industry that encompasses strategies and initiatives aimed at maximising the economic potential of footballers and their brands. One of the primary economic drivers of athlete activation is sponsorship and endorsement deals and transfers. In recent years, with the rise in popularity of social media platforms, athletes have found new ways to communicate with their fans and increase revenues. Footballers with strong personal brands and a significant fan following are more attractive to corporate sponsors on and off the field of play (Välkkynen and Niinikoski, 2017). However, the delicate balance of loyalty persists in relation to fan loyalty between their club and player and players' loyalty between their club and moral compass. Regardless, it poses an interesting question: is the celebrity athlete pursuing the path of athlete activism for social good or purely for commercial gain?

Sponsorship deals can yield substantial financial rewards, ranging from lucrative contracts to product endorsements. Athlete activation helps athletes build and maintain marketability, increasing their earning potential through marketing partnerships (Smith et al., 2023). Furthermore, another economic dimension influenced by athlete activation is fan engagement. Athletes who actively engage with their fan base through social media, events, and interactive experiences can drive revenue for themselves and their affiliated teams or organisations.

Increased fan engagement can translate into higher ticket sales, merchandise purchases, and media rights deals. However, there are often conflicts of interest; for instance, David Beckham's lucrative ambassadorial role at the 2022 Qatar FIFA World Cup raised eyebrows about his support of a nation fraught with human rights issues. The decision to draught in celebrity athletes to influence viewers' perception of the nation was tainted by accusations of political sportswashing, and LGBTQ+ fan groups heavily criticised David Beckham for his decision to take the paid role (Sky Sports, 2023).

The digital realm, particularly social media and digital marketing, is a significant driver of athlete activation's economic impact. Athletes can leverage their online presence to reach a global audience, attract sponsors, and promote products or services (Smith et al., 2023). Companies, governments, and nations have become savvy to celebrity sportspeople's global reach and influence. However, effectively managing digital personas comes with challenges, such as maintaining authenticity while adhering to contractual obligations.

Athlete activation is a crucial component of the modern sports economy. It empowers athletes to maximise their earning potential, enhance fan engagement, and create lasting economic value. By strategically leveraging their personal brands, athletes and organisations can harness the economic dimensions of athlete activation to thrive in the highly competitive sports industry (Kaufman, 2008). Nevertheless, athlete activism has its risks and challenges. Footballers risk breaching their contracts if they bring the clubs' reputations into disrepute. This has been demonstrated beyond sports, recently when US artist Kanye West went on an antisemitic tirade, allegedly claiming he lost $2bn in a day on cancelled contracts when companies cut ties with him (Roush, 2023). It is a cautionary tale for celebrities who speak out.

Challenges, Risks, and Criticisms Associated with Athlete Activism

In the high-stakes world of contemporary football, where the economic stakes are considerable, the political expressions of players can influence their personal endorsements and their clubs' financial well-being. The debate intensifies when these expressions impact sponsorships and revenues, as stakeholders often adjust their support in response to public and financial pressures.

Athletes are advised to tread carefully with political statements, especially on international issues, as backlash from national authorities and public disapproval can result in negative financial and reputational consequences. The case of James McClean, a footballer who chose not to wear a poppy, a symbol with complex historical implications in British-Irish relations, exemplifies this. He endured abuse and threats for his stance (Campbell, 2023; McGreevy, 2021), while fines were imposed on players from the UK for wearing the poppy, contradicting Fédération Internationale de Football Association (FIFA)regulations yet supported by their associations (Gibson, 2016).

The authenticity of athlete-led initiatives is often scrutinised; fans champion true activism but are wary of what they perceive as mere public relations efforts. Genuine movements have been observed with protests for human rights, such as during the Qatar World Cup (2022), the Norwegian national teams' campaign for equal pay (Wrack, 2017), and the pushback from Spanish players post-Women's World Cup win (Valiente, 2021). The support for LGBTQ+ rights came to the fore at the 2022 Qatar World Cup, with players and fans defying FIFA's stance and figures like US Soccer captain Megan Rapinoe advocating for LGBTQ+ rights and gender pay equality (Whyatt, 2020).

Despite significant investment into Saudi Arabian football in recent years (Elsborg, 2023), situations in neighbouring Doha, including confrontations between morality police and protesters and the Iranian team's national anthem protest, brought to light football's significant political role (Doombos and Chamberlain, 2022). Governing bodies are thus in a challenging position, having to balance support for social values against the risk of political engagement that can sway fans and sponsors. Silence is not always an option despite possible repercussions, as demonstrated by the extensive anti-racism initiatives within football (MacIntosh et al., 2020).

Conclusion

The increasing trend of footballers engaging in social and political advocacy is set to grow as digitally savvy younger players gain prominence, blending sport with geopolitics. The football industry, including clubs, sponsors, and governing bodies, must recognise the sport's role as a conduit for societal change and will need to adapt and evolve to acknowledge that in today's world, football is more than just a game. As players are paid more, with greater financial rewards, tighter protection from agents, and substantial social media backing, athletes are more empowered to voice their opinions on important issues.

The traditional team hierarchy is being broken down and is giving way to individual voices, empowered by massive online followings to initiate change. This shift reflects a changing perspective on the roles of athletes as societal influencers. If we consider leading footballers Cristiano Ronaldo and Lionel Messi, their influence over fans, clubs, stakeholders, and even nations, and regions has increased with their rising popularity. Their global dominance has attracted hundreds of millions of followers (Economist. 2022; Lamberti, 2020; Ribeiro, 2016).

Athlete activation in the geopolitical economy of football reflects a broader shift in how society views the roles and responsibilities of public figures. As ambassadors of the world's most popular sport, footballers possess a unique power to influence and inspire. Navigating the intricate geopolitics presents challenges, but the capacity for footballers to inspire positive change is significant, ensuring the evolution of football's societal impact. Athlete activism has become a balancing act for clubs to manage while maintaining the status quo with their stakeholders. Reputational damage has become more difficult to manage in an era of player power.

References

Berman, S. (2023). A Guide to Athlete Activism. *Tackle What's Next*. https://www.tacklewhatsnext.com/Athlete-activism.
Calamur, K. (2016). Muhammad Ali and Vietnam. *The Atlantic*. June 4, 2016. https://www.theatlantic.com/news/archive/2016/06/muhammad-ali-vietnam/485717/.

Campbell, N. (2023). James McClean: 'I know other players who don't want to wear the poppy, but they don't want the hassle'. *Belfast Telegraph*. September 18, 2023. https://www.belfasttelegraph.co.uk/sport/football/james-mcclean-i-know-other-players-who-dont-want-to-wear-the-poppy-but-they-dont-want-the-hassle/a1117017136.html.

Ceithernach (2020). How a chariot race sparked off the bloodiest riots in history. *Medium*. June 23 2020. https://medium.com/@ceithernach/the-nika-riots-a4660f55ed22.

Common Goal (2020). Reconciliation through football: How Didier Drogba helped halt a civil war. 8 October 2020. https://www.common-goal.org/Stories/Reconciliation-Through-Football2020-10-08.

Crafton, K. L. (2021). Defining and addressing the intersection of sports, media, and social activism. *Honors Theses*. 1745.https://egrove.olemiss.edu/hon_thesis/1745

Dobson, M. and McVeigh, N. (2020). Marcus Thuram and Jadon Sancho both pay tribute to George Floyd after scoring. https://www.theguardian.com/football/2020/may/31/marcus-thuram-takes-knee-after-scoring-tribute-to-george-floyd.

Doombos, C. and Chamberlain, S. (2022). Iran soccer team refuses to sing national anthem before World Cup opener. *New York Post*. November 21, 2022. https://nypost.com/2022/11/21/irans-world-cup-team-refuses-to-sing-national-anthem/.

Economist (2022). Lionel Messi and Cristiano Ronaldo have forged modern football. November 17, 2022. Economist Culture. https://www.economist.com/culture/2022/11/17/lionel-messi-and-cristiano-ronaldo-have-forged-modern-football.

Elsborg, S. (2023). The expansion of Saudi investments in sport: From football to es-port. January 12, 2023. *Play The Game*. https://www.playthegame.org/news/the-expansion-of-saudi-investments-in-sport-from-football-to-esport/.

Gibson, O. (2016). England and Scotland players to defy FIFA and wear poppies in Armistice Day match. *The Guardian*. https://www.theguardian.com/uk-news/2016/nov/02/england-players-to-defy-fifa-ruling-and-wear-poppies-in-armistice-day-match.

Goodyer, T. (2017). Mohamed Salah and The Political Power of the Apolitical Entertainer. *Football Paradise*. October 2, 2017. https://www.footballparadise.com/mohamed-salah-and-the-political-power-of-the-apolitical-entertainer/.

Guardian (2018). LeBron James responds to Fox host's controversial 'shut up and dribble' comment. February 17. https://www.theguardian.com/sport/2018/feb/17/lebron-james-laura-ingraham-shut-up-and-dribble-fox-news.

Guiberteau, O. (2020). Didier Drogba: How Ivory Coast striker helped to halt civil war in his home nation. *BBC Sport*. March 31, 2020. https://www.bbc.co.uk/sport/football/52072592.

Kaufman, P. (2008). Boos, bans, and other backlash: the consequences of being an activist athlete. *Humanity & Society*, 32(3), 215–237.

Lamberti, B. (2020). *Celebrity endorser's role on brand equity: a qualitative study on Cristiano Ronaldo and Nike* (Doctoral dissertation, The IIE).

Lewis, T. (2020). Game changers: the new wave of athletic activism shaping Britain. *The Guardian*. https://www.theguardian.com/world/2020/sep/06/game-changers-the-new-wave-of-athletic-activism-shaping-britain.

MacIntosh, A., Martin, E. M. and Kluch, Y. (2020). To act or not to act? Student-athlete perceptions of social justice activism. *Psychology of Sport and Exercise*, 51, 101766.

Magee, W. (2022). The Radical Spirit of Doctor Sócrates. *Tribune*. November 29, 2022. https://tribunemag.co.uk/2022/11/the-radical-spirit-of-doctor-socrates.

Magrath, R. (2022). *Athlete Activism: Contemporary Perspectives* (p. 222). Oxfordshire: Taylor & Francis.

Marcus. J. (2018). Koreas to march under single 'united' flag in Olympic Games. January 17, 2018. BBC News | World | Asia https://www.bbc.co.uk/news/world-asia-42721417.

McGreevy, R. (2021). Royal British Legion stands by James McClean's right not to wear poppy. *Irish Times*. February 18, 2021. https://www.irishtimes.com/news/ireland/irish-news/royal-british-legion-stands-by-james-mcclean-s-right-not-to-wear-poppy-1.4488902.

Nair, A. and Sridhar, S. (2022). World Cup 2022: What is the OneLove armband and why did FIFA ban it? *Reuters*. November 29, 2022. Eds, Rutherford, P. https://www.reuters.com/lifestyle/sports/world-cup-2022-what-is-onelove-armband-why-did-fifa-ban-it-2022-11-24/.

Ribeiro, Rogerio B. (2016). The relationship between the behaviors of the top 50 most endorsed athletes in the world and the monetary value of their endorsement deals. *Undergraduate Honors Theses*. Paper 347. https://dc.etsu.edu/honors/347

Robson, H. (2023). The real story of the Christmas truce. Imperial War Museum (IWM). https://www.iwm.org.uk/history/the-real-story-of-the-christmas-truce.

Roush, T. (2023). Kanye West – Who Lost a Fortune after Antisemitic Tirade – Says He Likes Jewish People again. *Forbes*. March 25, 2023.

Saleh, H. (2018). Mo Salah brings hope and pride back to weary Egyptians. *The Financial Times*. Cairo. April 28, 2018. https://www.ft.com/content/119315c6-4a0f-11e8-8ae9-4b5ddcca99b3.

Sands, L. and Hudson, J. (2022). Rainbow-wearing soccer fans confronted at Qatar World Cup. *Washington Post*. November 22, 2022. https://www.washingtonpost.com/sports/2022/11/22/rainbow-flag-fifa-soccer-qatar/.

Sky Sports (2019). LeBron James applauds Colin Kaepernick for resolving collusion standoff with NFL. 17 February 2019. https://www.skysports.com/nba/news/36244/11639899/lebron-james-applauds-colin-kaepernick-for-resolving-collusion-stand-off-with-nfl

Sky Sports (2023). David Beckham 'proud' of Qatar ambassador role at World Cup despite LGBTQ+ rights criticism. Sky Sports News. 4 October 2023. https://www.skysports.com/football/news/11095/12976710/david-beckham-proud-of-qatar-ambassador-role-at-world-cup-despite-lgbtq-rights-criticism

Smith, L. (2019). Stand up, show respect: athlete activism, nationalistic attitudes, and emotional response. *International Journal of Communication*, 13, 22.

Smith, B., Tryce, S. A. and Ferrara, C. (2023). Which sway? Athlete activism, teammate allyship and fan patriotism. *International Journal of Sports Marketing and Sponsorship*, 24(3), 519–537. https://doi.org/10.1108/IJSMS-02-2022-0049

Valiente, C. (2021). Elite athlete activism for gender equality in sport: Women's football in Spain. In *Athlete Activism* (pp. 109–119). Abingdon: Routledge.

Välkkynen, L. and Niinikoski, M. (2017). Value and risks of athlete endorsements: Case study on NIKE, Inc. endorsed athletes Tiger Woods and Lance Armstrong. Masters' Thesis. University of Turku. https://www.utupub.fi/bitstream/handle/10024/143927/V%C3%A4lkkynen%20Liisa.pdf?sequence=1.

Whyatt, K. (2020). Megan Rapinoe, defiant as judge, throws out US Women's claim for equal pay with male counterparts. *The Telegraph*. May 2020. https://www.telegraph.co.uk/football/2020/05/02/federal-judge-dismisses-unequal-pay-claim-us-womens-soccer-team/.

Wrack, S. (2017). Norway's historic pay deal for women's team shows it can be done. *The Guardian*. https://www.theguardian.com/football/blog/2017/oct/17/norway-historic-pay-deal-for-womens-team-shows-it-can-be-done.

Younge, G. (2012). The man who raised a black power salute at the 1968 Olympic Games. *The Guardian*. March 30, 2012. https://www.theguardian.com/world/2012/mar/30/black-power-salute-1968-olympics.

8

ENVIRONMENT, CLIMATE CHANGE, AND FOOTBALL

Andy Carmichael

Football encompasses all aspects of the environmental debate. Hosting the game registers significant and measurable impacts on the planet, from building and sustaining venues, the manufacture of products in support of the sport, and the transport that gets people to the place of action. Simultaneously, football is impacted by a changing environment, from adjusting kick off times because of excessive temperatures to developing new pitch constructions to cope with extreme rainfall. A scarcity of natural resources, most particularly grassed areas to play on, stems the sport's development and its potential health benefits. Football generates economic activity, occupies a role in tourism, and for good or ill affects the happiness of a large sector of the community. The sport's position as 'the global game' provides opportunity for insight into the patterns of consumption and responses to climate change upon which our future depends. Its prominence as a cultural phenomenon with millions of followers accords football the potential to act as a vehicle for public engagement in a concern that belongs to all of us. Currently, however, the way football responds to environmental threats, begins to realise its potential as a mobilising force, and starts to understand what the future of the sport may look like requires major change.

While football at its most basic level of practice needs only the resources of a ball and two goals alongside its mental and physical performance (Reckwitz, 2002), the sport has grown to be so much more than that. Heavily organised, codified, and made competitive, at multiple geographical levels, there are laws with direct relevance to the environment, for example specifying clothing, equipment, and the playing surface, with league regulations that can stop the best team being promoted if their home arena does not meet a designated standard. This is applicable even in the non-professional and

DOI: 10.4324/9781003473671-9

community game and it creates a demand and a pattern of consumption for products with significant environmental footprints such as plastics, fertiliser for grassed pitches, and building materials.

At the elite level of football, individual club demands are especially high, and their performances generate large attendances who bring with them additional pressures. The energy used during a single match at a large professional club stadium, around 25,000 KWh, could power a dozen homes for a year (Keating, 2021). The annual waste of an English Football League One club was identified as 281 tonnes, with the aggregated figure for clubs across eight levels of the playing structure in England being three times that of the waste generated by the London Olympics (Dosumu et al., 2014). In the German Bundesliga, the average carbon footprint of a football fan attending matches was calculated at 311.1 kg of CO_2 emission (Loewen and Wicker, 2021). These footprints, of both clubs and their supporters, are made considerably worse by the travel involved in football, and particularly the mode of travel often used. Car use was the major factor in those Bundesliga spectator numbers, accounting for 70% of their emissions (Loewen and Wicker, 2021). Meanwhile, despite the relative size of the nation, air travel has become a highly popular way for English Premier League clubs to reach away fixtures on the basis that it affords players greater time to rest. The impact of such choices is clear, when Liverpool FC flew back to their home city from a match with Newcastle United the 33-minute flight generated 3,000 kg of carbon emissions. To have gone by coach would have taken around two and a half hours longer but reduced the carbon emissions by 2965 kg (Bruce Jones and Swarbrick, 2023).

Being a sport that is typically played outdoors, largely on natural surfaces, during times of the day suitable to attract an audience, football is an activity directly affected by climate change and the extreme effects of its, and others, impacts. The first week of the Persian Gulf Pro League scheduled for 3 and 4 August 2023 was cancelled as temperatures in Iran rose above 40°C (Tehran Times, 2023). The worldwide players union, Fédération Internationale des Associations de Footballeurs Professionnels (FIFPro), wants the recognised maximum much lower than this, calling for matches to be rescheduled when the recorded temperature is beyond 32°C (FIFPro, 2023a). At the other end of the scale, the La Liga match between Atletico Madrid and Sevilla due to be played just a month later was postponed due to forecasts of exceptional and dangerous rainfall, a fate that befell the Tottenham versus Leicester friendly match in July of 2023. While examples of weather stopping play can be found throughout sporting history human-induced climate change has led to a rise in the incidence and extent of temperature extremes and contributed to the increase of precipitation extremes (Stott, 2016). The Tottenham Leicester occasion particularly highlights the challenge at the heart of this issue when it is learned that the match was due to be played in Thailand, as a showpiece by the clubs, many thousands of miles from either of their home stadiums.

That global warming has been caused by human activities is unequivocal (IPCC, 2023). Temperatures are likely to rise to record levels by 2027 (World Meteorological Organization, 2023). Some 3.3–3.6 billion people now live in contexts highly vulnerable to climate change (IPCC, 2023). Large areas of the planet are witnessing a reduction in food security, impacts on human health, and increased risks to ecosystems (IPCC, 2023). These are obviously not consequences that can be ascribed solely to football, nor will how football singularly reacts be the solution. Football is, however, part of the cause, as responses to the climate crisis have thus far been inadequate, and electricity supply, transport, and construction, all things identified as features of football's modern incarnation, are sectors that have been declared in need of transformation (United Nations Environment Programme, 2022). Football is more than ever the sport of consumption (Sandvoss, 2004), and the desire to grow the game by reaching new audiences and markets jars with the need to redress environmental decline by adopting "new forms of living, working, and playing" (Shove, 2010, p. 1273). This need is here and now, with the call for systemic change that can generate "rapid and deep emissions reductions and transformative adaptation to climate change" (IPCC, 2023, p. 28) loud and clear.

Football's world governing body, Fédération Internationale de Football Association (FIFA), joined the UN Sports for Climate Action Framework in 2016, the first sports federation to do so. The Framework has the twin goals of establishing a path for sport in combatting climate change, while using sport as a vehicle for encouraging global action. FIFA suggest this voluntary pledge of theirs has been backed by "concrete actions to protect our planet" (FIFA, 2023). For the 2022 Men's World Cup Sustainability Strategy (FIFA, 2020) this appeared to be opportunities to mitigate the tournament-related emissions through energy efficient stadiums, low-emission transportation, and sustainable waste management practices. Closer examination, however, identifies the environment as only one of five pillars of activity in the strategy, the others being social, human, governance, and crucially, economic development. The "concrete actions", an ironic choice of adjective, are in fact a series of initiatives to encourage the host nation, not FIFA themselves, to achieve certain standards while backing the need for "the construction or refurbishment of at least eight stadiums, numerous training sites and supporting temporary infrastructure" (FIFA 2020, p. 65).

Herein lies the problem with football and its governing body's actions. The sport promulgates a message of minimising impacts that they continue to significantly contribute towards through their choices. The construction or refurbishment programme would not occur without the 2022 Men's World Cup being awarded to a country devoid of sufficient suitable stadiums to host matches. Tournament emissions would be lower if 31 other nations were not asked to travel to that country to participate. The Women's World Cup in 2023 was similarly called out on their supposed 'green credentials' with the 32 teams involved there accruing thousands of miles of air travel across the twin hosts of Australia and New Zealand (Garry, 2023). Rather than consider changes to the tournament format to reduce its footprint, FIFA has doubled down on their impact, expanding the 2026 World Cup to 48 teams, selecting three different countries as hosts, with the requirement to provide 16 stadiums for play.

FIFA is not alone in its quest for growth. The Union of European Football Associations (UEFA) is increasing the number of teams participating in the group stages of its Champions League competition from 32 to 36 in 2024. This increases the number of matches, and their attendant energy, waste, and travel impacts, from 125 to 189. The climate change priority for football should according to Mabon (2023) be reducing emissions through appropriate scheduling of matches and making better use of land transport. Instead, as Amann and Doidge (2023, p. 1) note, football governing bodies are simply "not addressing the root causes of climate change".

The last decade has, however, seen an awakening to environmental issues from within football. There was a time when the only name springing to mind might have been Forest Green Rovers, an English division two club declared by the United Nations in 2018 as the World's first carbon neutral football club (BBC, 2018). Clubs worldwide now trumpet their efforts, from Spanish club Real Betis' 'Forever Green' campaign to FC Osaka of the J-League signing up to the emissions targeting 'Science Based Targets Initiative'. Players have made their voices heard, alongside Hector Bellerin, there are such as Norwegian international Morten Thorsby and his 'We Play Green' Foundation, with FIFPro highlighting how their members are "using their platform to help the environment" (FIFPro, 2023b). Promoting and popularising this work are a range of campaign groups and active social media accounts, with the national press taking a periodic interest in such efforts. There are studies in the sport suggesting collective awareness and action can be an important driver of change (Amann and Doidge, 2022) and pressure may be brought to bear on football organisations through their stakeholders (Todaro et al., 2023) and institutional settings (Daddi et al., 2021).

However, the majority of this 'bottom up' activity is individual clubs, players, and supporters promoting behaviour change to those who follow the game. As broader studies show the relationship between behaviour and climate change is a complicated issue with most people unable to determine how their activity should change (Thøgersen, 2021). There is little by way of a unified and co-ordinated response to climate change and environmental damage across football, certainly not of the magnitude that is required on issues such as air travel to matches and the footprint of elite level events. Liverpool FC heralds their 'Red Way' sustainability strategy, which shows "a responsibility to use our voice and take demonstrable action against critical issues such as climate change" (Liverpool FC, 2023). That flight home from Newcastle suggests they are keener to use their voice than take demonstrable action.

Football as a sector reinforces information provision and inspiration as strategies to promote optional change in club and supporter behaviour. Football federations, clubs, and players now frequently reference the environment, sustainability, and climate change, and the work they are doing to reduce their impacts. That is positive, it is undoubtedly getting better, but there is an avoidance of the difficult questions that need to be asked and a sense of business as usual, or better, while attempting not to look out of step with public opinion. It is not difficult to find examples of relationships that undercut claims and pledges; one of the sponsors of the UEFA Champions League is Turkish Airlines, Hyundai cars is a FIFA partner, the wealth of the petroleum industry has been a powerful feature in football for the last two decades (Do et al., 2021). The environmental literature identifies that "profound" alterations are required to address the climate crisis (Whitmarsh et al., 2021, p. 76) and the scale and pace of those alterations "can no longer be reconciled with a massaged form of the status quo" (Stoddard et al., 2021, p. 679). Flying to matches relatively close to home, expanding tournaments to include more teams, increased travel, and additional construction, funding such activity through association with the very industries that accelerate the climate crisis, this is not acknowledging the scale of the problem. There need to be serious discussions about what football will look like in the future, when temperatures increase, when extreme weather is more frequent, when sea levels rise. There need to be questions asked about how we live, work, and play football, and the "big, big changes" (Bellerin, 2020) that will be necessary in future.

References

Amann, J. and Doidge, M. (2022). Climate change, catastrophe and hope in football fandom. In J. Cherrington and J. Black (Eds.), *Sport and Physical Activity in Catastrophic Environments*. London: Taylor & Francis.

Amann, J. and Doidge, M. (2023). 'I hadn't realised that change is not a difficult thing': mobilising football fans on climate change. *Sociology*. https://doi.org/10.1177/00380385221142211

BBC (2018). *Forest Green Rovers named 'greenest football club in world'*. Available at: https://www.bbc.co.uk/news/uk-england-gloucestershire-45677536 [Accessed 19 September 2023].

Bellerin, H. (2020). *Race against climate change live*. Available at: https://envision-racing.com/hector-bellerin-the-ev-driving-vegan-footballer-who-is-also-defending-the-planet/ [Accessed 1 August 2023].

Bruce Jones, L. and Swarbrick, A. (2023). *The English Premier League: Time to Get Green*? Available at: https://www.nortonrosefulbright.com/en/inside-sports-law/blog/2023/06/the-english-premier-league-time-to-get-green [Accessed 31 July 2023].

Daddi, T., Todaro, N. M., Iraldo, F. and Frey, M. (2021). Institutional pressures on the adoption of environmental practices: a focus on European professional football. *Journal of Environmental Planning and Management*, 1–23. https://doi.org/10.108 0/09640568.2021.1927679

Do, H. X., Nguyen, Q. M., Nepal, R. and Smyth, R. (2021). When pep comes calling, the oil market answers: the effect of football player transfer movements on abnormal fluctuations in oil price futures. *Energy Economics, 100*, 105325.

Dosumu, A., Colbeck, I. and Bragg, R. (2014). Greenhouse gas emissions: contributions made by football clubs in England. *Atmospheric and Climate Sciences, 4*(04), 642–652.

FIFA (2020). *The FIFA World Cup Qatar 2022™ Sustainability Strategy*. Zurich: FIFA Publications.

FIFA (2023). *Sustainability*. Available at: https://www.fifa.com/social-impact/sustainability [Accessed 31 July 2023].

FIFPro (2023a). *Extreme weather in football*. Available at: https://fifpro.org/en/supporting-players/health-and-performance/extreme-weather-and-climate-change/extreme-weather-in-football [Accessed 31 August 2023].

FIFPro (2023b). *Earth Day footballers using their platform to help the environment*. Available at: https://fifpro.org/en/supporting-players/player-influence/player-impact/earth-day-footballers-using-their-platform-to-help-the-environment/ [Accessed 31 August 2023].

Garry, T. (2023). Two countries, 10 stadiums, 32 teams, 70,000 miles – carbon footprint of Women's World Cup. *The Daily Telegraph*, 25 August.

IPCC (2023). Summary for policymakers.In H. Lee and J. Romero (Eds.). *Climate Change 2023: Synthesis Report. Contribution of Working Groups I, II and III to the Sixth Assessment Report of the Intergovernmental Panel on Climate Change*. Geneva, Switzerland: IPCC, pp. 1–34, https://doi.org/10.59327/IPCC/AR6-9789291691647.001.

Keating, D. (2021). *Will This Year's Euro Cup Have Lessons for Football's Climate Impacts?* In *Euro 2021 Football Cup: The Green Issue* (pp. 4–6), Euractiv Special Report. Available at: https://www.euractiv.com/section/energy/special_report/euro-2021-football-cup-the-green-issue/ [Accessed 31 July 2023].

Liverpool FC (2023). *Sustainability, The Red Way*. Available at: https://www.liverpoolfc.com/theredway [Accessed 25 September 2023].

Loewen, C. and Wicker, P. (2021). Travelling to Bundesliga matches: the carbon footprint of football fans. *Journal of Sport & Tourism, 25*(3), 253–272.

Mabon, L. (2023). Football and climate change: what do we know, and what is needed for an evidence-informed response? *Climate Policy, 23*(3), 314–328.

Reckwitz, A. (2002). Toward a theory of social practices: a development in culturalist theorizing. *European Journal of Social Theory, 5*(2), 243–263.

Sandvoss, C. (2004). *A Game of Two Halves: Football Fandom, Television and Globalisation*. London: Routledge.

Shove, E. (2010). Beyond the abc: climate change policy and theories of social change. *Environment and Planning A, 42*, 1273–1285.

Stoddard, I., Anderson, K., Capstick, S., Carton, W., Depledge, J., Facer, K., Gough, C., Hache, F., Hoolohan, C., Hultman, M. and Hällström, N. (2021). Three decades of climate mitigation: why haven't we bent the global emissions curve? *Annual Review of Environment and Resources, 46*, 653–689.

Stott, P. (2016). How climate change affects extreme weather events. *Science, 352*(6293), 1517–1518.

Tehran Times (2023). *PGPL matchweek 1 canceled due to extreme heatwave*. Available at: https://www.tehrantimes.com/news/487461/PGPL-Matchweek-1-canceled-due-to-extreme-heatwave [Accessed 31 July 2023].

Thøgersen, J. (2021). Consumer behavior and climate change: consumers need considerable assistance. *Current Opinion in Behavioral Sciences, 42*, 9–14.

Todaro, N. M., McCullough, B. and Daddi, T. (2023). Stimulating the adoption of green practices by professional football organisations: a focus on stakeholders' pressures and expected benefits. *Sport Management Review, 26*(1), 156–180.

United Nations Environment Programme (2022). *Emissions gap report 2022: the closing window – climate crisis calls for rapid transformation of societies*. Nairobi. Available at: https://www.unep.org/emissions-gap-report-2022 [Accessed 7 September 2023].

Whitmarsh, L., Poortinga, W. and Capstick, S. (2021). Behaviour change to address climate change. *Current Opinion in Psychology, 42*, 76–81.

World Meteorological Organization (2023). *WMO global annual to decadal climate update* (Target years: 2023–2027). Available at: https://library.wmo.int/records/item/66224-wmo-global-annual-to-decadal-climate-update [Accessed 7 September 2023].

9

HOW THE UKRAINE CONFLICT AFFECTS RUSSIAN FOOTBALL CLUBS

The Hostages of Big Politics

Timur Absalyamov and Mathias Schubert

Introduction

The development of the most popular sports in Russia, such as ice hockey and football, has mirrored the evolution of the country's economic, social and political life throughout the whole post-Soviet period. The infamous 1990s, characterized by an extreme economic and institutional crisis in Russia, saw outdated infrastructure, a massive exodus of the best Russian players, and clubs struggling to meet their ends (Veth, 2016).

Nevertheless, when at the beginning of the twenty-first century the country's economy began to rapidly catch up with more developed countries, so did the football industry. Finally being able to spend, Russian clubs entered the international transfer market as bulk buyers. At first, however, they were mostly buying affordable, not well-known players. This changed in 2003 when CSKA Moscow purchased Czech Jiří Jarošík and Croat Ivica Olić, both rising European stars. From that moment, clubs in Russia realized that they are able to sign high-class legionnaires and just in a couple of years the league's strength increased dramatically, reaching the sixth position in Union of European Football Associations (UEFA) ranking by 2008 (UEFA, n.d.). Landmark events of the era included CSKA winning the UEFA Cup in 2005 (being the first club from the post-socialist space to do so), Zenit's victories in UEFA Cup and UEFA Supercup in 2008, and the Russian national team's semi-final at the EURO 2008.

The league's competitive intensity was growing with every year: if from 1992 to 2001 Spartak Moscow won nine out of ten titles, the Russian Premier League saw four different champions from 2002 to 2009 (CSKA, Lokomotiv Moscow, Rubin Kazan, Zenit St. Petersburg). The appearance of eccentrically

DOI: 10.4324/9781003473671-10

rich Anzhi Makhachkala and the strengthening of the bottom clubs made the league even more competitive in the first part of the following decade.

Soon, however, things began to change. Russian football entered the era of stagnation and subsequent decline. Although there were various factors contributing to it, the main impactor was lying far outside the football domain.

Political Developments of 2013–2014 and Their Effect on Russian Football

The political developments in Ukraine in 2013–2014 and the following crisis in Russian-Ukrainian relationships largely affected all spheres of life in the region. Political course, social rhetoric and economic reality of the countries quickly mutated, and the state of affairs in football was not an exemption.

The first victim, though quite a controversial one, was the project of the Russian-Ukrainian united football league, an initiative promoted by renown Russian coach Valeri Gazzaev and leaders of the countries' richest clubs in 2012–2014 (Volotko, 2013). Due to the political situation as of 2014, the concept of the united league has become irrelevant and the local championships were not sacrificed for the sake of the big clubs (Jarosz et al., 2023).

While the failure of the united league project barely affected the actual status quo, some particular clubs experienced the conflict between two previously highly integrated countries at its fullest. FC Kuban Krasnodar, a Russian elevator team throughout the 2000s, finally became a serious power in the early 2010s and debuted in the Europa League in 2013. The golden era did not last though – in 2015–2016 the club's main investor (Ukrainian-Armenian entrepreneur Oleg Mkrtchan, head of a Ukrainian steel rolling corporation Industrial Union of Donbas) had to quit his football investments due to the problems his business experienced after the escalation of the Donbass crisis (Kuznetsov and Perova, 2015; Mun, 2019). Soon after Mkrtchan left his control share in the club, FC Kuban faced severe financial problems and eventually went bankrupt in 2018 (Mun, 2019).

Another Russian Premier League club seriously affected by the political situation was CSKA. Being a role model of a successful private club, it enjoyed generous investments from its owner Evgeni Giner. Originally moving to Moscow from Kharkiv, the entrepreneur kept a significant part of his business in Eastern Ukraine and began to experience troubles due to the new political and economic reality in the region (TASS, 2014). This coincided with Giner's spendings on the construction of the CSKA stadium, and, eventually, in 2019 he had to sell the club, thus ending the most successful era in CSKA's history (Filatov and Chunova, 2019).

The rest of the league was affected by the political situation less directly, though still noticeably. Following the first international sanctions on the Russian economy introduced in 2014, the value of the Russian Ruble dropped by

50%, heavily affecting financial capacities countrywide (Obizhaeva, 2016). The number of big spenders in the league shrunk rapidly. The competitiveness and quality of players gradually declined, which soon led to a decrease in European results and Zenit's domestic dominance (from 2019 to 2023 they had won all five titles).

The Sanctions of 2022: FIFA Ruling – The Heist of the Century?

Following the escalation of Russia-Ukraine conflict in February 2022, various stakeholders started to impose unprecedented sanctions on Russia in order to put pressure on its government, and many organizations made their own decisions suspending Russian memberships, cancelling events, and closing their operation in the country. The Fédération Internationale de Football Association (FIFA) and UEFA, for instance, suspended Russian clubs and the national team from all international competitions and revoked the 2022 Champions League final from St. Petersburg and 2023 UEFA Supercup from Kazan (FIFA, 2022a; UEFA, 2022, 2023). Such sanctions alone would seem to be a big hit on Russian football; however, the main strike came from FIFA's ruling on transfers.

On March 7, 2022, FIFA stated that "… foreign players and coaches will have the right to unilaterally suspend their employment contracts … until the end of the season in Russia" and later prolonged the suspension possibility for two more seasons (FIFA, 2022b, 2022c, 2023). What seemed to be a temporary measure to protect the players who did not feel comfortable staying in Russia, opened a Pandora's box. As most of the contracts were about to expire during the two and a half seasons of the rule's action (not knowing at the time being if the rule is going to be prolonged again), the 'temporary suspension' de-facto turned into a full contract termination. Neither FIFA did offer any compensation mechanism for the clubs, nor did it offer any other plausible solution on how to deal with the expiration of suspended contracts. Russian clubs suddenly lost their main assets for no compensation, the integrity of 2021/2022 season was ruined as the players massively left at the decisive stage, and transfer relations plunged into chaos.

The consequences of the FIFA ruling felt, arguably, most severe at FC Krasnodar and FC Rubin Kazan. The market value of players, who left Krasnodar for free, was totalling to around 80 million euros (Kokorin, 2022). Despite the loss, the team managed to finish the season properly. For Rubin, however, the situation went disastrous. Since 2019, the club's management was actively scouting for talented youngsters in order to sell them to European leagues and thus obtain financial stability. By 2022, the club had gathered a bunch of valuable players who showed an impressive progress. This, together with successful media campaigns, attracted interest from City Football Group (the owners of Manchester City and other clubs). Rubin's general director at the time, Rustem Saimanov, claimed that the plans included making it a Russian super club and the negotiations were at the advanced stage when the new geopolitical reality made the project impossible (Sports.ru, 2022). Instead of generous foreign investments, the club soon lost eight players due to the FIFA rule and consequently lost eight out of ten remaining games, ending in relegation. Although the total value of gone players was estimated to 49 million euros (Transfermarkt.com, n.d.a), the real losses were much higher as the footballers were supposed to be sold on better conditions: Before FIFA's decision, Rubin was asking 30 million euros for the club's main star, Georgian winger Khvicha Kvaratskhelia, arguably the biggest talent from ex-USSR countries of the last decade (SportBO, 2021). However, in March 2022, he terminated the contract, went to Georgian side Dinamo Batumi, and from there was sold to Napoli in the summer (Alfimov, 2023). A year later Kvaratskhelia was named the best player of the 2022/2023 season in Italy's Serie A and led Napoli to the long-awaited champions title, raising his market value to 80 million euro (Serie, 2023). Saimanov's management team was sacked later in 2022, drawing a finish line on their effort to build a successful financial model at Rubin. Thus, the geopolitical affairs and the following FIFA's decision cost Rubin one of their best talents in history, a place in the Premier League, the majority of the main squad, dozens of millions of euros, and probably the investment deal of a lifetime.

While the consequences of the FIFA ruling have not been as dramatic for all clubs, the imperfections of the decision were popping up also elsewhere. Several cases highlighted the underdeveloped nature of FIFA's action: Norwegian player Erik Botheim, who moved to FC Krasnodar from Bodø/Glimt for a fee of 8 million euro, suspended the contract and left Krasnodar before playing a single official game (Kurchavova, 2023). In May 2022, he terminated the contract (though FIFA ruling only allowed suspension), arguing that Krasnodar did not pay a signing bonus of 1 million euro. The bonus, however, was allegedly supposed to be paid later than the date Botheim suspended his contract. Both sides addressed FIFA's jurisdiction, with Botheim wanting his bonus and Krasnodar wanting player's disqualification due to contract violation (Kurchavova, 2023). FIFA took the side of Botheim, obliging Krasnodar to pay a half of the bonus (Belous, 2023). As a result, we see, on the one hand, a club that paid 8 million euro for a transfer, never used the player, while still owing him half a million euro. On the other hand, we have a footballer, who managed to get the signing bonus for the contract he has terminated and sign with a new club with no consequences.

Another notable case was Serbian defender Silvije Begić. He suspended his contract with Rubin just to sign with another Russian club, Ural Yekaterinburg (Kurchavova, 2022). The football community met the transfer with an irony regarding the motives of his contract suspension.

Moreover, while the initial FIFA's decision gave the footballers time until April 7, 2022, to decide whether they are suspending their contracts or not, the June 2022 extension opened the window again. Such extensions created a situation when every incoming transfer carried huge risks for Russian clubs, since any, even a newly purchased, player could leave with no fee anytime. Only in the 2023 edition FIFA acknowledged the flaws and stated that from 2023/2024 season only the players who had already left Russia in spring of 2022 can keep suspending their contracts, and such players cannot sign with another Russian club (FIFA, 2023).

Curiously, FIFA's decision was applied to Ukrainian clubs in a very similar manner. By way of example, Darijo Srna, sportive director of Shakhtar, claims that FIFA destroyed the team as it lost 14 foreign players due to the rule and requested a compensation of 50 million euros in the court (Vysotsky, 2023). In this context it is worth mentioning that the text of FIFA's ruling states that it aims to 'protect the Ukrainian clubs'.

The drawbacks of FIFA's decision created controversial consequences and raised a number of ethical concerns. If the decision's goal was to protect the players, it remains unclear why it was only applied to foreign ones. Further, while the clubs lost their footballers without any compensation, they were still obliged to pay the remainders of the respective transfer sums (for players whose earlier transfer payments were split in parts, but who left due to FIFA rule). If Russian clubs are to be reintegrated in any observable future, then such rulings seem to be quite discriminatory. Many Russian clubs as well as Shakhtar went to the Court of Arbitration for Sport (CAS) in order to get a compensation from FIFA, but all of them lost (Vysotsky, 2023). Lastly, it seems legitimate to at least consider whether the signing of available players from Russian or Ukrainian clubs are in any way reconcilable with fair play principles (or should rather be viewed as predation under the given circumstances). And what can be said about the behaviour of players? While we see cases like Begić or Botheim, there are also others like Polish Sebastian Szymański from Dynamo Moscow, who denied the opportunity of leaving for free and transferred to Fenerbahce for a fee of 10 million euros (Suryaev, 2023). All of the above create a controversial precedent for the football transfer market and no one knows how it may backfire in the future.

The Sanctions of 2022: Sanctions on Financial Institutions as the Newest Obstacle for Football Transfers

Bans from competitions and the transfer ruling, however, are just drops in the ocean of various sanctions imposed by Western economies on Russia. The endless list of restrictions changed many aspects of Russia's everyday life, however, the most tangible sanctions for regular individuals and organizations are those on financial institutions. In March 2022, Visa and

Mastercard made the cards issued by Russian banks no longer accepted outside the country and online (BBC, 2022). Selected Russian banks were excluded from the Society for Worldwide Interbank Financial Telecommunication (SWIFT) system and could no longer perform international money transfers, while many banks in Europe even went beyond the official sanctions and stopped accepting transfers to or from Russia disregarding the presence of a respective Russian bank in the sanctions list (Forbes, 2022). In addition to that, the rate of Russian Ruble took an impressive rollercoaster ride: from pre-2022 rate of 80–85 Rubles for 1 Euro, the Ruble crashed to 140 Rubles for 1 Euro in March 2022, then surged to 60 Rubles for 1 Euro for the rest of 2022, and then steadily declined to the level of 110 Rubles for 1 Euro in August 2023 (WSJ, n.d.). Such turbulence in Russian economy obviously also affects football clubs.

In August 2023, FC Rostov was restricted by FIFA from registering new players due to a failure to pay Swedish side IFK Norrköping the remainder for a transfer that happened in 2020 (Suntsova, 2023b). However, Rostov actually did send the money, but the Swedish bank did not allow Norrköping to withdraw the funds and sent it back referring to political reasons (which is a part of the mentioned bigger problem of banks going beyond official sanctions) (Suntsova, 2023c). To solve the issue, the clubs cooperated and called FIFA for consultations on how to move on. Even though the final payment mechanism was not specified publicly, the case was resolved (Sports. ru, 2023).

Not everyone chooses the cooperation path though, and the biggest problems occur between Russian and English clubs. For example, West Ham United refused to pay CSKA the remainder for the 2021 Nikola Vlašić transfer, owing the Moscow club 17.43 million euro (Airapetov, 2023). According to CSKA, the club tried every possible way of peaceful resolution, but due to West Ham's unwillingness to cooperate, had to file a complaint to FIFA (Airapetov, 2023). FIFA ruled the case in favour of CSKA, obliging West Ham to pay the debt by July 31, 2023, otherwise the debt would raise to 25.62 million and West Ham would be banned from registering new players (Gevorgyan, 2023). Other Russian clubs won similar cases against English clubs as well (Golovin, 2022). However, FIFA allows a loophole, which we may assume West Ham and others are using (as they are still registering new players). If the debtor can demonstrate legal impossibility of money transfer, it can postpone the payment – and in the current times it does not seem hard to prove so (Airapetov, 2023). The indirect victim of the payment dispute is Dutch club Heerenveen: Not getting compensated for their players, CSKA itself opted for legal impossibility excuse and did not transfer the remaining 3 million euros for 2020 transfer of Chidera Ejuke, who suspended his contract and left Russia in 2022. Calling the situation annoying, the Dutch club admits that not much can be done if the second side does not want to cooperate (Suntsova, 2023a).

With so many grey zones in the rules, possibilities of transfer payments mostly depend on the actual will of the involved parties and the way they interpret the regulations.

For instance players still move between Russia and EU – most recent examples include transfers of Arsen Zakharyan from Dynamo to Real Sociedad, Théo Bongonda from Cádiz to Spartak, and Lucas Olaza from Real Valladolid to Krasnodar (Transfermarkt.com, n.d.b). This shows that in most cases the possibility of transfers is a matter of clubs' willingness to overcome the present difficulties. However, the lack of clarity in the rules leads to various interpretations. A recent journalist investigation, for example, suggests that transfers to and from Russia may violate the sanction regime (Smits et al., 2023). The journalists cite an expert saying that "… you are not permitted to make economic resources available, and a player is an economic resource. Making a player available 'for free' is also prohibited …" (Smits et al., 2023). Such an interpretation in the context of football seems problematic: if clubs must not make 'free agents' available for Russian clubs, that means they cannot allow players becoming 'free agents' at all; and if 'free agents' are limited in their choice where to play next, this could violate their human rights of freedom to move and choose the employment and bring football somewhere into pre-Bosman ruling times. But as the rules are still not written explicitly and exhaustively, discussions on the interpretations will most likely not end soon.

Conclusion

The Russia-Ukraine conflict of 2022 and its dramatic nature has touched the entire world. Totally unexpected developments were uncovering with a cosmic speed, and many aspects of life were rethought and reconsidered. Football was among many other areas, where the usual landscape had to change quickly. Like many other decisions of that time, FIFA's ruling probably was developed in a rush, without a proper assessment of likely consequences. What seemed to be a measure to protect footballers happened to be a legalized theft from Russian (and Ukrainian) clubs and a start of previously unseen transfer chaos. The 2023 FIFA adaptation stopped the chaos, although the harm done to the clubs by the initial decision is hard to overestimate. The global financial sanctions hardened the operation of football as well, affecting the possibilities of international trade and fulfilment of obligations. Nevertheless, despite the hostile environment, Russian football clubs so far demonstrated an impressive ability to adapt. To date, there were no bankruptcies, the clubs managed to keep business relationships with most of the European partners, and even came up with a Russian Cup reformation to substitute missing European games in the calendar. However, the long-term consequences of the international competition ban and the global sanctions are yet to be observed. Even if Russian football clubs try their best to dodge the obstacles, their actual future is first of all dependent on the future of the global geopolitical situation and the place Russia takes in it, as well as on the political and economic developments inside Russia itself.

References

Airapetov, V. (2023). Gendirektor CSKA: West Ham tak i ne rasplatilsya za Vlashicha. My obratilis v FIFA [CSKA director: West Ham haven't paid for Vlašić. We contacted FIFA] *Sport-Express,* 1 April. Available at: https://www.sport-express.ru/football/rfpl/news/v-cska-rasskazali-chto-vest-hem-do-sih-por-ne-rasplatilsya-s-klubom-za-vlashicha-2058342/ [Accessed 1 September 2023].

Alfimov, M. (2023). Tainstvennyy transfer Hvichi iz «Rubina» v 2022-m. Do sih por neizvestno, skolko poluchili kazantsy (i kak) [The mysterious transfer of Khvicha from Rubin in 2022. It is still unknown how much Kazanians received (and how)] *Sports.ru,* 12 April. Available at: https://www.sports.ru/tribuna/blogs/alfimov/3129885.html [Accessed 1 September 2023].

BBC (2022). "Visa and Mastercard suspend Russian operations," *BBC News,* 6 March. Available at: https://www.bbc.com/news/business-60637429 [Accessed 1 September 2023].

Belous, A. (2023). «Krasnodar» proigral sud Butheymu iz-za rastorzheniya kontrakta. FIFA obyazala klub vyplatit forvardu 500 tysyach evro [Krasnodar lost the trial to Botheim due to the termination of the contract. FIFA ordered the club to pay the striker 500 thousand euros] *Sports.ru,* 8 February. Available at: https://www.sports.ru/football/1114880733-krasnodar-proigral-isk-protiv-butxejma-fifa-obyazala-klub-vyplatit-ras.html [Accessed 1 September 2023].

FIFA (2022a). *FIFA/UEFA suspend Russian clubs and national teams from all competitions.* Available at: https://www.fifa.com/tournaments/mens/worldcup/qatar2022/media-releases/fifa-uefa-suspend-russian-clubs-and-national-teams-from-all-competitions [Accessed 1 September 2023].

FIFA (2022b). *FIFA adopts temporary employment and registration rules to address several issues in relation to war in Ukraine.* Available at: https://www.fifa.com/about-fifa/organisation/fifa-council/media-releases/fifa-adopts-temporary-employment-and-registration-rules-to-address-several [Accessed 1 September 2023].

FIFA (2022c). *FIFA extends temporary employment and registration rules to address several issues in relation to war in Ukraine.* Available at: https://www.fifa.com/legal/media-releases/fifa-extends-temporary-employment-rules-to-address-issues-relating-to-war-in [Accessed 1 September 2023].

FIFA (2023). *FIFA extends and adapts temporary employment rules to address issues relating to war in Ukraine.* Available at: https://www.fifa.com/legal/football-regulatory/media-releases/fifa-extends-and-adapts-temporary-employment-rules-to-address-issues-relating-to-war-in-ukraine [Accessed 1 September 2023].

Filatov, A. and Chunova, A. (2019). VEB.RF stanet osnovnym vladeltsem futbolnogo kluba CSKA [VEB.RF is going to become the main owner of CSKA] *Vedomosti,* 15 December. Available at: https://www.vedomosti.ru/business/articles/2019/12/15/818735-vebrf-tsska [Accessed 1 September 2023].

Forbes (2022). Kak perevesti dengi za granitsu: alternativy SWIFT, kotoryye ispolzuyut rossiyane [How to transfer money abroad: SWIFT alternatives used by Russians] *Forbes.ru,* 13 July. Available at: https://www.forbes.ru/finansy/471301-kak-perevesti-den-gi-za-granicu-al-ternativy-swift-kotorye-ispol-zuut-rossiane [Accessed 1 September 2023].

Gevorgyan, A. (2023). FIFA obyazala West Ham vyplatist CSKA 17.43 mln [FIFA obliged West Ham to pay CSKA 17.43 millions] *Championat.com*, 11 June. Available at: https://www.championat.com/football/news-5135181-fifa-obyazala-vest-hem-vyplatit-cska-eur-17-43-mln.html [Accessed 1 September 2023].

Golovin, A. (2022). Spartak suditsya s anglichanami, dengi TSSKA zastryali v Amerike, Rostov pobedil v FIFA. Kak sanktsii povliyali na nash futbol [Spartak is suing the British, CSKA's money is stuck in America, Rostov won FIFA. How sanctions affected our football] *Sports.ru*, 15 September. Available at: https://www.sports.ru/tribuna/blogs/golovin/3075859.html [Accessed 1 September 2023].

Jarosz, O., Kornakov, K. and Metelski, A. (2023). Transnational leagues and their role in projecting soft power. In S. Chadwick, P. Widdop and M. M. Goldman (Eds.), *The Geopolitical Economy of Sport: Power, Politics, Money, and the State* (pp. 49–63). Oxford: Routledge.

Kokorin, A. (2022). Na fone massovogo otyezda legionerov RPL uzhe polegchala na €160 mln, postradali prakticheski vse kluby [With massive departure of foreigners, RPL gets lighter by €160 mln, all the clubs suffered] *Sports.ru*, 30 March. Available at: https://www.sports.ru/tribuna/blogs/russian_football/3029280.html [Accessed 1 September 2023].

Kurchavova, L. (2022). Begich pereshel v «Ural». V marte on priostanovil kontrakt s «Rubinom» do leta 2022-go [Begic moved to Ural. In March, he suspended the contract with Rubin until the summer of 2022] *Sports.ru*, 8 September. Available at: https://www.sports.ru/football/1111743152-begich-pereshel-v-ural-v-marte-on-priostanovil-kontrakt-s-rubinom-do-l.html [Accessed 1 September 2023].

Kurchavova, L. (2023). Krasnodar ne vyplatil Butheymu 1 mln yevro podyemnyh v marte 2022-go – iz-za etogo kontrakt rastorgli. FIFA vstala na storonu igroka – teper klub dolzhen 500 tysyach evro [Krasnodar did not pay Botheim 1 million euros of lifting money in March 2022 – because of this, the contract was terminated. FIFA sided with the player – now the club owes 500 thousand euros] *Sports.ru*, 9 February. Available at: https://www.sports.ru/football/1114882986-krasnodar-ne-vyplatil-butxejmu-1-mln-evro-podemnyx-v-marte-2022-go-ime.html [Accessed 1 September 2023].

Kuznetsov, P. and Perova, A. (2015). "Kuban" vyhodit s dolgami odin na odin [Kuban is one on one with debts] *Kommersant*, 24 July. Available at: https://www.kommersant.ru/doc/2774339 [Accessed 1 September 2023].

Mun, R. (2019). Byvshyi vladelec Kubani v tyurme [Kuban's former owner is in jail] *Sports.ru*, 17 October. Available at: https://www.sports.ru/tribuna/blogs/innuendo/2605619.html [Accessed 1 September 2023].

Obizhaeva, A. (2016). The Russian ruble crisis of December 2014. *Voprosy Ekonomiki*, 5.

Serie, A. (2023), "BEST OVERALL 2022/2023," *News*, 4 June. Available at: https://www.legaseriea.it/en/media/serie-a/best-overall-2022-2023 [Accessed 1 September 2023].

Smits, H. W., Schramade, K. and Claessens, T. (2023). Dozens of European football clubs risk violating sanctions with Russia transfers, *FTM.EU*, 12 December. Available at: https://www.ftm.eu/articles/offside-deals-football-fouls-in-sanctions-against-russia?share=MfwXO9LMKHE6RtAzJsYvDr/Ohf/cEivqZrX+0g4o2zgBlCDqE7WLz okQTzNZCdl= [Accessed 14 December 2023].

SportBO (2021). Oleg Yarovinskiy: Nasha tsena za Hvichu – 30 millionov evro [Oleg Yarovinskiy: our price for Khvicha is 30 millions] *SportBO*, 2 May. Available at: https://sport.business-gazeta.ru/article/264576 [Accessed 1 September 2023].

Sports.ru (2022). Gendirektor «Rubina» podtverdil peregovory s holdingom «Man City»: «Byli ochen blizki i mogli sdelat superkomandu. Obstanovka izmenilas, k sozhaleniyu» [Rubin's CEO confirmed the talks with the Man City holding: "We were very close and could make a super team. Things have changed, unfortunately."] *Sports.ru*, 1 July. Available at: https://www.sports.ru/football/1110118002-sajmanov-podtverdil-peregovory-s-xoldingom-man-siti-my-byli-ochen-bliz.html [Accessed 1 September 2023].

Sports.ru (2023). FIFA snyala s Rostova ban na registratsiyu novichkov. Klub zayavil 7 igrokov v den matcha s Zenitom [FIFA removed the ban on registration of newcomers from Rostov. The club announced 7 players on the day of the match with Zenit] *Sports.ru*, 29 July. Available at: https://www.sports.ru/football/1115339058-rostov-zayavil-6-novichkov-na-rpl.html [Accessed 1 September 2023].

Suntsova, A. (2023a). Herenven zhdet ot CSKA yeshche 3 mln yevro za Edzhuke: Nas eto razdrazhayet. Mozhno obratitsya v MID, no tolko yesli obe storony zainteresovany [Heerenveen expects another 3 million euros from CSKA for Ejuke: It annoys us. You can contact the Foreign Ministry, but only if both parties are interested] *Sports.ru*, 8 June. Available at: https://www.sports.ru/football/1115214121-v-xerenvene-zayavili-chto-czska-dolzhen-3-mln-evro-za-edzhuke-my-poter.html [Accessed 1 September 2023].

Suntsova, A. (2023b). FIFA zapretila Rostovu registrirovat novichkov iz-za dolga za Almkvista. Oni ne sygrayut s Fakelom [FIFA banned "Rostov" from registering newcomers because of the debt for Almqvist. They won't play Fakel] *Sports.ru*, 23 July. Available at: https://www.sports.ru/football/1115323614-prezident-rostova-o-zaprete-fifa-na-registracziyu-novichkov-iz-za-dolg.html [Accessed 1 September 2023].

Suntsova, A. (2023c). Prezident Rostova o dolge za Almkvista: SHvedskiy bank vozarashchal nam dengi s pometkoy politika. Norcheping soobshchil FIFA, my s nimi v kontakte [The President of Rostov about the debt for Almqvist: The Swedish bank returned money to us with the note of politics. Norrköping told FIFA, we are in contact with them] *Sports.ru*, 24 July. Available at: https://www.sports.ru/football/1115325794-prezident-rostova-o-dolge-za-almkvista-shvedskij-bank-vozarashhal-nam-.html [Accessed 1 September 2023].

Suryaev, A. (2023). Dynamo obyavilo o prodazhe Shimanskogo Fenerbahche [Dynamo announces Szymanski transfer to Fenerbahce] *Sports.ru*, 12 July. Available at: https://www.sports.ru/football/1115290343-dinamo-obyavilo-o-prodazhe-shimanskogo-fenerbaxche.html [Accessed 1 September 2023].

TASS (2014). Evgeni Giner: iz-za krizisa na Ukraine u CSKA stalo menshe svobodnyh sredstv [Evgeni Giner: due to the crisis in Ukraine CSKA has less free funds] *TASS.ru*, 5 November. Available at: https://tass.ru/interviews/1599833/amp [Accessed 1 September 2023].

Transfermarkt.com (n.d.a). *Rubin Kazan – Club profile 21/22*. Available at: https://www.transfermarkt.com/rubin-kazan/startseite/verein/2698?saison_id=2021 [Accessed 1 September 2023].

Transfermarkt.com (n.d.b). *Russian Premier Liga – Transfers 23/24*. Available at: https://www.transfermarkt.com/premier-liga/transfers/wettbewerb/RU1 [Accessed 1 September 2023].

UEFA (no date). *Country coefficients. UEFA Coefficients*. Available at: https://www.uefa.com/nationalassociations/uefarankings/country/#/yr/2009 [Accessed 1 September 2023].

UEFA (2022). *Decisions from today's extraordinary UEFA Executive Committee meeting*. Available at: https://www.uefa.com/news-media/news/0272-148740475a92-1b97baa3e9d7-1000--decisions-from-today-s-extraordinary-uefa-executive-committ/ [Accessed 4 September 2024].

UEFA (2023). *2023 Super Cup relocated to Athens*. Available at: https://www.uefa.com/uefasupercup/news/027d-1727c00c9ab2-62be804330cf-1000--2023-super-cup-relocated-to-athens/ [Accessed 4 September 2024].

Veth, K. M. (2016). *Selling the 'people's Game': Football's Transition from Communism to Capitalism in the Soviet Union and Its Successor State*. PhD thesis, King's College London.

Volotko, L. (2013). "Tolstykh mne neinteresen - nam detei ne nyanchit!" ["Tolstykh is not interesting to me – we won't raise kids!"] *Championat.com*, 1 October. Available at: https://www.championat.com/football/article-3217151-valerij-gazzaev--ob-obedinjonnom-chempionate.html [Accessed 5 September 2024].

Vysotsky, V. (2023). Vazhnyy shag FIFA: legionery v Rossii i Ukraine bolshe ne mogut zamorazhivat kontrakty. Vse detali [An important step by FIFA: Legionnaires in Russia and Ukraine can no longer freeze contracts. All details] *Sports.ru*, 23 May. Available at: https://www.sports.ru/tribuna/blogs/odukhevremeni/3139757.html [Accessed 1 September 2023].

WSJ (no date). *EUR to RUB. Euro/Russian ruble historical prices, WSJ*. Available at: https://www.wsj.com/market-data/quotes/fx/EURRUB/historical-prices [Accessed 1 September 2023].

10

EMBRACED BY GAZPROM

Why Is the Business Model of FC Zenit Unclear to Scholars of Sports Management?

Sergey Altukhov and Veronica Astashkina

Introduction

Zenit Saint Petersburg Football Club has become Russia's football champion for five years straight. Perhaps, such a "tradition" will be continued this year. Fans, experts, researchers associate the main reasons for success and domination in the domestic Russian football market with the sustainable alliance with the state-owned Gazprom Corporation and the club's growing funding from the resources of this entity. However, the UEFA compliance audits did not reveal serious violations in the club's books and artificial budget inflation. Everything happens within the framework of the Regulations. But there are still questions to ask.

We aim to show only a small and non-core part of the football business of the state corporation, we will trace when and how the interests of a large industrial gas giant and an ordinary football club from St. Petersburg came together. Who benefits from this, and how did it become possible? A business model for filling the club's budget and a sponsorship card with a dozen and a half Gazprom subsidiaries, the formation of public opinion about the Zenit "people's" team through the efforts of reporters and commentators of the only Match TV channel owned by Gazprom Media, a number of football farm clubs and the level of corporate interests in the production and sports hierarchy are the new realities and dominants of Russian football. Successful marketing concepts of Russian football clubs still remain an "unexplored object" for both sports marketing theorists and practitioners who cannot understand the benefits of the parties involved in the development of football in Russia.

DOI: 10.4324/9781003473671-11

Theoretical Foundations of the Study

Management theories increasingly convince us that the contours of the relationship between the state and society have fundamentally changed (Rhodes, 1997). This is happening in various countries of the world and leads to changes in the world order. Management is no longer absolutized in the form of a single responsible governing body. Most often, various state institutions and public organizations are involved in the management process. Therefore, we turn to a comparative analysis of different management models and their transformation in accordance with changes in the external environment.

Common governance approaches used in sports include federal/unitary governance, system governance, joint governance, stakeholder governance and network governance (Harris et al., 2023).

The above-mentioned problems and the structure of federal/unitary governance are studied in the work (O'Boyle and Shilbury, 2016); system governance was presented in a study (Henry and Lee, 2004); forms and principles of joint governance were reflected in another study (Shilbury et al., 2016); stakeholders were managed by the same researchers a year earlier (Ferkins and Shilbury, 2015); the basics of network relationship governance are presented here (Chappelet, 2016).

We assume in this article that the structure of relations in Russian professional sports in the XXI century has become the basis for another form of governance in sports, which we will conditionally call "public-corporate governance in sport".

For You, for Us and for the Gas!

This is how the most popular toast sounds at feasts with representatives of the gas industry. Almost the youngest raw materials industry has become the most fashionable, the most promising and the most resource-intensive in just 50 years. It was Gazprom's gas revenues that made Russia a strong mining and trading power with "South" and "Nord" Streams of international transportation. And let no one be confused by the terrorist sabotage on the Nord Stream, and the problems that arose after that. It's unpleasant, but not tragic. The whole world is going through difficult times. And the perpetrators will be punished. The inconvenience of this situation was experienced, first of all, by the end users of the product in Europe. In winter, this is especially palpable and painful. Though this does not prevent Gazprom from developing its business projects and reinforcing the power of its empire with victorious achievements and trophy decisions.

We try to show only a small and non-core part of the football business of the state corporation, and trace when and how the interests of a large industrial gas giant and an ordinary football club from Saint Petersburg came together. Who benefits from this, and how did it become possible? In modern realities,

Zenit's five championships straight and a weighty claim to a sixth title cannot do without mentioning the Gazprom empire in this context of success and triumph. A business model for filling the club's budget and a sponsorship card with a dozen and a half Gazprom subsidiary, the formation of public opinion about the Zenit "people's" team through the efforts of reporters and commentators of the only Match TV channel owned by Gazprom Media, a number of football farm clubs and the level of corporate interests in the production and sports hierarchy are the new realities and dominants of Russian football.

How it all began? As they say in Russia, know how to do things, know how to have fun. They always knew how to have fun in Russia and everywhere. The first experience with the placement of gassers' money in Soviet football dates back to 1976. At that time, the senior officials of Orenburg oblast disbanded Lokomotiv, that played in the third division, in order to establish Gazovik football club and transfer the financing of the club to the Orenburggazprom gas production company and employ all the football players, coaches and staff of Lokomotiv there. That's how everyone lived in the USSR. Sports teams were assigned to industrial enterprises, law enforcement agencies or trade unions and were united into voluntary sports societies. If a football club was established at an enterprise, then football players were registered as sports instructors, and salaries and bonuses were received through the trade union committee. At that time, the Orenburggazprom company was headed by Viktor Chernomyrdin, the future prime Minister of the Russian Government. With his light hand, the cooperation of football and gas partners started.

This initiative did not go unnoticed in the gas industry, and gradually football clubs with a "gas" history began to be established. For instance, Moscow's Spartak has acquired a partnership with Urengoygazprom, an affiliate of Gazprom. The company's logo was placed on the team's kits in the 1995 and 1996 seasons. Astrakhangazprom acquired football club "Volgar" of Astrakhan and renamed it "Volgar-Gazprom". In Tomsk, Vostokgazprom, another Gazprom regional affiliate, became the general sponsor of the FC Tom Tomsk. But in all these cases, it was about financing sufficient for the third division. Gazovik-Gazprom FC from Izhevsk is considered to be the most successful among Gazprom clubs. Vladimir Tumaev, director of Spetsgazavtotrans, became the founder of the club, its president and a player who took to the field in official matches until the age of 58. And the club from Izhevsk was very close to reaching the top division of the Russian Football Championship. Thus, Gazprom's football clubs have left a noticeable mark on the football map of Russia.

Zenit Leningrad

Zenit FC won its main title of the USSR Cup winner in the military 1944, after the lifting the siege of Leningrad. But the club's structure and its circumstances were no different from hundreds of similar Soviet sports organizations. Since the late 1950s, the club has been on the balance sheet of the Leningrad Optical and Mechanical Association (also known as LOMO), which produced military optics and guidance systems. The name of the Zenit FC is a symbol of the upper point of intersection of the horizon with the celestial sphere. As you see, it indicates belonging to the military sports complex.

Right after the dissolution of the Soviet Union and the resulting economic crisis in the country, LOMO stopped funding the club. Leningrad City Council, the Leningrad Association of State Enterprises, Lenoblsovprof (Leningrad Regional Labor Unions Council), Lengorsportkomitet (Leningrad City Sports Committee) and Leningrad Football Federation became the new custodians of Zenit. In 1992, Zenit played in the first Russian Championship. However, at the end of the season, Zenit was relegated to the first division again. Anatoly Sobchak, the city's mayor, entrusted the rescue of the club to Vitaly Mutko, chairman of the mayor's committee on social issues. Mutko had to find sponsors who would take over the funding of the dying club and organize the work.

Over the next five years, the club has transformed. In 2001, Zenit had ten shareholders among its founders: Fertilizer manufacturer Eurochem (12%), Fund for the Development and Support of Mass Media (10.8%), IT company CJSC Computerland SPb (6%), Saint Petersburg Telephone Network (7%), bakery manufacturer Karavai (5%), Worldwide Fair "Russian Farmer" (5%). Vitaly Mutko owned 12% of the shares. But Gazprom's structures like Gazenergofinance (24%), Lentrasgaz (28%) were already the major shareholders and the largest sponsors of Zenit at the turn of the century. Cumulatively, Gazprom's affiliates owned 52% of the club's shares. Life was getting perfect, and the football club from Saint Petersburg became a prominent football force in the Russian Championship.

Restructuring of the Club's Management

In the early 2000's, big money came to Russian football. In 2001, Evgeny Giner became the owner of FC Central Sports Club of Army (CSKA), Spartak was acquired by Leonid Fedun and Vagit Alekperov, the Lukoil co-owners in 2003. They were ready to increase the clubs' budgets and Zenit with the level of funding that Gazprom's affiliates provided to it at that time, was uncompetitive. Vitaly Mutko brilliantly used his administrative connections and lobbied for the invitation of David Traktovenko and Vladimir Kogan, the Promstroybank SPB bankers, to be among the shareholders of Zenit. The bank was engaged in lending to the largest industrial enterprises of Saint Petersburg. Many of them were close to bankruptcy and eventually banks got the companies. In order to manage numerous assets, Kogan and Traktovenko established the management company Banking House Saint Petersburg. FC Zenit became one of the clients of this management company.

Technically, in 2002, the bankers purchased 24% of Zenit owned by Gazenergofinance and then bought out an additional issue and shares of some minority shareholders. As a result, Promstroybank received a control share in Zenit, and Lentransgaz retained a block of 25%, which allowed Gazprom representatives to participate in the club's life. Sergey Fursenko, head of Lentransgaz, became Gazprom's representative on the Zenit's board of directors in 2003.

At that time, Fursenko was not a well-known executive, but he had a very serious personal resource. In 1996, together with his older brother Andrey Fursenko, he co-founded the cottage cooperative (camping) "Ozero" ("Lake") in the Priozersky district of the Leningrad oblast. Among the other founders of the coop were Yuri Kovalchuk and Nikolai Shamalov, the future co-owners of the Rossiya Bank, and Vladimir Yakunin, the future president of JSCO Russian Railways.

The owners' alliance fixed the club's business pretty quickly. Zenit's budget immediately increased to $15 million in 2003, to $25 million in 2004, and to $45 million in 2005. The last figure already matched to the level of expenditures by the largest clubs of Moscow. In the mid-2000s, Giner and Fedun estimated the annual budget of CSKA and Spartak at around $50 million, respectively. But for the shareholders of Promstroybank, $50 million was already the limit. In 2005, Vladimir Kogan, the major shareholder of Promstroybank, announced a total sale of his assets in Saint Petersburg. He received the largest amount for the bank – VTB acquired it for $577 million. Meanwhile, Kogan and Traktovenko received $36 million for the 51% of the Zenit FC. Although the actual market value of unprofitable club without valuable real estate and titles was probably close to zero. Furthermore, Alexey Miller, who had been a fan of the club since childhood and became chairman of the Gazprom board of directors in 2001, was directly interested in the fate of Zenit FC. In the first season after the purchase by Gazprom, Miller became president of the club, and Zenit's budget grew to $60 million, in 2008 it reached the prestigious mark of $100 million. Opponents from Moscow fallen behind abruptly.

The Russian Football Economics

Except Krasnodar FC, the structure of the top Russian football clubs' economy is arranged uniformly. Zenit FC was no exception, but displayed the most extensive example of such a model of Russian football. In the framework of this model, the figure of the owner [company or individuals] is a formal affair. Indeed, profit or loss by the end of the year are reflected only on paper and do not affect the welfare of the owner in any way. Suffice it to recall how sanctioned VEB.RF has sold the majority of the stock in CSKA to an obscure Balance Asset Management. Another example is FC Rubin, where Rustem

Saimanov performed as both the owner and CEO until December 2022. Therefore, the fact that Gazprom does not directly own the club solves nothing. Accordingly, Zenit's official owner is not Gazprom, but Gazprombank, in which Gazprom directly owns less than half of the shares, but controls it through other affiliates.

But the most important thing for understanding the organizational structure of Russian clubs is elsewhere. Who is that perfunctory owner and whom does he represent? The answer on this question impacts on the source of funding processed into advertising deals that, in its turn, form a significant part of the budget. UEFA investigated these contracts in detail according to the previous version of the rules on financial fair play. A special commission and independent agencies assessed whether agreements had been signed on market terms or whether the owners were trying to artificially inflate the budget.

The information provided by Zenit to UEFA estimated Gazprom's contribution at €48.8 million, where €20.8 million was an advertising contract, and €28 million was an endowment. Nevertheless, UEFA Club Financial Control Body found Zenit violated Financial Fair Play Rules, but the sanctions turned out to be quite mild – Russian club fined €6 million, got limits on transfer expenses, strict monitoring for three years.

Zenit was found to be in violation of the rules of financial fair play, but got off lightly – €6 million in fines, limits on transfer expenditures, strict monitoring for three years.

But this story has served a good purpose for the club's owners. They began to split up advertising contracts and expand partnership niches. Is this what academics don't realize when they ask questions at conferences about how Russian football clubs manage to attract such generous sponsors with the lack of notable achievements and titles on the international stage? The capitalist form of production described by Karl Marx could not even dream or think about creating state corporations that can transform the tasks of the state through obtaining financial benefits from tax revenues and incomes in the context of business relations with commercial partners.

Right after the UEFA investigation, the list of sponsors and partners posted on Zenit's official website has expanded. Gazprom stands apart, but a large list of subsidiaries of the gas company has been added to it. Currently, Gazprombank, Gazprom Neft, Gazprom Export, Gazprom Mezhregiongaz, Gazprom Pererabotka, Gazprom Transgaz Saint Petersburg, two brands of Gazprom Neft product (G-Drive fuel and G-Energy engine oil) are officially represented as sponsors of Zenit FC, the corporate integrator of digital development Gazprom Neft Digital Solutions, as well as the former Gazprom insurance company SOGAZ (now controlled by Yury Kovalchuk's structures) and another former Gazprom affiliate, the petrochemical company Sibur (the major owners are Leonid Mikhelson and Gennady Timchenko).

Such a sponsorship contract-splitting between Gazprom's subsidiaries happened due to Zenit's desire to technically comply with the UEFA FFP rules. Under these circumstances, Zenit's budget continued to grow. Back in 2010, Alexander Dyukov, who replaced Sergey Fursenko as president of the club, stated that by 2014 the budget would grow to $150 million (at that time it was about $100 million), and this would allow Zenit to fight in European competitions. Dyukov is an old familiar to Alexey Miller. In 1998–99, they worked at the Seaport of Saint Petersburg, through which the main stream of Russian oil was exported. Dyukov was the CEO of the port, and Miller served as the investment director of the management company OBIP. Soon Miller became the head of Gazprom, and Dyukov run his petrochemical affiliate Sibur. A few years later, Dyukov turned executive of Gazprom Neft. In fact, it was Sibneft, which Gazprom acquired from Roman Abramovich for $13.1 billion and made corporate rebranding.

Where Is the Government Watching?

And here we come to the most significant question. Why does a gas company need such grandiose investments in Zenit FC? What is the point for Gazprom to spend so much money on marketing, and how does the state as a holder of the controlling stake in the company (50.2%) look at it?

Zenit executives insist that marketing contracts have a salutary effect on the business of Gazprom companies. Zenit executives insist that marketing contracts have a positive impact on the business of Gazprom companies. In 2017, Alexander Dyukov claimed that the partnership between Zenit and Gazprom is mutually beneficial. As the Chairman of the Gazprom Neft Management Board, he noted that the company is completely satisfied with its cooperation with Zenit. Sponsorship of the football club is viewed as an effective tool for promoting retail brands, such as gas station networks, Drive-café, G-energy, and G-drive, under which motor fuels, energy drinks, and various related products are sold to consumers. In a stagnating market, the company manages to increase sales every year and generate additional revenue. According to Dyukov, Gazprom Neft ranks first in Russia in terms of average daily fuel sales and sells more coffee in its cafes than any other gas station or coffee shop network.

Such statements can be treated with skepticism. Eventually, the dynamics of Gazprom Neft's revenue growth clearly depends on the conjuncture of oil prices on the global market, and not on the results of Zenit.

Another question is: since Gazprom's major holder is the government, then maybe the $2 billion that Gazprom spent on the football team, could it invest in healthcare or education?

Actually, this is not exactly the case. Certainly, the government is the major holder of Gazprom, but operating management issues, except for completely strategic and geopolitical ones, are in the hands of hired managers.

Excessive marketing costs could theoretically have a negative impact on the company's income. Nevertheless, in the case of Gazprom, the revenue indicator is much more significant than marketing costs that do not affect it at all. The government receives income from Gazprom in two ways: in the forms of taxes and dividends, which are paid to all shareholders in proportion to the size of the shares. And the first amount is much larger than the second.

A recent example: by the end of 2022, Gazprom's net income decreased by 40% to 1.2 trillion rubles, the second half of the year company run at a loss mainly due to a reduction of gas supplies to Europe (by more than 50%) and an increase in the tax rate on mining for Gazprom. The Board of Directors refused to pay dividends at the end of the year. However, the government is in the black: in the form of taxes for 2022, Gazprom paid more than 5 trillion rubles to budgets of all levels, which makes 18% of federal budget revenues. Dividends would have brought much less: in recent years, Gazprom's total dividend payments have been kept at 300 billion rubles – half was owed to the state.

Therefore, Gazprom's expenditures on Zenit FC do not seriously affect anything for the state, since Gazprom's revenue and taxes on gas production are essential to the state.

References

Chappelet, J.-L. (2016). From Olympic administration to Olympic governance. *Sport in Society*, *19*(6), 739–751. https://doi.org/10.1080/17430437.2015.11 08648.

Ferkins, L. and Shilbury, D. (2015). Board strategic balance: an emerging sport governance theory. *Sport Management Review*, *18*(4), 489–500. https://doi.org/10.1016/j. smr.2014.12.002.

Harris, S., Dowling, M. and Washington, M. (2023). Political protest and rule 50: exploring the polycentric governance of international and Olympic sport. *International Journal of Sport Policy and Politics*. https://doi.org/10.1080/19406940.2023 .2224345.

Henry, I. and Lee, P. C. (2004). Governance and ethics in sport. In S. Chadwick and J. Beech (Eds.), *The Business of Sport Management* (pp. 25–42). London: Pearson Education.

O'Boyle, I. and Shilbury, D. (2016). Comparing federal and unitary models of sport governance: a case study investigation. *Managing Sport and Leisure*, *21*(6), 353–374. https://doi.org/10.1080/23750472.2017.1289339.

Rhodes, R. A. W. (1997). *Understanding Governance: Policy Networks, Governance, Reflexivity, and Accountability* (p. 252). Milton Keynes: Open University Press.

Shilbury, D., O'Boyle, I. and Ferkins, L. (2016). Towards a research agenda in collaborative sport governance. *Sport Management Review*, *19*(5), 479–491. https://doi. org/10.1016/j.smr.2016.04.004.

PART II

Women's Football

11

EUROPE AND GEOPOLITICAL INFLUENCES ON WOMEN'S FOOTBALL FINANCE

Christina Philippou

Introduction

With the recent growth in women's football in Europe has come an interest from sponsors (Carp, 2022), broadcasters (Petty and Pope, 2019), and governments (DCMS, 2023). Where the funds for this investment have originated from (and why), and how geopolitically motivated regulations have shaped this growth are integral to understanding some of these changes. Geopolitics has affected women's football financial and commercial health both at national team and club levels, and this chapter looks at some of the hows and whys of this influence.

To do so, we must briefly consider the historical landscape of women's football, and how its evolution in Europe has affected the global state of women's football finances today.

England and the Ban on Women's Football

On 5 December 1921, the English FA banned the use of grounds belonging to football clubs affiliated with the FA for women's football (FA, n.d.), thus effectively imposing a ban on women's football as the teams were faced with having nowhere to play. In the geopolitical context, the global influence of the UK at the time ensured that what was in essence a country-specific reactionary protectionist measure (as women's football was seen, due to its wartime success, as a threat to men's football) spread beyond England to enact a barrier against women's football whose repercussions are felt to this day. This is despite the fact that the English had distanced themselves from the global football family – something that led to the establishment of FIFA as the world governing body (Conn, 2018).

DOI: 10.4324/9781003473671-13

European influence on FIFA was strong, with the continent providing all FIFA presidents prior to the appointment of João Havelange in 1974 (FIFA, 2024). The lack of gender diversity within the governing body did not help the commercial cause of women's football, even after the various bans began to be lifted. The diversity issue at governing body, league, and club level continues to affect the commercial potential and financial sustainability of football clubs to this day (Clarkson and Philippou, 2022). For example, Philippou et al. (2022) found two-thirds of clubs in the top four leagues of the men's professional game in England had all-male boards, while, in 2022 in the Women's Super League (WSL) in England, 7 of the 12 sides had all-male boards (Philippou, 2022a), something affecting the commercial potential at club level.

The English ban was eventually lifted on 19 January 1970, but lack of investment into the women's game continued for a number of decades. In the intervening time, while the women's game was still banned from the professional sphere, the men's game had hurtled towards the commercial success that it is today. The money in the professional men's game initially came through ticketing and sponsorship. As the leagues progressed and broadcasters realised the potential of sport in general and football in particular, broadcasting income became an increasingly important source for football clubs and sporting organisations from FIFA to individual leagues.

There is some evidence of some professionalisation of women's football despite the ban, with players from Dick, Kerr Ladies (a factory team from 1917 to 1965) "paid 10 shillings (50p) to cover their expenses" (The FA, n.d.). The English FA assumed commercial control of professional women's football by launching the WSL in 2011, although concerns were raised around the original structure based on traditional gender concepts (Woodhouse et al., 2019) and the type of commercialised match day experience (Fielding-Lloyd et al., 2020). In 2023, control of the WSL was passed on to NewCo, "an independent body where each club who participates in the top two tiers of women's football acts as shareholders" (The FA, 2023). It aimed to address issues such as the previous commercial prioritisation of men's football (Parry et al., 2023) but also to benefit from commercial partnerships associated with different values to that of the men's game, something often cited in reflections of fan experiences of women's football (Williams et al., 2023).

FIFA had started commercialising football through partnerships and collaborations in the 1980s (Homburg, 2008). These partnerships either bundled (a strategy used by product holders to increase income from their less important and less popular products by tying them into a deal with a very popular product) or excluded women's football, and the commercialisation of women's football did not start until decades later. One such example was the partnership with EA Sports from 1993 until 2023 (BBC, 2023), where women's football was first included in the game in FIFA 16 (Heckmann and

Furini, 2018) and a female footballer included on the cover for the first time in 2023 (EA Sports, 2022).

A similar pattern can be seen on the broadcasting front, where women's football, even at governing body level, continued to be packaged alongside the men's. The 2023 Women's World Cup was the first in which the women's offering formed part of a media rights sale independent of the men's. However, FIFA were publicly disappointed following the rights sale, with their president calling out European broadcasters for offering ten to a hundred times less than for the men's World Cup, despite viewing figures being in the region of 50–60% of the men's (FIFA, 2023). European broadcasters blamed location (as Australia and New Zealand time zones are not favourable for European viewing audiences (Ingle, 2023)), but it is also likely that the significant and unanticipated growth in interest in the time between setting budgets and bidding for the World Cup rights caught broadcasters unprepared. Media outlets criticised FIFA for chronically undervaluing women's football and for the delay in starting the rights bidding process (which resulted in rights not being confirmed until less than a month before the Women's World Cup was due to kick off, while, in contrast, men's World Cup rights were negotiated years in advance).

European Geopolitical Influences on UEFA and FIFA's Strategies in Relation to Women's Football Finance

But it is not just the strategies of governing bodies and clubs that have had an influence on women's football finances. Political and government bodies have also had an impact on the commercialisation and acceptability of women's football as a business. Regulations and policies in Europe have affected women's football commercial growth globally and can be seen through the effects of legislative and political actions taken in the continent.

The Council of Europe set out the legal groundwork for autonomy and self-regulation in sport through its European Sport's Charter which states that "voluntary sport organisations have the right to establish autonomous decision-making processes within the law" (Council of Europe, 2001). This right to autonomy has led to poor governance in a number of sports organisations (Chappelet, 2016) and included governance issues involving lack of diversity (Geeraert et al., 2015). The Council of Europe recognised problems arising in football as a result of poor governance and adopted the Good Football Governance Resolution (Council of Europe, 2018) to improve accountability and corporate governance in football in general. However, matters of governance progressively grew to overtly include equality concerns. The Council's Committee on Culture, Science, Education, and Media also highlighted the need for equality in football, suggesting to the industry that "a greater proportion of available resources should be allocated to measures to achieve these goals, including equal pay and rewards for women's teams" (Council of Europe, 2022).

Football's governing bodies have taken the lead from governments and political entities, as well as addressing the concerns of the increasingly vociferous calls for women's inclusion in the football industry, by stipulating conditions that include development and funding of women's teams. For example, UEFA introduced new licensing rules in 2022 whose objective was "to encourage men's football clubs to embrace women's and girls' football in all 55 UEFA member associations" (UEFA, 2022). In the same vein, both UEFA Financial Sustainability Regulations (UEFA, 2023) and the Premier League's Profitability and Sustainability Rules (Premier League, 2023) provide exclusions for spending on women's teams, effectively offering a financial inducement for investment.

Part of the reason for change in perspective from adrenal resources to an opportunity for investment and development is, of course, commercial, as the financial success of Euro 2022 highlighted a new market and demographic which the football industry could target. As building brand equity can further drive club revenue (Kerr and Gladden, 2008), increasing marketing and other resources in women's football through improved broadcasting and commercial partnerships has had a positive effect on the overall commercial outlook of women's football, something aided by football's resilience to economic recessions (Cox and Philippou, 2022). However, the financial situation at women's football club level is less positive, with strong revenue growth being marked by growth in both debt and losses (Clarkson et al., 2023).

The way that women's football is treated from the commercial and business perspective is increasingly converging with that of men's football, and that brings both opportunities arising from shared resources and risks of following widespread poor governance and business practices found in men's football (Philippou, 2022b). It also has the tendency to create comparisons between two sub-industries, men's and women's football, where one operates in an established and saturated market and the other is more akin to a start-up. This then leads to some commercial decisions which do not align with social and other expectations. For example, Mary Earps (Women's World Cup 2023 Golden Glove award recipient and England player) publicly questioned sponsor Nike over lack of availability of replica England women goalkeeper shirts during the Women's World Cup, which eventually led to two limited online releases of her replica shirts in October and December 2023 that sold out within minutes (Lee, 2023). It was reported that "Nike do not sell women's goalkeeper shirts because it is not part of their commercial strategy" (Batte, 2023), but, following a public outcry, Nike issued a statement that "We hear and understand the desire for a retail version of a goalkeeper jersey and we are working towards solutions for future tournaments, in partnership with FIFA and the federations" (Ostlere, 2023). In short, Nike and other commercial partners of women's football are starting to recognise the commercial value of the game.

Sovereign Wealth Fund and Private Equity Ownership in Europe

In addition to geopolitical effects on the finances of women's football caused by powerful federations and indirect political influence through laws and regulations in Europe, the effects of ownership have also had financial repercussions with a geopolitical twist.

The increase of the use of sport for geopolitical influence and soft power (Chadwick et al., 2020) is an important contributory topic that has been covered in more detail elsewhere in this book, but nevertheless remains a key reason for some commercial partnerships and investments. The increase in sovereign wealth fund ownership (for example, Manchester City, Newcastle United, and Paris Saint-Germain) and private equity ownership (for example, Chelsea, Liverpool, AC Milan, and Atalanta) in Europe has also had profound effects not just on the football industry as a whole, but on women's football specifically.

Sovereign wealth fund ownership has been linked to a strategy of on-the-pitch success for the club (men's, women's, and youth teams) at all costs, something that has flowed over into the management of the affiliated women's teams. For example, Manchester City has pumped in large funds into its women's football team, resulting in huge increases in their debt ratios (Clarkson et al., 2023), but also making it a fairly successful team with one WSL title and three Women's FA Cups since 2015.

Private equity ownership has also influenced the finances of women's football teams, often with a geopolitical aspect in the strategy. For example, the acquisition of Wrexham football club by two Hollywood stars in 2021 was in part fuelled by diversification of markets and public relations benefits arising from ownership of a Welsh football team by US owners: as part of the strategy of success in both performance and image, there has been both resourcing and integration of the women's team which has enabled their move to semi-professionalism and their promotion (Sutcliffe, 2023).

The effect of both sovereign and private equity ownership has also been to create a perceived demand for a luxury item (football clubs), and the increased visibility of women's football has led to more interest from potential commercial partners and owners seeking to increase their own portfolios for both commercial and image reasons. The potential of women's football has led to increased prices for women's football clubs, as seen by the prices paid for NWSL expansion teams (Herrera, 2023), as well as the creation of the first multi-club ownership group for women's football by investor Michele Kang (Linehan, 2023).

In conclusion, while the importance of professional football as a social and cultural entity is recognised by society (Hyndman et al., 2023), the commercial value of women's football is still affected by a protectionist economic measure enacted in 1921 and since repealed. The irony is that, while geopolitical influences negatively impacted growth for decades, it is geopolitical influences that are now acting as catalysts for explosive growth in women's football finances.

References

Batte, K. (2023) 'England Women's Mary Earps slams 'hugely hurtful' Nike for not selling her keeper shirt for commercial reasons – and reveals they brutally cut her from the photoshoot for the kit release', *Mail Online* (20 July 2023 edn). Available at: https://www.dailymail.co.uk/sport/football/article-12320083/England-star-Mary-Earps-blasts-Nike-hugely-hurtful-decision-not-goalkeeper-shirt-sale-Womens-World-Cup-not-available-Euro-2022.html.

BBC (2023) 'Fifa no more? EA Sports rebrands its biggest game', *BBC News*. Available at: https://www.bbc.co.uk/news/entertainment-arts-65244351 [Accessed 5 January 2024].

Carp, S. (2022) 'Three reasons why unbundling women's sponsorship works for Uefa, World Rugby and Fifa', *SportsPro Daily*, 22 July 2022. Available at: https://www.sportspromedia.com/insights/opinions/sportspro-blog/uefa-world-rugby-fifa-womens-sponsorship-rights-unbundling/?zephr_sso_ott=ND7t13 [Accessed 1 April2023].

Chadwick, S., Widdop, P. and Burton, N. (2020) Soft power sports sponsorship – a social network analysis of a new sponsorship form. *Journal of Political Marketing*, *21*(2), 196–217.

Chappelet, J.-L. (2016). Autonomy and governance: necessary bedfellows in the fight against corruption in sport. In I. Transparency (Ed.), *Global Corruption Report: Sport* (p. 372). Abingdon: Routledge.

Clarkson, B. and Philippou, C. (2022) Gender diversity and financial sustainability in professional football: a competitive strategy and proposed interdisciplinary research agenda. *Managing Sport & Leisure*, *29*(4), 681–685.

Clarkson, B., Plumley, D., Philippou, C., Wilson, R. and Webb, T. (2023). Money troubles and problems ahead? The financial health of professional women's football clubs in England. *Sport, Business & Management*, *13*(5), 563–581.

Conn, D. (2018). *The Fall of the House of Fifa*. London: Yellow Jersey Press.

Council of Europe (2001) *European Sport Charter (revised)*. Brussels (No. R (92) 13 REV).

Council of Europe, Committee on Culture, S.E.a.M. (2022) *Football governance: business and values* (Doc. 15430). Available at: https://pace.coe.int/en/files/29767/html.

Council of Europe, Parliamentary Assembly of the Council of Europe (2018) *Good Football Governance* (Resolution no. 2200). Available at: https://assembly.coe.int/nw/xml/XRef/Xref-XML2HTML-en.asp?fileid=24444&lang=en#:~:text=Footb all%20does%20not%20belong%20to,play%20down%20and%20trivialise%20 overindulgences.

Cox, A. and Philippou, C. (2022) Measuring the resilience of English Premier league clubs to economic recessions. *Soccer & Society*, *23*(4–5), 482–499.

DCMS (2023). *Raising the bar – reframing the opportunity in women's football*. Available at: https://www.gov.uk/government/publications/raising-the-bar-reframing-the-opportunity-in-womens-football/raising-the-bar-reframing-the-opportunity-in-womens-football.

EA Sports (2022) *EA SPORTS™ Unveils FIFA 23 Cover Athletes Kylian Mbappé & Sam Kerr*. Available at: https://ir.ea.com/press-releases/press-release-details/2022/EA-SPORTS-Unveils-FIFA-23-Cover-Athletes-Kylian-Mbapp–Sam-Kerr/default.aspx [Accessed 5 January 2024].

FA, T. (n.d.). *The Story of Women's Football in England*. Available at: https://www.thefa.com/womens-girls-football/heritage/kicking-down-barriers [Accessed 4 January 2024].

Fielding-Lloyd, B., Woodhouse, D. and Sequerra, R. (2020). 'More than just a game': family and spectacle in marketing the England Women's Super League. *Soccer & Society*, 21(2), 166–179.

FIFA (2023). Broadcasters urged to pay a fair price for FIFA Women's World Cup™ media rights. Available at: https://inside.fifa.com/about-fifa/president/news/broadcasters-urged-to-pay-a-fair-price-for-fifa-womens-world-cup-tm-media-rights.

FIFA (2024). *Past presidents*. Available at: https://www.fifa.com/about-fifa/president/past-presidents [Accessed 5 January 2024].

Geeraert, A., Mrkonjic, M. and Chappelet, J.-L. (2015). A rationalist perspective on the autonomy of international sport governing bodies: towards a pragmatic autonomy in the steering of sports. *International Journal of Sport Policy*, 7(4), 473–488.

Heckmann, P. L. and Furini, L. (2018). The introduction of women's teams in FIFA 16 and how Brazilian women reacted to it. *Estudos em Comunicação*, 1(26), 247–260.

Herrera, S. (2023) 'NWSL commissioner Jessica Berman reveals expansion details: League eyes two new teams for 2026 season', *CBS*, 9 September 2023. Available at: https://www.cbssports.com/soccer/news/nwsl-commissioner-jessica-berman-reveals-expansion-details-league-eyes-two-new-teams-for-2026-season/.

Homburg, H. (2008). Financing world football. A business history of the Fédération Internationale de Football Association (FIFA). *Zeitschrift für Unternehmensgeschichte/Journal of Business History*, 53(1), 33–69.

Hyndman, N., Lapsley, I. and Philippou, C. (2023) Exploring a Soccer Society: dreams, themes and the beautiful game. *Accounting, Auditing & Accountability Journal*, 37(2), 433–453..

Ingle, S. (2023) 'Fifa threatens Women's World Cup broadcast blackout in Europe', *The Guardian*. Available at: https://www.theguardian.com/football/2023/may/02/fifa-threatens-womens-world-cup-broadcast-blackout-in-europe-offers-rights-infantino.

Kerr, A. K. and Gladden, J. M. (2008). Extending the understanding of professional team brand equity to the global marketplace. *International Journal of Sport Management and Marketing*, 3(1–2), 58–77.

Lee, A. (2023). 'Mary Earps's England goalkeeper shirt sold out within 5 minutes, but when will it be restocked?', *Independent*, 12 December 2023. Available at: https://www.independent.co.uk/extras/indybest/outdoor-activity/football/mary-earps-goalkeeper-shirt-england-nike-b2399993.html.

Linehan, M. (2023). 'Washington Spirit, Lyon owner Michele Kang buys London City Lionesses', *The Athletic*, 15 December 2023. Available at: https://theathletic.com/5140139/2023/12/15/michele-kang-london-city-lionesses-2/.

Ostlere, L. (2023). 'Nike U-turns on selling Mary Earps' England goalkeeper jerseys', |*Independent* (26 September 2023 edn). Available at: https://www.independent.co.uk/sport/football/mary-earps-goalkeeper-hit-england-nike-b2418592.html.

Parry, K. D., Clarkson, B. G., Bowes, A., Grubb, L. and Rowe, D. (2023). Media framing of women's football during the COVID-19 pandemic. *Communication & Sport*, 11(3), 592–615.

Petty, K. and Pope, S. (2019). A new age for media coverage of Women's sport? An analysis of English media coverage of the 2015 FIFA Women's World Cup. *Sociology*, 53(3), 486–502.

Philippou, C. (2022a). 'Euro 2022: why women's football remains dominated by the men's game', *The Conversation*.

Philippou, C. (2022b). 'How women's football can avoid being corrupted when more money comes its way', *The Conversation*.

Philippou, C., Clarkson, B., Pope, S., Jain, S., Parry, K., Huang, X., Plumley, D. and Cox, A. (2022). *The Gender Divide That Fails Football's Bottom Line: The Commercial Case for Gender Equality*: Fair Game. Available at: https://static1. squarespace.com/static/6047aabc7130e94a70ed3515/t/6225fcd351786a64ba44 21b0/1646656733257/The+Gender+Divide+That+Fails+Football%27s+Bottom+L ine+-+Fair+Game+Report+March+2022.pdf [Accessed 4 April 2023].

Premier League (2023). *Handbook: Season 2023/24*. Available at: https://www.pre-mierleague.com/about/publications [Accessed 4 January 2024].

Sutcliffe, R. (2023). 'Wrexham Women enter a new semi-professional era with grand ambitions', 15 September 2023. Available at: https://theathletic.com/4852620/2023/09/15/wrexham-women-enter-a-new-semi-professional-era-with-grand-ambitions/.

The FA (2023). *Nikki Doucet appointed as NewCo CEO*. Available at: https:// womensleagues.thefa.com/nikki-doucet-appointed-as-newco-ceo/ [Accessed 4 January 2024].

The FA (n.d.). *The Story of Women's Football in England*. Available at: https://www. thefa.com/womens-girls-football/heritage/kicking-down-barriers [Accessed 4 January 2024].

UEFA (2022). *UEFA Executive Committee approves first dedicated women's football licensing regulations*. Available at: https://www.uefa.com/news-media/news/0275-151c94376657-090c3bee485f-1000--uefa-executive-committee-approves-first-dedicated-women-s-// [Accessed 4 January 2024].

UEFA (2023). *UEFA Club Licensing and Financial Sustainability Regulations*. Available at: https://documents.uefa.com/r/UEFA-Club-Licensing-and-Financial-Sustainability-Regulations-2024-Online.

Williams, J., Pope, S. and Cleland, J. (2023). Genuinely in love with the game' football fan experiences and perceptions of women's football in England. *Sport in Society*, 26(2), 285–301.

Woodhouse, D., Fielding-Lloyd, B. and Sequerra, R. (2019). Big brother's little sister: the ideological construction of women's super league. *Sport in Society*, 22(12), 2006–2023.

12

THE PARADOX OF FRENCH WOMEN'S FOOTBALL

Lindsay Sarah Krasnoff

It was the FIFA World Cup 2023 ad that went viral, generated global discussion, showed the art of the possible (*Reuters*, 2023a). A nearly two-minute spot by French telecoms giant Orange began with Kylian Mbappé, Antoine Griezmann, and other Les Bleus stars electrifying crowds in a series of dazzling plays and goals. 'This is the football we love' the ad proclaimed halfway through. 'Only Les Bleus can give us these emotions,' it added before viewers were informed of the dupe: 'But that's not them you've just seen.' The segment was actually footage of Les Bleus, the national women's team; the players' gender obfuscated by VFX technology, effectively a deep fake video (*Orange – la Compil des Bleues (English version)*, 2023). Orange explained to *Business Insider* that they wanted to show just how much general audiences undervalued and at times ridiculed the women's game. '[T]he skills of the players are very impressive, and matches can bring as much emotion as those of men … We wanted to rectify the truth and change these ideas' (Kirschner, 2023).

It was not the only part of that summer's Team France campaign to garner worldwide attention and tease the country's ability as an influence in women's football. Hervé Renard, named Les Bleus head coach in late March, was the first manager to guide two separate squads at World Cups six months apart and the first to leave a men's national team coaching position for a women's.[1] Renard earned platitudes from his squad as they progressed to a tension-filled quarterfinal against Australia. Still, despite a plethora of talent that included veteran defender Wendie Renard (no relation) and France's all-time highest-scoring player Eugenie Le Sommer (93 goals), the team lost on penalties, 6-7, to the co-hosts.

DOI: 10.4324/9781003473671-14

These vignettes illustrate the possible for France. At both the elite and professional levels, the country can at times lead and help set the conversation. Yet, there remain startling gulfs, from national team results and domestic competitions to cultural perceptions and attitudes, despite significant twenty-first-century progress. That's the paradox of French women's football.

A Complicated History

Women's football mirrors the larger contradictions within French sport. The country's citizens helped shape the international sporting landscape more than a century ago and today the French Ministry of Foreign Affairs' sports diplomacy policy is viewed as a golden standard (Parrish, 2021). French national teams and elite athletes regularly dominate the top rungs of international competition, from football, basketball, and handball to fencing, judo, skiing, and swimming, while its sportspeople excel within the top professional championships, notably stars Mbappé and Griezmann, alpine skiing's Tessa Worley, or basketball's Naismith Hall of Famer Tony Parker and recent seven-foot-four NBA sensation Victor Wembanyama. Yet, France has long lacked a national sports culture, despite attempts to inscribe it since the 1975 Mazeaud Law first mandated sports as an integral part of the country's cultural fabric (Krasnoff, 2012).

This striking juxtaposition extends into women's football where the push/pull between glimmers of leadership and torpor is rooted in the game's development. Football was imported from Britain in the late nineteenth century but was viewed, like so many other sporting domains in France, as a masculine endeavor (Prudhomme-Poncet, 2003). Conditions fostered by the First World War, during which women entered the workforce in unprecedented numbers, enabled a brief dawn of the women's game. Paris served as the initial hub, site of the first women's match on September 30, 1917, and other games soon followed (Prudhomme-Poncet, 2003; Williams, 2021). These matches were not part of mainstream culture and received little-to-no mediatization, effectively remaining hidden from popular view. Yet, in 1920 a squad representing France played their English counterparts, Dick Kerr Ladies; when the two captains kissed cheeks in a friendly pre-match gesture, the game provided the world's first 'viral' football moment (Krasnoff, 2018; Williams, 2021).

France was thus an early international influencer alongside England. But such examples obscure the game's minimal impact domestically. The number of Frenchwomen who played remained small, estimated at roughly 200 in 1922, but a mere trickle a decade later; the French league ceased organization in 1937, and the game was finally outlawed by the Vichy Government in 1941 (Prudhomme-Poncet, 2003). At issue was that physical culture for Frenchwomen centered around activities perceived as more 'feminine' such as swimming, dancing, calisthenics, and even basketball (Bordieau,

1998; Holt, 1991; Stewart, 2001; Thibault, 1987). There were also gendered medical arguments for what was 'safe' or what was 'ideal' for women to play in order to be healthy, as there were in other countries of the era (Krasnoff, 2019b).

It wasn't until the second wave of feminism of the late 1960s that women's football revived and provided a new opportunity to influence globally. The first clubs formed in the mid-1960s, notably in Reims (Leclercq, 2019), and France played the Netherlands on April 17, 1971, for a 1-0 win in front of 1,000 spectators, a match formally recognized retroactively by FIFA as the 'first' women's international (*First ladies pave the way*, 2020). Later that summer, France was one of six countries represented at the second Women's World Cup. The tournament, sponsored by Martini & Rossi, was not sanctioned by FIFA but managed to set enormous attendance records as more than 100,000 fans in Mexico City twice filled Azteca Stadium; France placed fifth after a 3-2 defeat of England (FIFA World Football Museum, 2019).

It was a remarkable achievement, for the game domestically was viewed as a parody. Frenchwomen who played were negatively stigmatized, told they were too masculine, tomboys, lesbians, not 'real women,' and more, cultural attitudes that persisted well into the twenty-first century (Krasnoff, 2019b; Prudhomme-Poncet, 2003). Thus, despite being part of the international forefront of WWI-era growth and post-1968 revitalization, the game in France remained stunted and lacked cultural relevancy, even as girls and women continued to play.

Leadership and Gulfs with Elite Football

France made progress within the rungs of elite football after 1998. The legacy of a FIFA World Cup victory on home soil that summer translated into new opportunities for women in and around the game. It inspired fresh generations of French girls to the game and the number who enrolled in clubs increased. The French Football Federation (FFF) subsequently launched an elite training program in the National Football Institute at Clairefontaine to develop future Les Bleus and provide them with the same sporting, scientific, and technical expertise as their male counterparts (Krasnoff, 2019b).

This formation, which brought the country's best young players together, was known for its quality and rigor. It was also a way for aspiring female players to interact with the country's elite boys and, at times, the World Cup winners themselves. Former international and current FFF Secretary-general Laura Georges, one of the first to go through the program, noted its uniqueness. 'You are taught by some of the best coaches in France,' she relayed of the experience (Krasnoff, 2019b). Other countries did not offer such possibilities at that time, not even the game's then-dominant powerhouses the United States, Norway, and Germany.

In this endeavor, France led. The same system that produced some of the best male players in the world began to produce some of the best females, too. Among its alumni were Georges, Louisa Necib Cadamuro, arguably one of the best midfielders in the world, and current Les Bleus powerhouse Delphine Cascarino. The latter was one of the first to matriculate through the program once it relocated from Clairefontaine to the National Institute of Sports (INSEP) in Paris in 2014 (Krasnoff, 2019c; McCann, 2015).

Investment in elite formation paid dividends thanks to player accomplishments on-pitch. When FIFA launched its first-ever women's world ranking in 2003, France were seeded ninth. Over the next several years, the team's standing improved; in March 2005 they ranked fifth and broke into FIFA's top three in 2014, a rung they held for three years. Since June 2018, Les Bleus are consistently considered among FIFA's top teams and as of March 2024, are classed as third-best in the world, ranked higher than the United States (fourth) for the first time (FIFA, 2024).

Despite being at the forefront in detection and training, a glaring gap remains. The national team has not yet won a World Cup, European Championship, or Olympic medal. Les Bleus were semi-finalists at World Cup 2011, Olympics 2012, and Euro 2022, but a podium finish remains elusive.[2] On February 28, 2024, France were crowned vice champions of the first-ever UEFA Women's Nations League competition following a 0-2 loss to Spain in a match that underscored the work still to be done to attain an allusive championship title.

The relative lack of results impacts, but is not solely responsible for, a lack of consumption and mediatization. Television viewership of the national team has improved. Some 1.5 million tuned in for France's December 1, 2023, League of Nations win over Austria (FFF, 2023b), and the largest television audience for a non-World Cup or Euro match was set February 24, 2024 when 1.9 million French watched their team beat Germany in the UEFA Women's Nations League semifinal in Lyon (*France-Allemagne : l'audience TV*, 2024) That's a far cry from the team's viewership record to date, their June 23, 2019 World Cup knock-out win over Brazil, which netted 11.9 million (FFF, 2023a). Such numbers are better contextualized in comparison to neighboring England, where some 17.4 million watched the Lionesses win the 2022 Euro final on television and 12 million in the United Kingdom caught Spain's defeat of England at the FIFA 2023 final; just 5.6 million in Spain did so (*Reuters*, 2023b).

In-person spectatorship for the national team similarly leaves room for improvement. A record 45,595 people watched the France-United States World Cup 2019 quarterfinal, but that was an outlier with a significant number of US fans who traveled for the match (FFF, 2023a). More indicative is the recent record set for a non-World Cup match on home soil, when 30,267 people showed up at Lyon's Groupama Stadium for the Nations League semifinal (Benjamin, 2024). Thus, although a leader in investment in detection, formation, and elite-level results, there remains a disconnect with France's ability to influence thanks in part to cultural proclivities.

A Yawing Gap between the Best and the Rest

The paradox between being a leader at the global level in certain ways yet lagging in others extends to the professional game. The country's topflight championship, D1 Arkema, boasts two dominant clubs: Paris Saint-Germain (PSG) and Olympique Lyon (OL) Féminin, the winningest professional football club in the world (Smith, 2019). While both teams attract some of the world's best talent, for more than 15 years Lyon has led the way as a beacon for what greater gender equality in club football can look like. The *Lyonnaises* are known for access to the same facilities as the men's side, as well as high-level investment in coaching, medical, and support staff thanks to long-time trailblazing president Jean-Michel Aulas (Krasnoff, 2019a). The ways that Aulas' team dominated European competition egged on counterparts throughout Western Europe to also start investing in their women's sides, a competition of ego as much as an on-pitch one (Krasnoff, 2019a). Although American investor Michele Kang became the majority owner and Chief Executive Officer in May 2023, her mission to create the world's first global super club between Lyon and her two other professional women's teams, the Washington Spirit (NWSL) and London City Lionesses (NewCo), promises to maintain OL Féminin's mantle as an influential leader (Shephard, 2023).

The top D1 clubs also lead in youth detection and development. This was a function originally tasked to the FFF after 1998, since 2010 OL Féminin, PSG Féminin, and one of their closest competitors, Paris FC, have amped up their women's youth academies. Today's current generation of Les Bleus are predominantly formed through the pro club system, like Renard (OL) and PSG alumnae Marie Antoinette Katoto, Khadidiatou Diani, and Grace Geyoro.

Yet, despite the *rayonnement* of these sides, the remainder of the league remains far behind. Not all D1 players are fully professional. As of May 2021, just 81% of players in French women's football earned their primary income solely from the sport, compared to 85% in Italy, 91% in England, and 100% in Spain (FIFA, 2021). The FFF hopes to fully professionalize all of D1 by 2026 but remains behind its European neighbors in this endeavor (Britton, 2023; Hernandez, 2023). It's an interesting contrast for, domestically, female footballers are among the highest earning *sportives*, second only to their basketball counterparts, earning an average of €3,500 per month, €800 more than the average handball player's monthly salary yet €200 less than basketball (Statista, no date).

Spectatorship remains an area of needed growth and was negatively impacted by the Covid-19 pandemic (as was the broader D1 ecosystem). In-person attendance is small compared to European neighbors. The average attendance for D1 during the 2022–23 season was 841, up from 676 in 2021–22 and 444 during the pandemic-stunted 2020–21 season (Two Circles, 2023). For comparison, the Women's Super League (WSL) had an average 6,961 in-stadium spectators per game during the 2022–23 season, the Frauen-Bundesliga 3,057, and Sweden's Damallsvenskan 849 (Two Circles, 2023). Television diffusion of D1 matches through subscription network Canal+, a contract first signed in 2018, is set to continue through 2029 (Ouest-France, 2023). Yet, at times conditions around D1 stadiums are lamentable and result in poor-quality broadcasts while poorly lit pitches are also problematic for television viewers and players alike (Houeix, 2023). It's thus little surprise that Canal + or other potential suitors have yet to invest significant money in the league's broadcast rights.

Changing the Culture

One of the underlying currents that shape the paradox of women's football is the cultural regard, or lack thereof, of the game. Socio-cultural values are slower to change than on-pitch or structural issues and the game remained tinged with negative social stereotypes, although far less so than even 20 years ago. The generation that moved Les Bleus into the international limelight in the 2000s attempted to reset the public narrative. Some adopted a very stylized, 'feminine' appearance with just-so makeup, manicured nails, and fashion, while others posed for a 2009 nude calendar that sought to break the mold. Billed as personal choices, these were natural self-expressions for some, but others did so by 'choice,' one made for their public image – and that of the game (Barbusse, 2016).

FIFA World Cup 2011 was a watershed moment. That year, Les Bleus were able to break through public consciousness thanks to French disaffection for a men's team whose players appeared coddled and uninterested in representing the best of the nation (Krasnoff, 2017, 2019b). It helped that Georges, Renard, Le Sommer, and their teammates enjoyed a deep tournament run, knocked out in the semifinals by the United States, 3-1. As a result, women's football became less a parody and more an entertainment forum, and with it, taken a bit more seriously.

Host duties for FIFA World Cup 2019 continued to drive gains in popularity, mediatization, and consumption of women's football that, while incremental, began to move the needle. The FFF's investment of resources, including marketing Les Bleus and Les Bleus together as one football family, helped. So, too, did continued efforts from Aulas and OL Féminin's global dominance. As a result, by February 2024, the number of women and girls in France who hold a football license reached a record-high of 247,160, a 12% increase from the 2022–23 season (FFF, 2024)

Public support for the women's game markedly improved, too. Some 88% of French polled admitted that World Cup 2019 provided a favorable image of the sport ('Baromètre sport: Bilan de la Coupe du monde féminine', 2019). Yet, a series of scandals that pitted key national team players against then-Coach Diacre, those of sexual harassment that plagued FFF leadership, and the fiasco over lack of a television contract for FIFA 2023 until five weeks prior to the tournament's start left a sour image of the game, according to mid-fielder Sandie Toletti (Hernandez, 2023). Early indications are that the summer campaign and subsequent dominance in League of Nations play have begun to turn the tables once again as Les Bleus seek to seduce ahead of hosting the 2024 Olympics.

Conclusion

The paradox of French women's football is that at both the elite and professional levels, the country can lead internationally and help set the conversation. Yet, there remain startling gulfs within the sport, from national team results and domestic competitions to cultural perceptions and attitudes. Although the United States is a trailblazer in women's football, France is an influencer in how football diplomacy can be used in multidimensional ways through the FFF's Iraq initiative. In tapping into the federation's reputation for elite youth and coaching development, the FFF since 2021–22 has partnered with its Baghdad-based counterpart to train 200 Iraqi women's national team players, coaches, and federation managers (*Women's Football*, 2023).

The endeavor raises a litany of questions. First and foremost is how and why the FFF created a women's football diplomacy initiative with the Iraq Football Association and why the Iraqis wanted to engage with the French in this endeavor. France's reputation for detecting and training up elite talent appears to hold primacy. And perhaps French women's football's uphill struggles to gain traction and cultural relevancy are attractive to an Iraqi FA whose members also face certain negative social taboos for playing football.

Forthcoming host duties for the Paris 2024 Summer Games also focus a multidimensional spotlight on French sport. It forced change within the FFF's executive rungs as new president Philippe Diallo and Aulas, who heads a special mission on women's football, seek to shore up the game on all sides ahead of the Opening Ceremony. It remains to be seen whether or not part of the Olympic legacy will include more concrete advances in women's football infrastructure and cultural regard to help bridge these gaps and enable France to flex its role more fully as a global football influencer.

Notes

1 Renard gained international acclaim at Qatar World Cup 2022 when, as coach of Saudi Arabia, his squad stunned the world with a 2-1 victory over eventual tourney champions Argentina. His March 2023 designation as France manager capped a tumulus start to the year for the French Football Federation. In February, then-FFF president Noel le Graet resigned due to a sexual harassment scandal and in early March controversial Les Bleus head coach Corinne Diacre was fired.
2 France won the SheBelieves Cup, an invitational tournament organized each March by the US Soccer Federation.

References

Barbusse, B. (2016). *Du sexisme dans le sport*. Paris: Anamosa (Hors collection). Available at: https://www.cairn.info/du-sexisme-dans-le-sport–9791095772132.htm.
'Baromètre sport: Bilan de la Coupe du monde féminine' (2019). Odoxa. Available at: https://www.odoxa.fr/wp-content/uploads/2019/07/Odoxa-Barometre-Sport-RTL-Groupama-Bilan-CDM-feminine.pdf.
Benjamin (2024). 'Près de 2 millions de de téléspectateurs ont suivi la demi-finale de la Ligue des Nations', *Sport Fémimin*, 26 February. Available at: https://www.sportfem.fr/pres-de-2-millions-de-de-telespectateurs-ont-suivi-la-demi-finale-de-la-ligue-des-nations/ [Accessed 11 March 2024].
Bordieau, P. (1998). *La domination masculine*. Paris: Seuil.
Britton, T. (2023). '« C'est une question de timing » : le football féminin français à la croisée des chemins', *Ouest-France.fr*, 17 February. Available at: https://www.ouest-france.fr/sport/football/d1-feminine/c-est-une-question-de-timing-le-football-feminin-francais-a-la-croisee-des-chemins-49fcdab4-ac7f-11ed-b6e3-38da84828b93 [Accessed 26 December 2023].
FIFA (2021). 'Share of players in women's soccer leagues that have soccer as their primary source of income in Europe as of May 2021 [Graph]'. Available at: https://digitalhub.fifa.com/m/3ba9d61ede0a9ee4/original/dzm2o61buenfox51q-jot-pdf.pdf.
FFF (2023a). *Équipe de france feminine palmares et histoire*. Available at: https://www.fff.fr/selection/3-equipe-de-france-feminine/palmares-et-histoire-des-bleus.html [Accessed 26 December 2023].
FFF (2023b). *France-Autriche : l'audience TV*. Available at: https://www.fff.fr/article/11554-france-autriche-l-audience-tv.html [Accessed 26 December 2023].
FFF (2024). *8 mars 2024, record de licences féminines*. Available at: https://www.fff.fr/article/12073-8-mars-2024-record-de-licences-feminines.html [Accessed 11 March 2024].
FIFA (2024). *Women's Ranking March 2024*. Available at: https://inside.fifa.com/origin1904-p.cxm.fifa.com/fifa-world-ranking/women [Accessed 18 March 2024].
FIFA World Football Museum (2019). *The Official History of the FIFA Women's World Cup: The Story of Women's Football from 1881 to the Present*. FIFA.
First ladies pave the way (2020). FIFA. Available at: https://www.fifa.com/tournaments/womens/womensworldcup/france2019/news/origin1904-p.cxm.fifa.comfirst-ladies-pave-the-way-1414187 [Accessed 12 June 2022].
France-Allemagne : l'audience TV (2024). Fédération Française de Football. Available at: https://www.fff.fr/article/11996-france-allemagne-l-audience-tv.html [Accessed 11 March 2024].
Hernandez, A. (2023). 'Le football féminin français ne veut pas manquer le dernier train du professionnalisme', *Le Monde.fr*, 31 July. Available at: https://www.lemonde.fr/sport/

article/2023/07/31/au-dela-de-l-exposition-des-bleues-le-football-feminin-francais-ne-veut-pas-manquer-le-dernier-train-du-professionnalisme_6183938_3242.html [Accessed 26 December 2023].

Holt, R. (1991). Women, men, and sport in France, 1870–1914: an introductory survey. *Journal of Sports History*, *18*(1), 121–125.

Houeix, R. (2023). *En France, 'l'avenir du foot féminin dépend de la qualité de sa diffusion'*, *France 24*. Available at: https://www.france24.com/fr/sports/20230124-en-france-l-avenir-du-foot-f%C3%A9minin-d%C3%A9pend-de-la-qualit%C3%A9-de-sa-diffusion [Accessed 26 December 2023].

Kirschner, K. (2023). 'People are talking about this viral World Cup ad that uses deceptive editing in all the right ways', *Business Insider*, 22 July. Available at: https://www.businessinsider.com/viral-french-world-cup-soccer-ad-les-bleues-challenges-misconceptions-2023-7 [Accessed 24 December 2023].

Krasnoff, L. S. (2012). *The Making of Les Bleus: Sport in France, 1958–2010*. Lanham: Lexington Books.

Krasnoff, L. S. (2017). Devolution of Les Bleus as a symbol of a multicultural French future. *Soccer & Society*, *18*(2–3), 311–319. Available at: https://doi.org/10.1080/14660970.2016.1166775.

Krasnoff, L. S. (2018). 'How the Great War made soccer the world's most popular sport—and led to its first viral moment', *The Athletic*, 16 November. Available at: https://theathletic.com/653722/2018/11/16/how-the-great-war-made-soccer-the-worlds-most-popular-sport-and-led-to-its-first-viral-moment/ [Accessed 28 November 2020].

Krasnoff, L. S. (2019a). 'The house that Aulas built: Why the 2019 World Cup's biggest matches are being played in Lyon instead of Paris', *The Athletic*, 5 July. Available at: https://theathletic.com/1063798/2019/07/05/the-house-that-aulas-built-why-the-2019-world-cups-biggest-matches-are-being-played-in-lyon-instead-of-paris/.

Krasnoff, L. S. (2019b). The up-front legacies of France 2019: changing the face of "le foot féminin". *Sport in History*, *39*(4), 462–483. Available at: https://doi.org/10.1080/17460263.2019.1667420.

Krasnoff, L. S. (2019c). '"You open their minds": Why France moved their women's football academy away from Clairefontaine', *The Athletic*, 27 June. Available at: https://theathletic.com/1050454/2019/06/27/you-open-their-minds-why-france-moved-their-womens-football-academy-away-from-clairefontaine/ [Accessed 26 December 2023].

Leclercq, N. (2019). 'En 1968, à Reims, des pionnières qui avaient « juste envie de jouer au foot »', *Le Monde.fr*, 7 June. Available at: https://www.lemonde.fr/m-le-mag/article/2019/06/07/en-1968-a-reims-le-coup-d-envoi-du-football-feminin_5472549_4500055.html [Accessed 26 December 2023].

McCann, A. (2015). 'World Cup Players to Know: « Eugénie Le Sommer and Louisa Nécib, France's One-Two Punch »', *Grantland*, 20 May. Available at: https://grantland.com/the-triangle/world-cup-players-to-know-eugenie-le-sommer-and-louisa-necib-france/ [Accessed 26 December 2023].

Orange – la Compil des Bleues (English version) (2023). Available at: https://www.youtube.com/watch?v=QVNZRHIZVL8 [Accessed 22 December 2023].

Ouest-France (2023). 'Equipe de France, D1 Arkema… La FFF a enfin trouvé ses diffuseurs pour le football féminin', *Ouest-France.fr*, 13 June. Available at: https://www.ouest-france.fr/sport/football/equipe-de-france-feminine/equipe-de-france-d1-arkema-la-fff-a-enfin-trouve-ses-diffuseurs-pour-le-football-feminin-d636d2a2-09e8-11ee-9bb1-5bd217959d48 [Accessed 26 December 2023].

Parrish, R. (2021). *Promoting a Strategic Approach to EU Sport Diplomacy Final Report*. Edge Hill University. Available at: https://www.edgehill.ac.uk/wp-content/uploads/documents/Final-Report-DEC-2021-.pdf.

Prudhomme-Poncet, gas (2003). *Histoire du football féminin au XXème siècle*. Paris: L'Harmattan.

Reuters (2023a). 'Fans rave about French Women's World Cup ad with unexpected twist', 15 July. Available at: https://www.reuters.com/sports/soccer/fans-rave-about-french-womens-world-cup-ad-with-unexpected-twist-2023-07-15/ [Accessed 24 December 2023].

Reuters (2023b). 'Women's World Cup final draws record TV figures in Spain, England', 22 August. Available at: https://www.reuters.com/sports/soccer/womens-world-cup-final-draws-record-tv-figures-spain-england-2023-08-21/ [Accessed 26 December 2023].

Shephard, S. (2023). 'Late drama, grand ambitions – and big sunglasses: Michele Kang arrives at London City', *The Athletic*, 18 December. Available at: https://theathletic.com/5144338/2023/12/18/london-city-lionesses-michele-kang/ [Accessed 26 December 2023].

Smith, R. (2019). 'The World's Most Dominant Team Isn't Who You Think', *The New York Times*, 17 May. Available at: https://www.nytimes.com/2019/05/17/sports/olympique-lyon-womens-champions-league.html [Accessed 1 August 2022].

Statista (2024) 'Football in France,' January 10. Statista: Hamburg.

Stewart, M. L. (2001). *For Health and Beauty: Physical Culture for Frenchwomen, 1880s–1930s*. Cambridge: Cambridge University Press.

Thibault, J. (1987). Les origines du sport féminin. In P. Arnaud (Ed.), *Les Athlètes de la République*. Privat, pp. 331–339.

Two Circles (2023). 'Average match attendance of selected women's soccer leagues in Europe from 2021/22 to 2023/24' [Graph]. Statista: Hamburg.

Williams, J. (2021). *The History of Women's Football*. Barnsley: Pen & Sword History.

Women's Football (2023). France Diplomatie, April 12. Available at: https://vimeo.com/816932114/5c06a12ac0 [Accessed 26 December 2023].

13

GENDER PAY INEQUALITY IN AFRICAN FOOTBALL

A Pale of Two Halves

Shane Wafer and Nick Flowers

Football can be viewed as being a game of balance – the perfect unity between art and skill (Leonard, 2016). A sport where anyone, anywhere, can at any time "pick" up a ball and instantaneously be transformed into their idols – whether that is Messi, Ronaldo, Putellas, or Marta. Football, renowned for its fervent following and international appeal, has showcased both men's and women's teams in the grandest of arenas – from iconic cathedrals like the Santiago Bernabéu to the Maracanã. Yet, behind the roar of the crowds and the glory of victory, an unsettling disparity persists. In the world of football, where passion and talent collide on the pitch, the beautiful game has not remained untouched by the intricate web of geopolitical factors that shape our global landscape.

As we delve into the heart of this chapter, we turn our attention to a subject that has, for far too long, cast a, at times clandestine, shadow over the sport's egalitarian spirit: the gender pay gap (Garris and Wilkes, 2017). The gender pay gap in football is a global problem (Archer and Prange, 2019), but it is particularly pronounced in Africa (Shehu, 2020). In many African countries, female footballers earn a fraction of what their male counterparts do, even when they are just as, if not more, successful. This is due to a number of identifiable factors, including historical biases, economic inequality, culturally embedded sexism, and a general lack of investment in women's football by governing federations.

In this chapter, we embark on a journey to explore the multifaceted dimensions of the gender pay gap in African football and dissect the geopolitical forces that have contributed to its enduring existence in the continent. By unravelling the various layers of this issue, we hope to shed light on the paths forward, offering potential solutions and highlighting the importance

DOI: 10.4324/9781003473671-15

of continued advocacy for gender equality in the sport we all hold dear. The hope is that through greater awareness of this prevalent issue, football federations throughout Africa can take concerted efforts to help bring about the elimination of the gap entirely.

A Global Gap

It should be noted as a preliminary point that the gender pay gap in football is not merely a localised problem; it reverberates across continents and cultures, revealing itself as a global concern (Hoffmann et al., 2002). From North America to Europe and Asia, women's national football teams have consistently found themselves battling for equal pay and recognition in a sport predominantly dominated by their male counterparts (Williams, 2019).

Indeed, across the Fédération Internationale de Football Association's (FIFA) 211 affiliated member associations (FIFA, 2022), a little over 6% offer equal pay for their male and female national teams. While precise research on the exact countries is hard to attain, it appears that these are the following countries who have taken steps to eliminate the gap: Australia, Brazil; England, Norway, New Zealand, Wales, the United States of America (Hruby, 2023), Netherlands (KNVB Media, 2022), Ireland (Euronews, 2021), Spain (Marsden and Llorens, 2022), South Africa; Zambia (Michollek, 2023), and Sierra Leone (Brown and Eulich, 2020).

What is perhaps most shocking, and best highlighted by the case of the United States, is that oftentimes the female national team will be far more celebrated than their male counterparts on the field. It seems incongruous then that relative mediocrity of a male team is rewarded while the success of the female team is belittled. However, this appears to be the exact state of play for the 199 countries yet to "bridge the gap". The gap in football is a pervasive issue with profound implications on a global scale. This disparity extends beyond just the players' salaries and touches various facets of the sport, from investment to media coverage and leadership positions within football organisations.

One of the primary drivers of the gender pay gap in football is the unequal investment in women's teams compared to their male counterparts. Historically, men's football has garnered substantially more funding, leading to better facilities, coaching staff, and resources. This disparity in investment has a direct impact on the quality of play and the ability of female players to reach their full potential. Consequently, it has resulted in a significant gap in remuneration between male and female players.

Another critical factor contributing to this wage gap is the disparity in sponsorship and media coverage. Men's football receives far more extensive media attention and sponsorship deals, translating into higher revenues for clubs and governing bodies. This unequal distribution of resources not only affects player salaries but also hampers the growth and visibility of women's football. Moreover, limited opportunities for women in coaching and administrative roles within the sport play a role in perpetuating the gender pay gap. The underrepresentation of women in leadership positions not only hinders their ability to advocate for equal pay but also reinforces the systemic biases that exist in football.

In recent years, there have been positive developments aimed at addressing this issue. FIFA has taken steps to bridge the pay gap, including increasing prize money for women's tournaments such as the FIFA Women's World Cup (Worden, 2023). Furthermore, FIFA has been actively involved in promoting women's football development worldwide. The "FIFA Forward" programme, launched in 2016, allocates significant financial resources to help grow the sport, particularly at the grassroots level (FIFA, n.d.a). These funds are used to improve infrastructure, coaching, and the overall infrastructure for women's football in various countries.

However, despite these strides, there is still a considerable journey ahead to achieve true gender equality in football. The efforts to close the gender pay gap must continue, with a focus on creating equitable opportunities for female players, increasing visibility, and breaking down systemic barriers that have persisted for too long. Achieving this goal is not only a matter of justice but also essential for the growth and sustainability of football as a global sport. It is imperative that stakeholders at all levels, including clubs, national associations, and governing bodies, remain committed to this cause to ensure that female players receive the recognition and compensation they rightfully deserve for their exceptional contributions to the sport.

Yet, while the struggles of women football players in across these global regions have gained considerable attention and ignited important discussions, we must also shine a light on how this issue manifests within the African football landscape – as this continent's geopolitical framework provides an interesting lens for examining the issue of gender inequality.

Africa's Troubled Past Feeds Its Troubled Present

Within the African context, the gender pay gap in football takes on a unique dynamic, influenced by a blend of historical legacies, socio-economic challenges, and evolving societal norms. As highlighted above, only three of the Confédération Africaine de Football's (CAF) 54 members associations (CAF, 2023a) have, where applicable, enacted equal pay for their male and female national teams. Admittedly though, these enactments have all taken place in the last three years, with Sierra Leone in 2020 (Barrie, 2020), and Zambia in 2022 (Short, 2023) leading the charge. It should be noted that inequitable pay is merely one of the issues blighting African (and global) football, with wage theft, unsafe working conditions, harassment, and sexual abuse completing the long laundry list which scourges the sport (Worden, 2019). For purposes of the present discussion, only the gender pay gap is considered.

Historically, African nations have made significant strides in promoting football on both the men's and women's fronts. Today, 47 of CAF's members field female national teams (Lumumba, 2023). However, despite the scope of this perceived inclusivity, or parity of participation, female football players often earn a fraction of their male counterparts' salaries. The pay disparity remains a stark reality, one which seems to seep deep within the very fabric of the continent.

Historical Legacies

To understand the roots of this disparity, we must first acknowledge the historical legacies that have shaped African football. Many African countries were colonised by European powers, which left indelible imprints on the continent's sports infrastructure. At the Congress of Berlin in 1884, 15 European powers divided Africa among them, with the imperial powers having fully colonised the continent. This resulted in the exploitation of its people and resources (Facing History & Ourselves, 2022). The principal powers involved in the modern colonisation of Africa were Belgium, Britain, France, Germany, Italy, Portugal, and Spain (Keita, 1999). In fact, only the countries of Liberia and Ethiopia were free of colonial rule (Hasanova, 2020).

As a result, football (and more generally, most sports) was introduced and cultivated primarily as a male-dominated sport during colonial rule (Allen, 2014), and these early biases have persisted to this day. The outcome is the legacy and existence of latent gendered mechanisms through which these initial biases are amplified and perpetuated. This could manifest itself in the form of appointment to positions of power within federations, the efforts undertaken to secure lucrative sponsorship deals for female teams, and the general attitude and perception with which female football is treated. This point is perhaps best made by the quote that, "Gender inequality is not merely an echo of political promises or rhetoric in the discourse of global [']sport (for) development['] – it is a stark reality … that influences people in all spheres of their existence. Discriminatory effects based on gender parity in society, represent fluid and ever-changing realities embedded in socially constructed phenomena" (Burnett, 2018). While women's football has grown in popularity, it still struggles to break free from the shadows of these historical inequities. The deep-seated roots of these biases is further compounded when regard is had to the various socio-economic challenges present throughout Africa.

Socio-Economic Challenges

Socio-economic factors also play a significant role in perpetuating the gender pay gap in African football. Many female players face financial hardships such as reduced wages/bonuses, inadequate or ineffectual training facilities (Salaudeen, 2019), and limited access to professional opportunities compared to their male counterparts. CAF espouses that a women's top division competition is organised in 91% of CAF member associations (CAF, 2022). However, upon closer inspection, it is revealed that the current status of the top division competitions can be classified as follows: 67% (31) are amateur, 24% (11) are semi-professional, and 9% (4) are professional (CAF, 2022). These statistics point to a much deeper underlying issue than merely colonial heritage, and it speaks to the economic fibre underpinning the various countries and its impact upon resource allocation.

Many African countries are poor, and there is a large gap between the rich and the poor. Consider that for 2022, the United States of America had an estimated gross domestic product (GDP) of $26,854.599 billion (PopulationU, 2022). The amount placed America at the top of all countries worldwide. Meanwhile, Nigeria was the highest African country with a nominal GDP of $504.203 billion (IMF, 2022). The total for the continent was $2,988.527 billion (54 countries cumulatively representing only 11% of the United States of America's entire GDP) and an average of $55,343 billion (IMF, 2022). The stark reality of the discrepancy in GDP is frightening. This means that there is less money available to invest in women's football, and female footballers are often paid less than their male counterparts because they are seen as less marketable (this viewpoint being influenced by both a biased and economical perspective). This disparity in resources directly affects their earning potential and overall career development. Examining deeper still, the economic disparities between African nations further compound these issues, with some countries providing better support and compensation to their female players than others, whether in the form of a women's football department in the national federation, a developed women's football strategy, established women's football committees, or identifiable sponsor support (CAF, 2022).

However, there is not always a clear-cut link between the GDP of a country and the implementation of gender inequality remedial measures. Sierra Leone, Zambia, and South Africa sit 42nd, 20th, and 3rd, respectively, among the GDP rankings (IMF, 2022). Just because a country *has* money (determined relatively, of course) does not necessarily mean it *will* spend that towards women's football. The answer as to why perhaps lies in an examination of sexism within various African cultures.

Embedded Sexism

Sexism is another major factor contributing to the gender pay gap in African football. This is a pressing issue that reflects broader societal inequalities within the continent's sporting landscape. Despite the remarkable talent and dedication demonstrated by female footballers in Africa, they continue to face a multitude of challenges, with gender-based discrimination deeply ingrained in the sport's structures. This discrimination manifests itself in a myriad of ways, with a pronounced effect seen in instances of what and how women's teams wages are handled.

A fascinating study to expound upon this is that of the Nigeria women's national football team (the "Super Falcons"). The Super Falcons are, far and away, the most successful female team on the continent, having won 11 Women's Africa Cup of Nations titles (CAF, 2023b), by comparison, the male team has won three (Britannica, 2023), and being the only female team to have reached the quarterfinals of the FIFA Women's World Cup (FIFA, n.d.b) and Summer Olympics (Olympics, n.d.). Furthermore, the Super Falcons are the highest ranked African side at 32 (FIFA, n.d.d), having qualified for every edition of the World Cup – a total of nine tournaments since 1991 (FIFA, 2023). By every conceivable metric, Nigeria's female team is Africa's *most successful* women's team. Expanding further, they may just be *Africa's* most successful national team: boasting more continental titles than Egypt's male team (11 to 7) (Aluko, 2020), and more World Cup appearances than Cameroon's (nine to eight) (Soccernet, 2023). The only blemish on their impeccable record is the absence of an Olympic medal, of which only the Nigerian (Alaka and Eludini, 2023) and Cameroonian male teams can boast (FIFA, 2020).

And yet, one of the most successful teams in Africa's richest country faces countless inequities. From years-old bonuses and allowances (FIFPRO, 2023), to women players receiving around $3,000 for a win at major tournaments while the male players receive up to $10,000 (Joshua, 2023), it is evident that Nigeria has a big problem. Former Super Falcons' captain, Desire Oparanozie, recognised this point in 2019, stating, "We are the most successful female team in Africa, yet we have the largest disparities between men's and women's pay. I think we deserve equal pay. This big gap tells a different story and a proper rethink of this mode of payment could also help the women's game. We have done the nation proud and I think the results over the years are there for all to see" (Dehinbo, 2023).

So, what is happening here? One answer is that Nigerian is strongly embedded in patriarchal traditions. Culture shapes the prevailing gender relationships, with one unable to exclude culture from gender because gender is a product of culture (Okpokwasili and Dukor, 2023). This practice is not solely confined to Nigeria but can be seen in various traditional African marital practices (Bassey and Bubu, 2019). This problem compounds with the effect of religion and other historically entrenched biases (Levey and Cheng, 2022). Women may have their achievements belittled, even undermined (by way of wage theft, or unequal pay), because it is not their role to be playing a "male" sport. Their successes represent a slight to the fragile male ego, whose own sporting accomplishments cannot compare, resulting in them lashing out due to the bruising (English, 2020). Cultural sexism thereby inflates the egos of men, this, when coupled with positions of power, i.e., within football federations, directly impacts how women footballers are to be treated.

Despite this position, meaningful change is still capable of being attained as recent examples suggest, although it is not as widespread as hoped.

Winds of Change or Challenge?

On the positive side, African societies are evolving, and gender norms are gradually shifting. Women's football is gaining more visibility, and talented female players are emerging as role models, inspiring future generations of African girls to pursue their football dreams. The most successful female team (America) achieved its long-awaited pay equality in 2022 after "six years of federal complaints, three years of litigation and decades of domination" (Cohen, 2022), having built their case off of the back of accused violations of Title VII of the Civil Rights Act (employment discrimination) and the Equal Pay Act (Das, 2022). South Africa also implemented similar measures, but it took the women's team winning its first continental title to spark action on the national federations part (how the Super Falcons must shudder) (Dindi, 2023).

FIFA recently adopted an extensive human rights framework and women's football strategy, which explicitly includes gender equality and, thus, equal pay (FIFA, n.d.c). The framework's "three key objectives serve as 'common carriers' for both long-standing institutional interests (in power, profit, and prestige) and newer institutional interests (in women footballers, women's football, and women in football governance)" (Krech, 2020). Such a strategy is also mirrored in a similar one adopted by CAF (Ahmadu, 2020). In theory, these point towards positives which *should* ensure change. However, the efficacy of the systems is very much in doubt. A FIFPRO report claims that 29% of players were not paid for taking part in qualifying tournaments for the 2023 World Cup and when athletes were paid it was often based on match performance (Lloyd, 2023). Each national federation is annually funded by FIFA, but "money intended to build women's sport is too often siphoned off by national federations before it reaches the players who earned it" (Worden, 2023). Furthermore, "due to the dynamics between FIFA and its member associations, pay parity cannot be achieved by a member association when its purse strings are controlled by FIFA" (Poppelwell-Scevak, 2022). All of this raises the question of what is a female athlete supposed to do when their national labour laws fail them, the very federation protecting their interest are tainted, and the global body pays lip-service? The answer is elusive, tied up in a labyrinthine mix of politics, culture, governance, and law.

Conclusion

The road to gender equality in football remains long and challenging, as deeply ingrained historical biases, cultural and societal attitudes continue to influence the allocation of resources and opportunities within the sport. However, it is important to raise awareness of the problem and to work towards eliminating it. By making concerted efforts investing in women's football and by paying male and female national teams equally, African football federations can play a leading role in promoting gender equality in sport. In this regard, the words of Cyril Ramaphosa, South Africa's President, ring prophetic, "[e]qual pay for work of equal value is one of most fundamental tenets of gender equality. The sporting fraternity is neither exceptional nor is it exempt. That female athletes should still earn less than their male counterparts is an affront to [] sports-women, more so at a time when the achievements of some of [the] women's sports teams surpass those of [the] men's teams" (Salt, 2023). The same pay for the same 90 minutes of play. Seems simple, does it not?

References

Ahmadu, S. (2020). *Caf launches first-ever African strategy for women's football | Goal.com South Africa*. [online] Available at: https://www.goal.com/en-za/news/caf-launches-first-ever-african-strategy-for-womens-football/1aofu6gyfwct21rxoll7050jy2.

Alaka, J. and Eludini, T. (2023). *27 years after Nigeria's football took off at the 1996 Olympic Games*. [online] Premium Times Nigeria. Available at: https://www.premiumtimesng.com/sports/sports-features/614340-27-years-after-nigerias-football-took-off-at-the-1996-olympic-games.html.

Allen, D. (2014). "Games for the Boys": Sport, empire and the creation of the masculine ideal. In Hargreaves, J., & Anderson, E. (Eds.). (2014). Routledge handbook of sport, gender and sexuality (pp. 21–29). Routledge.

Aluko, I. (2020). *Top African National Football Teams | Africans in Sports | Your Home to All Things African Sports*. [online] Available at: https://africansinsports.com/top-african-national-football-teams/.

Archer, A. and Prange, M. (2019). 'Equal play, equal pay': moral grounds for equal pay in football. *Journal of the Philosophy of Sport*, 46(3), 416–436.

Barrie, M. F. (2020). *Sierra Leone women welcome life-changing equal pay*. [online] Available at: https://www.bbc.com/sport/africa/54194133.

Bassey, S. A. and Bubu, N. G. (2019). Gender inequality in Africa: a re-examination of cultural values. *Cogito*, 11(3), 21–36.

Britannica, T. Editors of Encyclopaedia (2023). *Africa Cup of Nations | History, Winners, Trophy, & Facts | Britannica*. [online] Available at: https://www.britannica.com/sports/Africa-Cup-of-Nations.

Brown, R. L. and Eulich, W. (2020). *More nations ending soccer's gender wage gap: 'This could change things'*. [online] Available at: https://www.csmonitor.com/World/2020/0928/More-nations-ending-soccer-s-gender-wage-gap-This-could-change-things.

Burnett, C. (2018). Politics of gender (in) equality relating to sport and development within a sub-Saharan context of poverty. *Frontiers in Sociology*, 3, 27.

CAF (2022). *CAF Women's Football Landscape Report*. [online] Available at: https://www.cafonline.com/media/hedpebel/caf-womens-football-landscape-report-2022.pdf.

CAF (2023a). Member Associations. [online] Available at: https://www.cafonline.com/member-associations/.

CAF (2023b). *TotalEnergies CAF Women's Africa Cup of Nations*. [online] Available at: https://www.cafonline.com/caf-womens-africa-cup-of-nations/.

Cohen, L. (2022). *U.S. women's national soccer team formally signs years-in-the-making equal pay deal after defeating Nigeria in friendly.* [online] www.cbsnews.com. Available at: https://www.cbsnews.com/news/uswnt-formally-signs-equal-pay-deal-soccer/.

Das, A. (2022). U.S. Soccer and Women's Players Agree to Settle Equal Pay Lawsuit. *The New York Times.* [online] 22 February. Available at: https://www.nytimes.com/2022/02/22/sports/soccer/us-womens-soccer-equal-pay.html.

Dehinbo, T. (2023). *Gender Pay Parity: Should men and women national teams receive equal pay?* [online] Nairametrics. Available at: https://nairametrics.com/2023/01/31/gender-pay-parity-should-men-and-women-national-teams-receive-equal-pay/.

Dindi, S. (2023). *No-one will get more: Safa president Jordaan confirms equal pay for Bafana and Banyana.* [online] Available at: https://www.timeslive.co.za/sport/soccer/2023-06-23-no-one-will-get-more-safa-president-jordaan-confirms-equal-pay-for-bafana-and-banyana/.

English, C. (2020). Elite women athletes and feminist narrative in sport. *Sport, Ethics and Philosophy, 14*(4), 537–550.

euronews (2021). *Irish Football Association introduces equal pay for men and women.* [online] Available at: https://www.euronews.com/2021/08/31/irish-football-association-introduces-equal-pay-for-men-and-women.

Facing History & Ourselves (2022). *Colonial Presence in Africa | Facing History and Ourselves.* [online] Available at: https://www.facinghistory.org/resource-library/colonial-presence-africa.

FIFA (2020). *Africa's golden Olympic history.* [online] Available at: https://www.fifa.com/tournaments/mens/mensolympic/tokyo2020/news/africa-s-golden-olympic-history.

FIFA (2022). *Member Associations.* [online] origin1904-p.cxm.fifa.com. Available at: https://www.fifa.com/about-fifa/associations.

FIFA (2023). *Nigeria's all-conquering Super Falcons target FIFA Women's World Cup progress next.* [online] Available at: https://www.fifa.com/fifaplus/en/articles/nigerias-all-conquering-super-falcons-target-fifa-womens-world-cup-progress-next.

FIFA (n.d.a). *FIFA Forward Programme.* [online] Available at: https://www.fifa.com/football-development/fifa-forward.

FIFA (n.d.b). *FIFA Women's World Cup USA 1999™.* [online] Available at: https://www.fifa.com/tournaments/womens/womensworldcup/usa1999.

FIFA (n.d.c). *Women's Football Strategy.* [online] Available at: https://www.fifa.com/womens-football/strategy/strategy-details.

FIFA (n.d.d). *Women's Ranking.* [online] Available at: https://www.fifa.com/fifa-world-ranking/women?dateId=ranking_20230825.

FIFPRO (2023). *FIFPRO Statement: Nigeria women's national team.* [online] Available at: https://fifpro.org/en/who-we-are/what-we-do/foundations-of-work/fifpro-statement-on-behalf-of-nigeria-women-s-national-team/.

Garris, M. and Wilkes, B. (2017). Soccernomics: salaries for World Cup Soccer athletes. *International Journal of the Academic Business World, 11*(2), 103–110.

Hasanova, A. (2020). *Colonized African countries in the 21st century.* [online] pickvisa.com. Available at: https://pickvisa.com/blog/colonized-african-countries.

Hoffmann, R., Ging, L. C. and Ramasamy, B. (2002). The socio-economic determinants of international soccer performance. *Journal of Applied Economics, 5*(2), 253–272.

Hruby, E. (2023). *Wales women's national soccer team reaches equal pay deal.* [online] Available at: https://justwomenssports.com/reads/wales-womens-national-team-equal-pay-uswnt/.

IMF (2022). *Report for Selected Countries and Subjects World Economic Outlook database: October 2022.* [online] Available at: https://www.imf.org/en/Publications/WEO/weo-database/2022/October/weo-report?c=612.

Joshua, P. (2023). Africa: Why Isn't FIFA Red Carding Africa's Soccer Bodies Over Women's Low Wages? *allAfrica.com*. [online] 18 Jul. Available at: https://allafrica.com/stories/202307180431.html.

Keita, L. (1999). Africa and its linguistic problematic. *Quest, 13*(1–2), 27–35.

KNVB Media (2022). *KNVB beloont OranjeLeeuwinnen vanaf juli gelijk aan de mannen.* [online] Available at: https://www.onsoranje.nl/node/80269.

Krech, M. (2020). Towards equal rights in the global game? FIFA's strategy for women's football as a tightly bounded institutional innovation. *FIFA's Strategy for Women's Football as a Tightly Bounded Institutional Innovation, 25*(1), 12–26.

Leonard, A. (2016). *The relationship between art and football: Guardiolismo and Expressionism.* [online] These Football Times. Available at: https://thesefootball-times.co/2016/07/26/the-relationship-between-art-and-football-guardiolismo-and-expressionism/.

Levey, S. and Cheng, L. R. L. (2022). The impact of bias and discrimination. *Communication Disorders Quarterly, 43*(4), 215–223.

Lloyd, O. (2023). *FIFPRO calls on better conditions for female footballers after pay disparities.* [online] Available at: https://www.insidethegames.biz/articles/1138147/fifpro-world-cup-qualifying.

Lumumba, E. R. (2023). *'Empowering Equality: The Rise of Women's Football and Inclusive Sports Infrastructure in Africa'.* [online] Available at: https://www.linkedin.com/pulse/empowering-equality-rise-womens-football-inclusive-sports-lumumba/.

Marsden, S. and Llorens, M. (2022). *Spain women to receive equal bonuses.* [online] Available at: https://www.espn.com/soccer/story/_/id/37629321/spain-female-footballers-receive-equal-bonuses-new-agreement.

Michollek, N. (2023). *Africa's World Cup women raise unfair pay and sexual abuse – DW – 07/18/2023.* [online] Available at: https://www.dw.com/en/africas-world-cup-women-raise-unfair-pay-and-sexual-abuse/a-66265367#:~:text=Global%20gender%20pay%20gap&text=SAFA%20has%20announced%20equal%20pay.

Okpokwasili, O. A. and Dukor, M. (2023). The intersectionality of culture in gender relation in Nigeria. *Nigerian Journal of African Studies (NJAS), 5*(2), 52–59.

Olympics (n.d.). *Olympic Games Athens 2004.* [online] Available at: https://olympics.com/en/olympic-games/athens-2004/results/football/football-women.

Poppelwell-Scevak, C. (2022). The gender pay gap: how FIFA dropped the ball. *International Journal of Constitutional Law, 20*(1), 325–350.

PopulationU (2022). *Countries by GDP 2022.* [online] www.populationu.com. Available at: https://www.populationu.com/gen/countries-by-gdp.

Salaudeen, A. (2019). *African female footballers face uphill battle to play a 'man's game'.* [online] CNN. Available at: https://edition.cnn.com/2019/06/20/football/women-football-underfunded-africa-intl/index.html.

Salt, L. (2023). *Scoring own-goals: unequal pay in women's sports.* [online] Available at: https://www.ensafrica.com/news/detail/7417/scoring-own-goals-unequal-pay-in-womens-sport.

Shehu, J. (2020). Governmentality and gender equality politics in African women's football: A discourse analysis of selected media texts, Jean Monnet Working Paper 13/20 [online]. Available at: https://www.jeanmonnetprogram.org/wp-content/uploads/JMWP-13-Jimoh-Shehu.pdf.

Short, K. (2023). *Zambia Women's Team Makes Cup Debut.* [online] Available at: https://www.voanews.com/a/zambia-women-s-football-team-makes-world-cup-debut-/7188936.html.

Soccernet (2023). *Top 5 most successful African National teams – Soccernet NG.* [online] Soccernet.ng. Available at: https://soccernet.ng/2023/03/top-5-most-successful-african-national-teams.html#:~:text=1.

Williams, J. (2019). Upfront and onside: women, football, history and heritage special edition. Introduction: women's football and the# Metoo movement 2019. *Sport in History*, *39*(2), 121–129.

Worden, M. (2019). *Women soccer players' biggest challenge is changing FIFA itself.* [online] Available at: https://qz.com/1653596/fifa-womens-world-cup-players-deserve-better.

Worden, M. (2023). *Women's World Cup Shows Equality Still Has a Long Way to Go.* [online] Forbes. Available at: https://www.forbes.com/sites/minkyworden/2023/07/20/womens-world-cup-shows-equality-still-has-a-long-way-to-go/?sh=2fe813542f80.

14

EXPLORING THE INTERSECTION OF GENDER AND CLASS IN SPACE

The Case of New Generation Stadiums in Turkey

İlknur Hacısoftaoğlu and Rahşan İnal

Oblivion
The fans gone
The players in the changing room
The stadium lights off
The ball that bounced off the post
Lies forlorn where it rolled to a stop
The snowflakes whisper

Akif Kurtuluş (2017: 59)

Emerging as pivotal structures in societal and cultural landscapes, stadiums have evolved throughout history. The Fete de la federation, built in 1790 on the Champ de Mars in Paris, is the earliest permanent modern stadium with a capacity of acommodating a large audience of 400,000–600,000 spectators. This first stadium represented a crucial occasion, triggering a swift increase in the subsequent creation of stadiums. Nevertheless, modern stadiums surpass their original function as mere locations for sporting events and various organizations. These platforms now serve as arenas where policymakers demonstrate the symbolic power dynamics that are present in both national and international sports organizations. Another way stadiums help build and maintain national identities is by hosting sporting events. Furthermore, these impressive architectural structures function as platforms for the promotion and sale of diverse products, encompassing both sports-related and non-sports-related items, inside the capitalist marketplace. Moreover, historical stadiums possess a deep importance as warehouses of shared collective memory, especially impactful among the city's football aficionados (Bairner, 2001; Bale, 1986, 1993; Chapin, 2004; Church and Penny, 2013; Gaffney, 2010; Paramio et al., 2008)

DOI: 10.4324/9781003473671-16

Modern stadiums have evolved across decades, according to Sheard (2005); the late 19th-century first generation was huge yet uncomfortable. Stadiums of this time tried to accommodate as many spectators as possible, but comfort was the second goal. After television became popular, stadiums added restrooms, outlets, and food outlets. Sheard cites the 1972 Munich Olympics' Olympiastadion as an example of this generation. The American-led third generation turned stadiums into family-friendly entertainment hubs, inspired by Disneyland. This period's stadiums had comfortable seating, stands, lights, and restaurants to serve families.

Third generation stadiums were conceptualized as "new generation", "postmodern" (Bale, 2000; Paramio et al., 2008) or "gentrified"[1] in terms of their form and content in this period when neoliberal economic policies became widespread all over the world. While this transformation in stadiums sharpened the class barriers in the space, they continued to exist as men's spaces, thus continuing to reproduce gender inequality. Building upon this historical transformation, this paper aims to critically examine class and gender encounters in Turkish stadiums as a space, employing participant observations on match days and conducting informal interviews with fans during these observations.

Historical Process and Transformation of Stadiums in Turkey: Stadiums as a Gendered Space Reflecting the Transformation of the Societies

Following World War I, football was introduced to cities like Istanbul and Izmir in the Ottoman Empire by the British. Initially, it became a sport practiced by both British and non-Muslim Ottoman inhabitants. Nevertheless, within a few periods, it garnered widespread adoption among a substantial populace in numerous provinces, particularly in major urban centers. Football clubs and leagues developed as a result of this, and male football players had their own fields—that is, pitches—in "squares, meadows, and fields" (Yüce, 2019).

The emergence of contemporary sports stadiums in Turkey may be traced back to an organized and systematic strategy following the establishment of the nation state. The inaugural stadium, a prominent symbol of urban and architectural progress throughout the Republican era, was the Ankara Stadium, which officially opened on December 17, 1936. During the stadium's opening ceremony, İsmet İnönü, the prime minister at the time, succinctly describes the significance of stadiums in the sports policy of the "new" state. He states that the leaders of Turkey will make every effort to establish stadiums everywhere, considering them to be as valuable as the most esteemed educational institutions. "The upcoming generation in Turkey, who will be responsible for the country's future, will be brought up in outdoor environments and public spaces" (Cumhuriyet Newspaper, 18 December 1936). Instead of being considered a recreational pastime, sports during this era served as a method for cultivating a new generation in accordance with the health and demographic policies of a recently formed nation-state (Akın, 2004). During the early period of the Republic, stadiums were constructed in city/town centers for public purposes. They served as venues for inclusive sports activities, promoting the physical well-being of the population and nurturing the future generations of the new regime. These stadiums also represented the emerging national identity of the "new" Turkey, where the founding of the nation state was commemorated and Grand National ceremonies took place (İnal, 2022). During this early period, football did not receive any assistance from the government and was not extensively practiced by the public. Furthermore, it was argued that football encouraged a passive involvement in sports as a spectator pastime, rather than active participation. Nevertheless, the public's fascination with football was unstoppable, leading to its rapid ascent as one of the nation's most beloved sports. The transformation that commenced in all regions and establishments of early post-Republican Turkey also became evident in sports. The popularity of football as a sport for spectators started to increase, and initial efforts were made to establish professional football leagues.

Following the year 1959, when the "Regulation on Professionalism in Football" was fully enforced, individuals representing capital, who had hitherto operated behind the scenes, progressively began to participate in the administration of football teams. Representatives of the capital now included the state and politicians in addition to the sports and football industries (Gökaçtı, 2008). The rising popularity of football led to a corresponding growth in the construction of stadiums specifically designed for football. By 1990, there were a total of 129 turf and 217 dirt pitches available for football matches (TFF, 1992). As capitalism underwent reorganization, football clubs underwent corporatization and football itself became commodified. However, by the 1990s, even the football pitches owned by the prominent football teams in Istanbul were deemed inadequate in comparison to those in Europe (Cumhuriyet Newspaper, 4 May 1988).

The significant metamorphosis of stadiums in Turkey occurred subsequent to the 2000s. Despite variations in historical chronology, stadiums underwent a transformation into venues of capital in accordance with neoliberal economic principles, similar to what occurred in Europe and America. Due to the spatial growth of capital, as described by Harvey (2002), several stadiums located in the city center were demolished and removed from the collective urban consciousness.

Although it is difficult to give an exact number, it has been determined that 21 of the 26 stadiums that have been closed are parks, and real estate with housing and commercial functions has been developed on the land of five stadiums. The number of stadiums under construction or planned is 17 and there are 57 stadiums in use (Yılmaz, 2022). If we ignore the capacity differences, the only difference between all the stadiums whose construction has been completed and London's Tottenham Hotspur Stadium is that they are located in Turkey.

Beşiktaş Stadium, one of the highly engineered venues analyzed in this paper, was "renovated" and "arranged" to cater to the affluent's needs by "renovating" the interior and exterior due to its prime downtown location. The stadium has since transformed into a venue where "football" serves as a hook to which all other things are connected and broadcasted via satellite.

Space at the Intersection of Gender and Class: New Generation Stadiums

The stadiums utilized by the so-called "big three" sports clubs in Istanbul were the initial stadiums to undergo gentrification.[2] Following the 1990s, the majority of sports clubs' boards of directors—which have since evolved into capitalist enterprises—are made up of males who represent capitalist organizations. In the present day, football has become a marketable product, with football players serving as workers and spectators as consumers, predominantly consisting of males. Unlike many commodities, football is promoted throughout its production in the stadium where it is produced, similar to certain sorts of services. The consumption of football extends beyond the stadium through live broadcasts, although the stadium remains the primary venue for consumption. Stadiums possess a value, commonly referred to as "use value". According to İnal (2022), a football company management has the potential to boost the club's profits by utilizing the stadium as a productive asset to generate "surplus value". Football teams seeking increased profitability aim to attract spectators to their stadiums who, on one side, preserve the enthusiasm of devoted fans, so ensuring their continued allegiance, while also transforming them into "customers" who contribute financially. Today's stadiums serve as arenas where football club owners want to maximize revenue per seat. They clearly display class distinctions through the availability of high-priced lodge rentals for the entire season and a defined pricing hierarchy for seats based on their location on the field.

"Passion is beyond price"

For traditional football fans, watching matches in stadiums that are "Temples of the Earthbound Gods" gives them a sense of privilege (Gaffney, 2010). "Ordinary" spectators may watch the match on a screen, but watching football live in the venue is one of the signs of being a fan, but today, in gentrified stadiums, "season ticket prices" make it difficult for the working class to enter the stadium gates. The annual increase in season ticket prices makes the presence of the fans in the stadium an inconvenience. In fact, in contrast to the potential earnings generated from sponsorship, the sale of team and stadium naming rights, leasing VIP boxes, TV rights, and merchandise sales, the total income from ticket sales appears significantly inconsequential. This transformation in creating value not only alters marketing tactics but also revolutionizes stadium cultures. A deliberate initiative has been undertaken to dismantle the proletarian, masculine fan culture (Zinganel, 2010). When proletarian masculine fan culture gradually transforms, the tension, collision, and conflict between different spatial logics continue (Knoblauch and Löw, 2020) and, lower and middle classes make effort to maintain their seats in the stadium. Despite everything, the male fan who does not want to lose his presence in the stadium pushes his budget for his passion, this sacrifice is related to the strength of the fan identity that men in a football country have built since childhood.

The stadium serves as a center for developing a sense of community among men (Bromberger, 2010). Situated at the center of the network of relationships that fans build at home and around the venue, the stadium is enveloped in a powerful performance of emotion. The uniqueness of the stadium as a spatial entity is closely related to its architectural structure, which is distinctly surrounded by social relations, strongly preserving the bond between space and man, and man's desire to belong to the indispensable space (Bale, 1993; Berking, 1998; Frank and Steets, 2010).

Stadiums are a clear symbol of men's passion for the game, their undeniable commitment to the game is symbolized by stadiums. As expressed by a fan in one of the informal interviews we conducted on the day of the match, coming to the stadium is the place where fan identity is constructed.

Based on our pre-match and in-game observations, we have identified the following patterns. The stadium is a venue influenced by the interconnected social networks where men do not attend alone, but rather with groups of friends with whom they collectively indulge in their shared interest as fans. Although the aspect of being a member of the community remains, it has undergone a transformation in gentrified stadiums. In our interview with a middle-aged male fan, the fan criticized Beşiktaş stadium for changing with the industrialization of football and stated that they could no longer watch live and cheerful matches together: "We watch matches in rows where we sit, there is no old cheerful match watching".

The stadium area also fosters a significant bond between father and son through their shared passion for a particular sports team. Dads take their boys to the stadium to instill in them their passion for football and pass on their fandom as a legacy. During the match we observed, that fathers and sons were sitting next to us, in the back row and diagonally. While we were sitting in a pub where fans were sitting before the match, a father and son were sitting at the next table. In one of our informal interviews, the father, who had come with his son, said that he had brought his son to the Beşiktaş stadium so that he could breathe the stadium air and thus have a Beşiktaş identity. This bond between father and son is centered on action and emotion, not words, and the son's first visit to the stadium is like a rite de passage, one of the stages of the son's process of becoming a man (Hacısoftaoğlu, 2018). In the father-son interview we conducted, for the father, the stadium is a place where all men watch the match together and is a part of the ritual. For the sons, on the other hand, the stadium is known for being a consumption center and the finely calculated hierarchical categorization between the seats is accepted as a natural part of the stadium's structure. For the son, there is no nostalgic longing for the pre-new generation stadiums, no desire for the period when male fans were as one with their banners.

"It shouldn't be this hard to go to a match"

Not only match ticket prices, but also the practice of buying electronic tickets "Passolig", which started in Turkey in 2014, is another limitation of stadiums as panopticon spaces. With the Passolig application, the purchase of match tickets is connected to a singular center (*Passolig*, 2023). Spectators are obliged to record their identity and settlement information on their passolig cards when purchasing match tickets. The system claims to provide security measures in stadiums, it builds the system based on securitization and criminalizes the fan.[3]

The initial stage of securitization commences with the Passolig application while acquiring tickets. The registration and use of a Passolig card for ticket purchase is a meticulous and rigorous procedure involving the verification of identifying information. As the authors of this study, we have personally undergone the process of obtaining a Passolig card, which involves declaring our identity and specifying the tickets that can be purchased based on the team we support during matches. This declaration holds significance for individuals of all ages, including youngsters. It informs the child who enrolls with a team for their matches and possesses a Passolig card that their fan identity cannot be altered thereafter. The second phase involves organizing coordination meetings between the police forces and the clubs in order to guarantee security and disclose any planned chants and banners that will be displayed at the stadium venue. The security forces provide comprehensive explanations to the clubs regarding the allocation of police personnel and the measures taken to ensure security within and around the stadium, with particular emphasis on the entrances. From our observations of the match, it is evident that the searches conducted at the entrance to the stadium represent the utmost level of securitization. Both flags and other materials, as well as hard objects like money, make-up, mirrors, and any food or drink, are prohibited from being brought into the stadium. The fan exhibiting criminal tendencies enters the stadium and observes the match from their designated seat.

However, due to the current stadium construction, the ability for fan groups to collectively move around is limited compared to previous circumstances.

Beşiktaş Stadium: An Emblematic Instance of Gentrified Stadiums in Turkey

Beşiktaş Gymnastics Club (BJK) was founded in 1903. At first, they played their matches at Papazın Çayırı, Union Club, and Taksim Stadium like other Istanbul football clubs. In 1933, they moved to Şeref Stadium, which they built themselves on a ruined land they rented from the state on the shore of the Bosphorus, and then to the current Beşiktaş Stadium, built by the state and opened in 1947. In 1998, the club reached an agreement with the state and leased the stadium for 49 years, after which the ownership of the stadium was fully transferred to the club (BJK, 2023; GSGM, 2014; TFF, 1992).[4] This stadium, which overlooks the Bosphorus from its stands, is integrated with the historical texture of Istanbul. The Istanbul Municipality and the club had disagreements about the expansion of the stadium for many years. However, when the President of the Republic approved the project presented to him, the dispute was closed. The stadium was built in 2013 by being pulled down towards the sea and its construction was completed in three years. The stadium was designed as a multifunctional venue with shops, a museum, a conference hall, concerts, meetings, a restaurant, and lounges for VIP customers. In the club's definition, it is "a living space that can be visited and spent time every day, not only on match days" (BJK, 2023).

Beşiktaş Stadium rises in the center of Beşiktaş, one of the largest and most populous districts of Istanbul. It is one of the symbols of the neighborhood with its eye-catching architecture and size. On match days, the vitality of the stadium, which becomes the heart of the neighborhood, affects the whole place. We observed that not only the stadium but also the area around the stadium on match days is an area where fans live their identity, have fun together with other men, spend time, consume alcohol, and prepare for the match. The spaces around Beşiktaş Stadium vary as open and closed areas. Middle and upper-class fans, mostly men, spend time and drink alcohol before the match in bars and restaurants close to the stadium. Younger and lower-class men prepare for the match in squares and parks close to the stadium, start cheering, and wear and buy jerseys and scarves. During match days, individuals who are not fans, particularly women, tend to avoid the Çarşı area, which is both the symbolic location of the Beşiktaş Club in the center of the Beşiktaş district and the name of a fan group associated with the club. However, they cannot help but notice the immense football enthusiasm that extends to the streets on the outskirts of the stadium, filled with men's voices. The pedestrian zone stretching from Çarşı to the stadium transforms into an impressive carnival.

Conclusion

The stadium space, which we can call the embodiment of men's passion for football, also serves as a profitable source of income today. These stadiums, which have been gentrified with the transformation in recent years, have led to a change in the class composition and positioning of men watching the match. For the male fan, whose class position significantly determines where he is in the social hierarchy between men, it has become difficult to take part in this new stadium if he belongs to the lower classes. For the working-class man who carries his fan identity with a strong emotional attachment, the stadium where he displays his fan identity loses its working-class qualities day by day. The seats are made comfortable and redesigned to increase the comfort of the middle and upper class and to facilitate viewing. Within this redesign, security and control are tightened and its characteristic of being a gentrified space as a safe and controlled space is reinforced. However, despite all these difficulties, the indispensable place of fandom in the culture of masculinity enables the stadium to carry a more heterogeneous class identity compared to other gentrified spaces. Although being seen as unconventional by many fans and is said to damage the myth of unrequited and unexpected love of the fans, men from different classes strive to take their place in the stadium and be a part of this ritual despite all kinds of difficulties. The pre-match demonstrations around the stadium continue to function as a manifestation and visual representation of the common collective memory of the fan community. Despite the extensive surveillance and security measures in place, the seats and toilets in the stadium are constantly vandalized after each match due to the unruly behavior of the spectators. The space of football continues to be the field where both love and rage can be projected, the space where the intense relationship of man with emotion is embodied.

Notes

1 Gentrification, the conversion of socially marginal and working-class areas of the central city to middle-class residential use, reflects a movement, which began in the 1960s, of private-market investment capital into downtown districts of major urban centers (Zukin, 1987). This process can also be observed in the "renovated" stadiums in Turkey.

2 This stadium has been used by BJK throughout its history. Although the stadium is currently named after its sponsors, it is likely to change again in the coming years. We have chosen to refer to the stadium as Beşiktaş Stadium in order for readers to identify it with the club.

3 A case study illustrating the ineffectiveness of these measures in ensuring stadium security (BBC News, 2023).

4 Most of the stadiums in Turkey were built by the state with public funds or their construction was financially supported (GSGM, 2014).

References

Akın, Y. (2004). *Gürbüz ve Yavuz Evlatlar Erken Cumhuriyet'te Beden Terbiyesi ve Spor.* İstanbul: İletişim.

Bairner, A. (2001). *Sport, Nationalism, and Globalization: European and North American Perspectives.* Albany: State University of New York Press.

Bale, J. (1986). Sport and national identity: a geographical view. *International Journal of the History of Sport, 3,* 18–41. Available at: https://doi.org/10.1080/02649378608713587.

Bale, J. (1993). The spatial development of the modern stadium. *International Review for the Sociology of Sport, 28*(2–3), 121–133. https://doi.org/10.1177/101269029302800204.

Bale, J. (2000). The changing face of football: stadiums and communities. *Soccer & Society, 1*(1), 91–101. Available at: https://doi.org/10.1080/14660970008721251.

BBC News (2023). 'Turkey referee punched: Ankaragucu president Faruk Koca arrested after attack', 12 December. Available at: https://www.bbc.com/sport/football/67691038.

Berking, H. (1998). Global flows and local cultures. Über die Rekonfiguration sozialer Räume im Globalisierungsprozeß. *Berliner Journal für Soziologie, 8*(3), 381–392.

BJK (2023). *Tesisler.* Available at: https://bjk.com.tr/tr/cms/tesisler/6/25/.

Bromberger, C. (2010). Sport, football and masculine identity. In S. Frank and S. Steets (Eds.), *Stadium Worlds: Football, Space and the Built Environment* (pp. 181–194). The architext series. London and New York: Routledge.

Chapin, T. S. (2004). Sports facilities as urban redevelopment catalysts: Baltimore's Camden Yards and Cleveland's Gateway. *Journal of the American Planning Association, 70*(2), 193–209. Available at: https://doi.org/10.1080/01944360408976370.

Church, A. and Penny, S. (2013). Power, space and the new stadium: the example of arsenal football club. *Sport in Society, 16*(6), 819–834. Available at: https://doi.org/10.1080/17430437.2013.790888.

Cumhuriyet Newspaper (1936). 'Ankara Stadyumu Büyük Merasimle Açıldı', 18 December, p. 1.

Cumhuriyet Newspaper (1988). 'Derwall Emekli Oluyor', 4 May, p. 12.

Frank, S. and Steets, S., Eds. (2010). *Stadium Worlds: Football, Space and the Built Environment.* London and New York: Routledge.

Gaffney, C. T. (2010). *Temples of the Earthbound Gods: Stadiums in the Cultural Landscapes of Rio de Janeiro and Buenos Aires.* Austin: University of Texas Press.

Gökaçtı, M. A. (2008). *Bizim İçin Oyna.* İstanbul: İletişim.

GSGM (2014). *'Bakanlıktan Beşiktaş ve Galatasaray Kulüplerine Açıklama'.* Available at: https://shgm.gsb.gov.tr/HaberDetaylari/3/22031/bakanliktan-besiktas-ve-galatasaray-spor-kuluplerine-aciklama.aspx

Hacısoftaoğlu, İ. (2018). Futbolda Erkekliğin Gür Sesi: Taraftarlığın Cinsiyetle Olan İlişkisi Nedir? *The Blizzard Dergisi, 1*(1), 111–122.

Harvey, D. (2002). *Spaces of Capital.* London and New York: Routledge.

İnal, R. (2022). Stadyomdan Arenaya Türkiye'de Stadyumların Dönüşümü/From "Stadyom" to Arena Transformation of Stadiums in Turkey. *Praksis, 4*(60), pp. 93–112. Available at: https://search.trdizin.gov.tr/tr/yayin/detay/1174404/stadyomdan-arenaya-turkiyede-stadyumlarin-donusumu.

Knoblauch, H. and Löw, M. (2020). The re-figuration of spaces and refigured modernity – concept and diagnosis. *Historical Social Research, 45*(2), 263–292. Available at: https://doi.org/10.12759/HSR.45.2020.2.263-292.

Kurtuluş, A. (2017). *Hayat Saat Farkıyla.* Translated by Sinan Fişek. İstanbul: Can.

Paramio, J. L., Buraimo, B. and Campos, C. (2008). From modern to postmodern: the development of football stadia in Europe. *Sport in Society, 11*(5), 517–534. Available at: https://doi.org/10.1080/17430430802196520.

Passolig (2023). *What is Passolig?* Available at: https://www.passolig.com.tr/nedir.

Sheard, R. K. (2005). Foreword Stadia and arena through the ages. In P. Thompson, J. J. A. Tolloczko and J. N. Clarke (Eds.), *Stadia, Arenas&Grandstands. International Conference 'Stadia 2000'* (pp. xvii–1). London & New York: Routledge.

TFF (1992). *Türk Futbol Tarihi (1904–1991)*. İstanbul: Türkiye Futbol Federasyonu.

Yılmaz, Ö. (2022). *Hiçliğin Ortasında Mimarlık: Türkiye'nin Stadyumları*. Available at: https://www.arkitera.com/gorus/hicligin-ortasinda-mimarlik-turkiyenin-stadyumlari/.

Yüce, M. (2019). *Osmanlı Melekleri: Futbol Tarihimizin Kadim Devreleri: Türkiye Futbol Tarihi – Birinci cilt*. İstanbul: İletişim.

Zinganel, M. (2010). The stadium as cash machine. In S. Frank and S. Steets (Eds.), *Stadium Worlds: Football, Space and the Built Environment* (pp. 77–97). London and New York: Routledge.

Zukin, S. (1987). Gentrification: culture and capital in the urban core. *Annual Review of Sociology*, *13*, 129–147. Available at: https://www.jstor.org/stable/2083243.

PART III
Ownership and Investment

15

MULTI-CLUB OWNERSHIP

An Ominous Future

Steve Menary

As football emerged from the worst of the Covid-19 pandemic that savaged the global economy, a new saviour appeared through the emergence of multi-club ownership (MCO) groups. Clubs whose finances were weakened by the virus began to be acquired in ever increasing numbers.

Establishing exact figures for the full size of MCO remains problematic as this is a constantly shifting market with stakes increasingly bought and sold, while other holdings may not be publicly known. In 2022, Union of European Football Associations' (UEFA's) annual benchmarking report identified around 180 clubs caught up in MCO but research for this chapter identified 325 clubs around the world whose owners or significant shareholders own or have meaningful interest in another club at the start of November 2023.

These clubs or stakes were owned by 120 different groups or individuals and 31% of these clubs are in Europe, but the phenomenon stretches across the globe and now takes in every single one of Fédération Internationale de Football Association's (FIFA's) six confederations. The focus remains on clubs playing in the top tier, which makes up 52% of teams within MCO networks, with the remaining 48% of the global number of clubs identified in this research playing at the second tier or below at the start of November 2023.

As Chinese owners began to withdraw from overseas football club ownership, a wave of private equity and venture capital companies, primarily from North America, became the driver for acquisitions and football clubs became a recognisable asset class for the financial industry. UEFA estimated that 27 MCO groups – a third of the total identified in their 2022 research – were from the United States of America (UEFA, 2023a, p. 210), while 9 of 16 takeovers in Europe were by American investors (UEFA, 2023a, p. 205) (Table 15.1).

DOI: 10.4324/9781003473671-18

TABLE 15.1 Breakdown by confederation

Confederation	D1	D2	D3 & below	Total
UEFA	100	58	52	210
AFC	24	4	4	32
CONMEBOL	12	3	3	18
CONCACAF	26	13	7	46
CAF	7	4	7	18
OFC	1	0	0	1
Total	170	82	73	325

This is reflected in the money spent on merger and acquisition deals in football, which in 2019 was valued at $240m but had risen to just under $5bn by 2022 and was predicted to double to more than $10bn in 2023 (Pitchbook 2023, p. 2). However, a more sobering statistic for those championing the rise of MCO is that only 20% of MCO groups identified in this study were composed of four or more clubs, while 59% of portfolios featured just two clubs (Table 15.2).

UEFA seeks to separate the definition into multi-club "where a party exerts control and/or decisive influence over more than one club, while 'multi-club investment' refers to a situation where a party has investment interests in more than one club (without exerting control or influence)" (UEFA, 2023a, p. 206).

The success of the phenomenon remains mixed. The largest portfolio of club ownership or stakes is held by City Football Group (CFC) with 12 clubs. This is a portfolio ultimately controlled and financed by a nation state, the United Arab Emirates, which is endowed with massive wealth from natural resources. This is reflected in the success of this portfolio: in 2022, CFC subsidiaries Manchester City, Melbourne City, Mumbai City, and Yokohama F Marinos all won their respective titles.

The success of MCO at a wider level is less marked. In the 2022/23 season, two English clubs, Ipswich Town and Sheffield United, were promoted, while Toulouse won the *Coupe de France*, but four Belgian clubs then in MCO structures – RFC Seraing, Oostende, KAS Eupen, and Virton – were relegated, as was English Premier League club Southampton, while in Mexico Dorados de Sinaloa finished bottom of their league.

TABLE 15.2 Size of MCO groups

Six clubs+	7
Five clubs	3
Four clubs	14
Three clubs	25
Two clubs	71
Total	120

The ultimate success of MCO will be better judged from a greater distance, but the rise of the phenomenon has concerned many football stakeholders from governing bodies to fan groups and player bodies. UEFA has warned: "The rise of multi-club investment has the potential to pose a material threat to the integrity of European club competitions, with a growing risk of seeing two clubs with the same owner or investor facing each other on the pitch" (UEFA, 2023a, p. 8).

There have been multiple examples of supporters opposing the purchase of their clubs and this even deterred CFC's proposed acquisition in 2022 of Dutch club NAC Breda (The Guardian, 2022). Niamh O'Mahony, chief operating officer and head of governance at Football Supporters Europe, comments: "There are some good owners who respect the heritage of clubs, but there's an awful lot where we don't know what motivates them. The [MCO] model seems to be to run a club on the cheap, bring in players on the cheap and get them capped and then sell them on. Then replicate this multiple times in other countries" (PlaytheGame.org, 2021).

In addition to supporter objections, the rise in cross-ownership increases the risk of financial contagion should the ultimate beneficial owners or majority stakeholders of one large MCO group run into financial problems. Clubs are increasingly stretching payments for players as UEFA acknowledges: "In general there has been a trend over the years to buy now pay later, with long-term (due in more than 12 months) payables increasing in share from 29% at the end of FY2016 to 44% at the end of FY2022" (UEFA, 2023a, p. 15). If one MCO group collapses, this would create a domino effect with unpaid transfer debts hitting clubs across Europe and further afield, while also impacting on players.

UEFA's latest benchmarking report claimed that the 180 clubs caught up in MCO in 2022 had 6,500 players under contract (UEFA, 2023a, p. 211). Using the same metric as UEFA's report of 36.1 players per club, the research for this article suggests that nearly 12,000 players are at clubs whose owners own or have a meaningful stake in another club.

Given that the full extent of MCO is hard to gauge and the likelihood that there are more than 309 clubs involved, then the number of players caught up would again be larger. This must be a concern as the owners of MCO portfolios are often exposed to other commercial businesses that have the potential to drain money out of football. The increasing number of players involved in these structures also concerns global players' union, International Federation of Professional Footballers (FIFPRO), whose director of legal affairs Roy Vermeer commented. "[MCO is] much more than the integrity of the Champions League and teams playing each other. Behind the scenes there is so much more like moving players around and non-sporting motives" (PlaytheGame.org, 2021).

Non-sporting motives should be a cause for a concern if, for example, an investor comes to a club offering to cover wages – the largest part of club expenditure – but forgo any official shareholding in the club in favour of offering to introduce their own players and technical staff. This was the modus operandi of one of the largest MCO groups ran by Eric Mao, whose investments covered clubs in Portugal, Ireland, Romania, Latvia, the Czech Republic and Spain, and were later uncovered as part of a huge match-fixing scandal (The Black Sea, 2018).

At least one figure involved in developing an MCO portfolio of clubs has been banned for a national association for not reporting knowledge of match-fixing. This was in 2015 and before the MCO group they are now involved with (SBS, 2023), but as the financial chasm between the top and bottom of European football grows, a repeat cannot be discounted, as the suitability of the owners of MCO groups continues to be found wanting.

In March 2021, Luxembourgish entrepreneur Flavio Becca, who then controlled Swift Hesperange in his native Luxembourg and Royal Excelsior Virton in neighbouring Belgium, was handed a two-year suspended prison sentence and fined €250,000 for abusing company assets (Delano.lu, 2021). The same year, the Noah Group MCO portfolio halved in size after three foreign players at Noah Jurmala in Latvia were banned and fined €1,000 each for match-fixing (Eng.lsm.lv, 2021), while another subsidiary, German club KFC Uerdingen, nearly collapsed due to financial problems (World News Today, 2021). Noah exited Latvia and Germany but retained control of Yerevan FC in its native Armenia and ACN Siena in Italy. In 2023, Andy Pilley, who had built up an MCO portfolio of clubs in England, the Republic of Ireland, South Africa, and the United Arab Emirates, was sentenced to 13 years in jail for fraud unrelated to his football ownership (National Trading Standards, 2023).

A number of countries do run additional eligibility checks on potential new club owners involving fit-and-proper persons tests and proof of funds, and UEFA has claimed that rules on ownership were in place in 23 members by 2022 (UEFA, 2023a, p. 208), but these do not appear to preclude involvement with the sports betting industry. This study found nine clubs – eight in Europe, one in Africa – in four MCO groups controlled by leading figures in the betting industry, while one of the investors in Chelsea also had a stake in a leading sports data company (Daily Mail, 2022).

Regulation of owners and the burgeoning trend of MCO at a continental level remains laissez fare and inconsistent. Informal links have long existed between clubs around the world, but regulations were first tested in Europe in 1999 by the ownership of Glasgow Rangers, Slavia Prague, Athlitikí Énosis Konstantinoupóleos (AEK) Athens, Vicenza Calcio, Basel, and Tottenham Hotspur by investment group English National Investment Company (ENIC). When AEK and Sparta were drawn together in European competition, a rule was instigated banning clubs with the same majority shareholder playing each other in European competition.

This was tested again when, after another UEFA investigation, two Red Bull subsidiaries – Leipzig and Salzburg – were allowed to compete in the 2017/18 Champions League after board changes. Six more clubs controlled by three different owners were allowed to compete in European competition after a UEFA ruling and similar changes were made before the 2023/24 season, but no wider regulation has been instigated (UEFA, 2023b). With football seemingly permanently in thrall to the commercial potential of investors and owners, these decisions certainly did little to deter further investment.

US owners continue to seek opportunities, but these are typically private equity or venture capitalist groups, which will have identified an exit before they even made their investment. "I'm not bothered about our current owners, as we can negotiate with them. I'm more concerned about who comes next," says Carsten Sloth, leader of a fan group at leading Danish club Brøndby, which is controlled by the Global Football Holdings MCO group (Menary, 2023).

The Middle East is likely to produce the next wave of investors. In 2021, Saudi Arabia's Public Investment Fund took control of English Premier League club Newcastle United as part of an MCO plan that two years later saw the PIF purchase four leading Saudi clubs. However, the Saudi state is also the ultimate beneficial owner of four other clubs in the same country, which makes this the second largest MCO (OffthePitch.com, 2023).

Middle Eastern interest in MCO portfolios is certainly growing and range from the Abu Dhabi controlled CFC to Qatari ownership of six clubs including French giants Paris Saint-Germain and the Bahraini investment group Infinity Capital, which owns Cordoba in Spain and a stake in Paris FC. The United World Group is also controlled by Saudi Prince Abdullah bin Mosaad bin Abdul Aziz Al Saud owned five clubs at October 2023, while another Saudi businessman, Turki Al-Sheikh, owns La Liga side UD Almeria and is president of Sudanese club Al-Hilal.

State involvement in a large portfolio is not restricted to the Middle East. The Hungarian government, whose prime minister Viktor Orbán has long shown an affinity with football, has invested €55m on clubs in Hungarian-speaking regions of Croatia, Romania, Slovakia, Ukraine, Serbia, and Slovenia (Investigative Journalism for Europe, 2018). These investments in stadia and academies in the form of grants, which are not included in this research, are aimed at influencing Hungarian speakers in these countries, but those of the Middle Eastern countries have larger ambitions.

Europe remains the focus with 104 of the 114 MCO groups identified in this research controlling one or more European club, while 28 have clubs in North America. Any consolidation of ownership or stakes in European clubs – put at more than 200 in this study – could pose a significant problem for football in the continent. If a small cabal of owners control a large number of leading European clubs, UEFA potentially becomes unnecessary. As the game's governing bodies wave through MCO, this should be a concern for UEFA.

FIFA has so far eschewed any involvement in the regulation of MCO, but this looks unavoidable as the world body seeks to expand its Club World Cup idea, where the prospect of two clubs from the same MCO clashing seems inevitable. For the game's governing bodies, simply ignoring the rise of MCO and influence seems impossible but so does making any changes to a seemingly unstoppable phenomenon with significant consequences for the game.

References

Daily Mail (2022). EXCLUSIVE: LA Dodgers owner Todd Boehly – a leading candidate in the £3bn battle to buy Chelsea from Roman Abramovich – has a £120MILLION betting stake in Russia… but American billionaire's involvement is not significant. Available at: https://www.dailymail.co.uk/sport/sportsnews/article-10673749/Chelsea-takeover-bidder-Todd-Boehly-holds-shares-betting-firm-operating-Russia.html [Accessed 3 November 2023].

Delano.lu (2021). 2-year suspended sentence, €250,000 fine for Flavio Becca. Available at: https://delano.lu/article/delano_2-year-suspended-sentence-eu250000-fine-flavio-becca [Accessed 3 November 2023].

Eng.lsm.lv (2021). Three FC Noah Jūrmala soccer players banned for match fixing. Available at: https://eng.lsm.lv/article/culture/sport/three-fc-noah-jurmala-soccer-players-banned-for-match-fixing.a412246/ [Accessed 3 November 2023].

Investigative Journalism for Europe (2018). Hungarian Football Funds. http://www.investigativejournalismforeu.net/projects/investigating-hungarian-public-money-in-the-football-clubs-of-neighboring-countries/ [Accessed 3 November 2023].

Menary, S. (2023). Interview with author on 23 June 2023.

National Trading Standards (2023). Andrew Pilley sentenced to 13 years in prison for fraud. Available at: https://www.nationaltradingstandards.uk/news/andrew-pilley-sentenced-to-13-years-in-prison-for-fraud/ [Accessed 3 November 2023].

OffthePitch.com (2023). Saudi's Public Investment Fund just set up the world's second biggest MCO in plain view. Its influence is already being felt across Europe. Available at: https://offthepitch.com/a/saudis-public-investment-fund-just-set-worlds-second-biggest-mco-plain-view-its-influence-already [Accessed 3 November 2023].

Pitchbook (2023). Private Capital in European Football. https://pitchbook.com/news/reports/q3-2023-pitchbook-analyst-note-private-capital-in-european-football [Accessed 4 October 2024].

PlaytheGame.org (2021). Spree of buying clubs threatens football integrity. Available at: https://www.playthegame.org/news/spree-of-buying-clubs-threatens-football-integrity/#:~:text="It%27s%20much%20more%20than%20the,number%20of%20clubs%20in%20MCOs. [Accessed 3 November 2023].

SBS (2023). South Melbourne deny Pagniello involvement in A-League bid. Available at: https://www.sbs.com.au/sport/article/south-melbourne-deny-pagniello-involvement-in-a-league-bid/2reiktj8z [Accessed 6 November 2023].

The BlackSea.eu (2018). Eric Mao: the Asset Stripper of European Football. Available at: https://theblacksea.eu/stories/football-leaks-2018/eric-mao-asset-stripper-european-football/ [Accessed 3 November 2023].

The Guardian (2022). City Football Group plan to buy NAC Breda fails after supporter backlash. Available at: https://www.theguardian.com/football/2022/apr/22/manchester-city-football-group-plan-to-buy-nac-breda-fails-after-supporter-backlash [Accessed 3 November 2023].

UEFA (2023a). The European Club Footballing Landscape. https://ecfil.uefa.com/2023 [Accessed 4 October 2024].

UEFA (2023b). The CFCB renders decisions on multi-club ownership cases for the 2023/24 UEFA club competitions. Available at: https://www.uefa.com/news-media/news/0283-186f6a2609f6-77d919fb7eff-1000--the-cfcb-renders-decisions-on-multi-club-ownership-cases-for/ [Accessed 3 November 2023].

World News Today (2021). KFC Uerdingen objects: crisis club defends itself against point deduction. Available at: https://www.world-today-news.com/kfc-uerdingen-objects-crisis-club-defends-itself-against-point-deduction/ [Accessed 3 November 2023].

16

RE-CONCEPTUALISING MULTI-CLUB OWNERSHIP IN FOOTBALL

A New Definition and Typology of MCO

Michael Anagnostou and Argyro Elisavet Manoli

Introduction

While it has been argued that three ownership structures can be identified in football: private ownership, public ownership, and member associations (Rohde and Breuer, 2017), a new form of ownership has appeared in recent years, the so-called multi-club ownership (MCO). MCO has emerged as one of the fastest-growing trends within the financial ecosystem of football, with a rising number of instances observed globally (CIES, 2024; UEFA, 2023).

Investment funds originating from either generic private business investments and conglomerates, sports and entertainment conglomerates, football holding groups and individuals – like wealthy football club owners and wealthy investors – have been mixed together, creating new hybrids and ownership links and associations with other football clubs (directly and indirectly), changing the landscape of football club ownership. It is in fact estimated that currently, more than 230 clubs worldwide are part of a multi-club investment structure (UEFA, 2023). In this chapter, we aim to untangle this web of MCO offering a new and more encompassing definition of this phenomenon as well as introducing a more illustrative typology of how it manifests in modern-day football.

Definition of MCO

It is worth noting that UEFA (2023, p. 206) defines MCO as "a situation where a party exerts control and/or decisive influence over more than one club", while "'multi-club investment' refers to a situation where a party has investment interests in more than one club (without exerting control or influence)".

DOI: 10.4324/9781003473671-19

According to Breuer (2018), MCO is "a situation where a single investor (either an individual or a legal entity) holds shares of two or more clubs competing with each other in one or several tournaments" (p. 132).

However, Breuer (2018) also argues that the definition of MCO should not be limited to cases where a single investor holds majority shares in two or more clubs participating in the same tournaments. Instead, he proposes that a broader definition should be used which should reflect the definition of OECD (Organization for Economic Co-operation and Development) for associated enterprises. He believes that this broader approach is more fitting for the complex structures of sports, which involve clubs, leagues, sponsors, and broadcasters.

More specifically, article 9 of the OECD's model tax convention (OECD, 2017) defines "associated enterprises" as those where one person or enterprise in a Contracting State directly or indirectly participates in the management, control, or capital of an enterprise in another Contracting State. This broad definition includes direct and indirect influence and does not set a specific capital share threshold, thus encompassing various forms of influence beyond just capital share.

Taking all the above into consideration, as well as the different ways in which MCO manifests in modern-day football, we propose a new and better encompassing definition of MCO in football as "the simultaneous capital ownership and/or controlling power and influence in the operations of more than one football club by individuals, private equity firms, conglomerates, football holding groups, sovereign funds or any other entities".

As part of the definition, we note the nature of ownership group, which we argue significantly influences the underlying motivations driving the projects and the business model of the enterprise. Although, media attention is attracted to famous investment groups involved in many clubs (such as the City Football Group, 777 Partners, Red Bull, and Eagle Football Holdings), the most common model of MCO appears to be the ownership of just two clubs (Sportbusiness.com, 2024). Most often, MCO formations do not exceed more than three clubs, as investors focus mainly on majority stakes (UEFA, 2023). However, there are cases where minority investors acquire the management and control of a club such as the INEOS group agreement for the control of operations in Manchester United with only 27.7% stake (Harris, 2024). As such, it is apparent that MCOs can take different shapes and forms that might deviate from our preconceived perceptions.

Three Types of Multi-Club Ownership and Investment

Through our analysis, it emerged that there exist three distinctive types of owners and investors who are involved in multiple football clubs and MCO strategies, representing three corresponding broad categories or types of

MCOs. While these three types often interact, overlap, and mix through shared investments, creating new hybrid schemes and complicating even more the football ownership ecosystem, they simultaneously represent three discrete types of MCOs in terms of their operationalization, which can be better appreciated through diverse theoretical frameworks as we will discuss in this section.

Type 1: Private Equity Firms MCO

There are two kinds of private equity (PE) firms involved in football: (a) the generic business PE firms that manage investment funds in various business and industries and (b) sports and entertainment PE firms that tend to manage investments in sports, entertainment, and media industry (Hunter, 2021).

Private equity firms collect available funding from various investors such as institutions, pension funds, insurance companies, and individuals in order to invest it in buying equity in companies (Gilligan and Wright, 2020; Kaplan and Strömberg, 2009; Sauer et al., 2024). Private equity firms endeavour to secure returns by adhering to a business model that involves the acquisition of companies. They guide these enterprises through phases of performance enhancement and the augmentation of their intrinsic value. Once these improvements are realized, they ultimately divest these investments, capitalizing on the increased enterprise value (Barber and Goold, 2007). PE firms sometimes oversee the management and provide funding to companies, expecting a return on their investment within a specific period (Gilligan and Wright, 2020; Kaplan and Strömberg, 2009; Sauer et al., 2024). In the case of football, we have seen PE funds lending capital to clubs, purchasing media rights, buying shares of a club, or even buying a league or competition (World Football Summit, 2022).

The enhancement of value within PE ventures can be achieved through various mechanisms, including the leverage effect, operational improvements, and multiple expansion. Contextual factors play a crucial role in shaping the strategic decisions these firms make regarding business and portfolio management. As Krysta and Kanbach (2022) elucidate, these context factors encompass the characteristics of both the investor and the portfolio company, as well as aspects related to the buyout and the broader environment. As Sauer and colleagues (2024) argue PE funds are investing in the world of football in an increasing rate, aiming to generate value, and thus represent the first type of MCOs identified.

Type 1 MCOs can be better understood through the lens of Capital Investment Theory, which suggests that an investment should be selected if its return or profitability is greater than the investor's cost of capital (Alkaraan and Northcott, 2006; Cooremans, 2011; Maritan, 2001; Sauer et al., 2024), and Portfolio Diversification Theory, which captures the process of allocating wealth across a variety of assets, in order to reduce the risk and minimize both the probability and the potential severity of portfolio loss, through a multilateral insurance in which each asset is insured by the remaining assets (Koumou, 2020). Combining these theories allows us to understand that type 1 MCOs which are created by PE funds and their corresponding investments are driven by the funds' interest to increase the value and return of their investments through appropriate management, while minimizing any potential risk through the simultaneous investment in multiple football clubs.

Type 2: Football Holdings and Groups MCO

This type of ownership has the characteristic of football-focused ownership. In this case we note the pattern of holding groups of football clubs or wealthy individuals who own a club and progressively start investing and expanding in majority or minority ownership of other football clubs. Through such strategies they achieve resource maximization, synergies in scouting and talent identification, player development, and career pathways and growth (World Football Summit, 2022).

This type of MCO can be better understood through the lens of horizontal integration (Kumar and Kumar, 2019) which occurs when a company expands its operations by acquiring or merging with other companies at the same level of the value chain, typically in the same industry. Instead of solely relying on internal efforts to grow, some companies opt to expand their industry presence by acquiring or merging with competitors. This strategic approach is referred to as horizontal integration (Morris and Hodges, 2016, p. 150).

Horizontal acquisitions generate value by leveraging cost and revenue synergies. These synergies arise when the combined value of the newly merged (through a merger or an acquisition) firm is greater than the sum of the individual values of the two separate companies (Capron, 1999). In this case, MCO by an organization or an individual that are already investing in a football club and are subsequently investing in other clubs through an expansionist approach can be considered as horizontal integration in football, or as type 2 MCO. Horizontal integration, as viewed through the resource-based view (RBV) theory, can help organizations exploit better their internal capabilities to achieve a competitive advantage in the marketplace (Madhani, 2010). In the case of type 2 MCOs, we therefore see numerous potential benefits emerging through the better utilization of the internal capabilities, which collectively might be able to lead to previously unachievable results (Barney, 1991). Foremost, the pooling of resources is allowed, leading to significant financial and operational efficiencies. Clubs can consolidate their administrative functions, reduce costs, and leverage shared facilities and staff, thus optimizing their overall expenditure. This integration also enhances the talent pool by facilitating the movement of players between affiliated clubs, fostering the development of promising athletes through more robust and diverse training programmes.

Moreover, horizontal integration can expand a club's market presence and fan base, creating synergies in marketing, merchandising, and sponsorship opportunities. By uniting under a common brand (as is the case in some MCOs), clubs can increase their bargaining power with broadcasters and sponsors, leading to more lucrative deals. Additionally, this strategy can lead to a more robust and competitive team structure, improving on-field performance and increasing the likelihood of success in domestic and international competitions. The emergence of such benefits points to the phenomenon of disintermediation, which while previously linked only to vertical integration (Lazonick and Teece, 2012), can be seen in this case in the horizontal integration in type 2 MCO. Disintermediation refers to the removal of intermediaries from a supply chain, or simply put to the "cutting out the middlemen" in different transactions. In type 2 MCOs, it could be argued that they can facilitate the removal of many intermediaries, by cutting out the middlemen such as agents, brokers, feeder clubs' payments, and/or buying clubs profits (depending on the role of each player transaction), as well as achieving synergies in areas such as funding, scouting, talent development, and sponsorships.

What differentiates type 2 from type 1 is that Football Groups are solely focused in football clubs investments making use of their in-depth knowhow and expert knowledge, and RBV capabilities, not aiming for short-term exits. On the other hand, type 1 MCO may have various investment activities either in generic business or in entertainment, media, and/or other sports.

Type 3: Sovereign Funds MCO

Sovereign wealth funds, state-owned investment entities, allocate resources into tangible assets, managing these holdings as part of the investment reserves of their respective nations (Yang, 2015). These funds have ventured into the realm of football club investments. Much like their acquisitions of high-value assets such as real estate and art, these funds pursue investments in football clubs as part of their quest for enduring, prestigious assets (Sauer et al., 2024). The main motivations behind this emerging type 3 MCOs could be considered the potential indirect returns and spillover effects on other businesses owned by the sovereign wealth funds (Marin and Lee, 2020), as well as network-building strategies or political influence guiding such investments (Chadwick et al., 2016; Xue et al., 2020). It is also noted that especially for some countries that have been heavily relying on the generation of income produced by a very small number of industries (e.g. carbon fuel), investing in overseas assets such as football clubs through sovereign funds can allow them to diversify their economic activity and potentially mitigate any future risk (Amara and Al-Emadi, 2018).

What differentiates type 2 from type 3 MCOs is not only the fact that the former tend to be exclusively football-focused, but also and most importantly, that the latter are not primarily motivated by the RBV theory, and thus the effort to better exploit their internal capabilities in order to achieve a competitive advantage (Madhani, 2010). Instead, type 3 MCOs are being created by nations, states, and various entities which utilize sport to build and wield power, seeking strategic advantages by managing resources within networks where sport is integral (Chadwick, 2022). The geopolitical economy of sport therefore sees this type of MCOs as tools strategically employed and appropriately positioned geographically to shape international perceptions and behaviours towards a country, facilitating political objectives. They also view MCOs as a means to foster extensive networks of relationships, power, and influence that transcend the sport itself. At the same time, and maybe to a lesser extent, type 3 MCOs can assist in sustaining jobs, generating export earnings, and enhancing national economic output, thereby contributing to a nation's economic health, while simultaneously assisting in potentially acquiring new resources including labour, capital (socio, cultural, and political), intellectual property, and entrepreneurship (Chadwick, 2022). All the above motives and aspirations also differentiate type 3 MCOs (Sovereign Funds) from type 1 (investments by PE firms).

Figure 16.1 captures the three types of MCOs discussed above and illustrates that, although discrete, overlaps exist among the different types.

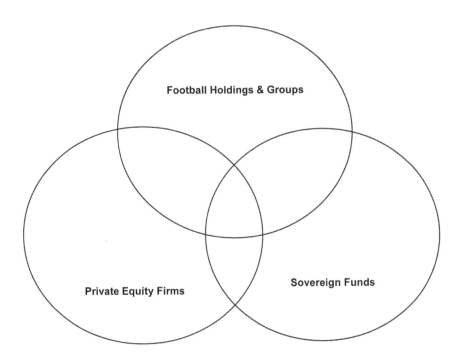

FIGURE 16.1 The Typology of Football MCO

Conclusion

The future of MCO in football appears poised for significant evolution, as demonstrated by the rapid increase of MCOs noted in the past years. As different forms of individual investors and investment funds continue to recognize the immense value and potential of football worldwide, the trend towards acquiring multiple clubs is likely to accelerate. As such, the introduction of a typology for MCO in football holds substantial value, offering a structured framework to analyse and understand the complexities of this emerging phenomenon. A well-defined typology enables scholars and practitioners to categorize various ownership models based on criteria such as ownership structure, strategic objectives, and operational synergies. By distinguishing between different forms of MCO – whether driven by financial diversification, capabilities harvesting, or geopolitical reasons – this framework provides deeper insights into the motivations and potential impacts of such investments. Moreover, it facilitates comparative studies, allowing for a systematic evaluation of the outcomes associated with each type. This, in turn, could inform policy discussions on regulatory practices and competitive fairness, ensuring that the sport's integrity is maintained amid increasing questions on the proliferation of MCOs. Ultimately, a typology of MCO not only advances academic discourse but also aids stakeholders in navigating the intricate landscape of modern football, fostering a more nuanced and strategic approach to governance and management within the sport. In this very much expected increase in MCOs in global football, understanding the different ways in which the phenomenon can materialize, as well as the details behind its using and potentially further enhancing the typology of MCOs presented in this chapter, can help enrich our understanding of MCO and investment in football, its motivations, and potential implications, as the phenomenon continues to develop.

References

Alkaraan, F. and Northcott, D. (2006). Strategic capital investment decision-making: a role for emergent analysis tools?: a study of practice in large UK manufacturing companies. *The British Accounting Review, 38*(2), 149–173.

Amara, M. and Al-Emadi, A. (2018). Business and governance of football in Qatar. In *Routledge Handbook of Football Business and Management* (pp. 539–547). Abingdon: Routledge.

Barber, F. and Goold, M. (2007). The strategic secret of private equity. *Harvard Business Review, 85*(9), 53.

Barney, J. (1991). Firm resources and sustained competitive advantage. *Journal of Management, 17*(1), 99–120.

Breuer, M. (2018). Multi-club ownerships. In M. Breuer and D. Forrest (Eds.), *The Palgrave Handbook on the Economics of Manipulation in Sport* (pp. 115–134). London: Palgrave Macmillan.

Capron, L. (1999). The long-term performance of horizontal acquisitions. *Strategic Management Journal, 20*(11), 987–1018.

Chadwick, S. (2022). From utilitarianism and neoclassical sport management to a new geopolitical economy of sport. *European Sport Management Quarterly, 22*(5), 685–704.

Chadwick, S., Widdop, P. and Parnell, D. (2016). The guanxi of football: From British railways to Hollywood A-listers, a world of connections lies beneath Chinese football investments. Available at: https://www.policyforum.net/the-guanxi-of-football/

CIES Sports Intelligence (2024). *Club ownership in European football, foreign investments, private capital & multi-club ownership.* CIES Sports Intelligence. Available at: https://www.cies.ch/uploads/media/20240306_ClubOwnership_01.pdf.

Cooremans, C. (2011). Make it strategic! Financial investment logic is not enough. *Energy Efficiency, 4*(4), 473–492.

Gilligan, J. and Wright, M. (2020). *Private Equity Demystified: An Explanatory Guide.* New York: Oxford University Press.

Harris, R. (2024). Sir Jim Ratcliffe completes purchase of Manchester United stake – taking control of football operations from Glazers. *Sky News.* Available at: https://news.sky.com/story/sir-jim-ratcliffe-completes-purchase-of-25-stake-in-manchester-united-13076565.

Hunter, A. (2021). Liverpool boost as owners confirm $735m RedBird deal for stake in FSG. *The Guardian.* Available at: https://www.theguardian.com/football/2021/mar/31/liverpool-boost-as-owners-confirm-735m-redbird-deal-for-stake-in-fsg.

Kaplan, S. N. and Strömberg, P. (2009). Leveraged buyouts and private equity. *Journal of Economic Perspectives, 23*(1), 121–146.

Koumou, G. B. (2020). Diversification and portfolio theory: a review. *Financial Markets and Portfolio Management, 34*(3), 267–312.

Krysta, P. M. and Kanbach, D. K. (2022). Value creation in private equity portfolio companies: a structured review of evidence and proposed framework. *Venture Capital, 24*(3–4), 203–286.

Kumar, B. R. and Kumar, B. R. (2019). *Mergers and Acquisitions* (p. 1). Berlin: Springer International Publishing.

Lazonick, W. and Teece, D. J. (Eds.) (2012). *Management Innovation: Essays in the Spirit of Alfred D. Chandler, Jr.* Oxford: OUP.

Madhani, P. M. (2010). The resource-based view (RBV): issues and perspectives. *PACE, A Journal of Research of Prestige Institute of Management, 1*(1), 43–55.

Marin, B. and Lee, C. (2020). Exploring new trends of sport business: Japanese companies' investment in ownership of foreign football clubs. *Sport in Society, 23*(12), 2031–2054.

Maritan, C. A. (2001). Capital investment as investing in organizational capabilities: an empirically grounded process model. *Academy of Management Journal, 44*(3), 513–531.

Morris, J. O. H. N. and Hodges, T. (2016). Strategic Management 2E (p. 150).

OECD (2017). *Model tax convention on income and on capital 2017 (Full Version), Article 9: Associated enterprises.* Retrieved May 26, 2024, from https://read.oecd-ilibrary.org/taxation/model-tax-convention-on-income-and-on-capital-2017-full-version_64c1a893-en#page1.

Rohde, M. and Breuer, C. (2017). The market for football club investors: a review of theory and empirical evidence from professional European football. *European Sport Management Quarterly, 17*(3), 265–289.

Sauer, T., Anagnostopoulos, C., Zülch, H. and Werthmann, L. (2024). Creating value in football: unveiling business activities and strategies of financial investors. *Managing Sport and Leisure,* 1–21. Available at: https://www.tandfonline.com/doi/full/10.1080/23750472.2024.2314568

Sportbusiness.com (2024). Multi-club ownership: The unproven concept transforming football. Retrieved May 24, 2024, from https://www.sportbusiness.com/multi-club-ownership-report/.

UEFA Intelligence Centre (2023). The European club footballing landscape, club licensing benchmarking report. Available at: https://editorial.uefa.com/resources/027e-174740f39cc6-d205dd2e86bf-1000/ecfl_bm_report_2022_high_resolution_.pdf.

World Football Summit (2022). A special report on football ownership and governance. Available at: https://worldfootballsummit.com/wp-content/uploads/2022/12/Report-WFS-22-1.pdf.

Xue, H., Watanabe, N. M., Chen, R., Newman, J. I. and Yan, G. (2020). Football (as) Guanxi: a relational analysis of actor reciprocity, state capitalism, and the Chinese football industry. *Sport in Society*, *23*(12), 2005–2030.

Yang, L. (2015). The rise of the Middle East sovereign wealth funds: causes, consequences and policies. *Journal of Middle Eastern and Islamic Studies (in Asia)*, *9*(2), 16–37.

17

THE DEVELOPMENT, STRUCTURE, AND OPERATIONS OF THE CITY FOOTBALL GROUP

Abhishek Khajuria

Introduction

Football has evolved ever since the game was first played in an organized league manner in late 19th century. The same way, football clubs as operating entities have also evolved. The earliest football clubs were primarily meant for recreation, both for those playing and for the watching public and were run by students, churches and the like. Many of them also ran as factory teams with the workers playing in the teams. When professionalism came in the game, things began to change. There also emerged a small number of businessmen who came to own the football clubs but still, they were run as a community concern. However, with the advent of broadcasting (and the revenue thus earned), slowly and gradually, owning football clubs became primarily a thing of the super-rich. One of the super-rich who comes to mind is Italian media tycoon Silvio Berlusconi, who became the owner of Italian club AC Milan in the 1980s. The formation of the Premier League in 1992 and English football becoming the richest the world over as a consequence of it has been something which has had far-reaching impacts on the game in every dimension one can imagine. The increased visibility has led to the most successful clubs becoming what some like to call "super clubs" boasting fans all around the world. Football has become a business in itself and the game is just not for those 22 players on the pitch and the fans in the stands. It is packaged as an entertainment product for the billions watching on their screens all over the globe. This "product" is just not the game. It also includes team merchandise, YouTube videos, exclusive access to various benefits through memberships, esports among others. This global reach has led to the emergence of fan bases whose loyalty is no longer to

DOI: 10.4324/9781003473671-20

club located in their vicinity. Rather, they follow a club located thousands of kilometres away and football thus, has become something, which transcends borders with an ease never seen before. This has attracted different types of owners to the business of owning a football club. Today, we see owners ranging from investment firms to Hollywood stars to multinational firms to nation states. The most unique model among ownerships of football clubs is, perhaps, the nation state one. While it is not as widespread as other kinds of ownerships, it might prove to be the most consequential of them all. While there are clubs like Paris Saint German owned by the Qatari Investment Authority and Newcastle United owned by the Saudi PIF, the behemoth among them all is the City Football Group (CFG) (whose jewel in the crown is Manchester City in a network of 13 clubs all around the globe), majority owned initially by the Abu Dhabi United Group (ADUG), now under ultimate parent company Newton Investment and Development LLC (CFG, 2023). CFG is the focus of this chapter. After looking at the origins and the history of the group, the chapter looks at the structure of the CFG and unpacks how the organization functions. While looking at the on-field successes and successes off it, an attempt has also been made to delve into the issues and controversies which have arisen with the ownership by Abu Dhabi of a number of football clubs around the world which started with Manchester City in England.

The City Football Group: Origins and History

The CFG was established in 2013. The website of CFG describes it as the "owner of football-related businesses in major cities around the world, including football clubs, academies, technical support and marketing companies" (CFG, 2023).

Though many trace the origins of the CFG to the acquisition of Manchester City Football Club by Sheikh Mansour bin Zayed Al Nahyan led ADUG in 2008, it is inaccurate. Seeds for CFG were sown when Ferran Soriano became the CEO of Manchester City in 2012. When CFG was formed in 2013, Soriano became the CEO of the whole group, a role in which he serves into this day. Before joining City, Soriano earlier had served as the Economy vice-president at FC Barcelona from 2003 to 2008 (Planellas, 2020; Rivolo, 2021). During his tenure, Barcelona became the fastest growing football club in the world. The club's revenues increased from 123 to 308 million Euros and it also turned profitable (Rivolo, 2021). The multi-club ownership model on which the CFG operates today was first mooted by Soriano to his bosses at Barcelona. However, the idea was ultimately shot down. He elaborated on his ideas for management of the football business in his book published in 2011 titled "Goal: The Ball doesn't go in by Chance" where he argued for innovation and a new way to surge ahead from the rivals (Planellas, 2020). His plan was essentially to turn a football club from a one city venture to "global entertainment companies like Walt Disney" (Lee et al., 2020a; Rivolo, 2021).

When Soriano joined City, he was met by owners who were equally ambitious as him if not more. There were no financial constraints here as Abu Dhabi's petrodollars were funding these investments (Chadwick, 2019). Added motivation for the owners was that the success of Manchester City and other teams of the CFG was going to be a positive marketing for the UAE in general and the emirate of Abu Dhabi in particular (more on that in a later section).

After CFG was set up, the first step towards internationalization was taken when New York City FC was established in 2013 (first started playing in 2015) in partnership with the New York Yankees (Lee et al., 2020b; Planellas, 2020). The next club to come into the fold was Melbourne Heart FC in 2014 which was renamed to Melbourne City FC the same year (CFG, 2023). Next up were Yokohama F. Marinos in Japan (in 2014 as well) where CFG took a minority stake (CFG, 2023). In April 2017, CFG bought Club Atletico Torque, playing in Montevideo, Uruguay (CFG, 2023). In 2020, it was renamed as Montevideo City Torque (CFG, 2023). The acquisition of Girona FC in Spain took place in August 2017 when CFG bought 44.3 per cent of the club (CFG, 2023). Sichuan Jiuniu in China and Mumbai City FC in India were acquired in February 2019 and November 2019, respectively (CFG, 2023). In the case of Mumbai, CFG bought a 65 per cent stake in the club (Chadwick, 2019). In 2020, Lommel SK in Belgium and Troyes in France became part of the group in May and September, respectively (CFG, 2023). The more recent acquisitions have been of Palermo FC in Italy and Bahia in Brazil in July 2022 and May 2023, respectively.

Apart from the 12 clubs which are fully part of the CFG, there is a 13th club which is a partner club. Club Bolivar of La Paz in Bolivia became the first partner club of CFG in January 2021 allowing it to "access a wide breadth of expertise, proprietary technology, best practice, and strategic advice developed by City Football Group through its multi-club structure" (CFG, 2023).

Structure

In terms of the structure of the club, if we look at the stakes in CFG, it was completely owned by ADUG till 2015. That year, the first investment into the group was announced. A 13 per cent stake of the club was bought by Chinese firms China Media Capital and investment firm CITIC Group for a sum of 298 million Pounds ($400 million) (Lee et al., 2020a). American private equity firm Silver Lake became part of the ownership in November 2019. It bought a 10-per cent stake for 373 million Pounds ($500 million) (Lee et al., 2020a). On 25 July 2021, CFG came under the parent ownership of Newton Investment and Development LLC (CFG, 2023). It is an Abu Dhabi registered company which is completely owned by Sheikh Mansour

(CFG, 2023). Silver Lake have also increased their stake in the CFG in the recent past. The last of expansions of Sliver Lake's shares took place in November 2022 when it bought the majority of the shares held by China Media Capital which led to the latter vacating its seat on the CFG board with its chairman Li Ruigang stepping down (Cunningham, 2022). Consequently, they hold 18.16 per cent of the group with more than 81 per cent being held by Sheikh Mansour (CFG, 2023).

Now when it comes to unpacking the functioning of CFG which in itself is a behemoth of an organization, we need to look at the executive structure across the length and breadth of the group. Each club in the group has one football director and one officer who looks after the executive affairs of the respective club. The terminology for the latter is not uniform across all the clubs in the group though most of them use the term CEO. Both the top officials of every club have to report to the CFG headquarters in Manchester (Rivolo, 2021).

The business workings of the club revolve around targeting those football markets around the world which have high football demand but comparatively low competition (Rivolo, 2021). In addition to that, marketing and player development form the other two important pillars of the CFG's functioning (Lee et al., 2020b; Rivolo, 2021). When clubs are bought, the target is to have them playing like Manchester City. Thus, the target is to have the same style of football played across teams from all the genders and age-groups across the continents. This comes in handy when players move from one team to another within the group. To fulfil these objectives, knowhow, resources and technologies and best practices are shared across the group. These range from coaching to physiotherapy to recovery techniques among others (Lee et al., 2020b; Rivolo, 2021).

When it comes to marketing, most of the deals for commercial partners for the group are struck in such a way that they cover most of the clubs of CFG. The major partners of the CFG are Etihad Airways, Puma, Nissan, Xylem and Asahi Super Dry (CFG, 2023). It is worth highlighting here that all the clubs in the group have a number of other partners in their individual capacity. Partnering with CFG gives brands a marketing opportunity which other clubs can only provide when they are on pre-season tours. As the group owns clubs in four continents and across markets, it gives a never seen before exposure to the brands (Rivolo, 2021). With every new acquisition of a club, the aim is to create a virtuous cycle of more fans, more partnerships, more revenues which in turn help to produce better players who either can become club mainstays and reach to the pinnacle that is Manchester City or give CFG a profit after they are sold (Lee et al., 2020a, 2020b; Rivolo, 2021). The latter is the focus of the player development strategy of the CFG headed by Brian Marwood who is the managing director of global football of CFG (Lee at al., 2020b).

On-field and Off-field Successes of CFG

When it comes to on-field successes, we need to look no further than Manchester City. The club has been totally transformed in the last 15 years. They were once termed "the noisy neigbours" by the legendary Sir Alex Ferguson who managed cross-town rivals Manchester United. But in the last decade and a half, they have become the most successful English club domestically while also adding continental success by winning the Union of European Football Associations (UEFA) Champions League for the first time in the club's history in 2023. The latter achievement also made the club only the second English club ever (there a handful of few on the continent) to win the "treble" of the Premier League, FA Cup and the Champions League after Manchester United. New York City FC who compete in the Major League Soccer (MLS) in the US have mostly finished in the top three in their conference. The club won the MLS in 2021 (Jackson, 2023). While Melbourne City added a league and cup each to its cabinet, Yokohama F. Marinos won its first league title in 15 years in 2019 to which it added another one last year (Jackson, 2023). While Mumbai City has also won silverware, success has arrived in different forms for other clubs. Most notable among them has been Girona. After getting promoted to the La Liga for the first time in the club's history, they finished tenth (The World Game, 2017). Though they were relegated to the second division the next season, after getting promoted in 2022, they are presently leading the charts in the La Liga (Jackson, 2023). CFG has also invested in esports with Kieran Brown signed in 2016 to play for Manchester City in tournaments organized by Fédération Internationale de Football Association (FIFA) (Simic, 2022). The group also has a partnership with Blue United Corporation, a company which has portfolio in esports like Blue United eFC (Simic, 2022).

The off-field successes of CFG are spearheaded by Manchester City. The club earned a record revenue of 712.8 million Pounds in the 2022–23 season (Unwin, 2023). Apart from that, CFG has built a world-class academy system starting from Manchester and aim to take it to all the clubs in the group. The group also works in the community through various initiatives which are carried out in a number of cities around the world (Manchester City, 2023). Through a programme called City in the Community (CITC), Manchester City in 2022–23 engaged more than 18,000 people in the Greater Manchester Area (Manchester City Annual Report 2022–23, 2023, p. 53). The club was also named the most valuable football club brand in the world while it also earned a profit of 121.7 million Pounds from player trading in 2022–23 (Manchester City, 2023, p/66; Manchester City Annual Report 2022–23).

Another aspect which needs to be looked at is the benefit which is accrued to Abu Dhabi due to CFG. There has always been an argument made that the CFG is a vehicle for increasing the soft power of Abu Dhabi and promoting it. Indeed, research has shown that CFG has been able to act as a soft power resource for Abu Dhabi (Jackson, 2022, pp. 208–234). It has contributed to a positive image for the emirate due to the number of fans its clubs have earned. But to what extent that has happened still remains inconclusive. It has also acted as a diplomatic network by virtue of its presence in 4 continents and 13 countries around the world (Jackson, 2022, pp. 208–234). The emirate's citizens also look up to what CFG has achieved and see it as something they relate to (Jackson, 2022, pp. 208–234). Added to these benefits, Abu Dhabi has been seen as a symbol of innovation (Jackson, 2022, pp. 208–234). This has attracted investment. An example is the relationship of Abu Dhabi with China which has led to important agreements. During his 2015 visit to the UK, Chinese President Xi Jinping visited Manchester City's training complex, the Etihad Campus (Jackson, 2022, pp. 208–234). A few months after that, China Media Capital and CITIC Group bought a 13 per cent stake in CFG (Lee et al., 2020a). After that, important agreements between the UAE and China were signed. During Sheikh Mohammad bin Zayed's (the then Crown Prince of Abu Dhabi) visit to China in December 2015, the UAE and China announced the establishment of a joint strategic investment fund worth US$10 billion (Jackson, 2022, pp. 208–234).

Manchester City has allowed Abu Dhabi to expand its real estate portfolio in Manchester. The result has been the construction of new homes in the Ancoats and New Islington areas and a student village at The University of Manchester (Jackson, 2022, pp. 208–234). Real estate has also been developed around the areas of the other CFG clubs (Jackson, 2022, pp. 208–234).

Issues and Controversies Surrounding CFG

There have been a number of issues and controversies with regard to CFG which have been almost as old as the acquisition of Manchester City itself. First of all, Manchester City are for football purists, a club which has not gone through an organic transition to become a bigger club. They accuse the club of "buying trophies" rather than winning them. On top of that, they have also been accused of violating Financial Fair Play (FFP) rules on numerous occasions by using inflated sponsorship valuations and the like. When in 2011, Etihad Airways signed a 10-year deal with Manchester City for shirt sponsorship and stadium-naming rights valued at 400 million Pounds, John W. Henry, the owner of Liverpool FC, famously tweeted, "how much was the losing bid?" (Lee et al., 2020a). There are currently under investigation for violating Premier League's financial rules on a mammoth 115 counts with the matter set to go for a trial (Summerscales, 2023). The charges date from 2009–10 to 2017–18. "Financial doping" is the term that has been used in this regard (Summerscales, 2023). On the continental level as well, City were initially banned by UEFA for two years from the Champions League due to the failure to comply with the FFP rules. However, in 2020, the Court of Arbitration for Sport overturned the ban while also reducing the fine imposed on the club from 30 million Euros to 10 million Euros (Conn, 2020). Throughout the years, whenever the allegations have been made against them, City and CFG have always denied any wrongdoing and claimed innocence.

Perhaps the biggest controversy which surrounds the CFG is that the whole venture is just a smokescreen, a humongous effort at sportswashing (Lee et al., 2020a). Human rights organizations like Human Rights Watch (HRW) and Amnesty International have accused the owners of CFG in engaging in an exercise of covering over human rights abuses and "launder the image" of Abu Dhabi (Conn, 2013). The Emiratis have consistently argued against the allegations saying that the authorities follow due process and labour reforms have been introduced and whatever difference is there about the UAE and Abu Dhabi's image, is due to unawareness of Emirati culture and values which City wants to show to the world (Conn, 2013). The involvement of the UAE in regional disputes like the war in Yemen and the Qatar blockade and continued concerns over the treatment of migrant workers have also resulted in a sort of "soft disempowerment" which is generally referred to as a negative publicity and a negative impact on the image of a country and the opposite of what the achievement of soft power envisions (Jackson, 2022, pp. 208–234).

On the footballing side, there is another issue which arises. This relates to the nature of multi-club ownership and the fact that two clubs owned by the same entity could end up in a same competition like Champions League or other competitions which maybe a threat to the integrity of the competition. It will be interesting to see if any two European clubs owned by CFG end up in the same competition, what would happen then. Precedent is there where UEFA allowed RB Leipzig and Red Bull Salzburg to participate in the Champions League (Ogden, 2023). However, Salzburg are known by the name FC Salzburg in continental competitions and both the Red Bull clubs had to prove they were not "controlled" by the same people (Ogden, 2023). CFG would also have to prove the same although the synergy with which the group operates will make it an interesting case if and when the time comes.

In April 2022, the acquisition of NAC Breda of the Netherlands by CFG fell through after a fierce backlash from the fans of the club. They raised a banner inside the club stadium: "Stay out of our territory, NAC is not a City Group story" (Hytner, 2022). Although a 7 million Euro deal had already been agreed, CFG ultimately decided to drop the plans to acquire the club (Hytner, 2022).

Conclusion

Thus, in conclusion, it can be said that in a decade of existence, CFG has changed the way in which the business of football is conducted and has proved to be a major disruptive force in the sport. The football empire which it has built and the synergy with which the clubs of the group work has led to a model of ownership which has become a benchmark for all its competitors. As much as they are envious of it, it wouldn't be incorrect to say that they are impressed by it in equal measure. The teams play superb quality of football on the pitch which is backed by excellent marketing and player development strategies off it. This has given rise to record revenues. The crown jewel of the group, Manchester City F.C., is one of the biggest clubs in the world today. Other than that, it has also been a useful soft power vehicle for the emirate of Abu Dhabi and the UAE. It has helped Abu Dhabi become an attractive destination for investments and helped increase the emirate's real estate portfolio, thus, becoming a perfect example in the age of geopolitical economy of sport. The CFG has also earned goodwill with the help of the community initiatives it has launched and the people it has helped. However, there have been controversies as well and it hasn't always been a smooth sailing, the failure to acquire NAC Breda being one example. CFG has been labelled as an instrument of sportswashing for the UAE in general and the emirate of Abu Dhabi in particular by many. There have been investigations on the allegations of breaching financial rules in the case of Manchester City. The group has always dismissed all the allegations levelled and fought back as well as was the case when the Champions League ban was successfully overturned and the fine reduced. The controversies and challenges have not deterred CFG though. The group has continued to expand, an example being the acquisitions of Palermo F.C. in Italy and EC Bahia in Brazil in around a year after the NAC Breda deal fell through. It has continued to innovate and evolve. The road ahead will not be easy but with its resources and the experience it has accumulated in the last decade, CFG looks well placed to preserve and expand its empire and keep fighting to stay at the pinnacle of world football.

References

CFG (2023). City Football Group, *City Football Group*, accessed via https://www.cityfootballgroup.com.

Chadwick, S. (2019). The Disney of sport: How Manchester City's owners are leading a global sports-entertainment business. *Scroll.in*, 2 December, accessed via https://scroll.in/field/945504/the-disney-of-sport-how-manchester-citys-owners-are-leading-a-global-sports-entertainment-business.

Conn, D. (2013). Abu Dhabi accused of 'using Manchester City to launder image'. *The Guardian*, 30 July, accessed via https://www.theguardian.com/football/2013/jul/30/manchester-city-human-rights-accusations.

Conn, D. (2020). Manchester City's Champions League ban lifted by court of arbitration for sport. *The Guardian*, 13 July, accessed via https://www.theguardian.com/football/2020/jul/13/manchester-city-champions-league-ban-lifted-cas-court-of-arbitration-for-sport.

Cunningham, E. (2022). Silver Lake expands City Football Group stake to 18% with CMC stepping back. *Sportcal*, 25 November, accessed via https://www.sportcal.com/news/silver-lake-expands-city-football-group-stake-to-18-with-cmc-stepping-back/?cf-view.

Hytner, D. (2022). City Football Group plan to buy NAC Breda fails after supporter backlash. *The Guardian*, 22 April, accessed via https://www.theguardian.com/football/2022/apr/22/manchester-city-football-group-plan-to-buy-nac-breda-fails-after-supporter-backlash#:~:text=A%20group%20of%20NAC%20fans,a%20campaign%20on%20social%20media.

Jackson, R. (2022). Assessing sports diplomacy as a soft power tool: the case of Abu Dhabi's City Football Group. *LSE Journal of Geography and Environment*, 1, 208–234.

Jackson, J. (2023). City Football Group: who are the 13 club and how are they faring? *The Guardian*, 2 December, accessed via https://www.theguardian.com/football/2023/dec/02/city-football-group-who-are-the-13-clubs-and-how-are-they-faring.

Lee, S. et al. (2020a). Special report: City Football Group. Part one-empire building. *The Athletic*, 9 December, accessed via https://theathletic.com/2244423/2020/12/09/city-football-group-manchester/.

Lee, S. et al. (2020b). Special report: City Football Group: Part two-does it work? *The Athletic*, 10 December, accessed via https://theathletic.com/2244579/2020/12/10/cfg-manchester-new-york-city-soriano/.

Manchester City (2023). Global Projects. *City Football Group*, accessed via https://www.mancity.com/community/global-projects.

Manchester City Annual Report 2022-23 (2023). Reports. *Man City*, accessed via https://www.cityfootballgroup.com/information-resource/reports/.

Ogden, M. (2023). The issues with multi-club ownership, from City Football Group to Red Bull and more. *ESPN*, 15 July, accessed via https://www.espn.in/football/story/_/id/38008353/the-issues-multi-club-ownership-city-football-group-red-bull.

Planellas, M. (2020). From FC Barcelona to City Football Group. *Do Better by esade*, 23 January, accessed via https://dobetter.esade.edu/en/football-management.

Rivolo, M. (2021). City Football Group: The Building of an Empire. *Medium*, 5 July, accessed via https://medium.com/the-buildup-play/city-football-group-the-building-of-an-empire-3cbba09e948f.

Simic, I. (2022). City Football Group announces collaboration with Blue United Corporation. *Esports Insider*, 17 January, accessed via https://esportsinsider.com/2022/01/city-football-group-blue-united-corporation-fifa.

Summerscales, R. (2023). Would Relegation Even Be That Bad for Manchester City? *FanNation Futbol*, 18 November, accessed via https://www.si.com/fannation/soccer/futbol/features/would-relegation-even-be-that-bad-for-manchester-city#:~:text=It%20is%20alleged%20that%20City,is%20basically%20what%20is%20alleged.

The World Game (2017). Girona promoted to La Liga for first time in 87 years. *The World Game*, 5 June, accessed via https://web.archive.org/web/20171201134250/https://theworldgame.sbs.com.au/article/2017/06/05/girona-promoted-la-liga-first-time-87-years.

Unwin, W. (2023). Manchester City post Premier League record revenue of £712.8m. *The Guardian*, 15 November, accessed via https://www.theguardian.com/football/2023/nov/15/manchester-city-post-premier-league-record-revenue#:~:text=Manchester%20City%20post%20Premier%20League%20record%20revenue%20of%20£712.8m,-Income%20increases%20by&text=Manchester%20City%20have%20announced%20record,by%20Manchester%20United%20last%20month.

18

THE BENIGN, BRILLIANT, AND BEAUTIFUL SOFT POWER OF QATAR'S PARIS SAINT-GERMAIN

Thomas Ross Griffin

Introduction

When Qatar won the rights to host the 2022 FIFA World Cup, the small Gulf nation appeared to have reached the mountaintop in its efforts to use sport as a means of generating soft power. Joseph Nye defined this concept as "the ability to get what you want through attraction rather than coercion or payments" (2004, p. x) and over the past decade, it has become a virtual ever present in discussions of Qatar's sporting endeavours. What Qatar *wanted* in bidding to host the World Cup, many academics suggest, was to be recognised as a modern and progressive Islamic state whose social framework was composed of the same abilities, values, and ideals as those found in the civil societies of the Global North. However, winning the hosting rights for FIFA's flagship tournament was not Qatar's only attempt to exert soft power through football at the time. Approximately six months after the announcement in Zurich in 2010, the government-owned wealth fund Qatar Sports Investments (QSI) purchased French football club Paris Saint-Germain (PSG). Yet while the 2022 World Cup inspired a slew of academic work from fields as disparate as international relations, human rights, business management, and cultural studies amongst others, by comparison, Qatar's ownership of PSG received remarkably little scholarly attention. Although many academics give passing mention to the relationship, Amara and Garcia's article (2013) on the French media perception of the takeover is the first of only a handful of peer-reviewed studies to provide prolonged insight into the relationship between Qatar and the Parisian football club. This was followed by Chanavat and Desbordes's work (2017) on the QSI-led efforts to transform PSG into a global brand, and by Koch's study that asks if "the academic fixation with soft

DOI: 10.4324/9781003473671-21

power in studying Gulf sports investments" (2020, p. 357) actually inhibits a proper understanding of how Qatar uses the club to generate soft power. The last article of note is recent work by T.R. Griffin (2024) on Qatar's ownership of PSG in which he argues that the team is a mechanism used by the state to perform a bespoke national identity overseas. Yet while each of the aforementioned authors generally interprets the QSI purchase of PSG within the nexus of soft power, none offers decisive insight as to whether Qatar's tenure as owner of the club has been a soft power success or failure. As such, shedding further light on this question is the primary goal of this chapter.

Method

One of the central criticisms of Nye's definition of soft power is that it is inherently vague and gives little indication as to where soft power originates from or how to measure it accurately. Alexander Vuving attempts to bring some degree of clarity to Nye's original description by breaking the concept down into three "variants of soft power" (2019, p. 23), benign power, brilliant power, and beautiful power. Vuving argues that they symbolise "kindness, competence, and commitment" (2019, p. 23), respectively, and the ability to demonstrate these "virtues" (2019, p. 23) is what generates the sense of attraction essential to the performance of soft power. While Vuving does not identify a means of measuring soft power, his taxonomy does at least allow some further clarity in ascertaining whether a state actor's efforts to exert soft power have been successful or not. Qatar's ownership of PSG is examined within this framework.

Benign Power

The attractive quality that defines benign power in Vuving's model is primarily one of kindness. He suggests that benign power in turn generates soft power when one practices "prosocial behavior such as being nice, helping, support, caring, sharing, respect, and benignity" (2019, p. 28). Qatar's PSG has made significant efforts in this regard to transform the club into a mechanism that demonstrates these qualities to the civil societies of Western Europe. QSI has deliberately and publicly aligned PSG with positive values that insist upon compassion and respect for others by using the club to promote several campaigns against homophobia, racism, and fan violence (Edwards, 2022; PSG, 2022). The creation of the PSG Foundation in 2018 is also a notable example of this version of soft power. Established by Qatari club president, Nasser Al-Khelaifi, the foundation is an outreach programme that provides educational, sports, and other support services to at-risk children and young adults in the local Parisian community (PSG, 2018). However, the ill feeling towards Qatar that emerged in the run-up to the 2022 World Cup has often overshadowed the benign power elicited by these actions. The series of controversies surrounding the tournament included accusations of corruption in the bidding process, repeated allegations that thousands of migrant construction workers had died building infrastructure works necessary for the event, and reports of the oppressive and often restrictive circumstances in which both Qatar's LGBTQ+ community and women citizens existed. Qatar's other most high-profile foray into the world of football, PSG soon found itself enmeshed in these World Cup controversies. Newspaper articles discussing these issues frequently included at least passing reference to Qatar's ownership of the Parisian team (Gibson, 2014; Ronay, 2019) as part of a wider sports-washing scheme. Nasser Al-Khelaifi acting as a de facto spokesperson for his country when pressed about these World Cup controversies increased this equivalency made by many Western media outlets (Sky News, 2022). So too, paradoxically, did the stellar performance of the club's most prominent stars, Kylian Mbappé and Lionel Messi, throughout the World Cup itself. They eventually played against each other in what Adam Crafton (2023) later described as "a PSG final". The closing image of the tournament, that of Shaikh Tamim bin Hamad Al-Thani, Qatar Emir, QSI founder, and regular attendee of PSG games at the Parc des Princes presenting Messi with the World Cup trophy cemented this link. The World Cup was to be the means with which Qatar introduced itself to the global community as a modern, progressive Islamic state. However, the image of the nation most commonly presented by the Western press was that of an uncaring and cruel society intent on exploiting the vulnerable and less fortunate in order to achieve its goal of hosting the world's most prestigious sporting event. Due to its highly publicised links to Qatar, PSG has found it incredibly difficult to separate itself from such an image, which in turn affected any benign power that the state hoped their ownership of the team would generate.

Brilliant Power

Vuving explains brilliant power as "the ability to do something successfully or efficiently" (2019, p. 34). Repeated displays of brilliant power result in greater respect, admiration, and privilege towards the instigator. As others seek to share in their glory, soft power in the guise of brilliant power is formed. It differs from benign power in that others are attracted to the holder's demonstrations of competence rather than kindness. As Vuving notes, "success is perhaps the most universal and most effective index of competence" (2019, p. 38), and PSG's success under the management of QSI has been unprecedented. Prior to the takeover, trophies were hard-won, unexpected, and rare, with only two Ligue 1 titles and a handful of domestic cups and one European Cup Winners Cup in the club's 38-year history. Over the past 12 years, however, PSG has won nine Ligue 1 titles and 12 domestic cups, and while the UEFA Champions League continues to evade PSG, they have become an ever-present in the final rounds of the competition. The methods used to achieve this level of success were not subtle however. Boosted by Qatar's hydrocarbon riches, the QSI takeover heralded the beginning of a Galactico era in Paris, one that saw world transfer records topple and eye-watering salaries paid to the game's most glamorous superstars. The arrival first of Zlatan Ibrahimovic, Edison Cavani, and Thiago Silva was superseded in later years by that of Neymar, Kylian Mbappé, and Lionel Messi as the name PSG became a catchword for the best footballers in the world. Given its enormous investment into the club over the past decade and more, it is clear that QSI purchased PSG to demonstrate to a Western sporting environment that Qatar's association with excellence was a rising tide that could lift all boats. The manner in which the team easily overcame the best efforts of less glamorous domestic opposition was testament to this quality. Yet this performance of brilliant power has also had its issues. Rather than being respected and admired for their successes, the club and its owners frequently found themselves criticised by rivals, journalists, and other commentators within the game who repeatedly argued that financial doping rather than on-field performances was the sole reason for the French team's change in fortunes since 2011 (Slater, 2022). In addition, the club's repeated inability to win the much more difficult UEFA Champions League, a competition in which the financial advantages PSG enjoys over its domestic rivals are greatly diminished by the presence of Europe's most elite teams, has meant that team's litany of success since 2012 has generated little meaningful brilliant power for its owners. Wealth rather than exceptional ability is seen as the catalyst to PSG's newfound success (White, 2022; White and Devin, 2018). Its achievements, while laudable, are expected rather than admired, while its failures are often celebrated. Both undermine the hoped for show of excellence that generates brilliant power.

Beautiful Power

The essence of beautiful power according to Vuving comes from a sense of "shared values, identities, beliefs, and aspirations" (2019, p. 40), one that forges a common identity between parties that creates the attraction necessary for the exertion of soft power. Equipped with unrivalled riches, the owners of PSG went to great lengths to assert such an equivalence between their team and Europe's footballing elite in order to generate this kind of soft power. Yet despite being cast in an identical mould to Europe's super-clubs and enjoying similar success, PSG is repeatedly seen as different to its peers, thus placing the common identity required to generate beautiful power permanently out of reach. PSG's association with Qatar's World Cup controversies as well as the myriad accusations of financial doping levied at the club over the past decade have contributed to this isolation. However, another explanation as to why this is so is the unprecedented manner in which the Parisian team steamrolled its way to the top table of European football alongside its equally wealthy and successful peers from Spain, Germany, Italy, and England. These clubs (a small group loosely consisting of Real Madrid, Barcelona, Bayern Munich, Juventus, A.C. Milan, Internazionale, Manchester United, Manchester City, Liverpool, Arsenal, and Chelsea) sit at the pinnacle of Europe's football pyramid. Small in number, their financial strength, longevity, success, and ability to ring-fence the sport's best players imbued each of them with what Elias and Scotson describe as a "group charisma" (1994, p. 104) or sense of superiority that distinguished them from younger or less successful rivals. Prior to the QSI takeover, as a club established as recently as 1970 and one that only ever enjoyed sporadic success, PSG was widely accepted as a lesser member of this community. However, since 2011, PSG has consistently refused to adhere to this unspoken, long-standing status quo. Enabled by QSI's considerable wealth, it has outspent historically elite clubs in the race for player resources, competed against them in European competition, and usurped several of their representatives in important positions of power and influence within UEFA and the European Club Association (ECA). Yet ironically, rather than allowing PSG to share in the group charisma that defines Europe's elite, one that could generate the beautiful power desired by the club's owners, these actions are perceived as the havoc that a state club can wreak upon the tradition and established practices of the sport as it seeks to fulfil its own ambitions. While once it may have been hoped that the QSI purchase of PSG would allow the latter to be recognised as a peer by what we can describe as the 'old clubs' of Europe, instead it has only created an indelible difference between the Parisian team and their rivals, one that makes any projection of beautiful power virtually impossible.

Conclusion

While the QSI takeover of PSG has transformed an under-achieving football team into one of the most glamorous clubs in European football, one for whom silverware has become customary, the soft-power ambitions that motivated Qatar's purchase of the club have not enjoyed the same success. A number of significant obstacles have prevented PSG from becoming an effective mechanism to make the state more attractive to others, particularly the civil societies of the Cultural West. Due to a combination of World Cup controversies, accusations of financial irregularity, and the Parisian team's status as a state club, the required feelings of kindness, competence, and sameness that coalesce to generate soft power are often noticeably absent from the discourse surrounding PSG. Despite Qatar's best efforts, the QSI-owned PSG is consistently seen as a parvenu that has little regard for the pre-existing social hierarchies, practices, or ideals of European football. Are there hopes for change in the future? As time passes, the issues related to Qatar 2022 will decrease in relevancy to the common perception of PSG, while continued successes will normalise its status as a member of Europe's elite to newer generations of football fan. Furthermore, recent decisions to abandon the Galactico approach to player transfers (Crafton and Hay, 2022) in favour of a more cohesive team approach, thus bringing the club more into line with the practices of its rivals, should diminish the animosity shown to PSG by those who insist that its status as a state club gives the Parisians an unfair advantage. Whether these factors allow PSG's Qatari owners to be viewed in a more benevolent light in the years ahead remains to be seen. But they at least offer the chance of a reset in its soft power ambitions for the club.

References

Chanavat, N. and Desbordes, M. (2017). Towards a globalization of the brand Paris Saint-Germain. In N. Chanavat, M. Desbordes and N. Lorgnier (Eds.), *Routledge Handbook of Football Marketing* (pp. 217–250). New York: Routledge.

Crafton, A. (2023). 'Qatar and the truth about Tottenham, Manchester United, and Liverpool'. *The Athletic*. Available at: https://theathletic.com/4112890/2023/01/24/qatar-spurs-man-united-UUliverpool?source=user-shared-article [Accessed 18 September 2023].

Crafton, A. and Hay, A. (2022). 'PSG president: We don't want flashy, bling-bling anymore'. *The Athletic.*. Available at: ttps://theathletic.com/4175061/2022/06/21/psg-president-we-dont-want-flashy-bling-bling-anymore/ [Accessed 1 October 2023].

Edwards, D. (2022). 'PSG wear special rainbow flag numbering on shirts as Ligue 1 acknowledges International Day Against Homophobia'. *Goal*. 15 May. Available at: https://www.goal.com/en-qa/news/psg-wear-special-rainbow-flag-numbering-shirts-ligue-1-acknowledges-international-day-against-homophobia/blt042452ee633514f2 [Accessed 2 October 2023].

Elias, N. and Scotson, J. L. (1994). *The Established and the Outsiders*. London: Sage.

García, B. and Amara, M. (2013). Media perceptions of Arab investment in European football clubs: the cases of Málaga and Paris Saint-Germain. *Sport & EU Review*, *5*(1), 7–29.

Gibson, O. (2014). 'Why PSG and the World Cup will not be enough for football-hungry Qatar'. *The Guardian*, 3 April. Available at: https://www.theguardian.com/football/2014/apr/03/psg-world-cup-football-tv-rights-qatar [Accessed 3 October 2023].

Griffin, T. R. (2024). Identity matters: Qatar and Paris Saint-Germain. *Journal of Arabian Studies*, *13*(1), 73–90.

Koch, N. (2020). The geopolitics of Gulf Sport Sponsorship. *Sport, Ethics and Philosophy*, *14*(3), 355–376. https://doi.org/10.1080/17511321.2019.1669693

Nye, J. S. (2004). *Soft Power: The Means to Success in World Politics*. New York: Public Affairs.

PSG (2018). *About the Paris Saint-Germain Foundation*. Available at: https://en.psg.fr/teams/club/content/about-the-paris-saint-germain-foundation

PSG (2022). *Against racism and anti-Semitism, #Signalez*. Available at: https://en.psg.fr/teams/club/content/against-racism-and-anti-semitism-signalez-ligue-1-psg-paris-saint-germain [Accessed 15 October 2023].

Ronay, B. (2019). 'Sportswashing and the tangled web of Europe's biggest clubs'. *The Guardian*. Available at: 3Thttps://www.theguardian.com/football/2019/feb/15/sportswashing-europes-biggest-clubs-champions-league-owners-sponsors-uefa [Accessed 24 September 2023].

Sky News (2022). *World Cup: I am 'so proud' of Qatar, says Al-Khelaifi*8. Available at: https://www.youtube.com/watch?v=7E3namCXz00 [Accessed 3 November 2023].

Slater, M. (2022) 'La Liga vs Ligue 1 and the bitter war of words after Mbappe chose PSG over Real Madrid'. *The Athletic*. Available at: 3 3Thttps://theathletic.com/3332826/2022/05/31/psg-mbappe-la-liga-tebas/ [(Accessed 28 September 2023].

Vuving, A. (2019). The logic of attraction: outline of a theory of soft power. *SSRN*, 1–50. https://doi.org/10.2139/ssrn.3637662

White, A. (2022). 'PSG's latest Ligue 1 title feels empty, unsatisfying and unexciting'. *The Guardian*. Available at: https://www.theguardian.com/football/2022/apr/25/psg-latest-title-feels-empty-unsatisfying-unexciting [Accessed 24 September 2023].

White, A. and Devin, E. (2018). 'PSG are champions but their 'project' is under more pressure than ever'. *The Guardian*.. Available at: https://www.theguardian.com/football/2018/apr/16/psg-ligue-1-title-project-monaco [Accessed 15 October 2023].

19

ANALYZING UNSUCCESSFUL EXAMPLES OF GULF OWNERSHIP AND INVESTMENT IN EUROPEAN FOOTBALL

Kristian Coates Ulrichsen

Since the turn of the century, the Gulf States have become increasingly visible as investors, owners, sponsors, hosts, and participants in sports and sporting events around the world, including in football. The examples of Manchester City, under Abu Dhabi ownership since 2008, and Paris Saint-Germain, Qatari owned since 2011, as well as the more recent revival of Newcastle United since their takeover by a Saudi-led consortium in 2021, have fostered an impression that Gulf money invariably breeds success. High-profile sponsorship and stadium naming rights agreements with Gulf airlines has added to the association of regional brands with excellence and achievement. However, a review of Gulf (and Gulf-linked) engagements with European football teams over the past two decades uncovers more of a patchy record and offers some clarity on the ingredients that can determine likely outcomes of any such investment.

This chapter provides an overview of investments from the Gulf into European football that, for a variety of reasons, did not generate the returns, whether on or off the field, anticipated by owners or supporters. There are two sections to the chapter, which begins by exploring specific instances of Gulf-based investments which did fail to go as planned and ends by analyzing underlying and contingent factors that may contribute to an assessment of the range of results.

Initiatives Which Fall Short

Links between the Gulf States and European football go back five decades, although they accelerated significantly in scope, scale, and intensity in the 2000s. For many European football fans, the Gulf first appeared on the

DOI: 10.4324/9781003473671-22

horizon in 1977, when Don Revie left the England job to manage the UAE national team, earning himself a ten-year ban from the Football Association, later rescinded (Thani and Heenan, 2017, p. 1012). The following year saw Roberto Rivelino, the captain of Brazil and a World Cup winner in 1970, join Al-Hilal but plans to attract other stars, such as Zico, to Saudi Arabia fell through (Washington Post, 1978). In 1983, Gulf Air, then the carrier for Bahrain, Oman, Qatar, and the United Arab Emirates, became the first shirt sponsor of Chelsea, more than two decades before Emirates, Etihad, and Qatar Airways entered the game (Taylor et al., 2022, p. 368).

The acquisition of Manchester City by Abu Dhabi United Group, an entity controlled by Sheikh Mansour bin Zayed Al Nahyan, the Deputy Prime Minister of the UAE and a key member of the ruling family of Abu Dhabi, catapulted Gulf investment onto the football landscape in Europe (Financial Times, 2008). At around the same time, a trio of developments at other English clubs raised a series of issues around apparent shortcomings in due diligence and understanding of regional state-business relationships. Two of these cases unfolded simultaneously at Portsmouth and Notts County. In mid-2009, Suleiman Al-Fahim, an Emirati real estate developer and television personality, acquired Portsmouth, a heavily indebted Premier League club, from the Gaydamak family for an undisclosed sum. Described in British media as a 'property billionaire' and the 'Alan Sugar of Abu Dhabi' for his hosting of a Middle East reality show, Al-Fahim had risen to prominence in 2008 when he initially fronted the Abu Dhabi takeover at Manchester City before he was sidelined by the club's new ownership (Daily Mail, 2009; The Athletic, 2023).

Within weeks, it became apparent that Al-Fahim was struggling to secure the financing to service the club's debts, and in October 2009 90 percent of Portsmouth was acquired by Ali Al-Faraj, a Saudi businessperson. Media reporting suggested that Al-Faraj held 'a personal holding in billion-dollar petroleum giant SABIC,' the Saudi industrial giant (The Guardian, 2009), but he never attended a game and journalists who tried to flesh out his business career ran into dead ends (The Independent, 2009). In February 2010, Balram Chainrai, a Hong Kong businessperson who had loaned money to Al-Faraj to finance Portsmouth's costs, seized control of the club after Al-Faraj missed repayment deadlines (The Guardian, 2010a). The succession of owners and false promises, which culminated in Portsmouth entering administration, being deducted nine points, and getting relegated, led the Premier League to review and strengthen its Owners' and Directors' Test (Fox Sports, 2010). Years later, in 2018, Al-Fahim was sentenced (in absentia) to five years' imprisonment in Dubai after he was convicted of forging documents and misappropriating £5m from his wife to fund the purchase of Portsmouth (Arab News, 2018).

Founded in 1862, Notts County hold a claim to be the oldest professional football club in the world and were one of the 12 founder members of the

Football League in 1888. While the team narrowly missed out on the inaugural season of the Premier League, having been relegated from the old First Division in 1992, by 2009 they had fallen on hard times and were in League Two, the fourth tier of English football. In May 2009, the club was acquired by a 'Middle East-based consortium' which media reports linked to investors in Dubai and Qatar albeit through unfounded and later disproven claims (The National, 2009). It transpired eventually that the takeover was connected to a convicted fraudster based at the time in Bahrain and underwritten by a letter of guarantee of uncertain authenticity (These Football Times, 2016). While the new owners made headlines by appointing the former England manager, Sven-Goran Eriksson, as Director of Football and hiring Sol Campbell, a decorated former Arsenal and England defender, on a five-year contract, by the end of 2009 the financing had not materialized and the club was put up for sale, Campbell had left after playing one game, and Eriksson departed soon after (The Guardian, 2010b).

A different set of challenges confronted a third English club, the three-time First Division champions Leeds United who were, like Notts County, in a period of difficulty at the time of their takeover in 2012 by GFH Capital, a Dubai-based subsidiary of the Bahrain-headquartered Gulf Finance House (GFH). A prominent figure in the takeover and a lifelong Leeds supporter, David Haigh, became the managing director of Leeds, but amid a fracturing of business relationships in 2014 he was arrested in Dubai and accused of financial improprieties (The Guardian, 2015). Haigh's subsequent two-year ordeal, which included allegations of torture while in jail, came a month after GFH Capital sold 75 percent of Leeds to an Italian businessperson (Wall Street Journal, 2014). Ken Bates, the outspoken former chairman of Leeds who had sold the club to GFH, used characteristically blunt language as he described the ownership as 'totally untrustworthy, totally unreliable, and totally liars' in an interview with Yorkshire Radio (Arabian Business, 2014). Amid suggestions it had never possessed the capital to fund the club, GFH sold its remaining stake in Leeds in 2016 (Gulf Business, 2016) while Haigh established the legal advocacy group Detained International.

Underlying and Contextual Issues

The examples above illustrate a pattern of issues which raise questions about appropriate due diligence, on the side of existing owners selling clubs, and potentially opportunistic activity, on the part of individuals and entities who may have overplayed their credentials to get a seat at a perceived football 'gravy train.' Intermediaries of varying and questionable motivation may also have played a linking role connecting the two sides and seeking to capitalize on Western stereotypes of the Middle East that personal relationships and networks are the key to successfully doing business and concluding deals. Greek giants Panathinaikos of Athens were linked via intermediaries to at least two Saudi 'princes' in the early 2010s about whom there was much speculation but little hard fact. Such figures may have featured a decade later in another round of 'club hunting' including a possible bid for Newcastle United by Bin Zayed International which later tried unsuccessfully to acquire Derby County (The Athletic, 2020a). If, however, the intermediaries are credible and well connected, they can play a key role in making the right introductions, as was reportedly the case with the initial 'pitching' of Newcastle, a year after the Bin Zayed International talks, to the Public Investment Fund of Saudi Arabia in 2020 (Wall Street Journal, 2020). The role of British financier Amanda Staveley both at Manchester City around the time of the Abu Dhabi takeover in 2008 and later at Newcastle during the protracted Saudi-led acquisition in 2020-21 is also indicative of the importance of engaging with a suitable and appropriate interlocutor (Gulf States Newsletter, 2008, p. 15).

A separate challenge relates not to the intermediary or identity of the buying party, but to the positioning of the owner within the political (and state-business) landscape. This has been evident in the cases of several other Gulf-based acquisitions of European clubs which include members of ruling families, representatives of prominent merchant families, and officials close to the ruling elite. While each case is distinct, a theme which links them is that the owner did not have access to, or decision-making authority over, sovereign wealth or state-linked entities as seen in the Manchester City, PSG, and Newcastle cases.

In 2010, Malaga CF had narrowly avoided relegation from *La Liga* before the club was purchased by Sheikh Abdullah bin Nasser bin Abdullah Al Thani, a distant cousin of the Emir of Qatar and somewhat removed from the center of power in Doha. Performances on the field initially improved rapidly, to the extent that, in 2012, Malaga CF finished fourth in *La Liga* and qualified for the 2012–13 UEFA Champions League, where they were minutes away from reaching the semi-final before conceding two injury time goals against Borussia Dortmund. However, issues arising from the non-payment of debts and player wages led UEFA's Financial Control Committee to hand Malaga FC a two-year ban from European competition, later reduced to one year, which was upheld by the Court of Arbitration for Sport (El Pais, 2013). Relations between club and owner also soured as minority shareholders commenced legal action against Sheikh Abdullah which resulted in a court judgment in their favor in 2020 (Associated Press, 2020). As investment dried up and the club was placed in judicial administration, the team was relegated from La Liga in 2018 and, five years later, fell into the third tier of Spanish football for the first time since 1998 (Sur in English, 2023).

Twice winners of the European Cup during Brian Clough's spell as manager in the 1970s and 1980s, by 2012 Nottingham Forest had been outside the Premier League since 1999 and suffered the ignominy in 2005 of being the first former European champion to be demoted to their third domestic tier. Three members of the Al Hasawi family from Kuwait acquired Nottingham Forest in July 2012 after the club's previous owner died suddenly in February. Neither access to family wealth nor stewardship of Kuwait's most successful club, Qadsia SC, translated into success or stability during a five-year ownership which saw the team go through nine managers and finish in a lower position each year (The Athletic, 2020b). During this period, Nottingham Forest breached financial fair play regulations, fell behind on payments to clubs, agents, and suppliers, were placed under a transfer embargo, and ended up in a legal dispute with the Al Hasawi family over the terms of their eventual 2017 sale to Greek shipowner Evangelos Marinakis (Mayer Brown, 2020; Sky Sports, 2015).

Back in Spain, UD Almeria was a club which historically had played in the lower divisions but which spent six seasons in *La Liga* between 2007 and 2015. Four years later, with the team back in the second tier, the club was purchased by Turki Al Sheikh, chair of the General Entertainment Authority in Saudi Arabia and confidante of Crown Prince Mohammed bin Salman. Al Sheikh had spent a turbulent year in football in Egypt with a brief presidency of Al Ahly, which ended in supporter acrimony, followed by the presidency of Al Assiouty FC, which he moved 400 miles to Cairo and renamed Pyramids FC (Breaking the Lines, 2020). Under Al Sheikh's ownership, UD Almeria returned to La Liga in 2022, after seven years, but only narrowly avoided an immediate relegation back to the second division, and struggled thereafter. Their results on the pitch contrasted sharply with that of Girona FC, a club acquired in 2017 by City Football Group (CFG) which ended 2023 in second place in La Liga, behind only Real Madrid, with Almeria winless and bottom.

CFG, which is by far the most prominent and most successful example of multi-club ownership in contemporary football, is the extension of the Abu Dhabi-led project which has transformed Manchester City, albeit with additional investment from Chinese and American stakeholders. The lackluster performance of UD Almeria suggests that ownership by individuals close to centers of power, such as Turki Al Sheikh and his proximity to Mohammed bin Salman, is not in itself a sufficient guarantee of success. A similar trajectory may be seen in the case of Sheffield United and its ownership by Prince Abdullah bin Mosaad Al Saud, a much younger half-brother of the assassin who had shot and killed King Faisal in 1975. While the team rose from the third tier of English football to return to the Premier League in 2019 after a 12-year gap, the club failed to make a sustained challenge despite their owner's seniority within the Saudi sporting landscape which itself was on the cusp of transformative change.

The success stories of Gulf-based owners and investors in European football are more of an exception than the norm and illustrate the importance of being able to tap into and mobilize the weight of state-linked and sovereign resources that have led many critics to accuse them of 'sports-washing.' It is these 'other' examples of less successful involvement which can shed at least as much light on the range of factors whose presence, or absence, can help determine or predict outcomes in practice. Finally, it should not be supposed that the challenges and difficulties listed in this chapter are unique to the Gulf, as any review of the checkered record of Chinese and many American owners and investors, to say nothing of some of the other individuals linked to Derby County after the Bin Zayed bid fell through in 2022, reveals.

References

Arabian Business (2014). 'The Curious Case of David Haigh,' 31 October. https://www.arabianbusiness.com/politics-economics/the-curious-case-of-david-haigh-570059.

Arab News (2018). 'Ex-Portsmouth Owner Al-Fahim Jailed for Stealing £5m from Wife to Buy Club,' *Arab News,* 16 February. https://www.arabnews.com/node/1247246/sports.

Associated Press (2020). 'Court Suspends Qatari Owner of Spanish Club Malaga,' 20 February. https://apnews.com/article/ebb5080dd327f23fddb6691102c8f479.

Breaking the Lines (2020). 'Turki Al-Sheikh's Ill-Fated Involvement in Egyptian Football,' 19 June. https://breakingthelines.com/investigation-piece/turki-al-sheikhs-ill-fated-involvement-in-egyptian-football/.

Daily Mail (2009). 'Arab Billionaire Dubbed the Alan Sugar of Abu Dhabi Buys Portsmouth FC,' 28 May. https://www.dailymail.co.uk/news/article-1189159/Arab-billionaire-Sulaiman-Al-Fahim-dubbed-Alan-Sugar-Dubai-set-buy-Portsmouth.html.

El Pais (2013). 'Malaga Banned from Playing in Europe Next Season,' 11 June. https://english.elpais.com/elpais/2013/06/11/inenglish/1370965227_956594.html.

Financial Times (2008). 'Abu Dhabi Investors Buy Manchester City,' 1 September. https://www.ft.com/content/abf1a412-784f-11dd-acc3-0000779fd18c.

Fox Sports (2010). 'Premier League Introduces New Financial Rules,' 3 August. https://www.foxsports.com/stories/soccer/premier-league-introduces-new-financial-rules.

Gulf Business (2016). 'Bahrain's GFH Disposes of Remaining Leeds United Stake,' 15 September. https://gulfbusiness.com/bahrains-gfh-disposes-remaining-leeds-united-stake/.

Gulf States Newsletter (2008). 'Abu Dhabi Buyout of Manchester City FC Raises Questions of Ownership,' Vol. 32, No. 836, 12 September, 14–15.

Mayer Brown (2020). 'English Court of Appeal Considers Whether a Football Club was Entitled to Indemnity Payments Under an SPA,' 28 January. https://www.mayerbrown.com/en/perspectives-events/publications/2020/01/english-court-of-appeal-considers-whether-a-football-club-was-entitled-to-indemnity-payments-under-an-spa.

Sky Sports (2015). 'Sky Bet Championship: Nottingham Forest Vow to Make Outstanding Payments,' 4 February. https://www.skysports.com/football/news/11688/9699283/forest-to-make-outstanding-payments.

Sur in English (2023). 'Malaga CF Administrator Shoulders the Blame for 'Disastrous' Season but Does Little to Appease Fans,' 26 May. https://www.surinenglish.com/sport/malagacf/administrator-shoulders-the-blame-for-disastrous-season-20230526132440-nt.html.

Taylor, T., Burdsey, D. and Jarvis, N. (2022). A critical review on sport and the Arabian Peninsula – the current state of play and future directions. *International Journal of Sport Policy and Politics, 15*(2), 367–383.

Thani, S. and Heenan, T. (2017). The ball May be round but football is becoming increasingly Arabic: oil money and the rise of the new football order. *Soccer & Society*, *18*(7), 1012–1026.

The Athletic (2020a). 'Derby Takeover Doubts Grow Over Legal Bills,' 15 December. https://theathletic.com/2260813/2020/12/15/derby-takeover-sheikh-khaled/?source=emp-shared-article.

The Athletic (2020b). ''Like Having a Teenager Owning a Football Club': Fawaz Al Hasawi at Forest,' 31 May. https://theathletic.com/1845313/2020/06/01/fawaz-al-hasawi-nottingham-forest-pearce-davies-cotterill-freedman/.

The Athletic (2023). 'Manchester City and Abu Dhabi: Triumphant Passion Project or Geopolitical Powerplay?', 8 June. https://theathletic.com/4592794/2023/06/09/manchester-city-and-abu-dhabi/.

The Guardian (2009). 'Saudi Tycoon in Shock Portsmouth Takeover,' 4 October. https://www.theguardian.com/football/2009/oct/04/portsmouth-sulaiman-al-fahim-ali-alfaraj.

The Guardian (2010a). 'Balram Chainrai Becomes Portsmouth's Fourth Owner in a Year,' 4 February. https://www.theguardian.com/football/2010/feb/03/balram-chainrai-portsmouth-owner.

The Guardian (2010b). 'Sven-Goran Eriksson Leaves Notts County After Takeover,' 11 February. https://www.theguardian.com/football/2010/feb/11/sven-goran-erikkson-notts-county.

The Guardian (2015). 'How Prospective Leeds Buyer Ended Up in Dubai Prison over Fraud Allegations,' 4 February. https://www.theguardian.com/football/2015/feb/04/leeds-united-david-haigh-dubai-prison-fraud-allegations.

The Independent (2009). 'On the Trail of Portsmouth's Elusive Saviour,' 6 October. https://www.independent.co.uk/sport/football/news/on-the-trail-of-portsmouth-s-elusive-saviour-1798219.html.

The National (2009). 'The Curious Case of Notts County,' 29 July. https://www.thenationalnews.com/sport/the-curious-case-of-notts-county-1.486086.

These Football Times (2016). 'Notts County and the Bizarre Takeover of 2009,' 13 April. https://thesefootballtimes.co/2016/04/13/notts-county-and-the-bizarre-takeover-of-2009/.

Wall Street Journal (2014). 'Bahrain's GFH in Legal Spat with Ex-Leeds United Director David Haigh,' 12 June. https://www.wsj.com/articles/BL-250B-1715.

Wall Street Journal (2020). 'How a Reality-TV Producer Became Rainmaker to $300 Billion Saudi Fund,' 10 February. https://www.wsj.com/articles/how-a-reality-tv-producer-became-rainmaker-to-300-billion-saudi-fund-11581380021.

Washington Post (1978). 'Saudis Hook Rivelino, Eye Other Brazilian Stars,' 20 August. https://www.washingtonpost.com/archive/sports/1978/08/20/saudis-hook-rivelino-eye-other-brazilian-stars/3ddcf822-e287-4c15-84f5-eb5312ee55d0/.

20

RED BULL'S INVESTMENT IN GERMAN FOOTBALL

A Game Changer for the Bundesliga?

Daniel Ziesche

RasenBallsport Leipzig (RB Leipzig) polarizes. Opposing supporters denounce as morally wrong, as a plastic product and as the club that "destroys their sport". To others, it is perceived to bring more competitive balance to the monotonous Bundesliga, to reflect wider developments in one of the few thriving regions in Eastern Germany and to bring this part of the nation back on the map of top-class German football and challenge the dominance of clubs from the West (Machowecz, 2017; Ruf, 2009). From a structural viewpoint, its undemocratic practices are criticized, the lack of supporter involvement and the active disregarding of what is usually common practice in Germany's football system are a common point of critique. Yet again, others highlight the skilful bending of rules and point to the fact that money is pumped into other clubs as well. Still, issues of legitimization surrounded the club from the very day of its existence. Even over a decade after its incursion, clubs are still forced by their supporters to cancel test matches against the club; opposing fans credit the club with anger and open hate before, during and after matches (Bresemann and Duttler, 2017; Germann, 2013).

Yet, to football researchers outside of Germany and especially in the UK, RB Leipzig and its internal structure might not seem to be something worth of an extended investigation. However, within the German framework of league statutes and demands made to the internal structure of football clubs to be allowed to take part in the league competition (Wilkesmann and Blutner, 2002), RB Leipzig with its semi-corporate structure might well be the forefront of what could well turn out to be a turning point for the future of the German football system and its operating principles. Within the limited scope of this contribution, I will outline three potential game-changing dimensions, with regard to (1) the league's competitive balance, (2) the inner-league, club

DOI: 10.4324/9781003473671-23

structural alignment and (3) the legitimacy of the governing bodies in German football. The research covers the timespan from the foundation in May 2009 to the end of the 2022/23 season.

From Not So Humble Beginnings: The Birth of a Football Star

First of all, it is thus noteworthy that, different from other examples in Red Bull's football endeavours, e.g. in Austria or the USA, its German football branch did not start with taking over and rebranding a club but by founding a new one. Though, in taking clever steps in this process, the company literally skipped a few classes. Still, strategically, Red Bull had envisaged investing in a club in Eastern Germany as this former German Democratic Republic (GDR) territory lacked any noteworthy competitive team which can hold itself for a longer time in the top tier of German football. Furthermore, Red Bull did not intend for its team to start at the very bottom of the league pyramid – as a newly formed club would have to. After fan scenes at the larger traditional clubs reacted quite hostile to the planned engagement, Red Bull was forced to widen their search into the leagues below and found a suitable candidate in *SSV Markranstädt 05*. The team, based in a small town in the outer areas of Leipzig, had just freshly promoted to the fifth tier of the league pyramid, was willing to sell its starting licence for the new league to Red Bull and to re-establish itself at the bottom of the pyramid system. The proximity to Leipzig, a metropole with more than half a million inhabitants, a rich football culture but with its traditional clubs in ruins and an empty, newly built stadium was a key factor in this decision. Thus, in May 2009 Red Bull founded a new club, *RasenBallsport Leipzig*, which bought the starting licence for the fifth tier 2009/10 season from *SSV Markranstädt 05* and took over its first squad.

In their first season, the club directly promoted from fifth to fourth level and with the beginning of the next season, RB Leipzig relocated from Markranstädt to Leipzig and played henceforth in the Zentralstadion, which was shortly after renamed into Red Bull Arena. The Leipzig project turned out to be working out well, so that in May 2010 then Red Bull owner Dietrich Mateschitz announced a change in strategy and switched the focus of Red Bull's aspirations in European football from Red Bull Salzburg to RB Leipzig, making the former a de facto supply club in player talent for the latter (Fritz, 2015; Heßbrügge, 2016). After progress had been delayed by three consecutive seasons in the fourth level, Red Bull was able to fulfil its proclaimed plan of pushing RB Leipzig to the top of the German league pyramid by 2016 and qualify for Champions League tournament in their first season, as the Union of European Football Associations (UEFA) allowed the club to enter its competitions even though a second Red Bull backed club, *Red Bull Salzburg*, was also taking part (Smith, 2017).

Right from the start, announced investments in the total sum of 100 Million Euro over the course of seven years to reach this goal, exclusive of a 35 Million Euro investment for training and youth academy facilities (finished in 2015), made clear that Red Bull intends to stay and that RB Leipzig is a long-term investment for the company (Kroemer, 2015). The club based its sportive development on young talents and while the club's ability to pay much higher salaries than their rivals in the lower leagues certainly helped its ascent, it is noteworthy that it did rely on stars from other clubs but pursued the strategy of creating its own pool of top players. Certainly, though, the inner-Red Bull global networks aided that course significantly.

RB's ascent through the leagues altered the competitive balance in the lower leagues dramatically, and even at the top it is presenting one of the strongest contenders to challenge Bayern Munich for the title as it finished outside the top four only once in now seven 1st Bundesliga seasons and made runner-up twice. However, the club mostly intensifies competition especially among the runner ups, as the two-time cup winners have not yet managed to win the league, the title went to Bayern Munich in each of the seasons since RB's ascent to the 1st Bundesliga. In three out of 19 matches, RB was able to beat the club from Munich whose dominance remains unbroken and who celebrated the 11th consecutive title at the end of the 2022/23 season – the closest challengers were indeed old-time rivals Borussia Dortmund who managed to have the championship being taken from them on the last match day in 2023. With regard to the competition between the runner-ups, it could be argued that RB made matters worse for the Bundesliga. The club made it into the CL tournament in six out of seven seasons, thereby increasing competition for international qualification, which is what the clubs besides Bayern Munich strive for in German football. Given the stream of investment guaranteed by Red Bull, the club takes away revenue from international competition from clubs where this revenue is direly needed. On a very formal level, it could be argued that all that should not have happened. In the following, the club's structure and its conformity with the German football system will be scrutinized.

The Peculiarity of RB Leipzig: Structural Issues

According to its statutes, all members in the German football association, the *Deutsche Fußballbund* (DFB), have to be non-profit, charitable membership associations. As this model proved to be somewhat limiting to investor involvement it is possible for clubs to separate capital companies which operate on behalf of the membership association. Crucially, though, it is required that 50+1 of the votes in the capital company are owned by the membership association, theoretically barring investors from gaining a majority in votes and thereby full control of the club. This limitation does not extend to the majority in shares in the capital company. This is the heart and soul of the 50+1 rule which seen either as a protective mechanism against investor takeovers and thus nothing short of what keeps the heart and soul of football intact (Evans, 2013), or, it is criticized as unjust and impairing freedom of competition in an increasingly European football market (Lopatta et al., 2014). The issue for the integrity of the German game is (and was) that in 2009, there were already two exemptions to that rule: VfL Wolfsburg and Bayer 04 Leverkusen, the so-called *Werksvereine*. In both clubs, the companies of Volkswagen and Bayer have a majority in votes, respectively. The rule, which came to be known as "Lex Leverkusen", allowed bot clubs to stay in the competition. Further, in 2015, an exemption to the standing rules was added, as the *Deutsche Fußball Liga*, the daughter association of the DFB with its own capital company tasked with the operating business in the two *Bundesligas*, expanded the right to achieve a majority in votes to legal entities that sponsored the club considerably and without interruption for more than 20 years. The exemption needs to be applied for and granted by the German League Association (DFL) and the DFB (DFL, 2023, §8 (2); DFB, 2023, §16c).

Interestingly, the equally loathed and admired 50+1 rule itself is *not* the issue with RB Leipzig, but the basic principle of the membership association. The idea of the 50+1 rule demands that the member association is the owner of the majority of votes (50% plus one vote) within the assembly of stockholders in the capital company (DFL, 2023: §8 (3)). The club basically consists of its members whose interests the club represents and in whose interest the club (in an ideal scenario) acts. So, for the rule to effectively work (or to work at all) there needs to be a critical mass of members which are involved in elections and crucial decisions – as is a common practice in members' associations of all kinds all over Germany. In its statutes from 2009, RB differentiates between executive membership and full membership. Only the latter allows for active and passive voting rights. Executive members are those who participate actively in the sporting activities of the club, except the club's employees. At the time of founding, RB had 7 and in early 2014 11 full members. By 2023 this number has grown to 21 members, all of whom were in some way directly or indirectly connected to Red Bull. To set this number in relation: membership numbers of clubs in the top four tiers of the league pyramid are usually at least four-figured, most 1st Bundesliga clubs have six-figure membership numbers (Ziesche, 2017). In comparison to other members' associations in German football, the obstacles of becoming a full member at RB Leipzig have always been exceptionally high. The full membership fee is 800€ annually, exclusive of a one-time admission charge of 100€. By the club's statutes, the board is allowed to take six months for the decision over acceptance or non-acceptance of membership applications and can deny them without stating any reasons. By the time of the foundation of the club, RB Leipzig had seven full members – which is exactly the minimum amount required for founding a membership association in Germany. The obvious problems with regard to the close attachment of RB's executive board members (i.e. club members) to the company Red Bull raised the issue of a violation of the 50+1 rule. Back then, the club (rightly) dismissed these accusations by referring to its structure which was set up as an ordinary members' association with no separated structures which made the regulatory demands of the 50+1 rule not applicable. Yet, RB Leipzig's structural set-up could have – if at all – only be justified in the form of separated structures and applying for an exemption in the likes of Wolfsburg and Leverkusen (which likely would have failed). Yet, as RB did not have any separated structures it in fact violated the German law of associations as it was (and is) a closed club with two handfuls of members who steer the club in the interest of the company Red Bull.

Impact on the Legitimacy of the Governing Bodies

Seemingly, the DFL did not give RB an easy time when it came to granting the license once the club ascended to the 2nd Bundesliga, stating the club's membership admittance and company-like emblem as main issues. After a three-week stand-off, some sabre-rattling and RB's then owner Matteschitz's threats to withdraw from German football, the license was granted. On the one hand, the DFL certainly sought the avoid a legal battle over its statutes, which were then and possibly are still everything but watertight. On the other hand, RB made a move into the direction of the DFL and, as the head of the licensing committee announced, by a "binding statement to fill its bodies with predominantly independent members and to change the current emblem according to the requirements of the UEFA, the club has fulfilled the essential preconditions for participation in the gaming operations by consensus" (Harald Strutz, quoted in *Frankfurter Allgemeine Zeitung*, May 15, 2014). The initial demand of changing the membership admittance issue was left out of the agreement. As for the "binding statements" made by RB with regard to the recruitment of the executive board it remains questionable if and in how far a predominantly independent board will become a reality. With regard to the membership issue, RB introduced "supporting members" in the early months of the 2014/15 season as a new way to financially support the youth teams of the club. The possible fees vary from 70 to 1.000 Euro annually and include different presents or rewards; a right to vote is not part of them.

Halfway into its first 2nd Bundesliga season, on 2 December 2014, RB Leipzig had separated its professional football team and all teams down to the under-16-squad into a GmbH, the German equivalent to an LLC, thus following the example of other football clubs as described above. The decision is crucial: prior to the separation, RB Leipzig could claim not to violate the 50+1 rule as it was still a plain members' association with no separated capital company which means the rule could not be applied – though de facto, no members were allowed on a free and voluntary basis. Now, authorities will have a closer look in how far the majority in votes is really held by the members' association and not by the sponsoring company Red Bull. The comments on this step deemed the outer appearance of the club to be the main reason behind this decision. A larger involvement of investors (regardless of their actual financial contribution as money is clearly already abundantly available) might present the club in a more favourable (as in: more normal) light. With their local partners in Audi and Porsche RB Leipzig had already potent sponsors; yet, of course, they are not actually needed or wanted for shareholder participation – Red Bull owns 99% of RB Leipzig's capital company.

The promotion to the 1st Bundesliga for the 2016/17 season was equally carried out without any hindering on behalf of the league and football authorities (SID, 2016). However, the capital company forces the club to lay aside its restrictive communication policy and make parts of its finances publicly available. It has thus turned out that in 2015 RB Leipzig achieved a turnover more than two and a half times larger than the average turnover of its competitors in the 2nd Bundesliga. Furthermore, the sum of investments by Red Bull (52.3 Million Euro) is not listed as sponsor donations but have been designated as loans, which means that RB – at least theoretically – will have to pay the sums back (Kroemer, 2015).

The internal structure of the club also differs significantly from ordinary members' association's structures. RB consists of three organs, the (full) members' general assembly, the Honorary Council and the Executive Board. As RB does not accept any full members and fans are not part of what the club calls "executive members", fans only have the chance to register official fan clubs. Needless to say, this does not involve any rights with regard to participation in the general assembly let alone voting rights. Instead, new official fan clubs are presented in the stadium TV prior to home games and receive a printed truck tarpaulin banner for the fan club's representation in the stadium. By mid-2014, RB hosted 11 registered fan clubs which enjoy "advantages, for example with regard to ticket purchasing", by December 2023 there are 68 of these clubs. These "sham-memberships" as I have called them elsewhere (Ziesche, 2020, p. 42) are exact copies of the memberships available at Premier League clubs and comparable to an alleviated customer-status and leagues away from what German football authorities conceive under membership. However, excluded from the decision-making process, fans have organized themselves since 2013 in an umbrella association for the (official and non-official) fan clubs, the *Fanverband Leipzig*. With accession to the 2nd Bundesliga and the licensing issues, a compromise was worked out that required RB to allow for supporting memberships that cost between 70 and 1000€ annually and grant price reductions. Also, supporting members are allowed to the club's annual assemblies but are neither given active or passive voting rights. In March 2023, the club had 940 supporting members.

Given the comparably easy path with four football and league associations involved at different levels which had to accept RB Leipzig as to be in accordance with their statutes and granting the license to play, there is no reason that the blueprint which the club delivered should not be taken up by copycats to follow suit. Granted, it might take longer than elsewhere, but the prospect of participating in one of the top five football leagues in the world is surely worth the wait. To supporters, RB Leipzig is the epitome of the league and football associations' untrustworthiness (ranging from the Saxon football association up to UEFA), yet, in recent years they have provided enough fodder to undermine their legitimacy, apart from Red Bull's German football project.

Conclusion – The Sky Is the Limit?

After now 14 years of existence, it has to be stated that a normalization process has set in after an initial time of upheaval and opposition to RB Leipzig, mostly in the years after its inauguration and most widely during and after its ascent to the 1st Bundesliga. It is quite noteworthy that RB's huge funding and the consequences for the competitive balance in the leagues is neither among fans nor in the media a recurring topic any more. Investor involvement is a common practice at many clubs in the two *Bundesligas* and the latest events around the opening of the DFL for investors have taken the debate to a different level (Nahar and Bark, 2023).

Apart from the more ideational struggles among fans and football followers, there are very tangible issues regarding the conformity of the club structures with the demands made at different levels of the football pyramid. As a consequence of struggles between investors and clubs and the DFL/DFB as well as the symbol of RB Leipzig, the DFL and the German antitrust office sought to make the 50+1 rule juridically watertight and create a solid footing without pulverizing the existent exemptions, a process that took years and came to an end in early 2023. Ironically, while the Federal Cartel Office attested that the 50+1 rule was indeed anticompetitive, it considered it to be justified with regard to its sport-political purpose. The main complaint by the BKA (Federal Cartel Office) lay in fact with the existent exemptions of the *Werksvereine* (Leverkusen and Wolfsburg) as well as, since 2015 and until 2023, Hoffenheim. While RB Leipzig pops up here and there within the discussion, it is not mentioned within the compromise as it is technically not an exemption to 50+1, since the Verein has the majority in votes. The issue here is of a different nature: the Verein is a de facto exclusive club and not an open members association and a "resourceful interpretation of the law of associations", as the chief of the antitrust office once attested (qtd. in Hofmann, 2023).

This issue used to play a larger role in both fan and media discourses in the first years of the club especially but is now – if at all – rather indirectly addressed. Much more, nowadays, RB Leipzig has become the battleground about the interpretational sovereignty of tradition and football culture. Over the years, the RB Leipzig issue has grown from a regional into a national debate and, since the 2017/18 season, it is European in scale. At this level, issues that go beyond the internal, immediate club-structural kind move into focus. The ramifications of Red Bull's international football endeavours for the transfer-market as well as the effectiveness of punishments by the authorities will likely continue to fuel interest from all areas of football studies. Regarding anti-trust issues, it will be interesting to see how far Red Bull's football enterprise will be under scrutiny in future years as it might potentially use its company-owned, global network of clubs to circumvent rulings by UEFA or the DFB with regard to player transfers, something that has already happened in 2014 when RB Leipzig bought Sabitzer from Rapid Wien and then borrowed him to RB Salzburg as his contract only allowed a sale into a foreign country. This example shows what might be possible, if, say RB was ever to face a transfer ban similar to the likes of FC Barcelona or Real Madrid. Yet, at this level again, the money that Red Bull pumps into the sport might be regarded as a mitigating factor.

References

Bresemann, Patrick and Duttler, Gabriel (2017). Kritik an RasenBallsport Leipzig. Marketing contra tradition? In A. Schneider et al. (Eds.), *Fanverhalten im Sport* (pp. 137–158). Wiesbaden: Springer VS.

DFB (2023). Satzung und Geschäftsordnung. DFB/DFL Grundlagenvertrag, 1 October 2023. Available at: https://www.dfb.de/fileadmin/_dfbdam/293025-grundlagenvertrag.pdf [Accessed 27 December 2023].

DFL (2023). Satzung Deutsche Fußball Liga e.V., 10 October 2023. Available at: https://media.dfl.de/sites/2/2023/10/Satzung-des-DFL-Deutsche-Fussball-Liga-e.V.-Stand-10.10.2023.pdf [Accessed 27 December 2023].

Evans, Steven (2013). German football model is a league apart. *BBC*, 24 May 2013. Available at: https://www.bbc.com/news/business-22625160 [Accessed 27 December 2023].

Fritz, Thomas (2015). Wenn Red-Bull-Fans 'Scheiß RB Leipzig' singen. *Zeit Online*, 27 June 2015. Available at: https://www.zeit.de/sport/2015-06/rb-leipzig-salzburg-spielerwechsel [Accessed 27 December 2023].

Germann, Carsten (2013). Red Bull greift die Bundesliga an. *Handelsblatt*, 27 July 2013.

Heßbrügge, Rolf (2016). Farmteam für Leipzig. *11 Freunde*, 2 September 2016. Available at: https://11freunde.de/artikel/farmteam-f%C3%BCr-leipzig/512942 [Accessed 27 December 2023].

Hofmann, Benni (2023). DFL verschiebt 50+1-Abstimmung erneut, *Kicker*, 29 November 2023. Available at: https://www.kicker.de/dfl-verschiebt-501-abstimmung-erneut-981677/artikel [Accessed 27 December 2023]

Kroemer, Ullrich (2015). Wirtschaftsfaktor Red Bull: RB Leipzig spült Millionen in Leipzigs Kassen, *Mitteldeutsche Zeitung*, 6 August 2015. Available at: https://www.mz.de/sport/fussball/wirtschaftsfaktor-red-bull-rb-leipzig-spult-millionen-in-leipzigs-kassen-3075678 [Accessed 27 December 2023].

Lopatta, Kerstin, Buchholz, Frerich, and Storz, Benjamin (2014). Die '50+1'-Regelung im deutschen Profifußball – Ein Reformvorschlag auf Basis Eines Vergleichs der europäischen Top 5 Fußballligen/'50+1-rule' in German football – a reform proposal based a comparison of the European Big 5 football leagues. *Sport und Gesellschaft/Sport and Society*, *11*(1), 3–33.

Machowecz, Martin (2017). Leipzigs Fußball klappt nur, wenn alle dran glauben. *Zeit Online*, 31 March 2017. Available at: https://www.zeit.de/sport/2017-03/rb-leipzig-krise-analyse [Accessed 27 December 2023].

Nahar, Chaled and Bark, Marcus (2023). Investor steigt ein: Eine Milliarde Euro – was die DFL mit dem Geld plant. *Tagesschau.de*, 11 December 2023. Available at: https://www.sportschau.de/fussball/bundesliga/dfl-investor-einstieg-zukunft-konsequenzen-plaene-100.html.

Ruf, Christoph (2009). Red Bull in Leipzig: 'Wir würden selbst den Teufel mit offenen Armen empfangen'. *Spiegel Online*, 17 September 2009. Available at: http://www.spiegel.de/sport/fussball/red-bull-in-leipzig-wir-wuerden-selbst-den-teufel-mit-offenen-armen-empfangen-a-630820.html [Accessed 27 December 2023].

SID (2016). DFL: Keine Lizenzverweigerung – Bedingungen und Auflagen für einige Klubs. *Zeit Online*, 18 April 2016. Available at: https://www.zeit.de/news/2016-04/18/fussball-dfl-keine-lizenzverweigerung---bedingungen-und-auflagen-fuer-einige-klubs-18180407 [Accessed 27 December 2023].

Smith, Rory (2017). UEFA Approves Entry of 2 Red Bull-Branded Teams in Champions League. *The New York Times*, 20 June 2017. Available at: https://nyti.ms/2tKKCLl [Accessed 27 December 2023].

Wilkesmann, Uwe and Blutner, Doris (2002). Going public: the organizational restructuring of German football clubs. *Soccer and Society*, *3*(2), 19–37.

Ziesche, Daniel (2017). Well governed? Fan representation in German professional football clubs. In B. Garciá and J. Zheng (Eds.), *Football and Supporter Activism in Europe. Whose Game Is It?* (pp. 89–120). Cham: Palgrave Macmillan.

Ziesche, Daniel (2020). *Lower League Football in Crisis. Issues of Organisation and Legitimacy in England and Germany*. Cham: Palgrave Macmillan.

21

GLOBAL INVESTMENT AND CULTURAL TRADITIONS

Raymond Boyle and Richard Haynes

Introduction

Professional football in Europe is a highly commercialized and mediatized sport, which through television and social media networks has become both a media 'product' and part of a global entertainment industry. Conversely, football and football fandom have deep cultural roots in communities and families, which provide important social networks built on cultural traditions, values, and practices often placed in conflict with, and at risk by, global commercial interests. This chapter aims to investigate the social and ethical questions raised by the changing nature of professional football club ownership and commercial interests on the long-established cultural heritage of such clubs, their supporters, and values. It also seeks to set out an agenda for future research in this area of growing political and economic importance.

Football, Cultural Heritage, and Ownership

Football clubs are cultural institutions that have historically played an important role in the civic identities of towns, cities, and regions, as well as supporting local and national economies (Ginesta and San Eugenio, 2022). The place-based value of football club heritage in many communities is both highly significant and contested. Football's cultural heritage is based on topophilia of football grounds (the emotional attachment to place), the material heritage of club shirts, emblems, trophies, and popular cultural ephemera (Bale, 1996). It is also based on the intangible heritage of individual and collective memory of players, clubs, specific matches and competitions, the stories, songs and invention of traditions associated with clubs, and the cultural

DOI: 10.4324/9781003473671-24

and affective ties and values associated with identification of being a fan increasingly expressed through social media.

We also know that football is a media-related international business, even if also a particular cultural form deeply rooted in local, regional, and national traditions and identities (Gibbons, 2014; Goldblatt, 2007; Guilianotti and Robertson, 2009). Clubs are cultural institutions often playing an important role in the civic identity of cities and regions as well as being important financial players in city and national economies (Conn, 2005). In an era of globalization, sport, and football specifically, driven by television, has become a cultural form closely aligned with soft power and influence (Brannagan and Giulianotti, 2015; Connell, 2018). Ownership of either an existing top club or the purchase and investment in a club in order to propel them into the elite of the English Premier League (EPL) offers influence and international exposure for individuals, corporate businesses, and even states.

Patterns of Ownership

For most of the twentieth century across the UK football industry, ownership of clubs was dominated by the private company with the limited liability model. This model saw the vast majority of professional football clubs using a legal and financial framework that saw them exist as private companies owned by shareholders. This ownership model often saw a club being run by a dominant shareholder (often a local businessman, and it was usually a man) who helped financially underwrite the club (and usually its losses) through their own financial means (Dobson and Goddard, 2001). Montague describes it as 'an ownership structure of old: local businessmen done good, investing in their clubs almost as an act of philanthropy rather than for profit or a short cut to fame and success' (Montague, 2017, p. 2). With slight regional variations this model of football club ownership, enshrined in the regulations of the English Football League, dominated the ownership structure of the industry in the two main footballing nations of the UK, England, and Scotland, until the 1980s.

Since the 1980s three differing models of ownership have emerged across the UK. The first is the *Stock Exchange model*, which sees clubs listed as public companies on the London Stock Exchange, the Alternative Investor Market (AIM) or the PLUS Market and trading the shares of the club's holding company through these various financial markets. In the UK the English club Tottenham Hotspur were the first to list on the London Stock Exchange in 1983 using this to raise over £3m in capital through its share issue (Morrow, 1999). Despite this, there was no great appetite among football clubs to move from private to public companies for the rest of the 1980s and it would be the creation of the FA EPL and the securing of live television coverage rights to the league by Sky Television in 1992 that would act as the catalyst for significant change (Mihir, 2012; Ridley, 2012). We would argue that what began as the

FA Premier League and became the EPL was the first football league in Europe to be created by the demands of television and Sky specifically.

As significant television money from the pay-TV market came into elite English football the 1990s saw a rise in clubs floating on the various public listing financial markets. By 2000, there were up to 22 English football clubs who had moved from being private companies to being public limited companies (PLC). Television companies, such as Sky and the cable network NTL, also bought equity in clubs with a view to exploiting the valuable media rights associated with football, a process which received regulatory interest in the UK and Europe, including the blocking of Sky's bid to have a controlling investment in Manchester United (Brown and Walsh, 1999). However, as Walters and Hamil (2010, p. 20) argue, 'enthusiasm for investing in football clubs was short lived. Even by late 1997, the majority of listed clubs recorded share prices were substantially lower than their initial public offering.' A combination of low institutional demand and smaller supporter shareholders buying into a club for sentimental, rather than financial, reasons meant that share trading in the football industry was significantly lower than other sectors of the economy.

Once it became clear to football clubs that the PLC model was one limited in the additional revenue it could raise many returned to private ownership. During the 2000s, as substantial television money flowed into the Premier League and to a lesser extent the English Championship 14 English clubs delisted from public ownership including Chelsea in 2003, Manchester United in 2005 and Manchester City in 2007. Today, only Arsenal FC, owned by Arsenal Holdings PLC of the elite English football clubs, is on the London Stock Exchange. Many such as Tottenham Hotspur operate a labyrinthine ownership structure that sees Enic International Limited, registered in the Bahamas (offshore tax haven), owning 85.55% of Spurs. Joe Lewis, resident in the Bahamas, has the controlling 70.6% ownership of Enic; trusts of which chairman Daniel Levy and family are the beneficiaries and own the other 29.41%. From 2004, football clubs in the UK saw the arrival of a new dominant model of ownership, model of private foreign investment and influence.

Foreign Ownership Model

In many ways the limited liability model of ownership that stretched back into the nineteenth century origins of the football industry in the UK, have helped to facilitate the rise in foreign ownership and investment that has transformed the ownership of elite clubs in the last decade or so. It allowed companies to borrow money, but individual owners not to be liable for any debts run up by the company. In keeping with the rest of the UK economy, it also made football clubs in the UK significantly easier to purchase than any other country in Europe and the scale of foreign investment in the English game for example is on a greater scale than any other football league in the world (Robinson and Clegg, 2019).

From 2003, Montague (2017) notes that foreign ownership of football clubs has in part its roots in the collapse of the Soviet Union and the rise of the wealthy Oligarch. Some owners bought EPL clubs as both a passion project and a leisure activity. Some foreign owners acted like absentee landlords, while for others it was a business investment and a chance to diversify from their North American franchise interests into the EPL, which had become by the late 2000s one of the most affluent football leagues in world football. It is important to recognize that this was not a new process in the English game. Steel magnet Jack Walker invested heavily in Blackburn Rovers who became EPL winners in 1995, and Egyptian and Harrods owner, Mohamed al Fayed, invested heavily (estimated at £200m) in Fulham, then in the third tier of the English game transforming them into an EPL club.

What has been significant has been the *scale, international connections* and *influence* that these new owners have brought. Manchester City, for example, were purchased by Sheikh Mansour bin Zayed al Nahyan of the Abu Dhabi royal family in 2008. By 2019, the parent company (City Football Group) of Manchester City now owns seven football clubs around the globe including New York City FC and Melbourne City FC and are actively seeking to add to its portfolio by buying a club in India.

By 2016, over three quarters of EPL clubs were under foreign ownership or had significant foreign investment. Interestingly the buying spree extended well down the football leagues. There are four distinct global areas seeking to investment in the football industry in the UK. They tend to involve individuals (1) who have created their wealth in eastern Europe and Russia; (2) or come from the north American sports franchise business tradition. You also have (3) the middle east oil rich states, and finally (4) the Asian wealthy with Malaysia and more recently China supplying wealthy individuals and businesses that have secured the ownership or made significant investments in clubs in the UK.

Montague (2017) argues that rather than nationality what really connects these investors is their extensive wealth and global investments of which owning a UK football club has become part of their portfolio of international assets. However, more recently nation-states have invested in football as a form of soft power to influence wider perceptions of their regime's global reputation (Skey, 2023). The Saudi consortium led by their Public Investment Fund (PIF) which bought Newcastle United in 2021 is the most high-profile evidence of an emerging process of wider global sport investment to 'cleanse' the image of regimes. The potential impact of such investment on supporters is discussed below.

Supporters Trust Model

There is however a third ownership model. This sees a club being owned by a supporter's trust. Walters and Hamil (2010, p. 23) argue that a supporters' trust is 'an independent, not-for-profit, democratic, cooperatively owned organisation that seeks to influence the governance of a football club through improved supporter representation and also to develop stronger links among a club, a community and a supporter base.' This model seeks to re-establish the bond between supporters and club and to reinforce the club's sense of identity and connection with local, regional, and national fan bases, rather than focus on the transient international supporter seeking to invest in a successful brand through media and commercial engagement. The different models of ownership of UK football clubs raise an important question for how significant these differences are for the clubs, supporters, and wider stakeholders.

Does Club Ownership Matter?

The influx of foreign investment into UK football began in a sustained manner back in 2003, and significant change took place at clubs such as Chelsea in 2003 bought by Russian oligarch Roman Abramovich, Manchester United in 2005 bought by the US-based Glazer family, Liverpool in 2007 sold to American businessmen and Manchester City purchased by Sheikh Mansour bin Zayed al Nahyan of the Abu Dhabi royal family in 2008. More recently (2023) ownership patterns of professional football clubs have become an increasingly public issue of concern. The sale of Newcastle United for £300m in 2021 by retail businessman Mike Astley to a consortium led by Saudi Arabia's PIF has been the most publicly controversial example to date of such investment in the EPL. The sale sparked national media and social media debate regarding the association of PIF to Saudi human rights abuses and the use of investment in the EPL to broaden Saudi influence in global sport culture. The sale created mixed reactions among supporters of the club. A minority group of supporters formed NUFC Against Sportswashing to campaign against the takeover on human rights grounds. However, initial analysis of fan social media forums suggests there has been a form of 'motivated ignorance' by many Newcastle fans to the wider human rights issue, whose identity is invested in the success of the team rather than the ownership of the club (Jones et al., 2023). The Newcastle experience emphasizes the complex and contradictory forces surrounding international club ownership for many fans, with social and ethical questions set aside for sporting success.

Journalist and writer Henry Winter (2019) has documented the litany of clubs, beyond the elite EPL that reside in the English Football League (EFL), including Blackpool, Blackburn Rovers, Bolton Wanderers, Charlton Athletic, Coventry and Port Vale that are in jeopardy of going out of existence due to the mismanagement of owners (both British and foreign). In so doing he highlights the growing public and political concern about the lack of safeguarding from the regulatory authorities of these important civic institutions and the grassroots community response of supporters keen to protect these important cultural institutions.

Governance Issues

In his overview of football and governance Garcia (2017, p. 107) has noted that 'Football and governance are two concepts that were hardly linked in the past.' The last decade has seen governance issue move more centre stage with a range of stakeholders across the sport. In England, historically, the Football Association (FA) has played catch-up on governance issues as the ownership models associated with football clubs have evolved. Tottenham Hotspur's 1983 flotation as a subsidiary part of a larger company allowed the club to side step legislation (the FA's Rule 34) that restricted the level of dividend payments to shareholders. By the late 1990s these had been dropped and replaced in 2004 by what is now called the Owners' and Directors' Test (often still called the Fit and Proper Persons Test) which barred individuals with fraud convictions or previous bankruptcies from taking over at a Club. The links between the on-field success of contemporary football clubs and their financial health has received greater focus over the past decade (Plumley et al., 2017). UEFA, the governing body of European club football, has introduced Financial Fair Play mechanisms in order to maintain competitive balance in both domestic and pan-European competitions. Moreover, such regulation also seeks to prevent the polarizing tendencies of club football brought about by increased television income, commercialization of club assets, and globalization of brands.

After well over a decade of various consultations, the UK government, through its Dept of Culture, Media, and Sport (DCMS), finally published its report into the sport and the need for an independent football regulator in England. On the issue of ownership, it frames supporters concerns around the *cultural* role of the clubs.

> The Review found that the financial distress we have seen at some of English football's most historic clubs was partly down to i) acquisition by owners unsuited to the custodianship of these important cultural assets and ii) the appointment of unsuitable directors without a proper, transparent appointment process or assessment of skills or qualifications.
>
> *(DCMS, 2023, p. 46)*

In Scotland, supporter involvement in football clubs has found provision in The Community Empowerment (Scotland) Act 2016, which secures rights to influence, govern, bid, and buy football clubs in Scotland. The Act reflects academic research on supporters as stakeholders, which has often been equated with significant sporting, social and financial rewards which follow such involvement (Porter, 2019).

However, UEFA's annual Club Licensing Benchmarking Report (UEFA, 2023) continues to reveal stark differences both across and within European

Leagues in terms of the economic health of football. The motivations for foreign investment in football clubs, and their impact on the finances of clubs, have had a particularly pronounced effect on the Premier League in England. England has a disproportionately higher percentage of foreign owners than any other European league. Among the top leagues the EPL has some key distinctive characteristics: it has the highest rate of growth (driven by TV income); it has the highest average gate receipts per fan; it has the highest average revenue from sponsorship; the aggregate revenue of EPL is nearly double that of that in Spain and Germany; they have significantly higher fixed asset ownership (stadia, training facilities) than any other league; they have the highest player values on the balance sheet, which is accompanied by the highest average wage (148 Euros), nearly double that of the Spanish league. All these indicators are factors in the increasing interest of foreign investors in English club football, and the financial impacts they are having on the infrastructure of clubs, their players, media and commercial partners, supporters and local economies.

The healthy financial benchmarks of top-flight British football do not extend to the vast majority of domestic clubs. Beyond the public announcements of financial buoyancy and success propounded by many British clubs, is a different story of fan exploitation, crippling debt and the constant threat of bankruptcy and administration (Kennedy and Kennedy, 2012). 'Soft debts' in football clubs have frequently turned in to 'hard debts' due to poor financial management and governance, precipitated by poor sporting performance, among other factors (Beech et al., 2010). Crucially, media coverage of financial crisis in football often focuses on the sporting and social consequences of failure, rather than its impact on clubs as small businesses. This is suggestive that governance and accountability in football stretches beyond financial management into the realm of society and culture.

However, Garcia and Welford (2015) urge caution and more research around the complex nature of the ways that supporters seek greater transparency and accountability around club ownership. They argue 'The increased attention football supporters are now receiving in the academic literature, away from the well-established body of work around football hooliganism, is a welcome avenue into learning more about this hugely popular social activity. Yet we are still a long way from understanding fandom. The way supporters engage with their clubs is changing; the internet and global markets are accentuating this, and whilst the cost of tickets continues to rise and the gap between the top and the bottom continues to grow, changes will continue. It is imperative that research works to capture these changes, to understand how fandom is evolving' (Garcia and Welford, 2015, p. 524). More nuanced investigations into the relationships between supporters and the governance of the football industry are therefore required to provide fuller insights on how broader transformations both within football (such as ownership structures and engagement with fans) and outside the game (such as television and sponsorship interests or social media and commodified fan cultures in football) are changing the nature of fandom.

Conclusion

The research into the impact of commercialization of football on the cultural heritage and civic value of football remains underdeveloped. The football industry uses the historical traditions and cultural heritage of clubs to sustain new forms of commodification, globalization, and transnational ownership. While clubs as commercial entities and brands have prospered, these imperatives are frequently in tension with the social capital of supporters with deep familial and community ties to these organizations. The international ownership of European clubs has raised questions about the use of football club ownership as a form of 'sportswashing': the laundering of poor international reputations for human rights and environmental abuses, through sport as a form of 'soft power.' A new football research agenda is emerging around a series of key questions including how the ownership structures of football clubs, both local and international, impact on the cultural integrity of clubs in terms of their value and significance to local civic culture and heritage. The need to explore the ethical questions raised by different club ownership models across Europe and beyond is clear. It is important to understand the inclusion and diversity of football supporter involvement in local clubs and the compromises supporters make to international business and commercial interests in their clubs. This includes identifying how football clubs adhere to particular UN Sustainable Development Goals (SDGs) such as reduced inequality, sustainable consumer practices, or promoting peaceful and inclusive societies. Finally, how do the tensions between global commercial interests and the promotion of SDG's impact on the social and cultural integrity of a football club's heritage? In the UK, there will be much for the proposed English football Regular to grapple with, should it ever be finally set up.

References

Bale, J. (1996). Space, place and body culture: Yi-Fu Tuan and a Geography of Sport. *Geografiska annaler. Series B, Human Geography, 78*(3), 163–171.

Beech, J., Horsman, S. J. L. and Magraw, J. (2010). Insolvency events among English football clubs. *International Journal of Sports Marketing & Sponsorship, 11*(3), 236–249.

Brannagan, P. M. and Giulianotti, R. (2015). Soft power and soft disempowerment: Quata, global sport and football's 2022Worls up finals. *Leisure Studies, 36*(4), 703–719.

Brown, A. and Walsh, A. (1999). *Not for sale: Manchester United, Murdoch and the Defeat of BSkyB.* Edinburgh: Mainstream.

Conn, D. (2005). *The Beautiful Game: Searching for the Soul of Football.* London: Yellow Jersey.

Connell, J. (2018). Globalisation, soft power and the rise of football in China. *Geographical Research*, *56*(1), 5–15.

DCMS (2023). *A Sustainable Future Reforming Club Football Governance*. London: OGL.

Dobson, S. and Goddard, J. (2001). *The Economics of Football*. Cambridge: Cambridge University Press.

Garcia, B. (2017). Football and governance. In J. Hughson et al (Ed.), *Routledge Handbook of Football Studies*. London: Routledge.

Garcia, B. and Welford, J. (2015). Supporters and football governance, from customers to stakeholders: a literature review and agenda for research. *Sport Management Review*, *18*(4), 517–528.

Gibbons, T. (2014). *English National Identity and Football Fan Culture*. London: Ashgate.

Ginesta, X. and San Eugenio, J. (2022). Football fans as place ambassadors: analyzing the interactions between Girona FC and its fan clubs after its purchase by City Football Group (CFG), *Soccer & Society*, *24*(2), 258–272. https://doi.org/10.1080/14660970.2022.2069752.

Goldblatt, D. (2007). *The Ball Is Round: A Global History of Football*. London: Penguin.

Guilianotti, R. and Robertson, R. (2009). *Globalization and Football*. London: Sage.

Jones, I., Adams, A. and Mayoh, J. (2023) Fan responses to ownership change in the English Premier League: motivated ignorance, social creativity, and social competition at Newcastle United F.C. *International Review for the Sociology of Sport* [Online]. https://journals.sagepub.com/doi/10.1177/10126902231179067.

Kennedy, P. and Kennedy, D. (2012). Football supporters and the commercialisation of football: comparative responses across Europe. *Soccer & Society*, *13*(3), 327–340.

Mihir, B. (2012). *Game Changer: How the English Premier League Came to Dominate the World*. Singapore: Marshall Cavandish.

Montague, J. (2017). *The Billionaires Club: The Unstoppable Rise of Football's Super-Rich*. London: Bloomsbury.

Morrow, S. (1999). *The New Business of Football: Accountability and Finance in Football*. Hampshire: MacMillan Business.

Plumley, D., Wilson, R. and Ramchandani, G. (2017). Towards a model for measuring the holistic performance of professional football clubs. *Soccer and Society*, *18*(1), 16–29.

Porter, C. (2019). *Supporter Ownership in English Football: Class, Culture and Politics*. London: Palgrave.

Ridley, I. (2012). *There's a Golden Sky: How Twenty Years of the Premier League Have Changed Football for Ever*. London: Bloomsbury.

Robinson, J. and Clegg, J. (2019). *The Club: How the Premier League Became the Richest, Most Disruptive Business in Sport*. London: John Murray.

Skey, M. (2023). Sportswashing: media headline or analytic concept? *International Review for the Sociology of Sport*, *58*(5), 749–764.

UEFA (2023). *The European Club Footballing Landscape: Club Licensing Benchmarking Report Financial Year 2022*. Nyon: UEFA.

Walters, G. and Hamil, S. (2010). Ownership and governance. In S. Hamil and S. Chadwick (Eds.), *Managing Football: An International Perspective*. Oxford: Butterworth-Heinemann.

Winter, H. (2019) FA has lost its moral compass over club ownership. It's time for change. *The Times*, 5 September, p. 63.

22

AN OVERVIEW OF THE UK GOVERNMENT'S FAN-LED REVIEW OF FOOTBALL GOVERNANCE

Mark Middling and Christina Philippou

Introduction

On 24 November 2021, the UK government published its "landmark" Fan-Led Review of Football Governance (FLR) (DCMS, 2021; MacInnes, 2022 para. 2). The review, and subsequent regulation, has widespread implications to the geopolitical economy of football, as it is the most significant regulation to date to be enacted by a nation state to curb issues such as overspending by clubs, self-interest of owners and increase the protection of fan interests. It remains to be seen how other nations respond – whether they follow suit or work to gain national advantage by allowing their clubs to be governed and spend in ways that English clubs now cannot. Thus, overregulation could see a reduction of English Premier League (EPL) global commercial dominance if clubs in other nations were to be able to benefit from outspending English clubs on playing talent – and so the benefits of regulation must be balanced against the commercial success of English Football.

The review made ten strategic recommendations (split into 47 detailed proposals) for improved governance within the sport. The most significant outcome was the introduction of an Independent Regulator of English Football (IREF) by an Act of Parliament (Philippou, 2023) to oversee the finances and governance of clubs from the EPL down to the National League (tiers 1–5) (DCMS, 2021).

The review is not the first UK government investigation into the finance and governance of English football. Previous reviews included the Football Task Force of 1997 (Brown, 1999), an All Party Parliamentary Football Group Report in 2009 (García and Welford, 2015), reports by the UK government's Department of Culture, Media and Sport (DCMS) in 2011 and 2013 (DCMS, 2011, 2013, found in García and Welford, 2015), an expert working group on

DOI: 10.4324/9781003473671-25

supporter ownership and engagement in 2014 (DCMS, 2014) and a DCMS review in the wake of the demise of Bury FC in 2019 (Dutton, 2019). However, where all these reviews made recommendations, they were not converted into regulation, while the FLR has formed the basis of football governance legislation in the UK (DCMS, 2023).

The FLR aggregated many fan and expert views on the need for improvement in running the game in the 21st century (Maguire et al., 2023). It marked a significant shift in the UK government's attitude of involving themselves in the national sport, a far throw from the anti-football attitude conveyed by the Thatcher government of the 1980s (King, 1997; Tempany, 2016). As such, it was accused of being a populist move by a populist government (Reddy, 2021; Samuel, 2021) using the FLR and its recommendations in an attempt to gain votes (Wearmouth, 2023).

Why Was There Need for a Fan-Led Review?

The FLR was initiated due to a sequence of high-profile governance failings in English football (DCMS, 2021). These failings led to both the government and the opposition proposing a football industry review in their 2019 manifestos (Conservative and Unionist Party, 2019; Labour, 2019), looking at club finances, governance, and regulation (Crouch, 2021).

The failings include the indirect incentivisation of financial risks. As a club moves up the leagues, its centrally distributed revenue from TV rights increases. As such clubs in the EPL earn well in excess of £100m per season, compared to an average in the Championship (England's second tier) of around £35m (Deloitte, 2023). This leads many clubs to "gamble" their long-term future in a short-term attempt to achieve sporting and perceived financial success (Evans et al., 2022, Plumley et al., 2019). This is particularly significant in the Championship where clubs routinely spend more on their wages than they earn in total revenue (Philippou and Maguire, 2022). Solberg and Haugen (2010) found that clubs pursue this strategy or else face relegation as, if other clubs are willing to outspend them, it will be those clubs that attract the best talent and thus enjoy better on-pitch performances. However, Maguire and Philippou (2023) found that the majority of EPL teams also make a financial loss, which demonstrates that the strategy of spending one's way to the EPL may be flawed from a financial perspective.

Despite football's resilience to economic shocks compared to most industries (Cox and Philippou, 2022), the Covid-19 pandemic resulted in financial concerns (Alabi and Urquhart, 2023) as clubs were unable to welcome supporters through their gates (the main source of income for most clubs outside the EPL) thus highlighting the pre-existing financial frailty at many clubs prior to the pandemic (Philippou and Maguire, 2022). Many clubs are reported to have survived the pandemic due mainly to government and industry funding

(DCMS, 2021; Maguire, 2022) made in part due to English football's geopolitical importance.

Indeed, the FLR was triggered by the demise of Bury FC who were excluded from the football league in August 2019 after financial mismanagement (Halliday, 2019). Although the consequences for Bury were severe, their financial woes were not an isolated case. Other recent examples include Derby County FC who were relegated following a mandatory points deduction resulting from the club going into administration (BBC Sport, 2021a; Maguire et al., 2021), Macclesfield Town FC who went into liquidation in 2020 (Ducker, 2020), Bolton Wanders FC who went into administration in 2019 (BBC Sport, 2021a; Ducker, 2019), Reading FC who were relegated in 2023 due to successive points deductions for financial mis-management (Fisher, 2021), and Southend United FC who suffered multiple relegations and have struggled to pay their tax bills (Moore and Baugh, 2023).

Then came the proposed European Super League (ESL) which was a catalyst for the UK government to accelerate the FLR (DCMS, 2021). Here, England's "big six" clubs were to join another six elite clubs from across Europe to take part in a new closed league. However, the ESL was quickly abandoned, not due to the football authorities but because of immense fan and media pressure (Hamilton, 2021).

Thus, the ability of existing football bodies to govern the game has been questioned (DCMS, 2021; Wilson and Burt, 2023). Described as a "laissez-faire" approach to governance (Chadwick, 2009), currently the EPL and the EFL effectively regulate themselves – both are members associations and the members are the clubs (EFL, n.d.; EPL, n.d.) – which often results in poor governance outcomes (Geeraert, 2019). Therefore, the FLR forged ahead.

Football's Social Importance

The FLR, as its name suggests, has the protection of football supporters at its heart. It stressed the importance of football clubs to their local communities and the social importance that they play helping to gel communities together (DCMS, 2021). It describes clubs as "community assets" (p. 16), which Inglis (1991) describes as being as important to a locality as its libraries and law courts, and used by more people. Although there is a debate in academic literature about the degree of support of different types of fans (Davis, 2015; Giulianotti, 2002), to committed and loyal supporters, the connection with their clubs is much deeper than for a standard customer relationship as it is found to be part of a supporter's identity formation (Malcolm et al., 2000), and to many is a relationship as important to the individual as family members (Jones, 1998). The significance was highlighted when, in the wake of Bury's demise, some fans required mental health support (BBC Sport, 2019). Therefore, one of the main aims of the FLR was to prevent the financial collapse of more clubs and thus prevent the devastation to fans of more clubs entering administration or liquidation.

Further, clubs have significant community importance through their corporate social responsibility (CSR) activities that are argued to have a greater impact than other charities in delivering social good due to the association with the club brand (Kolyperas et al., 2016; Walters, 2009). This was highlighted by their role in various CSR initiatives during the pandemic where clubs created food banks and other social initiatives to support vulnerable and lonely people (Ahmed et al., 2023). However, clubs seem to have under-achieved in terms of social capital as club disclosure of their activities has been found to be limited despite the enhanced stakeholder positivity resulting from it (Raimo et al., 2021).

What Does the Fan-Led Review Cover

The main recommendation from the FLR was the introduction of an Independent Regulator for English Football (IREF) that would operate a licencing system for the men's game and oversee club governance and finances (DCMS, 2021). It would ultimately have the power to withdraw a club's licence if it felt that it was of high risk of insolvency.

The FLR therefore covered a variety of aspects. It included attempts to improve the long-term financial sustainability of clubs through improving internal finances through measures such as capital and liquidity limits, backed up by real-time financial monitoring systems and IREF to have power to intervene to bring clubs back to suitable financial level if limits were found to be breached.

The FLR also suggested improved Owners' and Directors' tests, designed to tighten the rules around who can own and make decisions within clubs. Most club boardrooms currently centre around a concentrated, unilateral, all-powerful ownership model with few directors with meaningful power (Middling, 2023; Morrow, 2016). A few clubs have external, non-executive directors as recommended in commercial industries (Solomon, 2021) such as Brentford (Trehan, 2021), but these remain a minority (Malagila et al., 2021).

There were also recommendations designed to give fans more say in the running of their clubs, and to protect them from changes to key heritage and culture elements, such as badge, club name, home shirt colours, and location of stadium, as happened, for example, at Leeds United FC (Hunter, 2013; Independent, 2018), Hull City FC (Hunter, 2015), Cardiff City FC (BBC News, 2012), and Wimbledon FC (Guardian, 2004).

Domestic Implications

After answering long-standing calls for an IREF (see, for example, Hamil, 1999; Roan and Scott, 2020), the report was applauded by a number of supporter and campaign groups (FSA, 2021) for its recommendation to protect the English game. In this way, the primary ramification of the FLR was that it removed the opportunity for English football to govern itself in a manner acceptable to most fan groups and other stakeholders (Crouch, 2021). As the recommendations become law, clubs have to adhere to IREF licencing system rules.

As a result, we could see fewer English clubs endure financial distress. If the recommendations were in place at the time, they would have likely helped to at least reduce the financial and governance issues seen at Bury FC and Derby County FC, due to tighter spending controls – an issue that was at the centre of both clubs' troubles (Middling, 2021).

The review could also see a more joined up approach to English football regulation (Maguire, 2022). The current regulatory system is made up of four independent bodies – the FA (mostly focusing on the England Team, the FA Cup, and grassroots football), the Premier League (the top tier of English football following a breakaway in 1992), the English Football League (the next three tiers of English football), and the National League (tiers 5 and 6).

Commentators have, however, argued that regulation has not fixed a number of other British industries such as energy, water, and financial services (Maguire, 2022; Shackleton and Hewson, 2022). Therefore, there is no guarantee that regulation will improve the situation in English football – indeed Burns and Jollands (2022) argue that an over-focus on financial value means not enough focus on the true meaning of the FLR – putting supporters at the heart of the game.

Global Implications

For English football to remain competitive in the global stage, some argue that a free market approach of open competition is preferable. By embracing the benefits and risks that come with the free market approach and avoiding the burdens arising from heavy regulation (Chen et al., 2011), English football can continue to enjoy the globalisation of the football product (Ludvigsen, 2020) and the geopolitically savvy expansion (Dashti et al., 2022) that has made the Premier League a global success – it is the highest grossing league the world, out-earning its nearest rival (Spain) by almost two to one with annual revenues in excess of €6bn (Deloitte, 2023). Similar arguments are made by Shackleton and Hewson (2022) who argue that such regulation could significantly hinder investment, including global investment, in the English game and will also be costly for clubs and leagues to implement. This could result in a decline in the success and competitiveness of English football on a European or global stage and shift the geopolitical sporting power.

This is perhaps becoming more of a predominant issue as the rise of the Saudi Pro-League has seen some high-profile players being bought by its clubs (BBC Sport, 2023). In the Saudi Pro-League there are no restriction on clubs' spending, which is backed by the state (Panja and Al Omran, 2023). As such, should it gain the power to outspend EPL clubs and attract more of the best playing talent, it could challenge the EPL as the most watched and commercially successful football league in the world (Deloitte, 2023). However, as match attendances are on average less than ten thousand (ESPN, 2023), it would seem to have a way to go.

Concerns such as these have led to a number of English clubs speaking out against the regulations. Angus Kinnear, CEO of Leeds United, claimed that the recommendations are "Maoist" and anti-commercial (BBC Sport, 2021b para. 5), and Aston Villa CEO, Christian Purslow, commented that "the regulator risks 'killing the golden goose' if we overregulate" (Maguire, 2022).

Another concern raised by critics is around the legality of IREF as the worldwide governing body of football, FIFA, is against government intervention in football (Pavitt, 2023). This was tackled in the follow up White Paper (DCMS, 2023) by ensuring that the IREF was independent of government, similar to the precedent of other countries, such as Spain, that have set financial regulations for clubs overseen by bodies independently of the relevant league(s).

Conclusion

In this chapter we have introduced the FLR and briefly considered its domestic and global implications. It is clear that there are issues in the governance and finances of English football, and the subsequent regulation has been welcomed by many. However, it remains to be seen whether the regulation will be a silver bullet to fix English football's issues and how it will impact English football's geopolitical economic position and international commercial success.

References

Ahmed, J. U., Hasan, M. K., Islam, Q. T., Uddin, M. J., Faroque, A. R. and Chowdhury, M. H. K. (2023). CSR in major European football leagues in the age of COVID-19: financial vulnerability, mental health and domestic violence. *Society and Business Review*, *18*, 439–462.

Alabi, M. and Urquhart, A. (2023). Football finance and Covid-19. *Sports Economics Review*, 4, 1–7.

BBC News (2012). Cardiff City FC confirm rebranding with new red shirts. Available at: https://www.bbc.co.uk/news/uk-wales-south-east-wales-18337392 [Accessed 3 November 2023].

BBC Sport (2019). Bury FC: Mental health support offered to club's suffering fans. *BBC Sport* [Online]. Available at: https://www.bbc.co.uk/sport/football/49586279 [Accessed 10 September 2019].

BBC Sport (2021a). Derby County officially enter administration and are deducted 12 points. *BBC Sport* [Online]. Available at: https://www.bbc.co.uk/sport/football/58649432.

BBC Sport (2021b). Leeds: Chief executive Angus Kinnear says some review calls 'Maoist'. Available at: https://www.bbc.co.uk/sport/football/59481154 [Accessed 12 December 2021].

BBC Sport (2023). Saudi Pro League: Neymar, Benzema, Mahrez – which players have joined Saudi teams this summer? Available at: https://www.bbc.co.uk/sport/football/66132139 [Accessed 10 September 2023].

Brown, A. (1999). Thinking the unthinkable or playing the game? In S. Hamil, J. Michie and C. Oughton (Eds.), *A Game of Two Halves? The Business of Football*. Edinburgh: Mainstream Publishing.

Burns, J. E. and Jollands, S. (2022). Examining accountability in relation to local football communities. *Accounting, Auditing & Accountability Journal*, *28*, 626–650.

Chadwick, S. (2009). From outside lane to inside track: sport management research in the twenty-first century. *Management Decision*, *47*, 191–203.

Chen, S., Sun, Z., Tang, S. and Wu, D. (2011). Government intervention and investment efficiency: evidence from China. *Journal of Corporate Finance*, *17*, 259–271.

Conservative and Unionist Party (2019). Get Brexit Done Unleash Britain's Potential, The Conservative and Unionist Party Manifesto 2019. Available at: https://www.conservatives.com/our-plan [Accessed 5 November 2023].

Cox, A. and Philippou, C. (2022). Measuring the resilience of English Premier League clubs to economic recessions. *Soccer & Society*, *23*, 482–499.

Crouch, T. (2021). Forward: Fan-Led Review of Football Governance. Available at: https://assets.publishing.service.gov.uk/government/uploads/system/uploads/attachment_data/file/1135464/Football_Fan_led_Governance_Review_v8Web_Accessible.pdf [Accessed 24 November 2021].

Dashti, A. A., Haynes, R. and Murad, H. A. (2022). The impact of media globalization of English football: the Kuwaiti experience. *International Journal of Sport Communication*, *15*, 158–166.

Davis, L. (2015). Football fandom and authenticity: a critical discussion of historical and contemporary perspectives. *Soccer & Society*, *16*, 422–436.

DCMS (2011). Football governance: Seventh report of session 2010–12. Available at: http://www.publications.parliament.uk/pa/cm201012/cmselect/cmcumeds/792/792i.pdf [Accessed 15 April 2022].

DCMS (2014). Government sets up experts group to forge stronger links between supporters and professional football clubs. Available at: https://www.gov.uk/government/news/government-sets-up-experts-group-to-forge-stronger-links-between-supporters-and-professional-football-clubs [Accessed 15 April 2022].

DCMS (2021) Independent report: Fan-Led Review of Football Governance: securing the game's future. Available at: https://www.gov.uk/government/publications/fan-led-review-of-football-governance-securing-the-games-future/fan-led-review-of-football-governance-securing-the-games-future#chap1 [Accessed 24 November 2021].

DCMS (2023). A Sustainable Future – Reforming Club Football Governance. Available at: https://www.gov.uk/government/publications/a-sustainable-future-reforming-club-football-governance [Accessed 23 February 2023].

Deloitte (2023). A balancing act: Annual review of football finance 2023. Available at: https://www2.deloitte.com/uk/en/pages/sports-business-group/articles/annual-review-of-football-finance-europe.html.

Ducker, J. (2019). Bolton enter administration and are hit with 12-point deduction for next season *The Telegraph* [Online]. Available at: https://www.telegraph.co.uk/football/2019/05/13/bolton-enter-administration-face-12-point-deduction-next-season/ [Accessed 17 September 2020].

Ducker, J. (2020). Macclesfield Town football club wound up with debts of £500,000: Club were relegated from League Two earlier this year, after failing to pay wages. *The Telegraph* [Online]. Available at: https://www.telegraph.co.uk/football/2020/09/16/macclesfield-town-football-club-wound-debts-500000/ [Accessed 17 September 2020].

Dutton, T. (2019). MPs call on EFL to apologise to Bury FC fans after 'avoidable' crisis. *Evening Standard* [Online]. Available at: https://www.standard.co.uk/sport/football/mps-demand-urgent-reform-after-avoidable-failures-led-to-bury-fc-crisis-a4278906.html [Accessed 10 November 2019].

EFL. n.d. The EFL: Who we are. Available at: https://www.efl.com/-more/all-about-the-efl/history/#:~:text=The%20EFL%20is%20the%20world's,global%20national%20and%20international%20success [Accessed 1 May 2022].

EPL. n.d. About the Premier League. Available at: https://www.premierleague.com/about#:~:text=The%20Premier%20League%20is%20a,to%20English%20and%20European%20law [Accessed 01 May 2022].

ESPN (2023). Saudi Pro League Performance Stats – 2023–24. Available at: https://www.espn.co.uk/football/stats/_/league/KSA.1/view/performance [Accessed 11 December 2023].

Evans, R., Walters, G. and Hamil, S. (2022). Gambling in professional sport: the enabling role of "regulatory legitimacy". *Corporate Governance: The International Journal of Business in Society*, 22, 1078–1093.

Fisher, B. (2021). Reading agree six-point deduction with EFL for breaching financial rules. *The Guardian* [Online]. Available at: https://www.theguardian.com/football/2021/nov/17/reading-agree-six-point-deduction-with-efl-for-breaching-financial-rules [Accessed 21 November 2021].

FSA (2021). Fan-led review: "Potentially a huge step forward". Available at: https://thefsa.org.uk/news/fan-led-review-is-a-huge-step-forward/ [Accessed 27 June 2022].

García, B. and Welford, J. (2015). Supporters and football governance, from customers to stakeholders: a literature review and agenda for research. *Sport Management Review*, 18, 517–528.

Geeraert, A. (2019). The limits and opportunities of self-regulation: achieving international sport federations' compliance with good governance standards. *European Sport Management Quarterly*, 19, 520–538.

Giulianotti, R. (2002). Supporters, followers, fans, and flaneurs: a taxonomy of spectator identities in football. *Journal of Sport and Social Issues*, 26, 25–46.

Guardian, T. (2004). Wimbledon become MK Dons FC. Available at: https://www.theguardian.com/football/2004/jun/21/newsstory.mkdons.

Halliday, J. (2019). Bury FC: despair as club is expelled from Football League after 125 years; Collapse of 11th-hour rescue deal on Tuesday night puts club's future in grave doubt. *The Guardian* [Online]. Available at: https://www.theguardian.com/football/2019/aug/27/bury-and-bolton-two-of-englands-oldest-clubs-face-tuesday-expulsion [Accessed 28 August 2019].

Hamil, S. (1999). A whole new ball game? Why football needs a regulator. In S. Hamil, J. Michie and C. Oughton (Eds.), *The Business of Football: A Game of Two Halves*. Edinburgh: Mainstream Publishing.

Hamilton, T. (2021). Super League collapses: How fan reaction, revolt helped end English clubs' breakaway. Available at: https://www.espn.co.uk/football/story/_/id/37616441/how-fan-reaction-revolt-helped-end-english-clubs-breakaway [Accessed 26 August 2021].

Hunter, A. (2013). Everton fans up in arms about club's redesigned crest. Available at: https://www.theguardian.com/football/2013/may/27/everton-fans-clubs-redesigned-crest [Accessed 5 November 2023].

Hunter, A. (2015). FA rejects Hull City application to change club's name to Hull Tigers. Available at: https://www.theguardian.com/football/2015/jul/11/fa-reject-hull-city-application-change-name-hull-tigers [Accessed 3 November 2023].

Independent (2018). Leeds United scrap new badge after furious backlash from fans. Available at: https://www.independent.co.uk/sport/football/football-league/leeds-united-badge-fans-petition-club-statement-new-plans-a8184696.html [Accessed 5 November 2023].

Inglis, S. (1991). *The Football Grounds of Great Britain*. London: Collins.

JoneS, I. (1998). *Football Fandom: Football Fan Identity and Identification at Luton Town Football Club*. [Unpublished PhD Thesis, University of Luton].

King, A. (1997). New directors, customers, and fans: the transformation of English football in the 1990s. *Sociology of Sport Journal, 14*, 224–240.

Kolyperas, D., Anagnostopoulos, C., Chadwick, S. and Sparks, L. (2016). Applying a communicating vessels framework to CSR value co-creation: empirical evidence from professional team sport organizations. *Journal of Sport Management, 30*, 702–719.

Labour (2019). It's time for real change: The Labour Party Manifeso 2019. Available at: https://labour.org.uk/wp-content/uploads/2019/11/Real-Change-Labour-Manifesto-2019.pdf [Accessed 5 November 2023].

Ludvigsen, J. A. L. (2020). The premier league-globalization nexus: notes on current trends, pressing issues and inter-linked "-ization" processes. *Managing Sport and Leisure, 25*, 37–51.

MacInnes, P. (2022). Main proposals of fan-led review of English football backed by government. *The Guardian* [Online]. Available at: https://www.theguardian.com/football/2022/apr/25/main-proposals-of-fan-led-review-of-english-football-backed-by-government [Accessed 30 April 2022].

Maguire, K. (2022). Fan-led review of football governance: a kick in the right direction or a Maoist collective power grab? *The Political Quarterly, 93*, 154–159.

Maguire, K., Day, K. and Kilty, G. (2021). Derby County in administration. *The Price of Football* [Online]. Available at: https://uk-podcasts.co.uk/podcast/price-of-football/derby-county-in-administration [Accessed 20 September 2021].

Maguire, K., Day, K. and Kilty, G. (2023). The Price of Football Podcast. Available at: https://play.acast.com/s/price-of-football.

Maguire, K. and Philippou, C. (2023). Still Ill? Assessing the Financial Sustainability of Football. Available at: https://assets.publishing.service.gov.uk/government/uploads/system/uploads/attachment_data/file/1178214/Research_report_-_Assessing_the_financial_sustainability_of_football__2023_.pdf [Accessed 20 June 2023].

Malagila, J. K., Zalata, A. M., Ntim, C. G. and Elamer, A. A. (2021). Corporate governance and performance in sports organisations: the case of UK premier leagues. *International Journal of Finance & Economics, 26*, 2517–2537.

Malcolm, D., Jones, I. and Waddington, I. (2000). The people's game? Football spectatorship and demographic change. *Soccer & Society, 1*, 129–143.

Middling, M. (2021). Football: English fans want an independent regulator – here's how it could help save clubs from ruin. Available at: https://theconversation.com/football-english-fans-want-an-independent-regulator-heres-how-it-could-help-save-clubs-from-ruin-172720 [Accessed 17 December 2021].

Middling, M. (2023). *Accounting for Supporters: A New Reporting Framework for the English Football League*. DBA, Northumbria University.

Moore, O. and Baugh, E. (2023). Southend United: Fans protest outside Ron Martin's home. Available at: https://www.bbc.co.uk/news/uk-england-essex-66211277.

Morrow, S. (2016). Football, economics and finance. In J. Hughes, K. Moore, R. Spaaij and J. Maguire (Eds.), *Routledge Handbook of Football Studies*. Oxon: Routledge.

Panja, T. and Al Omran, A. (2023). Saudi Soccer League Creates Huge Fund to Sign Global Stars. Available at: https://www.nytimes.com/2023/06/02/sports/soccer/saudi-soccer-messi-benzema-ronaldo.html [Accessed 11 December 2023].

Pavitt, M. (2023). 'FIFA to study plans for a UK Government appointed independent regulator' amid concerns the proposals could breach rules over political interference in football. Available at: https://www.dailymail.co.uk/sport/football/article-11798897/FIFA-study-plans-Government-appointed-independent-regulator-political-interference.html [Accessed 08 November 2023].

Philippou, C. (2023). English football is ready for a rule change when it comes to financial management. Available at: https://theconversation.com/english-football-is-ready-for-a-rule-change-when-it-comes-to-financial-management-217034 [Accessed 10 November 2023].

Philippou, C. and Maguire, K. (2022). Assessing the Financial Sustainability of Football. *DCMS* [Online]. Available at: https://assets.publishing.service.gov.uk/government/uploads/system/uploads/attachment_data/file/1071503/Assessing_the_financial_sustainability_of_football__web_accessible_.pdf [Accessed 12 March 2022].

Plumley, D., Ramchandani, G. M. and Wilson, R. (2019). The unintended consequence of financial fair play. *Sport, Business and Management: An International Journal*, 9, 118–133.

Raimo, N., Vitolla, F., Nicolò, G. and Tartaglia Polcini, P. (2021). CSR disclosure as a legitimation strategy: evidence from the football industry. *Measuring Business Excellence*, 25, 493–508.

Reddy, M. (2021). Distraction, Brexit, soft power: How the UK government used football for its populist principles. Available at: https://www.independent.co.uk/sport/football/brexit-government-pandemic-melissa-reddy-b1852807.html [Accessed 8 October 2023].

Roan, D. and Scott, L. (2020). Neville, Lewis & Bernstein lobby for independent football regulation to solve 'crisis'. *BBC Sport* [Online]. Available at: https://www.bbc.co.uk/sport/football/54558837 [Accessed 06 April 2021].

Samuel, M. (2021). Fatal flaws riddled this populist fan-led review of football by the Government … a healthy, open competition must be protected. Available at: https://www.dailymail.co.uk/sport/football/article-10243761/MARTIN-SAMUEL-Fatal-flaws-riddled-populist-fan-led-review-Government.html.

Shackleton, J. R. and Hewson, V. (2022). RED CARD: Why English football doesn't need an independent regulator (IEA Current Controversies No.84). Available at: https://iea.org.uk/publications/red-card-why-english-football-doesnt-need-an-independent-regulator/#:~:text=The%20Fan%20Led%20Review%20of,indicated%20support%20for%20an%20IREF. [Accessed 14/10/2023].

Solberg, H. A. and Haugen, K. K. (2010). European club football: why enormous revenues are not enough? *Sport in Society*, 13, 329–343.

Solomon, J. (2021). *Corporate Governance and Accountability* (5th ed.). Croydon: Wiley.

Tempany, A. (2016). *And the Sun Shines Now: How Hillsborough and the Premier League Changed Britain*. London: Faber & Faber.

Trehan, D. (2021). Brentford appoint Preeti Shetty and Deji Davies as independent non-executive directors. Available at: https://www.skysports.com/football/news/11748/12372560/brentford-appoint-preeti-shetty-and-deji-davies-as-independent-non-executive-directors [Accessed 14 December 2023].

Walters, G. (2009). Corporate social responsibility through sport: the community sports trust model as a CSR delivery agency. *Journal of Corporate Citizenship*, 35, 81–94.

Wearmouth, R. (2023). Can the Conservatives use football reform to rebuild Red Wall trust? Available at: https://www.newstatesman.com/politics/conservatives/2023/01/conservatives-football-reform-rebuild-red-wall-trust [Accessed 20 December 2023].

Wilson, J. and Burt, J. (2023). A football regulator should not have been needed, but game has only itself to blame. Available at: https://advance.lexis.com/document/?pdmfid=1519360&crid=73cbd639-4426-402d-8805-3a87640d0cc6&pddocfullpath=%2Fshared%2Fdocument%2Fnews%2Furn%3AcontentItem%3A67M5-GFJ1-JBNF-W2MC-00000-00&pdcontentcomponentid=389195&pdteaserkey=sr0&pditab=allpods&ecomp=twmyk&earg=sr0&prid=f2ead175-65f7-44d4-b648-80f1138a6bd1 [Accessed 20 December 2023].

23

THE 3P-MODEL IN GLOBAL FOOTBALL

Creating Value by Combining Passion, Profit, and Politics on Multiple Levels

Martin Carlsson-Wall and Kai DeMott

Global Football as a Field of Multiple Tensions

Football is a field that combines business with social and political elements like few other sectors. This becomes particularly visible as football clubs have progressed from local member-based entities toward becoming global brands (Andon and Free, 2019; Clune et al., 2019; Ferkins and Shilbury, 2015; Sam and Macris, 2014; Sherry et al., 2007). This commercialization process can be filled with conflicts as stakeholders mobilize clubs in different directions (Dowling et al., 2014; Gammelsæter, 2010;; Rika et al., 2016). As a result of these incompatible demands, football clubs increasingly face challenges of "having to be many different things to many different people" (Gammelsæter, 2010, p. 569).

In this chapter, we introduce what we call the "3P-Model" to help practitioners, policymakers, and academics to make sense of how sport, economics, politics, and geography interconnect and influence one another in the field of football, as well as to create a common language to manage competing stakeholder expectations. This 3P-Model is based on three levels of analysis – passion, profit, and politics – that are inherent to the geopolitical economy of sport. Using this tool, we highlight the need to deliver sporting success (Gallardo-Guerrero et al., 2008), while acknowledging that football clubs have an "ethical commitment" (Blumrodt et al., 2013) as they remain an important site for social responsibility in their local communities (Gammelsæter, 2010, 2021). Using illustrative examples, we argue that football is not "just another industry" (Gammelsæter, 2021) and that the navigation of passion, profit, and politics requires a holistic view where strategic issues in global football are analyzed on multiple levels.

DOI: 10.4324/9781003473671-26

The 3P-Model: Passion, Profit, and Politics on Multiple Levels

Figure 23.1 showcases the 3Ps and the five levels of analysis. Similar to a football club that can have an offensive or defensive playing system, we argue that there is no one best way for how to apply the model. Instead, the 3Ps make strategic choices explicit so that they can be debated and potentially adjusted to improve value creation in a club. In the coming sections, we will describe the passion, profit, and politics dimensions individually before demonstrating how a multi-level analysis can help football clubs navigate geopolitical elements and conflicting stakeholders demands in a better way.

The Passion Dimension

> [Football clubs are] a nexus of passionate interests. Fans, players, sponsors, club managers and the board are emotionally attached (in different ways and with different degrees of intensity) through diverse and changeable passionate interests, such as derbies or retaining the club's traditional membership-based structure. Passionate interests are matters that connect or 'hook' actors emotionally; whether this be pride (in the club's long history) or frustration (at the team's chronic inability to win derbies).
>
> *(Baxter et al., 2019, p. 21)*

The passion dimension describes the foundation of many football clubs: an emotional attachment of members, fans, and other stakeholders that creates togetherness and belonging (Baxter et al., 2019; Gammelsæter, 2010). FC Barcelona is a good example: with more than 144,000 members, the club's

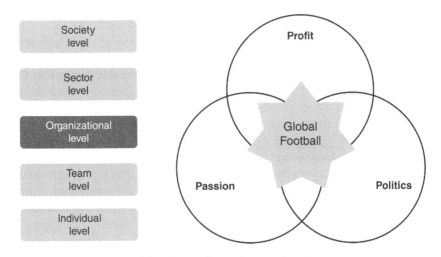

FIGURE 23.1   The 3P Model and its different levels of analysis

motto "Més que un club" (More than a club) demonstrates that the organization has a wider social and institutional impact in the region of Katalonia.

Understanding football clubs through the passion dimension allows us to make sense of why members are driven by a genuine commitment to societal or sports-related values. Any changes to the club, may it be commercial agendas (e.g. sponsorship) or political (e.g. ownership structure) can then become very sensitive to followers, creating a feeling that *their* club is being taken away from them. This becomes visible, for example, when the recruitment of external star players (Bolander et al., 2017) may be criticized by fans as opposed to the development of local players (Carlsson-Wall et al., 2016; Carlsson-Wall et al., 2024). For example, in FC Barcelona many of the star players such as Lionel Messi, Xavi, and Gerard Pique have grown up in the youth academy La Masia. In this way, they have internalized and embody the cultural norms and historical heritage of the club.

The Profit Dimension

On the other end of the spectrum, we find a profit-centered view of football clubs (Deloitte, 2020; McKinsey & Company, 2020). Today, few clubs thrive in the global football industry without the necessary business mindset. Even though strategic decisions may be made by members, managerial professionalism is needed. Historically, North American sports leagues such as the National Football League (NFL) and the National Basketball Association (NBA) have been pioneering best practice within the profit dimension. However, in recent years, we see how many clubs and leagues in Europe have started to assimilate, as it is increasingly common across Europe to work with American investors.

An interesting contrast to FC Barcelona in this regard is Paris Saint Germain (PSG). The main owner is Qatar Sports Investments, and in December 2023 the New York-based private equity company Arctos Partners acquired up to 12.5 percent of the club. The press release on PSG's website states that "the partnership will form the foundation of the next phase of PSG's global growth and drive forward the club's footballing and business success". Securing financing to build global brands is also important on a league level. For example, the American private equity company CVC has become a minority owner in LaLiga and in the end of 2023, and the German Bundesliga announced that they were seeking commercial partners for their media company.

The Political Dimension

Parallel to passion and profit, global football is also filled with politics. For many clubs, creating long-standing relationships with the city and communities, for example, is instrumental to manage ownership of real estate or hosting games. Studying Paris Saint-Germain, Cho et al. (2020) focus on how PSG's top management collaborated with different governance agencies in France. The authors describe how the relationship between "profit" and "politics" created a situation where violent and commercially less interesting fan groups were segregated at Stade de France from families and other affluent customer segments who could pay higher ticket prices. This illustrates how profit and politics dimensions reinforced each other and were even able to re-define and marginalize core elements of what had previously been considered "passion" in PSG.

The political dimension is also important in relation to the many leagues and federations that individual clubs are members of. For example, PSG is a member of the French football League 1, the European Club Association and often qualifies to Union of European Football Associations' (UEFA's) Champions League. In addition, many of the players for PSG play for national teams which are regulated by the Fédération Internationale de Football Association (FIFA). As such, politics as dynamics of organizing different clubs, geographies, and economics take place not only within a football club but also in relation to external stakeholders on different levels.

Applying the 3P-Model to Current Issues in Global Football

Having introduced the passion, profit, and politics dimensions, we now turn to the multi-level application of the 3P-Model. We illustrate two current issues in global football: the importance of data analytics in talent development and the growth of women's football.

Current Issue 1: Tensions Related to Data Analytics in Managing Talent Development

Arguably, developing and selling talent is one of the most critical geopolitical processes of a football club. In recent years, the systematic use of data analytics has become a common practice where many football clubs now have hired specialized data analysts. However, despite the many opportunities to improve talent development, there are also important conflicts of interests that can be uncovered if we apply the 3P-Model. Starting with the individual level, data analytics provide increased opportunities for "self-assetization" (Nappert and Plante, 2023). Football players such as Cristiano Ronaldo, Lionel Messi, and Erland Harland increasingly invest considerable sums in their own talent development by having specialized physiotherapists, nutrition experts, and data analysts to take their game. When both players and clubs invest in data analytics, it is not uncommon that tensions emerge between the two, for example, when data suggests that the player has reached a physical peak or the player's global brand should be used in a way that is in conflict with the football club.

Data analytics can also create tensions between the club and sector-specific norms. An interesting example of this is Red Bull. Originally a private company selling energy drinks, Red Bull has leveraged data analytics and talent development in new ways. Not only has Red Bull created a youth academy to produce new players, but the organization has also bought clubs across the world to maximize the "asset development" of individual players. From a profit dimension, this establishment of a multi-club platform makes perfect sense, while, from a passion perspective, this way of commercial player development violates many sector norms in football. For example, when the club is degraded to a "talent factory" rather than winning games, local supporters might protest. Furthermore, when commercial talent development is the main objective, it might also be difficult to develop strong relationships with the local city. Red Bull Salzburg, for example, could be argued to resemble a division of a large multinational company rather than being a local institution compared to other more "traditional" football clubs.

The scaling of talent development on an organizational level has also raised questions about data analytics and talent development on a society level. Even though football players have some unique characteristics, there are interesting similarities with other high-performing contexts – so-called "high-intensity organizations" (Carlsson-Wall et al., 2024) where there are clearly distinguishable stars (e.g. movie stars, music stars, investment banking stars, etc.). In these settings, the individual employee is constantly monitored, and the organization makes considerable investments in talent development. On the positive side, when incentives between the organization and the individual are aligned, this creates room for the "assetization" (Nappert and Plante, 2023) of players in football clubs. On the other hand, with constant monitoring of performance, we may also see an increase in pressure and burn-out rates, which warrants important questions about the relationship between the employee and the employer when passion, profit, and politics are analyzed on multiple levels.

Current Issue 2: Tensions Related to Growing Women's Football

A second issue that highlights the value of the 3P-Model is to identify tensions related to the growth of women's football. Prevailing gender inequalities in football along the combination of passion, profit, and politics is a complex issue. From a passion perspective, recent years have seen a growth in the celebration of women's football. For example, the FIFA Women's World Cup 2023 was a great success and the Australian national team ("the Matildas") have become local heroes and role models. From a profit and political perspective, this increase in passion drives many other promising areas, as market demand is growing and more young girls are starting to play football. Yet, the question remains: why is the development of women's football not progressing faster?

Mobilizing the 3P-Model, the answer might lie on different levels of analysis. Starting with the individual level, the large majority of women players suffer from vast pay-gaps and thus cannot have football as their only source of income. In many leagues, only the star players can earn a living by being professional athletes. This also means that training sessions for the team are suffering from accommodating the players' schedules. Arguably, if the majority of leagues could afford to employ all players as professionals (as men's leagues do), this would increase both personal well-being as well as the opportunity to improve sports performance.

On an organizational level, a challenge lies in infrastructure investments. Today, many top clubs in Europe have a competitive men's and women's team, in which all players are professional. Yet, these clubs often struggle with allocating funds between these two teams, not least as sponsors, spectators, and the optimization of capacity in stadiums puts strain on an equal distribution. The result is often a much tighter budget and profit squeeze which negatively affects the growth of women's football. Ideally, clubs would have the financial strength to invest in equal infrastructure to enable the women's clubs, for example, to play attractive games at the large stadiums and benefit from the same resources as the men's team. However, given the political and profit constraints, this is still far from reality. In many cases, women's football is still an "add on product" for many football clubs.

On a sector level, there are interesting tensions between profit and politics. More specifically, should gender equality be an issue that is handled through regulation (politics) or the free market (profit)? One could imagine a case where leagues democratically decide that all clubs need to be so called "double clubs" with both male and female teams. One can even go further and have regulation at the UEFA or FIFA levels about gender equality. On the other hand, there is also a case where commercial values drive the transformation toward gender equality. Since many corporate sponsors link their engagement with football to ESG goals, one might argue that it is faster to let the free market "make a business case" for gender equality (e.g., A22's proposal for a new European Super League includes 64 men's teams and 32 women's teams).

Finally, it is also worth noting that countries and geographies differ in their views on gender equality. While countries in Northern Europe normally have very strong institutional support for gender equality, there are significant differences in other countries across the world. As a consequence, even though general standards (and rules) are important to foster global change, contextual differences will most likely rely on local adaptations. Here, a business case for women's football is even more decisive. Will global investors preserve the current system and favor male football, or will they use the commercial potential in women's football and become a catalyst? We see from other industries that multinational corporations can both hinder and support change.

With the growth new ownership models (e.g., multi-club platforms such as Red Bull) will most likely increase their power in the future. Yet, it remains to be seen whether this new entrepreneurial culture will become a catalyst in terms of gender equality.

Conclusion

In this chapter, we have introduced the 3P-Model to create a common language about the geopolitical economy of sport among football practitioners, policymakers, and academics. Along two illustrative examples, we have shown how football clubs are challenged to balance passion, profit, and politics to become winners on and off the pitch. However, even though a balance between the 3Ps might come as no surprise, we also highlight the embedded nature of football organizations between matters of geography, politics, and economics. Regardless of if you are a club, a league, or a federation, the 3P-Model shows that tensions may occur between individual, team, organizational, sector, and society levels. We hope this framework can provide the cornerstone for future research, for example, developing it further and building in a temporal dimension: How do the 3Ps differ if you are new club or an existing club? In what ways does it become easier or more difficult to strike a balance? Using and developing the 3P-Model in such a way may aid in understanding the crossroads of global football facing geopolitical issues. Will global football become more commercial as the North American system, or might there be a backlash where supporters in Europe force stakeholders to become more passion oriented? We believe the 3P-Model can help practitioners, policymakers, and academics to make sense of these issues as they face an uncertain future in the geopolitical economy of sport.

References

Andon, P. and Free, C. (2019). Accounting and the business of sport: past, present and future. *Accounting, Auditing & Accountability Journal, 32*(7), 1861–1875.

Baxter, J., Carlsson-Wall, M., Chua, W. F. and Kraus, K. (2019). Accounting and passionate interests: the case of a Swedish football club. *Accounting, Organizations and Society, 74*, 21–40.

Blumrodt, J., Desbordes, M. and Bodin, D. (2013). Professional football clubs and corporate social responsibility. *Sport, Business and Management: An International Journal, 3*(3), 205–225.

Bolander, P., Werr, A. and Asplund, K. (2017). The practice of talent management: a framework and typology. *Personnel Review, 46*(8), 1523–1551.

Carlsson-Wall, M., DeMott, K. and Ali, H. (2024). Scaling and controlling talent development in high-intensity organizations: the case of a Swedish football club. *Accounting, Auditing & Accountability Journal, 37*(2), 480–501.

Carlsson-Wall, M., Kraus, K. and Messner, M. (2016). Performance measurement systems and the enactment of different institutional logics: insights from a football organization. *Management Accounting Research, 32*, 45–61.

Cho, C. H., Janin, F., Cooper, C. and Rogerson, M. (2020). Neoliberal control devices and social discrimination: the case of Paris Saint-Germain football club fans. *Accounting and Management Information Systems*, *19*(3), 409–443.

Clune, C., Boomsma, R. and Pucci, R. (2019). The disparate roles of accounting in an amateur sports organisation: the case of logic assimilation in the gaelic athletic association. *Accounting, Auditing & Accountability Journal*, *32*(7), 1926–1955.

Deloitte (2020). Annual Review of Football Finance 2020. Retrieved from https://www2.deloitte.com/ch/en/pages/technology-media-and-telecommunications/articles/annual-review-of-football-finance.html

Dowling, M., Edwards, J. and Washington, M. (2014). Understanding the concept of professionalisation in sport management research. *Sport Management Review*, *17*(4), 520–529.

Ferkins, L. and Shilbury, D. (2015). The stakeholder dilemma in sport governance: toward the notion of "stakeowner". *Journal of Sport Management*, *29*(1), 93–108.

Gallardo-Guerrero, L., García-Tascón, M. and Burillo-Naranjo, P. (2008). New sports management software: a needs analysis by a panel of Spanish experts. *International Journal of Information Management*, *28*(4), 235–245.

Gammelsæter, H. (2010). Institutional pluralism and governance in "commercialized" sport clubs. *European Sport Management Quarterly*, *10*(5), 569–594.

Gammelsæter, H. (2021). Sport is not industry: bringing sport back to sport management. *European Sport Management Quarterly*, *21*(2), 257–279.

McKinsey & Company (2020). The value pitch: the importance of team value management. Retrieved from https://www.mckinsey.com/industries/consumer-packaged-goods/our-insights/the-value-pitch-the-importance-of-team-value-management

Nappert, P. L. and Plante, M. (2023). The assetization of baseball players: instrumentalizing promise with signing bonuses and human capital contracts. *Accounting, Organizations and Society*, *105*, 101402.

Rika, N., Finau, G., Samuwai, J. and Kuma, C. (2016). Power and performance: Fiji rugby's transition from amateurism to professionalism. *Accounting History*, *21*(1), 75–97.

Sam, M. P. and Macris, L. I. (2014). Performance regimes in sport policy: exploring consequences, vulnerabilities and politics. *International Journal of Sport Policy and Politics*, *6*(3), 513–532.

Sherry, E., Shilbury, D. and Wood, G. (2007). Wrestling with "conflict of interest" in sport management. *Corporate Governance: The International Journal of Business in Society*, *7*(3), 267–277.

PART IV

The FIFA World Cup and Tournament Football

24

POLYCENTRIC FOOTBALL TOURNAMENTS

Robert Kaspar

The global market place for sports mega events has become more and more crowded over the past decade. Football mega events find themselves in a competition with all other single or multi-sports events to find a host country.

Polycentric sports mega events may provide a solution to make bidding and hosting of a sports mega event more attractive to host cities and countries again (Kaspar, 2014).

While the co-hosting of sports mega events was already discussed by Heere in 2012 (Heere et al., 2012), the term polycentric events was for the first time debated by Kaspar at the Lillehammer Sports Business Symposium in 2016 with members of the IOC (International Olympic Committee). At that time, the IOC was very reluctant to implement changes with the single Olympic village as a key obstacle to change towards polycentric formats.

In 2018 the Union of European Football Associations (UEFA) Euro 2020 was discussed ex-ante in a smaller study based on expert interviews (Stura et al., 2017).

The advantages of polycentric sports events arise around a series of venue management issues. The focus on the use of existing sports facilities in a larger geographic territory favours the often missing legacy as could be observed with the 2010 and 2014 International Federation of Association Football (FIFA) World Cups in South Africa and Brazil. In South Africa the key issues were the development of positive business plans and use of some World Cup venues. In Brazil there were major issues with corruption (AP, 2018) and the post-use of some venues (Brasilia, Manaus).

A polycentric tournament based on the use of existing stadia reduces the burden on governments to invest in new football venues if they have no clear legacy guaranteed. From a sustainability perspective any reduction of

DOI: 10.4324/9781003473671-28

building "white elephant" venues is necessary given the economic, social and environmental impact of building and maintaining larger football stadia.

From an events management perspective a polycentric format in a larger territory increases the accommodation capacity for all stakeholder groups to be taken into account. One of the arguments raised by Platini when lobbying for a pan-European UEFA Football Championship was to bring the matches to smaller countries that could not host the entire event on their own. From a host broadcasting and a spectator perspective there are hardly any disadvantages. The security may be seen as a positive aspect. If there is an incident in one country, matches could be shifted to venues in other countries on a short notice as the venues are already event ready.

Nevertheless a series of events management challenges arise that need to be discussed. First of all the travelling distances for the teams are an issue, but a study has proved that there was no impact on the performance of the teams in the UEFA Euro 2020/21 (O'Connor and Ehambaranathan, 2022). The major criticism comes from fans who may oppose the polycentric hosting format if the distances between the venues cannot be overcome by transport such as trains or buses. From a sustainability perspective it is also critical to increase the fan travel distances necessary to follow the teams.

For UEFA the 2020/21 meant an increasing complexity to guarantee the same standards across all host cities in terms of destination branding, security and safety and the live event experience to name a few of the challenges.

Football tournaments, in contrast to other sports mega events such as the Olympic Games, have increased both in the number of participating nations as well as require a minimum seating capacity in the venues. This growth poses an ever-increasing challenge to find host countries with existing stadia of the required size.

Additionally, new sports mega events have emerged and were promoted by the respective event owners. The European Olympic Committee launched the European Games in 2015 with the first edition in Baku, Azerbaijan. Europe was the last continent to organize a continental multi-sports summer sports mega event. ANOC (Association of National Olympic Committees) in 2019 organized their first multi-sports event, the World Beach Games. In 2019 the first World Urban Games took place in Budapest, an event owned by The Global Association of International Sports Federations (GAISF) (Kaspar, 2022, p. 278). Both multi-sports events are desperate to find host destinations for the future editions. A similar challenge to find host cities/countries in this overcrowded global sports mega event market place is evidenced by other multi-sports event owners such as the Commonwealth Games Federation.

On a global scale, the IOC was in a comfortable situation to select the host cities for the Olympic Summer or Winter Games from a large number of interested cities until the award of the 2020 Olympic Summer Games. From the 2022 Olympic Winter Games onwards, the number of cities interested to host this event shrunk to a small number with the 2022 event being chosen between Beijing and Almaty. The 2024 and 2028 editions of the Summer Games were awarded to Paris and Los Angeles in one session as there were no other cities in the entire world competing for the Summer Games. The low number of cities continued with the 2026 Olympic Winter Games being awarded to Milano/Cortina against its sole competitor, Stockholm. As a consequence the IOC adapted the requirements for the sports venues, eliminating the minimum seating capacity of sports venues and many other issues to attract more cities (IOC, 2020). The IOC also changed the allocation of the Olympic Games to a dialogue system rather than sticking to the old bidding version. In a rare decision in the sports world, the exclusive targeted dialogue for the Olympic Winter Games in 2030 (France), 2034 (Salt Lake City) (IOC, 2023) and a privileged exclusive dialogue 2038 (Switzerland) was agreed upon by the IOC session in 2023. With Brisbane to host the 2032 Olympic Summer Games the IOC has shifted back to traditional host cities with a focus on existing sports infrastructure after having been in Asia for three consecutive Olympic Games (Pyeongchang 2018, Tokyo 2020 and Beijing 2022) (Kaspar, 2018).

For the IOC and many other event owners the event always had to be organized in a monocentric format with only one host city and venues limited to only the host country. In other, especially European federations such as in handball, volleyball or basketball, the polycentric hosting format is now a common practice.

In football the organizing of polycentric global football tournaments started with the 2002 World Cup in South Korea and Japan.

Polycentric events encompass a minimum of two hosting countries and have a number of benefits such as the wider availability of existing sports venues, a larger accommodation base and to some extent being closer to a larger fan base as will be discussed later in this chapter. On the other hand, as evidenced by the too polycentric 2020/2021 UEFA European Championships, the event may be associated with a series of events management challenges (Stura et al., 2017).

FIFA has seen very similar developments in its quest for the designation of host countries. For the decision about the 2018 and 2022 World Cups an impressive number of nations entered a tough and controversial bidding competition that saw traditional football nations such as England, Spain and Portugal eliminated. According to the FIFA continental rotation system four European countries were bidding for the 2018 World Cup, two of them in a polycentric format involving two countries (Spain and Portugal, Belgium and the Netherlands). Five monocentric bids were presented by Qatar, the USA, Australia, South Korea and Japan for the 2022 World Cup. For the award of the 2026 World Cup, FIFA was confronted with only two bidders, a monocentric bid by Morocco and the successful polycentric bid by the USA with its neighbours Mexico and Canada. While FIFA did not officially change the system of deciding about future host countries, it emerged that for both the 2030 and 2034 World Cup only one bidder presented its proposal after intensive conversations taking place before the final deadline. The 2030 World Cup will see a polycentric format that goes beyond its principles. The polycentric tournament encompassing Spain, Portugal and Morocco as neighbouring countries fulfils the key requirements for a successful event with the teams and spectators in mind. Nevertheless, adding three polycentric matches in Latin America (Buenos Aires, Montevideo and Asuncion) stretches the idea of a polycentric format and may be more of a symbolic nature with all the disadvantages for the teams, spectators and media. For the 2034 edition of the World Cup Saudi Arabia is the only bidding country and it remains to be seen if it develops into a polycentric format given that Qatar may provide various world class venues built for the 2022 World Cup.

The FIFA Women´s World Cup has seen seven monocentric editions since its first edition in 1991. The 2023 edition was the first polycentric event being staged in Australia and New Zealand and for the 2027 edition one of the bidders is a polycentric format (Germany, Netherlands and Belgium).

On a continental level the UEFA European Championships were staged for ten times in a monocentric format with the 2000 edition co-hosted by the Netherlands and Belgium breaking the ground for a polycentric format. The 2008 (Austria and Switzerland) and 2012 (Poland and Ukraine) editions followed the success factors of organizing polycentric football tournaments only in neighbouring countries to the benefit of travelling teams, fans, media and other stakeholders. The 2020 edition that took place in 2021 was an interesting idea of former UEFA president Michel Platini to organize a European-wide tournament (Kaspar, 2022, p. 280). Finally, it took place in ten European cities and one Asian city encompassing enormous travel burdens. Additionally, it emerged that the events management challenges for UEFA were enormous. UEFA had to deal with 11 national security systems, face seven different currencies and operational issues guaranteeing similar performance levels across an entire continent. The impacts of the travelling challenges on the performance of the teams were analysed in a study in 2022, but the results did not confirm any disadvantage for any team with a higher travel distance covered (O'Connor and Ehambaranathan, 2022).

The upcoming 2028 edition will see a polycentric football tournament to be hosted in the neighbouring countries of England, Scotland, Wales, Northern Ireland and Ireland with one language, two currencies and convenient transport options for teams and fans. The 2032 edition again stretches the polycentric hosting format beyond its benefits. Italy and Turkey will use existing stadia, one of the advantages of the polycentric hosting format, but UEFA will see discussions about the allocation of the semi-finals and finals and transport and accommodation issues for teams and fans will emerge on a limited scale.

On the other continental federations, football tournaments have only seen very few polycentric hosting formats. In 2007, the AFC Asian Cup was organized in Indonesia, Malaysia, Vietnam and Thailand.

In Africa, the AFC Cup has a great potential for polycentric football tournaments, especially shared by neighbouring nations with the same language and pooling the existing football stadia into one tournament. It also allows smaller nations to co-host the tournament and bring it again closer to the fans. After one polycentric edition in 2012, only the 2027 AFC African Cup has been awarded to the neighbouring countries of Kenya, Tanzania and Uganda.

While in Latin America the Copa America has seen no polycentric football tournament to date, the CONCACAF Gold Cup in Northern and Central America is often co-hosted by two or three countries.

A bundle of challenges for future organizers of football tournaments in all continents remain. Polycentric football tournaments may in some scenarios be beneficial for future hosts with a focus on better sustainability and legacy.

In Europe, it will be increasingly difficult to find host countries for both men's and women's tournaments given the critical voice of the citizens on government spendings on sports venue infrastructure and security spendings. One option for UEFA is to enhance the share of television and sponsorship rights revenues directed into the hosting country. In certain regional scenarios a polycentric hosting format may yield all the benefits while minimizing the negative impacts. There are various geographic scenarios to be evaluated in the future in addition to the countries that have already explored polycentric hosting options such as Belgium and Netherlands, Austria and Switzerland and Spain and Portugal. Future potential hosting clusters may be Scandinavia including any of the Baltic countries. Another area with a strong passion for football may also consider a polycentric football tournament if they overcome their political challenges in the region (Slovenia, Croatia with the Western Balkan countries such as Bosnia and Hercegovina, Serbia, Montenegro, North Macedonia).

In Latin America, any two to three neighbouring countries may consider a polycentric tournament given the same language in most of the countries of the continent. The same applies to the Caribbean islands that could join forces for a future Gold Cup in the region. In the Middle East and other parts of Asia there are similar opportunities especially for smaller nations.

On a global scale the next FIFA Men's World Cup to be awarded is the 2038 one and if FIFA sticks to its continental rotation system the only option to bid for is the CONCACAF region as all other continents except Oceania will have hosted the World Cup by 2034 in the given timeframe (Foxsports, 2023). For the smaller FIFA Women's World Cup even more polycentric formats could be on the horizon from Scandinavia to Latin America.

There is a future for polycentric football tournaments if the event is hosted by countries in a certain geographic area that allows both teams and fans easy travel options between the host countries. Certainly the event will be smoother to organize if there is a limited number of languages, cultures and security systems involved.

References

AP (2018). 4 years later, graft taints 10 Brazilian World Cup stadiums. Last accessed 7 December 2023 via https://apnews.com/4-years-later-graft-taints-10-brazilian-world-cup-stadiums-fdbf477e6d504a4d91c4614b7746a4be.

Foxsports (2023). Why FIFA's new World Cup strategy could help the U.S. Last accessed 11 December 23 via https://www.foxsports.com/stories/soccer/why-fifas-new-world-cup-strategy-could-help-the-u-s.

Heere, B., Kim, C. Y., Yoshida, M., Ogura, T., Chung, K. S., Lim, S. Y. and Nakamura, H. (2012). The impact of World Cup 2002 on the bilateral relationship between South Korea and Japan. *Journal of Sport Management, 26*(2), 127–142.

IOC (2020). Contractual Framework for Hosting the Olympic and Paralympic Games. Last accessed 14 December 2023 via https://stillmed.olympic.org/media/Document%20Library/OlympicOrg/Games/Future-Olympic-Hosts/Contractual-framework-for-hosting-the-Olympic-and-Paralympic-Games-January-2020.pdf#_ga=2.226145818.1073018029.1582353916-147521303.1561554984.

IOC (2023). The French Alps and Salt Lake City-Utah invited into respective Targeted Dialogues to host the Olympic and Paralympic Winter Games 2030 and 2034. Last accessed 14 December via https://olympics.com/ioc/news/the-french-alps-and-salt-lake-city-utah-invited-into-respective-targeted-dialogues-to-host-the-olympic-and-paralympic-winter-games-2030-and-2034.

Kaspar, R. (2014). The event life cycle. In J. Beech, S. Kaiser and R. Kaspar (Eds.), *The Business of Events Management*. London: Pearson.

Kaspar, R. (2018). Smart Mega Events – How Have the IOC's "New Norm" Requirements Impacted the Sports Facility Concepts of the Cities Bidding to Host The 2026 Olympic Winter Games? (Practitioner Contribution EASM Sports Management Conference).

Kaspar, R. (2022). Hosting mega events in the Gulf. In D. Reiche and P. Brannagan (Eds.), *Handbook of Sports in the Middle East*. Abingdon: Routledge.

O'Connor, S. and Ehambaranathan, E. (2022). Evaluating the travelling inequality and final positions of teams in a European polycentric tournament: Euro 2022. *International Journal of Sport, Exercise and Health Research, 6*(1), 27–30.

Stura, C., Aicher, C., Kaspar, R., Klein, C., Schulz, S. and Unterlechner, S. (2017). The UEFA Euro 2020 as a pioneer project for multi-venue sports events. In M. Dodds, K. Heisey and A. Ahonen (Eds.), *Handbook of International Sport Business* (1st ed.) (pp. 26–36). Abingdon: Routledge.

25

A GEOPOLITICAL AND ECONOMIC ANALYSIS OF CHINA'S BID FOR THE FIFA WORLD CUP

Going It Alone or Co-hosting

Ren Huitao and Ma Yang

Football stands as the world's most influential sporting endeavour, and its premier event, the Fédération Internationale de Football Association (FIFA) World Cup, which occurs every four years, boasts a budget surpassing $15 billion. It not only holds the distinction of being the largest single-sport event but also stands as the most costly sporting spectacle (Matthias, 2020). Currently, the FIFA World Cup is undergoing changes to its format, to include 48 additional teams. These "gigantic" alterations further amplify pressure on host countries and host cities. In this grand context, joint hosting by multiple nations has emerged as the prevailing choice. The 2026 World Cup will be jointly hosted by the United States, Canada, and Mexico, while the 2030 World Cup will be cohosted by Spain, Portugal, and Morocco. FIFA President Gianni Infantino has also indicated that the days of a single nation hosting the World Cup may be in the past, as multinational cohosting can "ensure sustainability," aligning with current global trends.

Although the World Cup is typically seen as a major event that attracts the attention of football fans, broadcasters, and sponsors, it has also become a prominent academic topic in modern international relations, as it focuses on political manoeuvring and international cooperation surrounding major sporting events. Cohosting large-scale events is not a new concept. It is not only about reducing the burden of hosting costs but also strategically engaging in multilateral cooperation that goes beyond basic political and economic agreements. This inevitably gives rise to discussions in the realms of cultural and political geography (Nicholas and Lee, 2022). Furthermore, the joint bidding and hosting actions of these collaborating nations, as participants in global governance, are inherently built upon complex political relations and carry significant symbolic geopolitical significance (Beissel and Kohe, 2022).

DOI: 10.4324/9781003473671-29

China's passion for football mirrors that of other countries around the world, with an almost fanatical following during the FIFA World Cup. Questions such as "when will China reach the World Cup finals?" "when will China host the World Cup?", and "when will the Chinese team win the World Cup?" are frequently discussed among football enthusiasts and stakeholders in China. Currently, building upon its successful record of hosting events such as the 2008 Beijing Olympics and the 2022 Winter Olympics, China aspires to bid for the FIFA World Cup as a significant milestone in the country's future endeavours to host major sporting events. Given the prevailing trend of joint hosting, the choice China makes in this regard is of great interest. To better elucidate the decision-making process and the rationale behind China's bid, this study utilizes the geopolitical and economic framework proposed by Simon Chadwick (2022). The plan treats "China's bid for the World Cup" as an outcome influenced by geopolitical and economic factors, analysing it within the significant impact areas delineated by Simon Chadwick (2022).

The Bid to Host the World Cup Resulted from the Interplay between China's Natural Geography and Its Cultural Geography

China's natural geography poses challenges to the accommodation of extensive football activities, primarily due to the pressure on available space for football field construction. Football fields compete with other land uses, especially agricultural use, which is essential given China's need for sufficient land for farming and livestock production to support its large population. As of April 12, 2023, the Ministry of Natural Resources of the People's Republic of China released the "2022 China Natural Resources Statistics Bulletin," which indicated that China had a total of 127.601 million hectares of arable land and 264.273 million hectares of grassland. To ensure food security, the Chinese government adheres to the strictest farmland protection system known as the "1.8 billion mu redline," signifying that available land for public use, including sports facilities such as football fields, is limited. Currently, there are approximately 135,900 football fields in China, with 31,200 for eleven-a-side football, 43,200 for seven-a-side football, and 61,400 for five-a-side football. However, approximately 80% of these fields are located within school campuses.

China is a vast and populous superpower with a strong representation of football enthusiasts. According to data from FIFA's official website, China has more than 26 million football fans, defined as individuals who engage in football activities at least twice a week, which places the country first in the world in terms of football population. Additionally, China boasts a registered player count of 710,000, making it the 12th largest in the world. The FIFA World Cup typically centres on urban areas as host venues, a concept that aligns well with China's circumstances. Currently, China has achieved a 64.72% urbanization rate, with the total population in 661 cities exceeding 920 million people. Among these cities, 20 have populations exceeding 9 million, and 91 cities have populations exceeding 5 million. Many cities in China have cultivated a strong football culture, positioning themselves as "football cities" in urban identity and development strategies. In preparation for the 2023 Asian Cup, China initiated a nationwide project in 2019 to renovate and construct professional football stadiums in top the two tiers of cities. While some cities withdrew their bids to host the tournament, cities such as Tianjin (15.59 million), Shanghai (24.87 million), Chongqing (32.05 million), Chengdu (20 million), Xi'an (12.95 million), Dalian (7.48 million), Qingdao (10.34 million), Xiamen (5.31 million), and Suzhou (12.91 million) have already completed the construction of large football stadiums that meet FIFA's standards. China's football performance may not be at the highest level, but the enthusiasm for football events among urban populations is unparalleled.

The Bid to Host the World Cup Holds Significance as a Focal Point for Soft Power, Diplomacy, and Trade

Modern major sporting events carry a strong international dimension and serve as moments of utopian social interaction that few other forms of diplomacy can provide. The opening ceremonies of these events and the "peaceful battles" between nations on green fields garner significant attention and offer a sense of joy in the realm of imagined games. As noted by Wolfram Manzenreiter and John Horne (2007), the progress of East Asian football is closely linked to the expansion of global capital, nationalistic ambitions, and domestic policies. Beyond economic benefits, the will of nations in the entire East Asian region seems more pronounced, elevating football as a national endeavour within the modernization processes of Japan, South Korea, and China. In 2009, the newly elected President Xi Jinping made a public statement about football, expressing his personal hope that China could enter the finals and win the FIFA World Cup. The goal of "hosting or winning the World Cup" was incorporated into China's medium- to long-term development plan for sports, known as the "Sports Powerhouse Strategy" (Tien-Chin et al., 2016). The remarks of the national leader contributed to the integration of football into China's representation of cultural elements within its soft power. On September 23, 2023, during the opening ceremony of the Hangzhou Asian Games, President Xi Jinping once again emphasized the connection between major sporting events and Asia's development. He mentioned, "Over the past few decades, the Asian region has maintained overall stability, sustained rapid economic growth, and achieved the 'Asian miracle' where 'the scenery on this side is unique.'… As a community with a shared future closely connected by mountains and rivers and bonded by common humanity, we must use sports to promote peace, adhere to good-neighbourliness, mutual benefit, and resist Cold War mentality and confrontation between blocs. We aim to make Asia a stable anchor for world peace."

In addition to its diplomatic and soft power implications, the FIFA World Cup has also attracted attention in China for its economic impact, as the nation is an emerging economic powerhouse. During the quarter-final stage of the Qatar World Cup, China Central Television (CCTV), which holds the exclusive broadcasting rights for the World Cup, released statistics for mainland China. Since the start of the tournament, CCTV-5's viewership had grown by 498%, and its market share had increased by 420%. There was a significant increase in the number of younger viewers, with viewership among those aged 15–24 increasing by 985% and among those aged 25–34 increasing by 977%. Moreover, a multitude of Chinese companies, such as Alibaba, Wanda, Huawei, Hisense, Vivo, Mengniu, and Yili, have pursued international brand recognition through overseas sports marketing, establishing a prominent presence on the World Cup stage. Chinese investors are showing an increasingly fervent interest in international sporting events, playing a growing role in various aspects, including stadium construction, product promotion, and marketing of licenced products while participating in sponsorship of the World Cup. Driven by national policies, football and the football industry have gained significant attention and investment in Chinese cities. This heightened focus has led to a notable increase in the number of individuals participating in football activities and working in football-related fields. Investments in football and consumer engagement in sports are also on the rise.

Hosting the World Cup Is a Form of Networked Geopolitical and Economic Activity

In 2002, South Korea and Japan jointly hosted the World Cup, and South Korea's national team even reached the semifinals, bringing immense pride to South Korean people. The South Korean Football Association (KFA) expressed its desire to host the World Cup again approximately 20 years after their previous turn. The KFA proposed a joint bid by South Korea and China, but there was no response to this proposal from the Chinese Football Association (CFA).

Southeast Asian countries are also exploring the possibility of jointly bidding to host the FIFA World Cup, and the ASEAN Football Federation (AFF) has expressed support for the initiative to host the FIFA World Cup. In January 2011, discussions were held during the ASEAN Foreign Ministers' Informal Meeting and the ASEAN Coordinating Council Special Meeting, both held on the Indonesian island of Lombok, to explore the plans for ASEAN countries' joint bid to host this world-class sporting event. During the 34th ASEAN Summit held in Thailand on June 23, 2019, ASEAN countries welcomed and supported efforts to host the FIFA World Cup football tournament in the region. ASEAN expressed its desire to promote and support the endeavours of the national football associations in the region, as well as the AFF, towards this goal. Other Asian countries are actively using major sporting events to enhance diplomatic ties and build closer relationships between nations. For instance, football is seen as a potential facilitator within the context of the China-Pakistan Economic Corridor (Ali, 2022). The sport has the potential to diversify and strengthen the relations between China and Pakistan. However, these discussions have not received responses at the level of governmental or national football associations. In Asia, particularly in countries such as Japan and South Korea, the rising prominence of football is considered a crucial factor in aspirations for greater participation in global governance (Wolfram and John, 2007). This dynamic adds pressure to China's decision to proceed with joint bids to host major events.

Hosting the World Cup Serves as a Foundation for Achieving National Competitive Advantage

China follows a significant national strategy known as "Concentrating Power to Accomplish Big Things," which leverages its formidable capacity for social mobilization. This approach is a source of pride for the Chinese government and has been instrumental in various national endeavours. However, in the realm of football, this strategy has not been fully realized. Over the two decades from 1993 to 2013, Chinese football faced challenges in its professionalization and commercialization. A series of match-fixing scandals turned fans' enthusiasm into disappointment and shook the belief in a fully commercialized future for Chinese football. The development of the Chinese Super League (CSL) has continued to be significantly influenced by its political and economic environment (Li et al., 2024), leading Chinese football down a path of politically led commercialization (Yang and Markus, 2022). The Chinese central government initiated a series of reforms, including anti-corruption measures, in professional football. However, the future of Chinese football requires further structural changes in governance and government involvement (Fan and Lu, 2013). The reform of professionalism in Chinese football is a pilot project in the transformation of China's sports system. However, the effectiveness of these reforms has been limited due to confusion over the roles of governing institutions, thus resulting in weak governance and corruption issues in Chinese football (Runbin and Zhenpeng, 2022). Furthermore, the transition to professional football in China has encountered challenges stemming from the interaction between international football norms and traditional Chinese culture. For instance, from 1998 to 2009, bribing referees in the Chinese professional football league was common and considered an unwritten rule by all football clubs (Zheng et al., 2019).

China's extensive history has instilled a culture of reflection as the first course of action following any unsuccessful endeavour. Regarding the frequent losses of the national football team, professionals, fans, and football enthusiasts often point out issues related to youth development, grassroots participation, and the selection of talent for the national team. One of the most criticized aspects of Chinese football is its administrative structure. The governance system of Chinese football is not overseen by the CFA, which is the highest authority. While the chairperson of the CFA is also a vice director of the General Administration of Sport of China (GASC), the actual day-to-day affairs are managed by full-time vice chairpersons. Since its establishment in 1955, the CFA has had six chairpersons, but in reality, 11 individuals held leadership positions. Notably, figures such as Huang Zhong (1956–1979), Yuan Weiming (1986–1989, 1992–2014), and Cai Zhenhua (2014–2018) also served as vice directors of the GASC alongside their roles in football administration. Despite the convening of a general assembly, the vice chairpersons of the CFA and other decision-making members are typically selected through internal deliberations and elections within the GASC. Additionally, China has established institutions such as the National Sports Administration Football Management Centre and the Interministerial Joint Meeting Office for Football Reform and Development under the State Council to oversee football and drive reforms within the CFA. In 2016, the GASC underwent structural changes by disbanding the Football Management Centre, thereby implementing a separation between governance and operation. The CFA, now operating as a legal entity, assumed responsibility for supervising and managing various aspects of Chinese football affairs.

China's anticorruption efforts in football are moving into deeper waters, and it is worth noting that this campaign within the football sphere has the potential to bring about significant changes. According to the views of prominent Chinese sports scholar Yi Jiandong (2010), bidding for the World Cup may offer a valuable resource—the possibility of external influence—that could lead to improvements in the governance and administration of Chinese football.

Chinese citizens are a crucial factor. For football event broadcasting, the China Central Television Sports Channel (CCTV-5) stands as the exclusive broadcaster. CCTV essentially monopolizes the broadcast rights for all of China's national football team matches. However, they often opt to broadcast only matches with higher expected chances of winning, leading to a bias towards victorious outcomes. This frequently presents an overly optimistic view of Chinese football to the public, as they often see "winning" matches. Many of the television viewers for Chinese football events watch matches out of a sense of national pride (these same audiences rarely watch matches from professional football leagues, whether Chinese or Western). However, their focus on whether the team wins or loses often leads to a lack of "professional appreciation" for the technical aesthetics and tactical skills demonstrated by the players during the game, which results in limited aesthetic appreciation (these vast audience groups are often referred to as "casual fans" by professional football enthusiasts).

Win or lose, football can give people a stronger sense of national identity and strengthen the sense of national community, which has played a significant role in maintaining China's world-leading mass mobilization capacity and hierarchical administrative system.

Hosting the World Cup Serves as a Means of Acquiring Resources

Mega sports events are a special resource, and hosting the World Cup is not only an opportunity to actively integrate into the international community, but also a process to showcase the diversity of a country and its own culture. In modern times, China's integration into global economic, social, and cultural exchanges was mainly through its accession to the WTO, followed by the Beijing 2008 Olympic Games. In cultural exchanges represented by sporting events, China showcases the diversity of its political system, economic structure, nation, and history. The premise of recognition is to know and understand, and hosting the FIFA World Cup gives countries and football lovers around the world the opportunity to know China.

As a major cultural event, hosting the World Cup also brings the opportunity to reintegrate capital, high-level footballers and the football industry. China's soccer industry is mainly focused on the manufacture of supplies, especially soccer shoes, and China is still the world's largest soccer shoe contract factory. Hosting the World Cup provides strategic resources for the transformation of China's football industry to the service industry. In the process of hosting, global football governance authorities, affiliated events and intellectual elites will be introduced to this big event. Second, China's huge capital, labour and a large number of business organizations will be involved.

The World Cup will also bring new spirit and momentum to Chinese football. Whether it is the technical and tactical level of football, or the elite operation ability of football matches, the global scope is rapidly changing, from tactical concepts to technical training are rapidly improving. However, the level of professionalism, marketization, and internationalization of Chinese professional football is not sufficient, and the communication with international professional football is relatively small. The periodic dividends brought by hosting the World Cup can bring convenience to Chinese football in international exchanges.

Conclusions

Against the backdrop of an expanded World Cup final stage and evolving dynamics, recent trends have favoured joint hosting arrangements involving multiple countries. However, special considerations arise when we turn our attention to China. Whether we examine the success of the 2008 Summer Olympics or the 2022 Winter Olympics, both held in Beijing, we cannot discount the pivotal role played by China's unique geopolitical context, political system, cultural nuances, and socio-economic conditions in shaping these events. China's remarkable economic strides as a nation have also fuelled its enthusiasm for large-scale cultural endeavours. With an enormous population of football enthusiasts numbering hundreds of millions, China is well prepared to host the World Cup. However, its hosting approach appears to diverge from international norms. This study employs Simon Chadwick's (2022) geopolitical and economic framework to explore the possibility that China will opt for an independent bid, even though the prevailing trend leans towards joint hosting. The research contends that China is inclined towards the independent option, which has the potential to catalyse the further development of football within China to the fullest extent.

References

Ali, A. (2022). Just for kicks: football as a potential harmoniser in the China–Pakistan economic corridor. *Journal of Global Sport Management, 7*(3), 372–390.

Beissel, A. S. and Kohe, G. Z. (2022). United as one: The 2026 FIFA Men's World Cup hosting vision and the symbolic politics of legacy. *Managing Sport and Leisure, 27*(6), 593–613.

Chadwick, S. (2022). From utilitarianism and neoclassical sport management to a new geopolitical economy of sport. *European Sport Management Quarterly, 22*(5), 685–704.

Fan, H. and Lu, Z. (2013). The professionalisation and commercialisation of football in China (1993–2013). *The International Journal of the History of Sport, 30*(14), 1637–1654.

Li, H., Nabors, S., Nauright, J. and Bai, Y. (2024). Political economy and football in new market: the case of the Chinese Super League. *Sport in Society, 27*(2), 278–295.

Matthias, F. (2020). The game has changed – a systematic approach to classify FIFA World Cups. *International Journal of Sport Policy and Politics, 12*(3), 455–470.

Nicholas, W. and Lee, A. (2022). Uniting, disuniting and reuniting: towards a united 2026. *Sport in Society, 25*(4), 837–846.

Runbin, W. and Zhenpeng, R. (2022). Global vision and local action: football, corruption and the governance of football in China. *Asian Journal of Sport History and Culture, 1*(2), 128–160.

Tien-Chin, T., Hsien-Che, H., Alan, B. and Yu-Wen, C. (2016). Xi Jin-Ping's World Cup dreams: from a major sports country to a world sports power. *The International Journal of the History of Sport, 33*(12), 1449–1465.

Wolfram, M. and John, H. (2007). Playing the post-Fordist game in/to the Far East: the footballisation of China, Japan and South Korea. *Soccer and Society, 8*(4), 561–577.

Yang, M. and Markus, K. (2022). Doing it the Chinese way: the politically-led commercialization of professional football in China. *Journal of Global Sport Management, 7*(3), 355–371.

Yi, J. (2010). 12 reasons why China should bid for the football World Cup. *Journal of Sports, 17*(08), 25.

Zheng, L., Jian, D. and Bo, W. (2019). Bribing referees: the history of unspoken rules in Chinese professional football leagues, 1998–2009. *The International Journal of the History of Sport, 36*(4–5), 359–374.

26

FIFA WORLD CUP 2026, SOCCER'S NORTH AMERICAN SPORTING LEGACY

Vitas Carosella and J. Simon Rofe

The Origins of US Soccer

Contrary to a prevailing strand of popular opinion, Association Football or 'Soccer' has a long history in the United States. It is this history that bequeaths the 2026 FIFA Men's World Cup, a legacy that should not be underestimated or overlooked. Yes, for many generations soccer has been a mass participation sport for American children through to their teens when the so-called big four sports (American Football, Basketball, Baseball and Ice Hockey) take precedence for many as they feed through the college system into professional sports in the United States. The training ground provided by soccer of quick-wittedness, movement and overall fitness has spawned many professional sporting careers across the four main US sports. For those that continue to engage with and play soccer the success of the United States Women's Team has been another dominant narrative.

Furthermore, soccer has routinely been a game for migrant communities in the 'melting pot' of the United States, for hyphenated Americans: whether that is Scottish-Americans, German-Americans, Italian-Americans or in more recent times the collective expression for those from south of the Rio Grande, Latino-Americans. Whatever the vernacular, mindful it brings to the fore further questions of identity – some with potentially unpleasant, nee racist overtones, soccer has been a vehicle for sporting dialogue with the world in a nation that has historically modelled itself as a 'nation of immigrants.'

Indeed, the immigrant impact on US soccer was clear in the earliest days of a representative team. It was the migrants who came to the United States in the late nineteenth and early twentieth century who largely made up US teams in the first decades of the twentieth century. Players born overseas took

DOI: 10.4324/9781003473671-30

up a majority of names on the teamsheet for the first official fixture for a US team when they defeated Sweden 3-2 in August 1916. This came three years after the US Football Association was formed in Chicago in 1913 and welcomed into FIFA a year later. While the American Soccer League (ASL) prospered, like much else in the 1920s in the United States (Jose, 1998) it was based on company teams away from major US cities that enticed promising European players to the United States with the prospect of playing opportunities and a job on the way to citizenship. This meant opportunities for American-born players were limited in what international football took place in the 1920s, and that largely foreign-born players represented the United States in the first two Men's World Cups in 1930 and 1934. The former saw the US team finished third in the inaugural tournament, which remains the Men's teams' best ever performance.

Equally it is important to note that *before* the United States and European migration and settlement, historians have identified ball games akin to football being part of the cultures of various indigenous peoples across the North American continent. So, the legacy of soccer in the America's predates the United States, and there is a longer arc to the narrative that is bequeathed to the 2026 FIFA Men's United World Cup.

Arguably the most significant fixture for the US Men's soccer team in that arc in the twentieth century came in Belo Horizonte, Brazil at the 1950 FIFA Men's World Cup, when the team beat England 1-0 (FIFA https://www.fifa.com/tournaments/mens/worldcup/qatar2022/news/the-miracle-belo-horizonte-1165849). This is showcased in the movie *The Game of Their Lives* (2005) based on the novel of the same name by Geoffrey Douglass (1996); the narrative of US success in beating a supposedly all-conquering professional England team on the latter's World Cup debut with a team of amateur players pulled together at short notice bears a reasonable comparison with events. At least part of the reason for the compelling narrative was that the match became a key marker in English footballing history and then repatriated globally as England's own redemption story that culminated 16 years later when Sir Alf Ramsey – who played against the United States in Belo Horizonte – managed England to their sole World Cup win on home soil.

The more substantive legacy for this volume is to consider why the US soccer team's famous win against the odds did not see a generational shift in the place of soccer in the United States. The answer is necessarily multi-dimensional. Structural forces made it so the US win over England was a non-event. Press coverage of the US victory was minimal: the Baseball season was in full swing and the New York Yankees on their way to a World Series victory with a team full of hall of farmers; while American Football and Basketball respectively sought to challenge Baseball's predominance and their overlapping year-round schedules meant there was no 'window' for soccer to situate itself. Indeed, the post-war boom years saw the consolidation of other professional sports in the United States, and it would be a further generation before Base-ball – America's Game – was challenged by the National Football League (NFL) and National Basketball Association (NBA) after their respective merg-ers. Further structural factors mitigated against the victory in Belo Horizonte being pivotal for US soccer. Through the GI Bill (1944) many individuals who wouldn't have previously had access to college, and therefore college athletic programmes, ended up in sports other than soccer; it was not until 1959 that the National Collegiate Athletic Association (NCAA) recognised soccer. This served to focus minds and funnelled bodies away from cultures and environ-ments that spawned player development in the quintessential favelas of South America or the cobbled streets of industrialised Europe.

The Birth of the NASL and the Rise of Soccer in the 1970s

As soccer engulfed the rest of the world in the latter half of the twentieth century, and the allure of FIFA World Cup glory and money increased, the focus in the United States remained on the big four sports. The lack of media coverage and the abundance of other sporting and professional opportunities meant that soccer was not a priority for the average American in the post-war period. Despite the creation of the second iteration of the ASL, the game suf-fered from limited budgets, small-market teams and immigrant dominated fanbases, leading it to be absent for most of the American public.

From the latter half of the Truman presidency until the final year of Lyn-don B. Johnson's second term soccer remained a regionalised and divided sport (1945–1968). The absence of a national professional league led to semi-professionalism and stymied any momentum from the historic 1-0 victory over England in 1950 (Reese, 2023). In 1959 soccer was first sanctioned by the NCAA, the first collegiate national championship tournament was held, and 'the pipeline of soccer success shifted away from the streets and amateur and semi-pro leagues to the university' (Reck and Dick, 2015). The transition away from semi-professionalism saw institutions embrace the sport and offer schol-arships to players, aiding the growth of the beautiful game and giving way to the current pay-to-play club system that dominates American soccer today. Moreover, the adoption in colleges opened the door – following the model of other US sports – for the return of a fully professional domestic league.

In 1967 – on the back of the highly reported English World Cup triumph – soccer in the United States saw the creation of two professional leagues; the FIFA-approved United Soccer Association and the unsanctioned National Pro-fessional Soccer League, which benefited from a broadcast deal with national provider Columbia Broadcasting System (CBS). After one year of division, the two leagues came together in 1968 to form the North American Soccer League (NASL 1968–1984), giving professional soccer a level of prominence in the United States not seen since the 1920s. Nonetheless, while the NASL proved to be short lived – lasting only from 1968 until 1984 – it left an indelible mark on soccer culture in America, boosting youth participation and paving the way for the post-war hegemon to host its first FIFA Men's World Cup in 1994 and become the dominant force in women's football into the twenty-first century.

It is not an overestimation to say that without the NASL the United States would not have hosted the 1994 FIFA World Cup, let alone be awarded hosting rights for the largest ever World Cup in 2026. The NASL brought attention to the beautiful game in the United States by attracting some of the best talent in the world, notably Franz Beckenbauer, Johan Cruyff and Pelé. The growth of the sport even had political connotations. It was Secretary of State (1973–1977) Henry Kissinger who convinced Pelé to move to the United States (Zurick, 2023, Holmes, 2016), instead of hanging up his boots for good. Kissinger leveraged his political power to help grow the game in America – in part due to his personal fandom, in part because he saw the game could be used for political purposes – and used the transfer of Pelé from Santos to the New York Cosmos to strengthen ties between the United States and Brazil.

Once in the United States, Pelé did not disappoint. Over 10 million fans tuned in to watch the live broadcast of Pelé's debut for the New York Cosmos, and by the mid-1970s average stadium attendance was nearly 13,000 spectators. Even in the years immediately after the Brazilian's departure – 1977 to 1982 – the average attendance for a Cosmos game was 40,000 spectators.

Like many of the most successful enterprises in the United States, and previous iterations of US soccer, the NASL was built upon foreign labour. The league's over reliance on foreign superstars to score the goals and fill the stadiums was its eventual undoing. It left a dearth of talent funnelling into the national team, meaning that as the NASL boomed, the United States failed to produce enough high-level talent to qualify for a World Cup tournament until 1990. By the early 1980s the league was losing money and as foreign players left American shores, regulations were put in place to ensure a minimum number (3) of US and Canadian players were in the matchday teamsheet. This was not enough to save the league from its financial troubles and it folded in 1985, but not before inspiring the next generation to take up the sport.

It would not be until 1990 that the United States made its next World Cup, thanks in large part to the legacy left by the NASL. By the time the United States prepared to host the 1994 FIFA World Cup, the NASL was a fading memory, but its impact was enough to help give rise to the next ASL and continue the legacy of US soccer into the next millennia.

World Cup 1994 and the MLS

The opening match of the FIFA's men's World Cup on 17 June 1994 at Chicago's Soldier Field was a momentous occasion for a number of reasons: it marked the appearance for the first time since before the Second World War of a unified Germany team, as the successor to the West German team that had triumphed at Italia 90; it saw a red card for Bolivia's captain and star play Marco Etcheverry; and a quite remarkable penalty 'miss' by Diana Ross during the opening ceremony.

None of this served to capture the attention of anything but the most dedicated soccer fans in the United States on that day in June 1994, as the attention of the nation was captured by the drama provided by a televised pursuit of a White Ford Bronco containing Hall of Fame Running Back OJ Simpson along the freeways of Los Angeles. Even without the Simpson chase, coverage of the opening fixture was perhaps destined to be minimal as it had to compete with the final appearance of Arnold Palmer in golf's US Open; coverage of the New York Rangers' Stanley Cup victory parade; Game 5 of the NBA finals between the Houston Rockets and the New York Knicks; and Ken Griffey Jr tying Babe Ruth's record for home runs (30) before the end of June. All are captured in Brett Morgan's 30 for 30 film (2010) with the World Cup a supporting member of the cast. What is significant in explaining the legacy of soccer in the United States is what flowed from the 1994 World Cup: in short, Major League Soccer (MLS).

MLS was a direct outcome of the commitment made by the US Soccer Federation to host the World Cup. Alan Rothenberg, chairman of World Cup 1994, made the commitment to MLS six months before Germany played Bolivia in June 1994, pledging the League would begin in February 1995. However, the league's first match did not take place until April 1996 when the San Jose Clash defeated DC United 1-0 in the ten-team league. The narrative accompanying the MLS's first ten years tells a story of mixed fortunes. While the league expanded to 12 teams for four years between 1998 and 2001 on the back of a successful qualification by the US national team at World Cup France 98, the league itself took the decision to remove two Florida teams, Miami Fusion and Tampa Bay Mutiny, to cut the cost base for the League for the 2002 season, reducing the number of teams back to ten until the 10th anniversary of Robert Baggio's penalty miss that decided the 1994 World Cup final.

MLS Commissioner Don Garber recognised the challenge: 'I know many out there think this is the end of Major League Soccer, and that couldn't be further from the truth' he suggested. 'We simply could not find a solution that was economically feasible at this time, and we hope to return to the state of Florida when the league expands in future years' (http://news.bbc.co.uk/sport1/hi/other_sports/us_sport/1750024.stm, accessed 4 January 2024)

The history of the past 20 years has borne Garber out: between 2006 and 2016 ten new teams joined the MLS, and by 2025 a further ten teams will have joined. More specifically MLS returned to Florida with Orlando City in 2015, and then Inter Miami FC in 2020. Integral to the latter, was David

Beckham, who had joined the MLS from Real Madrid CF as a player in 2007 and would be the first amongst equals as the face of Garber's expansion of the MLS. The owners of the LA Galaxy, where Beckham would play for his five years in the MLS as a player winning two championships in his final two seasons, stated on his arrival, 'David is truly the only individual that can build the "bridge" between soccer in America and the rest of the world.' These words might be considered hyperbole, but what accompanied Beckham's time as a player was a recognition that the MLS was a meaningful location for elite soccer on the pitch, average crowds of over 20,000 supporters in the stands, and substantive investment off it. The expansion incorporated transitioning from traditional soccer hotbeds to big 'market' cities. Importantly these teams have had the support of those cities and their locales which has seen 11 purpose-built soccer first stadiums, which have in turn encouraged the development of indigenous fan cultures and mean that a Forbes report in February 2023 placed the average value of each of the MLS clubs at $579 million.

So while the first ten years were a challenge for the MLS, the League's growth since has been remarkable with potential owners now paying an entrance/expansion fee of $200 million to sit alongside the likes of David Beckham's Inter Miami, and Los Angeles FC – the first MLS club to be valued at more than $1 Billion dollars. Soccer is now the third largest sport by spectatorship in the United States, making the MLS also the seventh most-watched league globally.

The Road to 2026

Despite soccer's storied legacy in the United States – including its prominence in the 1920s, the shock the men's national team made on the international scene at the 1950 World Cup, the welcoming of global superstars to the NASL in the 1970s and the game's continued rise to prominence in the digital age thanks to the arrival of Beckham and now Messi – the beautiful game has traditionally been a sport that has captivated the American audience during World Cup years (male and female) and then faded into the background until the next international tournament began.

As the 2026 World Cup nears, the nature of soccer in the United States is changing. Due to a multitude of sociocultural and economic factors, soccer is more popular in the United States than ever before. While its dominant appeal amongst immigrant demographics is well documented, a Gallup (2023) poll shows that 8% of Americans now say soccer is their favourite sport to watch. In 2004 that percentage was just 2%, so now it is almost on par with that of America's pastime: baseball.

Improved viewership is partly due to the accessibility of the sport. Since 2015 NBC has broadcast a full slate of English Premier League games every weekend. In 2021 the broadcast giant began simulcasting games on its streaming service Peacock, bringing the English league to linear and streaming television across the United States (Appezzato, 2023). In recent years every single La. Liga Bundesliga, UEFA Champions League and Serie A match has also become available on streaming services and linear TV.

Access to foreign leagues and improving broadcast deals for domestic North American leagues like MLS, NWSL and Liga MX make it possible for Americans to spend their entire weekends watching soccer for the majority of the calendar year. At the same time, docuseries like Ryan Reynolds 'Welcome to Wrexham' and Emmy-winning show 'Ted Lasso' have created a diversified viewership by capitalising on the intersection of soccer and pop culture.

As viewership of soccer has gone up, so has participation. Studies by the National Federation of State High School Associations (Enten, 2022) show that roughly 40 years ago only 200,000 boys and girls played high school soccer, while almost 1 million boys played football. Today the gap is negligible with 800,000 boys and girls playing soccer in 2021. That represents a 300% growth in participation in just 40 years. This is partly due to safety concerns – soccer produces fewer long-term injuries, most notably concussions – but also because there is a growing association with soccer in the United States.

Millennials and Generation Z are accustomed to a world in which American female soccer players are competing for world titles, male players star for some of the best club sides in the world and Europe's biggest clubs tour the United States every summer. Soccer has moved beyond the immigrant communities it has long thrived in and is now part of mainstream American culture. This is evidenced by the fact that in 2023, the English Premier League overtook Liga MX – whose supremacy was largely based on capturing the attention of the large Hispanic population – as the most-watched league in the United States (Fansler, 2023).

Soccer's increased standing in US culture has seen the MLS and NWSL achieve record attendances in recent seasons, while franchise values and revenue streams continue to multiply. Even American businessmen have seen economic opportunity in the beautiful game, and their investments – primarily into the English Premier league – have strengthened US economic and cultural ties to the sport.

With the FIFA Men's World Cup – United 2026 – on the horizon, soccer in the United States is beginning to capture the attention of the mainstream in a way that it has done in other nations. This has only been multiplied by the arrival of multiple Ballon d'Or winner Lionel Messi at Inter Miami CF. What remains to be seen is if the newfound appeal of the sport will transition to success on the field, and whether or not the United States can successfully host the largest FIFA World Cup to date.

References

Appezzato, S. (2023). *Popularity of soccer soars in U.S. ahead of 2023-24 season – two River Times, Two River Times – The Two River Times is a weekly newspaper about life in Monmouth County, NJ, sold by subscription and on newsstands Friday*. Available at: https://tworivertimes.com/popularityofsoccersoars/ [Accessed 7 January 2024].

Douglass, G. (1996). *The Game of Their Lives*. New York: Henry Holt and Company.

Enten, H. (2022). *The US may have lost in the World Cup, but soccer is more popular than ever in America, CNN*. Available at: https://www.cnn.com/2022/12/12/football/soccer-popularity-us-world-cup-spt-intl/index.html [Accessed 7 January 2024].

Fansler, K. (2023). *Premier League is now the most-watched soccer league in USA, World Soccer Talk*. Available at: https://worldsoccertalk.com/tv/premier-league-is-now-the-most-watched-soccer-league-in-usa-20231228-WST-478701.html [Accessed 7 January 2024].

FIFA, *When England-USA served up one of the World Cup's biggest upsets*. Available at: https://www.fifa.com/tournaments/mens/worldcup/qatar2022/news/the-miracle-belo-horizonte-1165849 [Accessed 4 January 2024]

Gallup (2023). *Sports, Gallup.com*. Available at: https://news.gallup.com/poll/4735/sports.aspx [Accessed 7 January 2024].

Holmes, J. (2016). *How Henry Kissinger Convinced Pelé to Play Soccer in the U.S., Esquire*. Available at: https://www.esquire.com/sports/interviews/a44741/pele-interview/ [Accessed 6 January 2024].

Jose, C. (1998). *The American Soccer League – The Golden Years of American Soccer 1921–1931*. Lanham: Rowman & Littlefield.

NASL 1968–1984 (no date). *NASL*. Available at: http://www.nasl.com/a-review-of-the-golden-era [Accessed 6 January 2024).

Reck, G. G. and Dick, B. A. (2015). *American Soccer: History, Culture, Class*. Jefferson: McFarland.

Reese, D. (2023).*US Soccer history: 150 years and counting, World Soccer Talk*. Available at: https://worldsoccertalk.com/news/150-years-of-us-soccer-history-20221106-WST-406135.html [Accessed 6 January 2024].

Zurick, M. (2023). *Henry Kissinger, Pelé and the deal that changed American Soccer: 'my god!', Newsweek*. Available at: https://www.newsweek.com/henry-kissinger-pele-deal-that-changed-american-soccer-my-god-1848200 [Accessed 6 January 2024].

27

THE NATION BRANDING, PUBLIC DIPLOMACY AND THE 2023 FIFA WOMEN'S WORLD CUP

US against the World

Yoav Dubinsky

Introduction

The United States Women's National Team (USWNT) has been the standard for constantly raising the bar of women's football not just in terms of performance but also being a platform for generations of activist players who leveraged and their on-field success and fame to advocate for social causes, and predominantly gender equity and equality (Dubinsky, 2021, 2023a; Gitlitz, 2023). On-field, since the first FIFA Women's World Cup (WWC) in 1991 and the first women's Olympic football tournament in 1996 and as of the 2023 FIFA WWC in Australia and New Zealand, the USWNT has medaled in each of these major international events except for one, winning four world championships and four Olympic Gold Medals. Off-field, since the players of the 1999 winning team insisted the home WWC will be held in large football stadiums, marketing the tournament directly to students and through the community themselves, and winning the competition in a full Rose Bowl Stadium, USWNT players used their platforms to fight for change, on issues such as gender equality, LGBTQ acceptance, race, and others, even if it meant confronting American institutions such as their own federation and even the White House. Over the years, American governments used USWNT players for diplomatic purposes to showcase American lifestyle, and much like Brand America (Martin, 2007), the USWNT has also been associated with values such as freedom, capitalism and rebellion, along with arrogance and being self-centered (Dubinsky, 2021).

The USWNT headed to the 2023 WWC as a back-to-back defending champion after breaking ratings records while winning the 2015 WWC in Canada, and using the championship run in the 2019 WWC to further elevate

DOI: 10.4324/9781003473671-31

their demands from the US Soccer Federation for equal pay while also taking a stand against racial injustice at home (Dubinsky, 2021, 2023a; Gitlitz, 2023). Thus, the aspiration was to become the first men or women national team to win three consecutive world championships while winning their fifth, equaling the Brazilian men's achievement and through that establishing the place of the USWNT's historic significance for football, the most popular sport worldwide, at the very top. This chapter discusses the nation branding and public diplomacy implications of the USWNT's 2023 WWC campaign.

The USWNT and Brand America

To understand the significance of the USWNT to Brand America and to American society, one needs to go back to the Women's Rights Movement and Title IX, an amendment to the educational law that prohibits discrimination based on sex in any education institution that receives federal funds (Dubinsky, 2023a). In the realm of sports, the implication was that male and female student-athletes received equal opportunities regardless of revenue generation, which led to over ten times more girls and women participating in high school and collegiate sports. As the most financially impactful sport in the US collegiate system is American football generating billions of dollars to the system, and it is only played collegiately in Division I by men, this means that universities and colleges needed to provide the same level and amount of opportunities and scholarships to female student-athletes in team sports such as soccer, volleyball, lacrosse, and others without having a parallel men's team. The depth and breadth of female soccer talents coming out of the American collegiate system explains the American sustainable competitive advantage in international sports, why the USWNT is dominant in world championships and Olympic Games while the men's struggle, and how on-field performance is tied to a social movement and demand for change.

Although the USWNT won the first WWC in 1991, the landmark event was the 1999 WWC that was held on home soil (Dubinsky, 2021; Gitlitz, 2023). As mentioned, the athletes themselves pushed their federation to take the risk of empty stands and host the competitions in large stadiums that regularly hosted American football games. The players were also active marketing the tournament through schools and communities across the country, leading to over 90,000 fans coming to the final against China in the Rose Bowl Stadium. That proactive approach by players such as Mia Hamm, Julie Foudy, Cindy Parlow Cone who will later become the president of US Soccer, and Brandy Chastain who scored the championship clinching penalty and celebrated by taking her shirt of and staying with a Nike sports bra, set the tone to generations to come to further fight for gender equality and social justice. Players, such as Abby Wambach, Hope Solo, Alex Morgan, Carli Lloyd, and Megan Rapinoe, all grew up on or inspired by the 1999 team, and went on to breaking commercial rating records when winning the 2015 WWC, making the final the most watched soccer game in American history, all while representing different aspects of feminism, and becoming role models for the next generations of players.

The country image of the US has significantly deteriorated since the invasion of Iraq in 2003 (Martin, 2007). Joseph Nye (2008), who coined the term soft power as a way countries try to improve their image through attraction rather than military force, argued that the US needs to adapt a smart power approach of combining both soft and hard power. Following the 9/11 terror attacks, the US Department of State, the Bureau of Educational and Cultural Affairs, started to focus on sports diplomacy as part of American soft, to improve the international image of the country and spread American way of life (Bureau of Educational and Cultural Affairs, n.d.a, n.d.b). Part of the focus was on Title IX and women's sports, including through using USWNT players as envoys or establishing programs in the US where female leaders from different industries in different countries come to visit and are exposed to the benefits American women get through the sports system, including of course from soccer. According to Martin (2007) who analyzed Brand America, some of the values mostly associated with the US are freedom, capitalism, individualism, and rebelliousness, alongside self-concentration and arrogance. As seen from the US Department of State, American foreign policy sees the USWNT as a positive representation of what American values are.

Through the preparations, the tournament, and the aftermath of the 2019 WWC, payment issues and social activism were integrated within the USWNT (Dubinsky, 2021, 2023a; Gitlitz, 2023). Following the commercial success of the 2015 WWC, and the growing domestic support having the USWNT team jersey becoming the most sold Nike jersey in 2019, the players demanded better conditions from US Soccer beyond the latest collective bargaining agreement, and to equal the bonus payments the men receive, despite the different prize money FIFA awards to men's and women's tournaments. Furthermore, following incidents of police brutality, Megan Rapinoe was one of the first white athletes to join the wave of black athletes' activism protests and started to kneel when the American national anthem was played in international competitions (Dubinsky, 2021, 2023b; Fredrick et al., 2020). After US Soccer told her to stop, she stood and did not sing the words, along with other players who joined her. During the Presidency of Donald Trump, Rapinoe refused to visit the White House if the USWNT will win the WWC, which led to social media reaction by the president (Dubinsky, 2023b; Fredrick et al., 2020). The on-field and off-field success of the USWNT was well heard when the fans in Lyon chanted "Equal Pay" following the teams 2:0 victory over the reigning European champions, The Netherlands. In the following years, US Soccer apologized to Rapinoe for restricting her protests (Dubinsky, 2023a) and in early 2022 signed a new collective bargaining agreement, equaling payment bonuses to the men and receiving 22 million dollars in settlements (Bonesteel, 2022).

Along with being role models, the USWNT has also been polarizing due to their on-field and off-field behavior. The USWNT has traditionally been scrutinized for being politically liberal advocating for progressive causes and not necessarily reflecting the entire social fabric of America (Dubinsky, 2021). Furthermore, historically women's soccer in the US was associated with upper middle class and suburban lifestyle, and only in recent years the national team became more racially and ethnically diverse. The social activism of USWNT is driven from their financial profitability, thus, to continue to advocate effectively, they need to attract American audience to watch the competition, including through promos that glorify themselves on the expense of others. Furthermore, while the players fight for equal payment to leading male athletes, they are still better compensated than their female opponents, and when they were every classified as arrogant or bullies when celebrating a 13-0 win over Thailand in the first game of the 2019 WWC group stage (Dubinsky, 2021). Players also faced backlash from conservatives after a disappointing performance in the postponed Tokyo 2020 Olympic Games, where they settled for a bronze medal. Thus, domestically and internationally, the USWNT carries a baggage of representing America, with all its complexities.

US vs. The World

Despite disappointing Olympic Games and a series of loses to England, Spain and Germany in late 2022, the USWNT projected the typical American confidence. Before the 2019 WWC the broadcaster FOX and the USWNT promoted the competition with ads claiming, "All eyes on US" and framing the team as "Goliath", "Queen", perpetuating the narrative of being self-centered advertisement (Dubinsky, 2021). In 2023, the promotion focus was on "USA against the World" stating "the whole world was wondering what would it take to stop this U.S. team?" (FOX Soccer, 2023). Nike, the official apparel of US Soccer, along with other football associations, launched a campaign "What the Football" (Nike Football, 2023a) prior to the WWC celebrating the legacy of the 1999 USWNT and their influence on international football, and focusing specifically on "Megan Rapinoe All-American Hero" (Nike Football, 2023b). Under the Presidency of Joe Biden, the USWNT and the White House restored their relations, with the President awarding Rapinoe the Presidential Medal of Freedom (Lavietes, 2022), and the Bidens opening the official squad announcement of the USWNT for the 2023 WWC (US Women's National Team, 2023). USWNT participated in a campaign to encourage voting that was shared by former First Lady Michelle Obama (2023). During 2023 WWC, the US exercised sports diplomacy initiatives of gender equality, with First Gentleman Doug Emhoff leading the Presidential delegation in the opening ceremony and attending the first USWNT game against Vietnam (Frandino, 2023). During the tournament, Americans were involved with sports diplomacy conferences, including "Battle of the Sexes" winner Billie Jean King who led the formation of a professional women's tennis tour in the 1970s and spoke in the 2023 Equality Summit (The Wis Team, 2023). While off-field the USWNT, the White House, US Soccer, and commercial partners seemed to be more aligned than ever, and the squad itself was not just the most racially and ethnically diverse but also consisted of young and veteran players (Gitlitz, 2023), on the field the 2023 WWC was the worst major tournament the USWNT participated in, winning only one of the three group stages games before losing to Sweden in penalties in the first knockout round (Gitlitz, 2023). Through the tournament and especially after the elimination, critics of the USWNT, especially from the conservative side of the American political map ridiculed the players' behavior, framing them once more as arrogant (Reid, 2023).

Yet, to focus only on the USWNT, coaching changes, injured players, or roster issues, as the cause for their early elimination will not do justice with the progress of women's football worldwide (Biessel et al., 2023; Gitlitz, 2023). For the hosts Australia and New Zealand, the 2023 WWC was not only an opportunity to celebrate gender equality with New Zealand's Prime Minister Jacinda Ardern leading the draw of the competitions, and mixed-race Australian footballer Sam Kerr doing her iconic goal celebration flip was projected on the Sydney Opera House, but to honor indigenous culture (Biessel et al., 2023) as with ceremonies, land acknowledgements, and commemorations of Māori and other native tribes. For New Zealand the tournament played a developmental role, while in Australia broke attendance and viewership records, with the national team reaching the semifinal. The two finalists, Spain and England, both showed significant growth of interest in the club level during the recent decades, with women's teams selling out or breaking attendance records filling Stamford Bridge and the Emirates Stadium in Barcelona and bringing over 90,000 fans to the Camp Nou in Barcelona (Biessel et al., 2023). Yet, while in England The FA was promoting the women's national team and levering their hype and success as the Lionesses won a record breaking domestic European championship in front of 87,000 fans at Wembley Stadium, the Spanish football Association and the women's team were in constant struggles and disputes. The tension and mistreatment of women's football in Spain became evident to the world when during the cup lifting ceremony, Luis Rubiales the former president of the Spanish Football Association and Vice President of UEFA non-consensually kissed national team captain Jenni Hermoso, which led to international outrage and to him being banned (ESPN, 2024). The American sports system, including through football, had its fair share of history of sexism, abuse, and sexual violence (Dubinsky, 2023a), and USWNT were among those who publicly supported other international players in the

WWC who faced similar or even worse treatment and showed solidarity to the Spanish captain and to fellow players around the world who face their own domestic and international struggles, including the newly crowned world champions (Christenson, 2023; Gitlitz, 2023).

Conclusion

The 2023 WWC was a humbling experience for the USWNT, but nevertheless an opportunity to showcase American values, engage in diplomacy, and even leverage an on-field loss to border-crossing solidarity for gender equality and women's rights. On-field, the world has caught up, with European football clubs selling out stadiums and breaking recordings of attendance and viewership, more countries and regions investing in the women's game, and finding nation branding opportunities through participation and performance on a higher level. The European club system and the growth and development of the women's game around the world might mean that Title IX and the USWNT are going to face tougher competition moving forward, but the Americans are not going anywhere. The National Women's Football League (NWSL) dominating large markets and further expanding, breaking not just attendance records but Hollywood stars and other celebrities to invest. The 2026 FIFA World Cup will be held in the United States, Canada, and Mexico, which will lead to further investment in grassroots level for boys and girls. Two years later Los Angeles will host the 2028 Olympic Games, with the prestigious women's football tournament taking place on American soil and looking further down the line, the USA and Mexico are bidding together to host the 2031 FIFA WWC. Women's football and the activist approach of the USWNT are embedded within the fabric of American society, from young girls, through Title IX and into official foreign policy, and with unprecedent bloom in women's sports and with mega football events coming to the United States, this authentic connection will also manifest through nation branding and public diplomacy.

References

Biessel, A., Postlethwaite, V., Grainer, A. and Brice, J. E., Eds. (2023). *The 2023 FIFA Women's World Cup: Politics, Representation, and Management*. New York: Routledge.

Bonesteel, M. (February 22, 2022). A timeline of the U.S. women's soccer team's equal pay dispute with U.S. Soccer. *The Washington Post*. Retrieved from https://www.washingtonpost.com/sports/2022/02/22/uswnt-pay-lawsuit-timeline/.

Bureau of Educational and Cultural Affairs (n.d.a). Sports Diplomacy. *United States of America Department of State*. Retrieved from https://eca.state.gov/sports-diplomacy.

Bureau of Educational and Cultural Affairs (n.d.b). Sports Envoy. *United States of America Department of State*. Retrieved from https://eca.state.gov/sports-diplomacy/sports-envoy.

Christenson, M. (August 26, 2023). 'I'm disgusted': Alex Morgan leads support for Hermoso in Rubiales row. *The Guardian*. Retrieved from https://www.theguardian.com/football/2023/aug/26/im-disgusted-alex-morgan-leads-support-for-hermoso-in-rubiales-row.

Dubinsky, Y. (2021). Revolutionary or arrogant? The role of the USWNT in Brand America through the 2019 FIFA Women's World Cup. *International Journal of Sport and Society*, *12*(1), 147–164. https://doi.org/10.18848/2152-7857/CGP/v12i01/147-164.

Dubinsky, Y. (2023a). *Nation Branding and Sports Diplomacy: Country Image Games in Times of Change*. Cham: Palgrave Macmillan.

Dubinsky, Y. (2023b). Sports, Brand America and U.S. public diplomacy during the presidency of Donald Trump. *Place Branding & Public Diplomacy*, *19*(1), 167–180. https://doi.org/10.1057/s41254-021-00230-6.

ESPN (January 26, 2024). Former Spanish FA chief Rubiales' FIFA ban upheld on appeal. *ESPN*. Retrieved from https://www.espn.com/soccer/story/_/id/39393213/former-rfef-chief-rubiales-fifa-ban-upheld-appeal.

FOX Soccer (2023). USA vs. The World: What will it take to stop the USWNT at the 2023 FIFA Women's World Cup? *You Tube*. Retrieved from https://www.youtube.com/watch?v=cp6GXdnrHzE.

Frandino, N. (July 22, 2023). Second gentleman Emhoff cheers on US World Cup team in New Zealand. *Reuters*. Retrieved from https://www.reuters.com/sports/soccer/second-gentleman-emhoff-cheers-us-world-cup-team-new-zealand-2023-07-22/.

Fredrick, E. L., Pegoraro, A. and Schmidt, A. (2020). "I'm not going to the f***ing White House": Twitter users react to Donald Trump and Megan Rapinoe. *Communication & Sport*, 1–19. https://doi.org/10.1177/2167479520950778.

Gitlitz, R. (director) (2023). *Under Pressure: The U.S. Women's World Cup Team*. Netflix.

Lavietes, M. (July 7, 2022). Soccer star Megan Rapinoe receives Presidential Medal of Freedom. *NBC News*. Retrieved from https://www.nbcnews.com/nbc-out/nbc-out-proud/soccer-star-megan-rapinoe-receives-presidential-medal-freedom-rcna37141.

Martin, D. (2007). *Rebuilding Brand America: What We Must Do to Restore Our Reputation and Safeguard the Future of American Business Abroad*. New York: Amacom.

Michelle Obama (@MichelleObama) (July 21, 2023). I'm so proud of the talented @USWNT players representing us at the World Cup! X. Retrieved from https://x.com/MichelleObama/status/1682390032773156864.

Nike Football (2023a). What The Football. *You Tube*. Retrieved from https://www.youtube.com/watch?v=y5Jg9Wxc6yo,

Nike Football (2023). Let It Rip. *YouTube*. Retrieved from https://www.youtube.com/watch?v=yOOb52AJOzo.

Nye, J. S. Jr. (2008). Public diplomacy and soft power. *ANNALS of the American Academy of Political and Social Science*, *616*(1), 94–109.

Reid, A. (August 6, 2023). USA's 'arrogant' act backfires spectacularly in shock exit from Women's World Cup. *Y! Sport*. Retrieved from https://au.sports.yahoo.com/football-womens-world-cup-usa-arrogant-advertisement-backfires-after-sweden-loss-041931766.html.

The Wis Team (August 23, 2023). 2023 Equality Summit: Rewriting the future of soccer. *Women in Soccer*. Retrieved from https://womeninsoccer.org/2023-equality-summit-rewriting-the-future-of-soccer/.

U.S. Women's National Team (2023). IT'S HERE! We asked a few friends to help with this year's World Cup roster announcement. *X*. Retrieved from https://x.com/USWNT/status/1671540981244522498.

28

THE DIGITAL SYMBOLIC LEGACY OF THE RUSSIA 2018 FIFA WORLD CUP IN TIMES OF 'PLAGUE' AND WAR

Vitaly Kazakov

Introduction

On March 20, 2020, just over a week after the official designation of the Covid-19 outbreak as a pandemic by the World Health Organisation (WHO), another major international organisation marked a global event of its own. Namely, the chief governing body for football, Fédération Internationale de Football Association (FIFA), premiered on its YouTube channel an official documentary chronicling its most recent showpiece event, the 2018 Men's Football World Cup staged by Russia. According to the FIFA media managers, this tournament "produced countless moments that will endure in the collective memory of those who love the beautiful game"; the FIFA YouTube channel invited its followers to "relive" these memories with the help of the film (FIFA, 2020).

Global media events, like the Russia 2018 FIFA World Cup, have been conceptualised as a genre of media communication (Hepp and Couldry, 2010), whereby they "interrupt daily routines and schedules," and "electrify very large audiences" (Skey, 2021, p. 153). Because of their scale, reach of audiences, and broad emotional appeal, such events have been described as markers of breaks in "regular time" and as delineators between people belonging to certain generations, who experienced the events and were impacted by them in a communal fashion. Media events were even imagined as "electronic monuments" meant to be persevered in audiences' memories years after their conclusion (Dayan and Katz, 1992). These memories are imprinted not only in people's minds but also 'recorded' in both on- and off-line media materials: from newspaper articles

DOI: 10.4324/9781003473671-32

and social media posts, to photo albums and books, to documentaries such as the one produced by FIFA.

This chapter questions the 'stability' of media events as 'electronic monuments' and challenges the ingrained assumption by FIFA social media editors that there would be a lasting 'collective memory' of Russia 2018. Simultaneously, I explore how media events' remembering years after their conclusion affects the geopolitical economy of football tournaments, their political sponsors, and their audiences. The discussion addresses these issues by qualitatively examining the public engagement with FIFA's YouTube documentary through different timeframes and corresponding political and social issues affecting global audiences.

Soft Power and Disempowerment through Sports Media Events

In a previous volume of this publication, I suggested that the current academic and practice-based research overwhelmingly focuses on the perceived effects of events like World Cups *before* they actually take place or very shortly after their conclusion. Our understanding of "short-, medium-, and long-term reputational consequences and the effects of soft power (or otherwise)" is sadly lacking (Kazakov, 2023, p. 43). Whilst the hosting of major football and other events is increasingly linked to the concepts of 'soft power' or, conversely 'sportswashing' or 'disempowerment' effects (Boykoff, 2022; Brannagan and Giulianotti, 2018 and also see contributions across this volume), few scholars question how these effects have manifested themselves in practice after a tournament has taken place.

This chapter addresses this gap by examining how members of the public, who chose to engage with the recording of official FIFA 2018 documentary on YouTube, interpreted the significance of the World Cup as a media event. It examines how such engagement sheds the light on the public memory of the championship and its host, Russia, in the turbulent years since the World Cup conclusion. The YouTube documentary is just one element of the wider ecology of media materials produced by this global media event. Yet, assessing even a single archive of the event's memory can help us reflect on the complexity of public remembering of multifaceted events. An analysis of this single source—albeit a prominent component of the tournament's 'official memory' produced by its main organiser—highlights that such events cannot ever achieve a complete 'soft power victory', nor result in full 'soft disempowerment'. In fact, both effects coexist in the memory ecology of the media event, albeit each to a different extent. The 'collective memory' of the FIFA 2018 World Cup and other media events is made up of complex webs of often competing narratives and viewpoints which evolve with time.

Personal Memories of the Russia 2018 World Cup and the Covid-19 Pandemic

When FIFA released its 'Official Film' of the Russia World Cup on its YouTube channel, one of the hashtags used in the video description was "#WorldCupAtHome" (FIFA, 2020). The response to the pandemic was characterised by lockdowns and other curbs on public gatherings and mass events around the world. To counteract this physical isolation, people gathered online to socialise. Football enthusiasts watched recordings of older memorable games and tournaments at home, both on their own and together with others via online communications platforms. FIFA's social media managers astutely embraced this wave of nostalgia and catered to audiences yearning to connect with each other while in-person viewing was not possible.

The video at the centre of this discussion indeed reached an impressive audience: at the time of writing, the documentary has been viewed more than 11 million times and received 162 thousand likes. Though impressive in its scale, such large audience numbers are somewhat meaningless without further contextualisation. Importantly, the film also prompted 8,136 comments from YouTube users.

FIFA's social media managers encouraged user engagement by posting the first comment on the video shortly after uploading it. The comment read, "What is your favourite memory of Russia 2018?" and it resulted in 471 replies. Although the bulk of responses were generated in the first year after the video's publication, the thread has nevertheless continued to grow in the subsequent months, becoming an archive of public responses to the video itself, to new and older issues surrounding the Russian World Cup, and to relevant political and social issues like the Covid-19 pandemic and the war in Ukraine. This allows us to investigate how the 'electronic monument' of the World Cup as a media event has evolved over time.

The responses to the video reflect the strong emotional reaction the event generated and illustrate powerful ties between personal and communal experiences, not only of the World Cup as a sporting and media spectacle, but also major events surrounding it. Many of the comments mnemonically linked personal life events with the experience of watching or attending the tournament. The most liked comment, for example, read "My son was [born] on the day before Final and I watched France beat Croatia in hospital with him, my lifetime memory!" Another user from Switzerland reflected, "Literally each day I spent in Russia during those 31 days was memorable. People from all over the world had gathered there, united by one common feeling - Love for football. Thank you FIFA and Spasibo Russia" [sic]. Personal joys, sporting disappointments and other experiences at or of the event, whether in person or through mediation, are shared sincerely and with passion by the commentators on this YouTube thread. It is a clear reflection of the power and attraction of global media events like the World Cups to prompt its spectators into genuine, wholesome and good-natured reactions and engagement rarely seen elsewhere in the internet sphere.

The thread also captured users' sense of national pride, affection, and recollections of memorable games, teams, and individual performances throughout the tournament. Many of the users, for example, shared their admiration for the Croatian national team's impressive run to the final: "Croatia is such an inspiration. Proof that even the little guy can succeed," wrote one user. This is one example of the link between memories of the games, football as a sport and its power to inspire. At the same time, many posts linked memories of impressive performances and other sporting elements of the event to users' political and social lives. Another user wrote, "Proud to be Croat. I wish everyone a victory over this pandemic and look forward to playing football again. Greetings from Croatia." Here, the YouTube commentator, while sharing his feeling of national pride inspired by Croatia's football performance, also clearly discursively imagines a transnational community of YouTube viewers consuming the documentary, who through it come together to overcome the trauma of a major global crisis.

Individual memories of the event, as expressed through such comments, are ultimately imprints of users' construction of self, others, and the communities to which they belong. They also serve as reminders that popular sport media events do not take place in a vacuum, but rather reflect and further impact wider sociopolitical developments. Narratives of Croatia's run to the final ultimately become entangled with the international response to a pandemic: something that neither the event organisers, film producers, nor fans and audiences could have imagined as the tournament was taking place.

The Soft (Dis)Empowerment Legacy of Russia 2018: From Pandemic to the War

Since the documentary release coincided with the WHO's announcement, Covid-19 was the first major sociopolitical crisis to inform users' engagement with the video. Many of the comments shared in the months following its publication reflected that the quality of the tournament, organised well by Russia, had united fans around the world who were now experiencing the gloom of the pandemic. Many comments suggested that Russia staged a fabulous event, the memory of which can take 'us' as a global community through times of despair. One user shared: "this is the most incredible tournament. not even for the sport itself but for the unity, joy and pride it brings to people all across the world" [sic]. Likewise, the ability of the film to spur an emotional response from its viewers is praised in the comments. "A Fantastic film. Cried multiple times," and "Good film! In our country, everything is not so bad, as they like to say in different countries. Kind, friendly people is our pride,"[1] wrote users seemingly based in Russia. English-speaking viewers commented, "I wish there was an 'auto like' button that I could press that liked all the comments. So many beautiful comments, memories and moments. THANK YOU RUSSIA!!!!!" and "Ive seen the 2002, 2006, 2010, 2014, 2018, and the rigged 2022 World Cup. 2018 was the finest from start to finish in my opinion" [sic].

Such diverse comments, especially those remembering Russia positively as a host, resonate with the recollections of both journalists and academics (Crilley et al., 2022; Ronay, 2018), who wrote of an unexpected 'soft power effect' for Russia in the immediate aftermath of the event. Such accounts suggested that a pessimistic outlook on the event ahead of 2018 turned into a positive experience of a well-run mega-event staged by what was perceived by many attending and experiencing the event as a friendly and open country. This effect was aided by the high quality of football on the pitches and its media staging, which one could interpret as a case of effective public diplomacy through sport (Murray, 2018; see, for example, Rofe, 2018). It was this successful event, which was dubbed by many as the 'greatest World Cup ever' that was being fondly remembered by users at a time of the pandemic.

These reflections, as well as the tone of some of the comments, have since been abruptly challenged and recontextualised following Russia's full-scale invasion of Ukraine in February 2022. During this period, other 'memories' of the event emerged as this major geopolitical development caused many to re-evaluate the legacy of the Russian tournament (Pender, 2022; Ronay, 2022). The memory of Russia 2018 as an enchanting media event was transformed as many users started to view the tournament through a new lens. For example, in response to FIFA's question about viewers' favourite memory of the event, one user wrote, "How united we were... What have we become ..." Other users criticised Russia more overtly, suggesting the hosts used the event to 'sportswash' the regime and its actions on the geopolitical stage: "... and [then] Putin chose war"; "Thanks Russia for playing us all..."; "to fuck up absolutely everything. Thanks to the dictator in his bunker."[2] Lament, anger, and disappointment were just some of the sentiments towards Russia shared by YouTube users as they reflected on both the war and the World Cup. In this sense, the archive of World Cup-related memory on YouTube had turned into a 'monument' of soft disempowerment through sport and serves as an example of the loss of prestige and international influence through negative publicity linked to hosting of a sporting event (Brannagan and Giulianotti, 2018).

The interpretations of Russia 2018's legacy, however, were not uniform across the reflections shared in 2022 and 2023. There are examples of Russian users' comments mirroring blatant disinformation about the invasion of Ukraine, and trying to persuade others that the Russian offensive had a moral legitimacy. Interestingly, however, the thread did not turn into a polemic between critics and sympathisers in the wake of the invasion; rather, messages about the war have been limited to select sub-threads and individual comments.

During this time, much of the engagement continued to centre on the documentary itself, as well as fans' memories of the tournament and specific games. Another line of reflection was the anticipation for, and ultimately comparisons between, the Russian and Qatari World Cups. One user, for example, suggested:

> Ahhh its really painful to go from this kind of perfect World Cup to today's 2022 disgrace of a World Cup. Anyways a big Thanks for Russia and its beautiful peoples for the great memories, the quote at the beginning of the Video really touched me on how true it is.

Overall, the memory of and engagement with the Russian 2018 World Cup's legacy has been diverse and heterogeneous, and not a homogenous "collective memory" the FIFA producers had initially suggested (FIFA, 2020).

Conclusion

Ultimately, discussions prompted by the YouTube documentary were not just about sport, but also implicitly or explicitly reflected on major world events like the Covid-19 pandemic, the Russian invasion to Ukraine, and the political significance of the Qatar 2022 World Cup. As the discussion in this chapter has shown, the comment thread was far from being a uniform 'collective' of memories and interpretations.

In 2023, long after the war in Ukraine began, one user wrote:

> As an England fan I will always remember that great summer 🏴󠁧󠁢󠁥󠁮󠁧󠁿🏴󠁧󠁢󠁥󠁮󠁧󠁿🏴󠁧󠁢󠁥󠁮󠁧󠁿 Expectations were not very high and the country in general had rarely felt so disunited or lacking in belief yet this tournament rebuilt pride and faith into our national team and brought the whole country together, with great moments along the way.

This comment hints at the enduring ability of media events like the World Cup to serve as powerful prompts for international fans and observers of the game to share strong emotional reactions. They may discursively construct and imagine a collective 'us', but this uniformity is likely illusory and 'imagined': whether local, regional, national, or international, the collective 'us' relates differently to synchronous political, social, economic, and cultural contexts surrounding a sporting media event in question.

At the same time, memory of such events is not set in stone nor 'memorialised' in a static fashion. Instead, intervening developments serve as a prism that fractures people's reflections and prompts new interpretations. Both minor personal events and major global crises can have implications on viewers' impressions of the legacy of the media event, which lives on in archives like the video recordings and comment threads I studied here.

At the time of writing, it is hard to imagine a time when Russian sport will be reintegrated back into international competitions, nor when it will again act as host following a period that was once referred to as Russia's sports mega-event decade (Wolfe, 2021). The Ukraine invasion has meant that on the surface, any soft power 'gains' Russia made from hosting the World Cup and the Olympics have been almost entirely erased. Yet, the publics' enduring engagement with and reinterpretation of the World Cup as a media event shows how such media events resist utilisation as soft power tools by sponsoring states. These events have a life of their own and may have residual effects for their political sponsors—with Russia as a case in point.

Nevertheless, the limitations of the exploratory analysis provided here need to be acknowledged. As ever, online comments should be treated with caution, as there is potential they have been planted, or numbers inflated, with malicious intent. Both YouTube and FIFA also have the power to block and delete certain posts, thereby steering the online conversation. As such, the discussion here is not meant to represent a comprehensive overview of public attitudes nor does it claim to fully capture the 'public memory' of a global media event. Instead, it suggests further trajectories and opportunities for research to examine different sources or imprints of memory and symbolic legacies of past events. Both quantitative and qualitative methods need to be employed to test some of these findings in relation to the political significance of the remembering of football World Cups and other global sport media events.

Notes

1 Both comments translated from Russian by the author.
2 Last comment translated from Russian by the author.

References

Boykoff, J. (2022). Toward a theory of sportswashing: mega-events, soft power, and political conflict. *Sociology of Sport Journal, 39*(4), *Human Kinetics*, 342–351.

Brannagan, P. M. and Giulianotti, R. (2018). The soft power–soft disempowerment nexus: the case of Qatar. *International Affairs, 94*(5), 1139–1157.

Crilley, R., Gillespie, M. Kazakov, V. et al. (2022). 'Russia isn't a country of Putins!': how RT bridged the credibility gap in Russian public diplomacy during the 2018 FIFA World Cup. *The British Journal of Politics and International Relations, 24*(1). SAGE Publications: 136–152.

Dayan, D. and Katz, E. (1992). *Media Events: The Live Broadcasting of History.* Cambridge: Harvard University Press.

FIFA (2020). 2018 FIFA World Cup | The Official Film. Available at: https://www.youtube.com/watch?v=MiAcU2DvbXM [Accessed 17 October 2023].

Hepp, A. and Couldry, N. (2010). Introduction: media events in globalized media cultures. In N. Couldry, A. Hepp and F. Krotz (Eds.), *Media Events in a Global Age* (pp. 1–22). London: Routledge.

Kazakov, V. (2023) Public remembering of Sochi 2014 at a time of war: the Kremlin's soft disempowerment through sport. In S. Chadwick, P. Widdop, and M.M. Goldman (Eds.), *The Geopolitical Economy of Sport: Power, Politics, Money, and the State* (pp. 42–48). Abingdon-on-Thames: Routledge. doi. org/10.4324/9781003348238-7 [Accessed 17 October 2023].

Murray, S. (2018). *Sports Diplomacy: Origins, Theory and Practice* (1st ed.). Routledge new diplomacy studies. Boca Raton: Routledge, an imprint of Taylor & Francis.

Pender, K. (2022). History will judge IOC and Fifa as opportunistic hypocrites over Russia. *The Guardian*, 3 March. Available at: https://www.theguardian.com/sport/2022/mar/03/history-will-judge-ioc-and-fifa-as-opportunistic-hypocrites-over-russia [Accessed 3 March 2022].

Rofe, J. S., Ed. (2018). *Sport and Diplomacy: Games within Games*. Manchester: Manchester University Press. Available at: https://www.manchesterhive.com/display/9781526131065/9781526131065.xml [Accessed 20 September 2023].

Ronay, B. (2018). *How Football (Nearly) Came Home: Adventures in Putin's World Cup*. London: HarperCollins.

Ronay, B. (2022). Uefa and Fifa are too late: Russia's sportswashing has served its purpose. *The Guardian*, 25 February. Available at: https://www.theguardian.com/football/2022/feb/25/uefa-and-fifa-are-too-late-russias-sportswashing-has-served-its-purpose [Accessed 26 October 2023].

Skey, M. (2021). W(h)ither media events? Building a typology for theorizing exceptional events that break with the norm in a complex media landscape. *Communication Theory*, *31*(2), 151–168.

Wolfe, S. D. (2021). *More Than Sport: Soft Power and Potemkinism in the 2018 Men's Football World Cup in Russia*. Lausanne, Switzerland: LIT Verlag Münster.

29

THE FIFA WORLD CUP TELEVISION BROADCASTING IN AFRICA THROUGH PAY-TV

Shifting Flows

Gerard A. Akindes

Introduction

This chapter explores the historical transformation of the Men's FIFA World Cup (MFWC) broadcasting rights in Africa, focusing on the pivotal shift from exclusive Public Service Broadcaster (PSB) free-to-air (FTA) coverage until 2006, to the dominance of pay-TV broadcasters. The narrative unfolds through critical milestones, such as Arab Radio & Television (ART) securing exclusive rights for the 2006 MFWC in the Middle East and North Africa (Amara, 2007; Malkawi, 2007) and initiating a pay-TV monopoly over the MFWC broadcasting in North Africa.

In Sub-Saharan Africa, the transition to pay-TV occurred in 2014, challenging the traditional stronghold of the African Union of Broadcasting (AUB) and PSBs. This shift initiated a competitive landscape, with transnational pay-TV broadcasters contending for MFWC rights. The resulting dynamics opened doors for new entrants in the Sub-Saharan African media landscape, providing opportunities for emerging pay-TV broadcasters.

Analysing the 2018 and 2022 MFWC, the chapter examines the successful bids of Econet Media/Kwesé Sports and New World TV (NWT) for the MFWC broadcasting rights in Sub-Saharan Africa. This success came at the expense of PSBs and the AUB, underscoring the transformative influence of pay-TV broadcasters in reshaping the African sports broadcasting mediascape for the MFWC and major sporting events. Beyond historical analysis, the chapter overviews television evolution in Africa and explores the implications of MFWC broadcast rights shifting towards private media players and transnational pay-TV broadcasters.

DOI: 10.4324/9781003473671-33

The concluding discussion assesses the challenges faced by new entrants such as New World TV (NWTV) in a pay-TV sports media landscape dominated by four major groups: Canal+, StarTimes, beIN Sports, and Multichoice DStv/SuperSport. This comprehensive analysis sheds light on the intricate interplay of historical transitions, market forces, and emerging challenges that define the contemporary African sports broadcasting landscape. It demonstrates how the deregulation of media laws and the global liberalization of media ownership led to sports broadcasting transitioning from FTA PSBs to private transnational pay-TV and media corporations. This shift began in the 1990s, highlighted by BSyB acquiring rights to the English Premier League and Canal+ securing rights to Ligue 1 in France.

Pay-TV and the Constantly Changing Sports Broadcasting Mediascape

The advent of Direct-to-Home and Digital Terrestrial Television (DTT) has facilitated the rise of transnational broadcasters, fundamentally altering the relationship between sports and television. Pay-TV broadcasters, in particular, have emerged as pivotal financial contributors to professional sports, significantly impacting the revenues of major sporting events such as the MFWC.

While Africa, especially Sub-Saharan Africa, currently represents a comparatively minor share of these revenues in contrast to the United States, Asia, and Europe (FIFA, 2019) the region is witnessing a noticeable increase in pay-TV subscriptions. This surge has led to a paradigm shift in the revenue dynamics of professional sports in Africa. According to Digital TV Research, the period between 2021 and 2027 is expected to increase by almost 18 million new pay-TV subscribers in Africa, further setting pay-TV as a potential revenue generator for sports.

Notably, Canal+ and Multichoice/DStv collectively dominate a substantial 60% share of the pay-TV market in Africa (Pezet and Nébié, 2022). Multichoice/DStv and its 37% shareholder Canal+ lead to significant live sports content through pay-TV respective bouquets and channels. Other major entities in this domain, including StarTimes and beIN Sports, along with Canal+ and Multichoice/SuperSport, play a crucial role in shaping Africa's sports television broadcasting landscape. Through their offerings, these leading sports content providers enhance the media experience for African sports enthusiasts, delivering rich programming featuring international sporting events and competitions predominantly held outside the continent. As discussed in several publications, only a few football league matches in Africa are available on pay-TV (Owumelechili and Akindes, 2014). The following section presents the main types of television broadcasters defining the African television broadcasting landscape.

The Three Main Types of Television Broadcasters in Africa

Table 29.1 presents the three main types of television broadcasters actively broadcasting sports in Africa.

Transnational Pay-TV Broadcasters

Until the mid-2020s, the major transnational pay-TV sports broadcasters in Africa included Canal+, beIN Sports, Multichoice DStv/SuperSport, and StarTimes. These broadcasters operate across various countries or regions and typically secure broadcasting rights for popular international competitions and selected local and continental events. Except for Multichoice DStv/SuperSport, the dominant transnational broadcasters are non-African entities. This highlights how technological advancements facilitate transnational and transcontinental broadcasting reach for corporations with financial and technical capacities.

Public Service Broadcasting Free-to-Air Public (FTA)

All PSBs are pioneers in television broadcasting within African countries. Their sports broadcasting is FTA and confined to their national territory and

TABLE 29.1 The different types of television broadcasters in Africa

Type of broadcasters (pay-TV or FTA)	Broadcasters	Characteristics
Transnational pay-TV	Canal+, beIN Sports, DStv with SuperSport and StarTimes, Azam TV	These sports content providers operate across multiple countries or regions, typically securing broadcasting rights for popular international competitions. They also acquire rights for selected local and continental competitions to expand the diversity of content offered to viewers
Public service broadcaster (FTA)	All national public channels (FTA) are also the pioneers of television in most African countries	These broadcasters are often limited to national sports or international competitions as sub-licensees for national domestic audiences. As members of the African Radio and Television Union (AUB), they used to play a crucial role in acquiring sports rights across the continent
Private national pay-TV and FTA broadcasters	NCI in Côte d'Ivoire, LC2 in Benin, STv in Senegal, etc.	FTA television stations, with limited engagement in sports broadcasting rights or as sub-licensees

audience. These broadcasters are members of the AUB, which plays a crucial role in acquiring sports rights across the continent on behalf of its members.

National Private (or Pay) Television Broadcasters

The liberalization and democratization of media policies have paved the way for the emergence of privately owned national FTA or pay-TV broadcasters in numerous African countries. Notably, Azam TV in Tanzania and, more recently, NWTV in Togo stand out as among the few locally owned national pay-TV broadcasters actively competing for broadcasting rights for transnational audiences.

Several key characteristics define the main transnational pay-TV broadcasters in Africa. First, they dominate the broadcasting of the most popular European football leagues and competitions to African audiences. Second, their commercial presence has implicit linguistic exclusivity, with dominant broadcasting languages determining the preferred country and target audience for each broadcaster.

Canal+ primarily targets Francophone Africa, beIN Sports is present in North Africa and a few other Arabic-speaking countries, Multichoice/DsTv/SuperSport targets Anglophone and Lusophone Africa, and StarTimes operates across Francophone and Anglophone Africa (Akindes, 2017). Canal+, SuperSport, beIN Sports, and StarTimes, holding the largest pay-TV market share, effectively form an oligopoly. As transnational broadcasters, their significant transnational audiences and technical capacity provide a substantial competitive advantage, particularly in bidding for major events such as the European "Big Five" football leagues (English Premier League, Spanish La Liga, Italian Serie A, French Ligue1, and German Bundesliga) and globally widely watched competitions such as the MFWC, the Olympics, and the Africa Cup of Nations (AFCON). This dominance poses a significant barrier to entry for new players.

Despite the challenges and the barrier to entry posed by the dominant pay-TV broadcasters, the African mediascape continues to attract new players willing to compete for the broadcasting rights of international competitions. The competition was notably enabled when FIFA discontinued privileging the AUB and PSBs for MFWC broadcasting in Sub-Saharan Africa after 2014. This shift allowed transnational groups such as Canal+ Horizons, SuperSport, beIN Sports, StarTimes, and new entrants like Econet Media/Kwesé Sports and NWTV to enter the arena and bid for broadcasting rights.

MFWC Broadcasting Rights, a Competitive Ground in Africa

The initial years of FIFA World Cup (FWC) television broadcasting in Africa began with the global debut of the first MFWC broadcast. The 1966 MFWC marked the inaugural instance of global viewership, with 75 countries broadcasting the event live or through recorded films. In Africa, Sudan played a pivotal role by relaying all 32 competition matches in 16-mm format. Despite a complete ban on exports to Rhodesia, the country acquired films from the BBC and ITV, broadcasting 16-mm footage of 16 matches. Ethiopia and Mauritius also received matches for broadcast.

Morocco, Tunisia, and Algeria, being members of the European Broadcasting Union (EBU) and connected to the EBU terrestrial network, benefited from the Eurovision broadcast of the MFWC in Europe. Nevertheless, Africa, as a whole, remained minimally impacted by the event. Not only were no African teams represented at the 1966 MFWC due to the CAF boycott of the qualifiers, but most African countries had not yet established television broadcasting infrastructure in the 1960s.

By the early 1990s, however, all African countries had developed national public television broadcasting capabilities. Public service broadcasting initially monopolized television broadcasting for FWC events until the 2000s. This historical overview highlights the evolution of MFWC television broadcasting in Africa, from its early stages in the 1960s to the widespread national public television broadcasting capacity across the continent by the 1990s.

The End of a Monopoly on Broadcasting the MFWC by Public Television

The erosion of the monopoly on broadcasting the MFWC by PBSs began in 2006, when the private Saudi Pan-Arab channel, Arab Radio and Television (ART), secured the rights to broadcast the 2006 MFWC in Algeria (Amara, 2007). It was a significant shift for Algerians as the MFWC transitioned from being aired on free public television to pay-TV for the first time. In 2006, ART control of the MFWC in Algeria appeared as a geopolitical deployment of Saudi Arabia media in North Africa and the Middle East. However, in 2010, Al Jazeera Sports, known as beIN Sports, acquired ART, gradually extending its influence over MFWC broadcasting across North and Arabic-speaking Africa. Following its establishment in 2003, Al Jazeera Sports, now known as beIN Sports, quickly expanded its reach across North Africa and the Middle East. It emerged as a significant transnational sports broadcaster, playing a key role in Qatar's soft power geopolitical strategy.

Under the umbrella of beIN Sports, the landscape of MFWC television broadcasting has transformed, moving predominantly to pay-TV in North African and Arabic-speaking African countries. This transition includes regions beyond North Africa, encompassing countries such as Mauritania and Sudan and extending further to Somalia, South Sudan, Djibouti, and the Comoros. The entry of private broadcasters, particularly beIN Sports, has reshaped the accessibility and distribution of MFWC content, departing from the traditional model of exclusive airing on public television. beIN Sports shifted to pay-TV, the MFWC television broadcasting in North African and Arabic-speaking African countries while establishing the dominance of Qatar sport broadcasting and media influence.

In Sub-Saharan Africa, except South Africa, the switch to pay TV initially occurred pay TV when Canal+, and SuperSport were licensed to broadcast the 2014 MFWC. In 2014, Canal+ Africa acquired the rights to the MFWC in Brazil for its subscribers in Sub-Saharan Africa (Mohamed, 2014). The AUB also acquired the rights for public services broadcasting television in Sub-Saharan Africa, except for Nigeria and South Africa.

In Nigeria, Optima Sports Management International (OSMI) had already acquired the rights for the 2006 MFWC in Germany (*Daily Trust*, 2006). Public services broadcaster South Africa Broadcasting Corporation (SABC) maintains broadcasting rights on free public channels in parallel with SuperSport, which retains rights for the audience of its pay packages.

Despite the tipping of the MFWC television broadcasting to pay TV in North Africa and the AUB agreements with FIFA, the MFWC television broadcasting remained on public television in Sub-Saharan Africa. In 2008, FIFA announced the signing of a strategic cooperation with the AUB during its general assembly in Cotonou, Benin (FIFA, 2008). This strategic cooperation ended after the 2014 MFWC.

Full Privatization of the African MFWC Broadcasting Market

During the 2018 MFWC, a notable shift towards private players and pay television was observed. The strategic cooperation established in 2008 between FIFA and the AUB to ensure public television broadcasting of the MFWC in Sub-Saharan Africa was no longer applicable (FIFA, 2008). Contrary to the previous arrangement, a new entrant, Econet Media/Kwesé Sports, secured the rights to broadcast the 2018 MFWC in Russia for Sub-Saharan Africa, excluding South Africa.

In early 2017, Econet Media/Kwesé Sports TV (a division of the Econet group, Zimbabwe's largest telecommunications service provider) secured the rights to broadcast the 2018 MFWC in Sub-Saharan Africa. Subsequently, sub-licensing agreements were established with Econet Media/Kwesé Sports, allowing PSBs to broadcast selected games FTA. As shown in Table 29.2, the 2018 MFWC's primary broadcast rights licensees are now fully privatized. This shift reflects a significant transformation in the broadcasting landscape, moving away from the prior involvement of PSBs to a private players model dominated by transnational pay-TV. However, shortly after the conclusion of the 2018 MFWC, Econet Media/Kwesé Sports ceased its operations.

In Sub-Saharan Africa, PSBs, excluding SABC in South Africa, found themselves compelled to purchase the rights to broadcast the MFWC as sub-licensees through an African pay-TV broadcaster for the first time. Following

TABLE 29.2 Holders of television broadcasting rights for the 2018 MFWC in Sub-Saharan Africa

Rights holders	Type of broadcaster (pay-TV or FTA)	Territories
Econet Media/Kwesé Sports	Pay-TV and FTA	All territories in Sub-Saharan Africa, except South Africa
beIN Sports	Pay-TV	Algeria, Egypt, Morocco, Libya, Tunisia, Mauritania, Sudan, Somalia, and Comoros
SuperSport	Pay-TV	All territories in Sub-Saharan except South Africa, Mauritania, Sudan, Somalia, and Comoros
SABC	FTA	South Africa
StarTimes	Pay-TV	All territories in Sub-Saharan Africa, except South Africa
CANAL+	Pay-TV	All territories in Sub-Saharan Africa, except South Africa and Nigeria

Sources: FIFA.com (2022).

the conclusion of the agreement between the AUB and FIFA for broadcasting rights, PSBs were relegated to the role of sub-licensees, enabling only a partial broadcast of the 2018 MFWC matches.

Table 29.2 illustrates that the broadcasting rights for the MFWC in Sub-Saharan Africa are not exclusively held. Consequently, pay-TV companies such as Canal+, SuperSport, and StarTimes also secured the rights to broadcast the MFWC on their transnational pay-TV channels, albeit limited to specific countries and geographic regions by default. South Africa's public broadcaster, SABC, was the sole country in Sub-Saharan Africa to directly acquire broadcasting rights from FIFA without competing with transnational pay-TV broadcasters such as Econet Media/Kwesé Sports, Canal+, Super-Sport, and StarTimes. The Independent Communications Authority of South Africa (ICASA) sports broadcasting rule mandates that certain sporting events, including the MFWC, be nationally broadcast on free channels. This regulation enabled SABC to broadcast the World Cup in South Africa without biding against the pay-TV broadcasters.

The 2018 MFWC marked the inaugural instance where private rights holders took precedence over public television, requiring the latter to procure matches from Kwesé Sport to ensure access for viewers without a pay-TV subscription. The trend of television rights being held by private media is expected to persist in the 2022 MFWC. Unfortunately, Kwesé Sport ceased operations after the 2018 MFWC, preventing a comprehensive evaluation of the viability of acquiring MFWC broadcasting rights as a potential strategy to gain market share in the African pay-TV landscape.

In the late 1980s, deregulation in television, telecommunications, information technology, and media facilitated the rise of transnational television. This allowed Africa to become a significant market for global media corporations, particularly in sports broadcasting. Canal+ capitalized on the colonial legacy of the French language in Francophone Africa, while beIN Sport leveraged the historical and political significance of Arabic in North Africa and Arabophone nations. SuperSport took advantage of Anglophone Africa, benefiting from the linguistic legacy of British colonization. Additionally, the support of the Chinese government for StarTimes reflects China's soft power and economic investment in Africa. Privatization continues with a new player.

The privatization trend in MFWC broadcasting persists with the new pay-TV broadcasters. The 2022 MFWC in Qatar confirmed the challenges faced by the AUB in competing with private media entities. Ahead of the MFWC, a new entity emerged and swiftly positioned itself to secure the broadcasting rights for the 2022 MFWC in Sub-Saharan Africa, excluding South Africa. On July 26, 2021, FIFA officially announced that NWTV had successfully obtained the television rights for French-speaking Sub-Saharan Africa, covering the 2022 Men's FWC and the 2023 Women's FWC (FIFA, 2021). NWTV became the exclusive rights holder for all matches in the two premier men's and women's competitions across 19 French-speaking African countries (as of 2021).

Table 29.3 provides an overview of the holders of television broadcasting rights for the 2022 FWC in Sub-Saharan Africa. This development marks a continuation of the shift towards private entities in the realm of FWC broadcasting rights, exemplifying the ongoing transformation in the African sports broadcasting landscape.

An examination of the rights holders for the 2022 MFWC in Qatar reveals that NWTV possesses the rights for FTA, pay-TV, and mobile telephony in 19 French-speaking African countries. NWTV further sub-licensed these rights to

TABLE 29.3 Holders of television broadcasting rights for the 2022 FWC in Sub-Saharan Africa

Rights holders	Type of broadcaster (pay-TV or FTA)	Territories
beIN Sports	Pay-TV	Algeria, Egypt, Morocco, Libya, Tunisia, Mauritania, Sudan, Somalia, and Comoros
New World TV (NWTV)	Pay-TV and FTA	Nineteen French-speaking Sub-Saharan countries
SuperSport	Pay-TV	Forty English-speaking Sub-Saharan countries
SABC	FTA	South Africa

14 public television broadcasters and 12 private television or media groups across 26 countries. Richard Dimosi, the CEO of Media Business Solutions (MBS), the exclusive agent for NWTV, communicated that their collaboration extended to 38 Sub-Saharan African countries (personal communication, March 15, 2023). Dimosi specified that NWTV sub-licensed the rights for 24 out of the 62 matches of the competition to national public television for free, unencrypted broadcasting, with a preference given to matches featuring African teams (personal communication, March 15, 2023).

NWTV pay-TV services were accessible in 42 countries across Sub-Saharan Africa, excluding those covered by beIN Sports and South Africa. While the licenses for NWTV and Multichoice/DStv-SuperSport were initially confined to specific territories, factors such as satellite technology infrastructure, coupled with the appropriate satellite dish, decoder, and subscription, enable the reception of signals from NWTV and Multichoice/DStv-SuperSport throughout Sub-Saharan Africa.

According to Dimosi, NWTV's competitive edge played a crucial role in securing the 2022 MFWC bid. Dimosi emphasized that the affordability of subscriptions, priced at eight dollars, offered through mobile telephony applications, and the intentional use of African commentators speaking in national languages were pivotal aspects of NWTV's proposal (personal communication, March 15, 2023). Remarkably, for the first time in French-speaking Africa, MFWC broadcasting commentaries on pay-TV were provided in four national languages: Wolof, Ewe, Bambara, and Lingala. The subscription fees for NWTV, ranging from 2,500 CFA to 6,000 CFA (4–9 euros) (Repoux, 2022) per month, have proven affordable for audiences in French-speaking Africa. To enhance accessibility, NWTV developed applications for Android and Apple devices, facilitating Over-The-Top (OTT) streaming for the distribution of MFWC content.

The emergence of NWTV from Togo was celebrated as an African media outlet catering to African audiences. It marked the first instance where an African transnational media company effectively competed with European-based media and pay-TV corporations such as beIN Sports, Canal+, and StarTimes. This outcome holds significant geopolitical symbolism for Pan-Africanism. However, the economic implications are more complex, given shifts in mediascape post-2022 FIFA.

The 2022 MFWC confirmed the privatization of broadcast rights and the prevalence of pay-TV players for the MFWC in African television broadcasting. However, the licensing of the MFWC has several distinctive characteristics and implications for the African sports broadcasting mediascape.

Broadcasting rights are not exclusive in Sub-Saharan Africa—unlike in Arabic-speaking Africa, where beIN Sports has exclusive rights. Econet Media/Kwesé Sports did not challenge the dominance of Canal+, SuperSport, and StarTimes. License holders for the MFWC in Sub-Saharan Africa, Canal+,

SuperSport, and StarTimes, leaders of pay-TV in Francophone and Anglophone Africa, did not risk having their subscribers move to another pay-TV entity. Econet Media/Kwesé Sports entering the MFWC broadcasting competition affected essentially the AUB and PSBs. Econet Media/Kwesé Sports effectively served as a sub-licensor while ensuring the 2018 MFWC was available on FTA public and private television broadcasters.

After Econet Media/Kwesé Sports in 2017, NWTV won the tender for broadcasting rights before the AUB and Canal+ for Francophone Africa. Pay-TV winning the rights to the MFWC confirms the difficulty for the PSBs and the AUB in remaining economically viable competitors. African PSBs are not sufficiently financially and technologically endowed to compete on the rights market with a large-scale offer, digital satellite broadcasting, and mobile phone applications for major sporting events.

For Canal+, it was the first time they did not win a bid for a major event in Francophone Africa. It was also the first time after Multichoice/DStv in 1995 that Econet/Kwesé Sport, a sizeable African transnational pay-TV broadcaster, emerged to compete in a market dominated by the duopoly Multichoice/DStv and Canal+. Beyond the valuable Dimosi's descriptions of what made NWTV's bid competitive, it isn't easy to fully assess what factor gave a competitive edge to NWTV over Canal+. Nevertheless, it was a significant event in the Sub-Saharan African pay-TV mediascape. Canal+'s quasi-monopoly on pay-TV in Francophone Africa was challenged for the first time by an unknown new player a few years earlier.

The MFWC provided an exceptional opportunity for NWTV to enter the transnational pay-TV market in Sub-Saharan Africa. Without having the figures for subscriptions to NWTV and audiences and the income generated by sales of broadcasting rights to national public and private television, it appears that the acquisition of television rights and mobile telephony played an essential role and critical entry into the Sub-Saharan pay-TV landscape. However, for NWTV, one of the questions is the ability to gain market share in the pay-TV landscape after the 2022 MFWC, after the successful broadcast.

The 2022 MFWC broadcasting marked a noticeable entry of NWTV into the limited circle of pay-TV corporations in Africa. This was significant given the existing dominance of beIN Sports, StarTimes, Canal+, and SuperSport. Geopolitically, it held significance as NWTV, a corporation from the small West African nation of Togo, acquired rights to one of the biggest sporting events in the world, the MFWC. However, beyond the symbolism, the reality of the broadcasting rights fees paid by NWTV has limited economic implications for African football and the global geopolitical economy of sports broadcasting. This is evident in the fact that European football leagues and UEFA's competitions continue to attract the bulk of football broadcasting revenues globally.

Conclusion

Despite the continued importance of PSBs in ensuring widespread access to competitions such as the MFWC, their influence in the sports broadcasting landscape of Sub-Saharan Africa is waning. The landscape is evolving due to new entrants and their capacity to offer OTT services, contrary to the PSBs. Transnational television networks consolidate audiences, and their financial, commercial, and technological capacities dwarf those of PSBs or private national broadcasters. On a national level, the commercial model of pay-TV and sports broadcasting with subscription fees becomes economically impractical compared to the economies of scale achievable by large transnational groups. The 2022 MFWC further confirmed the challenges faced by the AUB and public television competing within the commercialized television rights market. As pay-TV and Internet penetration through mobile telephony continue to grow, the exclusive distribution of the MFWC in Africa through paid channels appears inevitable in the long run.

The acquisition of broadcast rights for the 2018 MFWC by Econet Media/ Kwesé Sports and the 2022 MFWC by NWTV in Sub-Saharan Africa exemplifies the transformation of the sports television broadcasting landscape, marked by the entry of new pay-TV transnational players. NWTV effectively capitalized on the opportunity presented by the 2022 MFWC to establish a foothold in the Francophone African pay-TV market. However, following the unsuccessful sports broadcasting and OTT business of Econet/Kwesé Sport, the critical question arises: How well can a new entrant navigate the challenges posed by the pay-TV oligopoly consisting of Canal+, SuperSport, beIN Sports, and StarTimes in Africa?

Can NWTV adopt an alternative business model that diverges from the prevailing neoliberal framework influencing the sports broadcasting economy, rather than solely relying on the MFWC and other major sports events, which often reproduce models with limited returns for African sports?

References

Akindes, G. (2017). Sports media complex and the business of football in Africa. In Dodds, M., Heisey, K., & Ahonen, A. (Eds.). (2018). *Routledge Handbook of International Sport Business*. New York: Routledge.

Amara, M. (2007). When the Arab World was mobilised around the FIFA 2006 World Cup. *Journal of North African Studies*, 12(4), 417–438.

Daily Trust (2006, April 20). World Cup: OSMI wins Nigerian broadcast rights. News section. https://allafrica.com/stories/200604200275.html.

FIFA (2008, October 29). 2010 FIFA World Cup™—All matches in Sub-Saharan Africa on free TV through strategic alliance with AUB. https://www.fifa.com/worldcup/news/all-matches-sub-saharan-africa-free-through-strategic-alliance-with-au-928395.

FIFA (2019). *2018 FIFA Financial Report*. Switzerland: FIFA. https://resources.fifa.com/image/upload/xzshsoe2ayttyquuxhq0.pdf.

FIFA (2021, July 26). New World TV awarded pay-TV rights. https://www.fifa.com/tournaments/mens/worldcup/qatar2022/media-releases/origin1904-p.cxm.fifa.comen-new-world-tv-awarded-pay-tv.

FIFA.com (2022). FIFA World Cup Qatar 2022 Media Rights Licensees, FIFA.com. Available at: https://digitalhub.fifa.com/m/203f2697ad928edb/original/FIFA-World-Cup-Qatar-2022-Media-Rights-Licensees.pdf [Accessed 10 April 2023].

Malkawi, B. H. (2007). Broadcasting the 2006 World Cup: the right of Arab fans versus ART exclusivity. *Fordham Intellectual Property Media and Entertainment Law Journal*, *17*(3), 591–610.

Mohamed (2014, April 23). Canal+ Afrique diffusera la Coupe du Monde 2014. *Media Sportif*, Articles en vedette section. https://www.mediasportif.fr/2014/04/23/canal-afrique-diffusera-la-coupe-du-monde-2014/.

Owumelechili, C. and Akindes, G. (2014). *Identity and Nation in African Football: Fans, Community and Clubs*. London: Palgrave Macmillan.

Pezet, G. and Nébié, S. E. (2022, September 29). Multichoice/Canal+: The future giant of African pay TV? *Dataxis*. https://dataxis.com/researches-highlights/779120/multichoice-canal-the-future-giant-of-african-pay-tv/.

Repoux, Sam. "New World Sport fait vibrer l'Afrique Subsaharienne au rythme de la Coupe du Monde de Football." *Sport Strtatégies* (blog), November 29, 2022. https://www.sportstrategies.com/new-world-sport-fait-vibrer-lafrique-subsaharienne-au-rythme-de-la-coupe-du-monde-de-football/.

30

COLOMBIA'S FAILURE TO HOST THE 1986 FIFA WORLD CUP

Jorge Tovar

Introduction

Historically, hosting the FIFA World Cup was an honor independent of its costs, supported mainly by the recognition earned by politicians in power. But costs matter. Uruguay hosted the first edition in 1930, not only because it won the 1924 and 1928 Olympics, but also because the government offered to pay the visiting teams' expenses and build an 85,000-capacity stadium (Goldblatt, 2007). Decades later, when major earthquakes hit Chile and Mexico in 1960 and 1985, both countries rose from the rubble to meet FIFA's expectations toward the 1962 and 1986 World Cups. In the lead-up to the 2014 World Cup in Brazil, large-scale protests erupted in response to public anger over the high costs and alleged corruption (Bailey et al., 2017).

Prioritizing national prestige and international recognition is not exclusive to Latin America. South Africa, the first African World Cup host in 2010, also caved to pressure exerted by FIFA and multinational corporations (Alegi, 2008). The ongoing conflict between FIFA and politicians eager for recognition with rising costs led to a wealthy nation lacking any football history to host the 2022 World Cup and three countries sharing the next one.

The global dilemma goes domestic every four years. Never, except once, has FIFA lost the battle. On October 25, 1982, Colombian President Belisario Betancur announced on national television that:

> having made democratic consultations, as I have done, on our real needs, the 1986 World Cup will not take place in Colombia. In this case, the golden rule that the World Cup should serve Colombia and not Colombia at the service of the World Cup multinational was not met. Here, we have

DOI: 10.4324/9781003473671-34

many other things to do, and there is not even time to attend FIFA's and its partners' extravagances. García Márquez [awarded the 1982 Nobel Prize in Literature] fully compensates us for what we may lose to showcase with the World Cup.

(Culturalia, 2018)

The President buried eight years of uncertainty and dreams in 44 seconds.

Despite Colombia's lack of a solid footballing tradition and adequate sporting, transportation, and touristic infrastructure, FIFA awarded Colombia the 1986 World Cup on June 9, 1974. Unlike previous South American hosts, Colombia had a below-average economy reliant on agriculture (23% of its GDP) and ranked 66th out of 154 countries in GDP per capita (Prados de la Escosura, 2009). The country joined Conmebol and FIFA in 1936 under the umbrella of Adefutbol, a regional organization that managed to take control of national football. Internal disputes in the 1960s between the professional branch (Dimayor) and Adefutbol led to the creation of the Colombian Football Federation (FCF), controlled by Alfonso Senior, the key figure in securing the bid. Former President of Millonarios, for pundits among the best teams in the world in the early 1950s, he became a top executive of FIFA (Silva, 2023).

The designation divided the country. Rhetorically, many opposed, defending the need to invest in elementary schools and hospitals. Additionally, FIFA's growing commercialization saw the tournament expand from 16 to 24 teams, making it financially unfeasible for Colombia's economy. This and a lack of national unity ultimately led to Betancur's withdrawal.

Exploring the Possibilities

Colombia secured the 1986 World Cup by impressing FIFA's executive committee with the novel aid of a video showcasing the country's beauty. Offering 12 cities as hosts, with stadium capacities ranging between 40,000 and 100,000 fans, but unclear on the costs of staging the event, Misael Pastrana, the Colombian president until August 1974, expressed his satisfaction, which revealed the "solid image that Colombia has in the world" (El Tiempo, 1974a). Alfonso López, elected president, declared that Colombia, "which struggles to overcome underdevelopment," has accepted FIFA's invitation because of the positive impact of the tournament on the country (Moncada, 1974).

Colombia lacked first-class stadiums, although Bogota's, Medellin's, and Cali's, the three largest cities, had potential. Connections between these cities were meager by road, nonexistent by train, and expensive by plane.

Critics argued that no stadiums suited for the World Cup existed, suggesting lavish spending diverting resources from critical needs, namely schools and hospitals. Additionally, the infrastructure was poor. According to the National Development Plan (PND) prepared by the Turbay administration, by December 1978, the country lacked highways and had only 12% of paved roads.[1]

The railway network was scarcer, with 2,911 operational kilometers, of which 582 km were in mountainous regions, the location of most major cities, including Bogota, Medellin, and Cali. Given the geography and the lack of alternatives, Colombia had developed a costly but functional air transportation system.

The Dream

Despite FIFA's expectation of immediate preparations under the incoming administration, neither López's nor the subsequent Turbay (1978–1982) PND mentioned the 1986 World Cup. The only action taken was the designation of an Evaluation National Commission (ENC) in July 1975, composed of cabinet members and other relevant official institutions. The high-level body did not meet until September 1976, designating five sub-commissions with no names of who would serve on them.

Ideas, but not actions, proliferated, such as Bogota's proposal to expand its stadium to a capacity of 80,000 fans (El Tiempo, 1977a). "FIFA News," as cited by El Tiempo in April 1977, praised the FCF building, the potential of an Official Country Club as the Media Center, and the creation of the ENC. However, concerns were growing within FIFA, forcing Havelange, FIFA's president, to travel to Colombia for the second time that year in December 1977. During a meeting with President López, Havelange received no assurance of the government's commitment beyond words on the "challenge" the event represented to the country (El Tiempo, 1977b). He deferred worries as he was still dealing with Argentina's ability to host the 1978 World Cup.

Havelange, Brazilian, defeated the incumbent Stanley Rous for FIFA's presidency in 1974, empathizing with Africa's requests for additional World Cup slots, promising an increase from 16 to 24 teams (Jennings, 2006). Africa, Concacaf, and Asia's votes led him to the presidency.

During that 1977 December visit, Havelange first suggested that Colombia might deal with 24 finalists. "Are there any studies over alternative venues for a 24 finalists World Cup?" he asked (El Tiempo, 1977b). With no plan for a 16-finalist World Cup, the ENC said they were only considering six cities. Havelange expected a 24-finalist Cup in Spain in 1982, which meant around ten venues for Colombia.

Unfulfilled Promises

In the following two years, the debate centered around the number of teams and the tournament's cost. In January 1978, Alfonso Senior, President of the FCF, utterly naïve, declared that Spain and Colombia rejected the 24-team tournament (El Tiempo, 1978a). In June 1979, FIFA announced that the 1982 World Cup would have 24 teams. With no confirmation for 1986, only a debacle in Spain would see FIFA regress to 16. Denial was Colombia's response. Hence, in October 1979, the ENC urged the FCF to have FIFA decide whether the 1986 Cup would have 24 or 16 teams. Spain was a success, and the 1986 host would receive 24 delegations.

Doubts about the costs were permanent. Attending an invitation to the 1974 World Cup final, incoming president López declared, "Our country battles to surface from underdevelopment, but the goal imposed by the 1986 World Cup will allow the overcoming and fulfillment of such great commitment" (Moncada, 1974). Colombia never figured out the cost of the World Cup.

The debate dealt initially with the amount that FIFA would pay and how much the government would need to invest. In a 1974 interview, Senior wrongly claimed that people in Colombia "assured that the '86 event will cost the country immense amounts of money. That is not true. The competition is financed directly by FIFA using just the television rights" (El Tiempo, 1974b).

Not until October 1978 did the government order a study to determine the costs (El Tiempo, 1978b). The National University, hired in January 1979, delivered the results in July, even though no government agency had signed the contract (El Tiempo, 1979a). The results gave insights into how revenues were to be shared. Once accounting for logistics costs, FIFA would receive 10%, the FCF 25%, and the remaining 65% shared between the competing teams. The government proposed sharing the 25% destined to the FCF.

According to the study, the World Cup required COP 4 billion, around USD 51 million in sporting infrastructure. The public sector additionally required COP 4.4 billion for communications and transportation infrastructure. Unable to commit, the government sought a "World Cup Law" to grant the President extraordinary powers for six months to establish a public and private entity to negotiate with FIFA and the FCF.

Early in 1980, the government filed the project, sparking Congressional and national debate. Proponents viewed hosting as a showcase, while opponents feared the financial strain. The latter prioritized investment in hospitals and schools, fearing a resource drain to the private sector. In March 1981, the House of Representatives voted against the project, which dampened the mood toward the Cup.

Facing mounting doubts, Havelange revisited Bogotá in August 1981, seeking to shore up support. Qualifying for the 1982 World Cup became crucial for momentum, but Colombia's national team campaign was disastrous, securing no wins and missing out on the tournament held in Spain.

With presidential elections on sight (March 1982) and a sluggish economy, political sentiment was against the World Cup. Furthermore, while visiting

Brazil, President Turbay declared that "the country has no money to devote COP10 or COP15 billion to the football tournament. We have more important needs than to watch football" (El Tiempo, 1981a).

Various organizations released additional studies to determine the cost of organizing the World Cup. A report released by the National Planning Department in November 1981 contradicted the National University study, claiming that the costs were underestimated. The report estimated that the government needed COP 10.1 billion for sporting, communications, and hotel infrastructure and an additional COP 2.7 billion for security and health, resulting in a public deficit of over COP 5.5 billion.

Even by November 1981, Congress was still weighing the pros and cons. One congressman cited a study claiming a COP 3 billion deficit. A congresswoman presented an alternative showing a surplus of COP 0.7 billion, while a third representative projected a surplus of COP 0.8 billion. Meanwhile, a fourth representative proposed deferring the discussion to the 1982 legislature. The nature of the studies got lost in time, but the law never made it through.

The next step was to create another commission, this time a private one, which would, ideally, fund the World Cup. It took four months, but by April 1982, the miracle occurred. A private corporation comprising many of the country's wealthiest economic organizations agreed to fund the tournament. The "Colombia Corporation 1986 Football World Cup" (CC86), supported by yet another study, this time by the National Financial Institutions Association (ANIF), proposed a low-budget World Cup. It suggested a stadium investment of only COP 0.6 billion and resolved the lack of hotels by facilitating private homes to house visitors.

Havelange did not concur because the "support and responsibility needs to be led by the government" (Fajardo, 1982). Remembering Turbay's words in Brazil just a few months earlier, FIFA needed assurance that there would be a free flow of currency, ease in visa issuing, the appropriate communications infrastructure, and access to flight adjustments when necessary.

Despite FIFA's position, in a futile attempt to promote official involvement, the CC86 funded an extensive publicity campaign during the 1982 World Cup. The delegation flew 30 tons of advertising material donated by over 20 Colombian companies. An airship would fly over Spanish skies with the legend (in Spanish) "Colombian Coffee. Colombia Corporation 1986 Football World Cup." It never did.

The divisions in the country were structural. In May 1982, Senior claimed that a World Cup needed government involvement (El Mundo Deportivo, 1982a). In July, President-elect Betancur publicly mentioned for the first time: "The World Cup for the good of my country, not my country at the service of a World Cup."

Complot?

A year after FIFA granted Colombia the World Cup, Pelé, the Brazilian super-star, debuted with the New York Cosmos as part of a long-term US hosting plan (Pelé, 2006). Pele would bring the passion, while Henry Kissinger (USA Secretary of State, 1972–1977) handled diplomacy.

The lack of progress in the 1986 World Cup organization encouraged other countries to pursue hosting the tournament. Indeed, as chairman of the North American Soccer League board, Kissinger soon clarified that his goal was to bring the Cup to the United States in "1986 or 1990" (El Tiempo, 1979b).

There were concerns about Colombia's ability to host a 24-team World Cup, to which altitude differences across cities increased criticisms from abroad. Bogotá, sitting at 2,600 meters, was now too high compared to sea-level cities like Barranquilla. On the latter, FIFA's head of press and public relations, René Courte, stated in September 1979 that it could be inconvenient to have Barranquilla and Bogota as host cities because of their substantial altitude differences (El Tiempo, 1979c).

More relevant, Senior, member of FIFA's Executive Committee, revealed in December 1980 that FIFA's vice president, Herman Neuberger, prepared for the Executive Committee a report exploring the possibility of having the 1986 tournament in the United States (El Tiempo, 1980). Although Senior mentioned that the report was rejected, it is evident that doubts about Colombia's ability to host the Cup successfully were increasing.

By 1981, Colombia's chances were slim. While Havelange declared support for Brazil if Colombia withdrew, Giulite Coutinho, head of the Brazilian Football Confederation, added that Brazil would only apply when Colombia officially resigned.

Despite Senior's knowledge of the US interest in hosting the 1986 Cup, he still trusted Havelange, even hailing him as Colombia's staunchest defender (El Tiempo, 1981b). As the Spanish tournament neared its end, things unraveled. Belisario Betancur, invited to the final, did not show up, underscoring the lack of official support toward Colombia 1986.

Significantly, the night before the World Cup Final, Havenlange and Neuberger dined with Gene Edwards, North American Football Federation President, and Henry Kisinger. Not surprisingly, Colombia received harsh and unexpected requirements a few months later. Sensing Kissinger's involvement, Alfonso Senior urged a South American boycott of a US-hosted World Cup (El Mundo Deportivo, 1982b). Simultaneously, Havelange again reiterated in August that the 1986 event could occur in Brazil (El Mundo Deportivo, 1982c).

FIFA's 1982 demands sparked outrage among many Colombians. These included airports and trains connecting all host cities, a media center, and stadium construction: 40,000 capacity for the first round, 60,000 for the second round, and 80,000 for the semifinals, the opening game, and the final.

Colombia would need to work from scratch and fund costly infrastructure. Adding to the pressure, FIFA imposed a deadline: November 10. Despite eight years of long-standing inaction, there was a widespread outcry against FIFA and an alleged complot against the country. The government saw a way out.

Alfonso Senior proposed to postpone the World Cup to 1994, while the FCF sought to negotiate with FIFA. It was a lost cause. Canada joined Brazil and the United States as candidates. If there were any doubts, Havelange declared in October, just days before Betancur's speech: "Colombia had the right to hold the Cup, but it is regrettable to see that after eight years - no program has been advanced." The train had passed.

One can imagine Edwards' and Kissinger's smile at the time. The World Cup would fly to the United States. However, they did not account for Guillermo Cañedo and the power of Mexican telecommunication moguls who obtained the 1986 Cup for Mexico. Kissinger had to wait until 1994.

Final Discussion

Colombia's bid to host the 1986 World Cup was ultimately unsuccessful due to a variety of factors, including economic constraints and political limitations typical of an underdeveloped economy. Leaders historically have concealed their inability to effectively plan and execute major initiatives by using the plight of the most unfortunate as a convenient cover. External factors also played a significant role. Colombia found itself caught in the midst of FIFA's structural shift within the geopolitical landscape of sports. In 1974, the World Cup was not the global event it would be in 1986 and beyond. The necessary investments increased substantially, favoring economies with deep pockets over those with a genuine interest in football as a sport.

Following Betancur's speech, Alfonso Senior said, "Colombia is a country of little significance that does not factor into world-changing events." Colombia, in 2022, still ranks low (59) in the United Nations logistics performance index, its transportation infrastructure is poor, its capital has unsuccessfully tried to build a subway line since the 1950s, informal workers surpass 50% of the labor force, and violence historically characterizes the country. It follows that the 1986 World Cup would not have been a development thrust, but not doing it had no positive effect either. The event reflects the country's inability to commit to long-term plans. High-end projects are easier for wealthier countries, but developing countries also require long-term commitments from politicians and society, which Colombia lacks.

FIFA's 1986 World Cup marked the dawn of a commercialization era that often superseded sporting priorities. Economic power fueled intense political battles for control, spiraling beyond manageable limits.

Note

1 Each incoming government in Colombia develops a PND which marks its policy roadmap over the following four years.

References

Alegi, P. (2008). 'A nation to be reckoned with': The politics of World Cup Stadium Construction in Cape Town and Durban, South Africa. *African Studies, 67*(3), 397–422.

Bailey, K., Oliver, R., Gaffney, C. and Kolivras, K. (2017). Negotiation "New" narratives: Rio de Janeiro and the "media geography" of the 2014 FIFA World Cup. *Journal of Sport and Social Issues, 41*(1), 70–93.

Culturalia (2018). Presidente de Colombia renuncia a realizar el mundial en su país. Available at: https://www.youtube.com/watch?v=rmyHCEc_yho (Accessed 2 March 2024)

El Mundo Deportivo (1982a). 'El M-86 no se hará sin apoyo del gobierno', 17 May, p. 27.

El Mundo Deportivo (1982b). 'Mundial-86: La Conmebol podría hacer boicot a EE.UU.', 17 May, p. 33.

El Mundo Deportivo (1982c). 'Havelange admite que Brasil puede organizar el M-86', 5 August, p. 16.

El Tiempo (1974a). 'Emocionado Pastrana Borrero', 10 June, p. 19A.

El Tiempo (1974b). 'Llegar a la presidencia de la FIFA', 15 July, p. 1C.

El Tiempo (1977a). 'Torre de 36 pisos para El Campín', 7 November, p. 2C.

El Tiempo (1977b). 'Hay que prepararse para una final de 24', 21 December, p. 1B.

El Tiempo (1978a). 'España no acepta 24 equipos', 14 January, p. 16B.

El Tiempo (1978b). 'Mundial-86 en entredicho', 4 October, p. 11A.

El Tiempo (1979a). 'La U. Nacional hará estudio del Mundial-86', 20 January, p. 3C.

El Tiempo (1979b). 'Kissinger en busca del Mundial-86', February 6, p. 1A.

El Tiempo (1979c). 'Courte recomienda 24 países para Mundial-86', 15 September, p. 8C.

El Tiempo (1980). 'Mundial-86 en FIFA'. 12 December, p. 3C.

El Tiempo (1981a). 'El Mundial 86 en veremos', 5 September, p. 3C.

El Tiempo (1981b). 'Buena acogida a Mundial-86', 7 January, p. 2C.

Fajardo, J. (1982). 'Mundial 86: habla Havelange', *Revista Semana*, No. 3 (May), p. 10.

Goldblatt, D. (2007). *The Ball Is Round: A Global History of Football*. London: Penguin.

Jennings, A. (2006). *Foul!: The Secret World of FIFA: Bribes, Vote Rigging and Ticket Scandals* (p. 61). London: HarperSport.

Moncada, A. (1974) 'Colombia se superará', *El Tiempo*, 10 July, p. 6C.

Pelé (2006). *Pelé. Memorias del mejor futbolista de todos los tiempos*. Madrid: Temas de hoy, Memoria Editorial.

Prados de la Escosura, L. (2009). Lost decades? Economic performance in post-independence Latin America. *Journal of Latin America Studies, 41*, 279–307.

Silva, M. (2023). *El major equipo del mundo*. Bogotá. Ed. Planeta.

PART V

Business, Society and Culture

31

FOOTBALL CONSUMPTION, NOSTALGIA, AND SOFT POWER

Definitely Maybe!

Paul Widdop and Simon Chadwick

Introduction

In the landscape of the geopolitical economy of football, the captivating interplay between foreign nation states and sovereign wealth funds investing in professional football clubs unfolds as a multifaceted intersection of sports, economics, and international relations. This intricate connected phenomenon, often scrutinized through the lens of soft power, illuminates a purposeful endeavour by nations to exert global influence through diplomatic channels. While scholars, including Chadwick (2022), Chadwick and Widdop (2018, p. 2019), Chadwick et al. (2020), and Grix and Brannagan (2016), have made commendable strides in unravelling the economic and geopolitical dimensions of these investments, a crucial gap still persists in comprehending the role of 'culture' in both its broad and narrow contexts. This is ironic given the importance placed on culture within management (Drucker, 2007), marketing (Belk, 2010; de Mooij, 2019; Holt, 2004), and consumption (Crossley, 2015; Stillerman, 2015; Warde, 2014). According to Williams (1976; see Crossley, 2015) 'culture' encompasses a dual interpretation that includes routine behaviours, beliefs, values, and norms shared by a community in its broad sense. In a narrower context, it intertwines with artistic realms such as football, fashion, and music, what musician Liam Fray had described as, 'The Holy Trinity,' occasionally homing in on specific entities within these domains. Currently, there exists a gap in our understanding of how the culture of football, embedded in places and symbolic sub-cultural codes, are intertwined with mechanisms of soft power. Furthermore, we explore how by adopting a cultural branding approach (Holt and Cameron, 2010), Football Clubs have successfully tapped into sub-cultures

DOI: 10.4324/9781003473671-36

and creatively cultivate and nurture relationships for mechanisms of soft power, which they have done through invoking nostalgia (Holbrook, 1993) consumable past (Brunk et al., 2018; Chadwick and Widdop, 2021), and cultural appropriation (Lin et al., 2023).

Definitely Maybe

In a season that left a distinguished mark on Manchester City's history, culminating in their 8th league title and 3rd English Premier League Championship, a crowd gathered on the home turf of the Etihad Stadium on 1 June 2022, the symbolic start to British Summertime. On this day, the Etihad's largest crowd of the season was assembled not to celebrate the football champions, but to pay homage to another cultural icon, a rock 'n' roll luminary, a son of Manchester, and notorious Manchester City supporter – Liam Gallagher.

The intertwined history of Gallagher and Manchester City traces back 26 years, to a momentous event that left an enduring imprint on the popular cultural fabric of Manchester and Britain. Amid the political optimism of the 1990s, catalysed in part by Tony Blair's New Labour and its Third Way, and set against the backdrop of the Britpop music and wider cultural movement, a group of Mancunians hailing from Burnage, a working-class suburb in South-East Manchester, 4 miles south of the Etihad, took to the stage at Maine Road, the place Manchester City called home for 80 years. This historic night witnessed 40,000 people congregating to witness the convergence of music, culture, and football – the five lads, Liam and Noel Gallagher, Paul 'Bonehead' Arthurs, Paul McGuigan, and Alan White, collectively known as Oasis, emerged on stage as the cultural pioneers of and embodiment of Britpop. A cultural tour de force that propelled British youth sub-culture to the world.

Britpop, a quintessentially indie music scene, broke into mainstream ascendancy in the mid-1990s, with bands like Blur, Pulp, Suede, Elastica, and Menswear. Yet, it is Oasis that remains the most symbolic representative of this genre. Beyond the musical homage to British rock 'n' roll heritage, echoing The Beatles, The Who, The Kinks, and The Jam, Oasis set themselves apart with their swagger, personalities, and distinctive fashion. Brothers Liam and Noel Gallagher, influenced by subcultures such as The Mods of the Sixties, Suedeheads of the Seventies, and the terrace culture of the Eighties, donned attire that epitomized the movement, making them the ringleaders of Britpop fashion – Parkas, Fred Perry polo shirts, Retro Adidas Originals, Fila, Burberry, and Ben Sherman shirts buttoned to the top, Levi's 511 jeans, and Clark's desert boots. As with all music and youth movements, fashion was a form of cultural code (Holt and Cameron, 2010) for this movement.

As Gallagher took to the stage at the Etihad with his signature swagger and style, just outside the stadium on Joe Mercer's way the club shop – a testament to the new era of football commercialization, the then English champions seized the opportunity to unveil their new kit for the upcoming 2022/23 campaign, a standard practice during summertime as teams across the country embark on their marketing campaigns accompanying new kit launches. However, Manchester City, particularly since their takeover by the City Football Group, distinguishes itself by employing a unique marketing cultural branding approach. The marketing and creative teams surrounding Manchester City demonstrate mastery in utilizing cultural codes and nostalgia to construct a consumable past.

Notably, the club emphasized that the 2022/23 kit was designed to celebrate iconic teams of the past and in particular club legend, Colin Bell. The homage was apparent in the new kit's resemblance to the 1970s attire, with the central positioning of the badge reminiscent of the legendary Number 8 worn by Bell during his heydays at Maine Road. However, what adds an extra layer of fascination are the other cultural codes interwoven into the kit's design. That year's kit, its promotional material, and advertising draw inspiration from its close connection to Britpop and in particular its cultural chief icons, Oasis.

Projected from the club shop's window facade was the marketing staple, 'Play Forever' – a clear and unmistakable nod to Oasis' third single, 'Live Forever,' from the debut album 'Definitely Maybe.' Furthermore, while the kit pays homage to Bell's City, it also mirrors the style, colours, and trims of the T-shirts worn by Oasis members and their legions of followers. Front and centre in the marketing campaign is Phil Foden, another androgynous charismatic Mancunian frontman, exuding a swagger. In the marketing material, Foden meticulously mimics the famous onstage stance – head to the side, hands behind the back – made iconic by Liam Gallagher. The cultural codes are clear, this was a campaign embedded in the culture of 1990s Manchester.

The significance of football's affinity for history becomes evident in its ability to transport us to a different time, providing an escape from the world we've created. It breaks the stranglehold of individualism, presenting an alternative way of being – a collective, entwined in social relationships, belonging to a tribe and a city. Nostalgia, often perceived negatively in consumer behaviour, takes on a different hue in football. Fans don't merely long for the good old days; they share stories of past triumphs, reliving moments like Colin Bell's goal against Burnley. This mechanism of reliving the past is not exclusive to football; it parallels the dynamics of music movements. The subcultures of music and football converge, creating a powerful force of symbols – clothing, style, mannerisms – conventions, and norms that construct a glorified past. A past that, perhaps, doesn't precisely reflect reality but resonates deeply within the collective consciousness.

The intersection of this holy trinity – football, music, and fashion – serves as a dynamic arena for the interplay of symbols and narratives. By tapping into collective memory, capitalism doesn't merely exploit socialism; it markets and exploits the mechanisms around collective identity and belonging within subcultures to sell football kits and increasingly other forms of merchandise such as training kits. The association with Oasis, Liam Gallagher, and the cultural codes of Britpop positions the Manchester City owners strategically in the marketplace. It signifies a club in touch with its supporters' past, woven into their collective history. Even those who weren't part of the Britpop movement recognize the signalling emanating from the Etihad. Further, by celebrating the past, the marketing campaigns extract the negatives (drugs, toxic masculinity, violence, and misogyny (see Millward et al., 2017)) from the movement and project the positives onto the club and its owners.

This then raises a critical question concerning what Manchester City's Abu Dhabi owners gain from this consumable past, beyond the obvious aim of selling as many kits as possible to boost club revenues. It's improbable that the Gulf owners inherently recognize Oasis, Britpop, and the distinctive swagger of Mancunians, or that they would like to be symbolically associated with some Gallagher's and the Britpop's movements vices. However, nostalgic soft power becomes a means to foster legitimacy and acceptance. By tapping into subcultures and their conventions, the club leverages soft power as an attractive force, changing perceptions of overseas owners who might be deemed out of touch. As explored in various contexts, soft power becomes a tool to convince others that shared values and aspirations underpin the club's ethos.

As the crowd at the Etihad vibrates to the beats of Liam Gallagher's 'everything's electric,' it's conceivable that more than a few among them were donning the new City kit. It marks a coming together of music, football, and fashion – the holy trinity – creating a powerful force that extends beyond the realms of sport and attire. For Manchester City and its owners, the consumable past isn't merely an effective marketing tool for selling shirts; it's a strategic component in the broader game of legitimacy and soft power. The intertwining narratives of music, football, and fashion form a tapestry that binds the club to its supporters and projects an image of cultural connectivity in the ever-evolving landscape of modern football.

Cultural Branding Strategy and the Manchester City Paradox

Examining Manchester City's consumable past reveals a seamless alignment with Douglas Holt's theoretical framework of cultural branding (Holt, 2004, 2020; Holt and Cameron, 2010). Holt's thesis emphasizes the co-creation of meanings within a cultural context, so therefore finds resonance in the intricate fusion of football, music, and fashion narratives within the club's marketing approach. The celebration of iconic teams and players constitutes a cultural mythos rooted in football history, yet it's the infusion of Britpop culture, particularly the explicit homage to Oasis, which elevates the narrative to wider social significance. The 'Play Forever' tagline, resonating as a cultural mantra, links Manchester City to the timeless essence of Oasis and the Britpop era, showcasing how cultural branding transcends traditional football marketing.

Holt's framework further underscores the strategic selection of Phil Foden, embodying the mannerisms reminiscent of Liam Gallagher, as the campaign's face. Foden becomes a conduit for connecting with a specific subculture, embodying the body and cultural codes associated with Britpop. The adoption of fashion reminiscent of Oasis, both by Foden and in marketing materials, enhances this subcultural connection, positioning Manchester City as culturally relevant. The paradox emerges in the realm of soft power, as Holt's framework suggests cultural branding can challenge the status quo. While the Gulf owners may not inherently grasp Oasis or Britpop nuances, the strategic use of nostalgic soft power fosters a sense of legitimacy, aligning the owners symbolically with the cultural values and aspirations of the supporters. Manchester City's evolution from a traditional football club to a cultural curator exemplifies Holt's notion of continuous brand identity evolution. The club's consumable past becomes a dynamic cultural artefact, weaving football, music, and fashion narratives into a cohesive brand story that transcends conventional football marketing boundaries.

References

Belk, R. W., Ed. (2010). *Research in Consumer Behavior (Research in Consumer Behavior)* (Vol. 12, pp. 183–208). Leeds: Emerald Group Publishing Limited. https://doi.org/10.1108/S0885-2111(2010)0000012010.

Brunk, K. H., Giesler, M. and Hartmann, B. J. (2018). Creating a consumable past: how memory making shapes marketization. *Journal of Consumer Research, 44*(6), 1325–1342. https://doi.org/10.1093/jcr/ucx100.

Chadwick, S. (2022). From utilitarianism and neoclassical sport management to a new geopolitical economy of sport. *European Sport Management Quarterly, 22*(5), 685–704. https://doi.org/10.1080/16184742.2022.2032251.

Chadwick, S. and Widdop, P. (2018, November 20). Saudi Arabia's growing sporting influence. Asia and the Pacific Policy Forum. https://www.policyforum.net/saudi-arabias-growing-sporting-influence/.

Chadwick, S. and Widdop, P. (2021, March 26). Soft power songs: PSG, rap and the State of Qatar. *GeoSport*. https://www.iris-france.org/155771-soft-power-songs-psg-rap-and-the-state-of-qatar/.

Chadwick, S. and Widdop, P. (2021, October 22). Football's Consumable Past and the Soft Power of Nostalgia. *GeoSport*. https://www.iris-france.org/161937-footballs-consumable-past-and-the-soft-power-of-nostalgia/.

Chadwick, S., Widdop, P. and Burton, N. (2020). Soft power sports sponsorship – a social network analysis of a new sponsorship form. *Journal of Political Marketing*. https://doi.org/10.1080/15377857.2020.1723781.

Crossley, N. (2015). Relational sociology and culture: a preliminary framework. *International Review of Sociology, 25*(1), 65–85. https://doi.org/10.1080/03906701.2014.997965.

de Mooij, M. (2019). *Consumer Behavior and Culture: Consequences for Global Marketing and Advertising* (3rd ed.). Thousand Oaks: Sage.

Drucker, P. F. (2007). *The Essential Drucker* (1st ed.). Routledge. https://doi.org/10.4324/9780429347979.

Grix, J. and Brannagan, P. M. (2016). Of mechanisms and myths: conceptualising states' "Soft Power" strategies through sports mega-events. *Diplomacy & Statecraft, 27*(2), 251–272. https://doi.org/10.1080/09592296.2016.1169791.

Holbrook, M. B. (1993). Nostalgia and consumption preferences: some emerging patterns of consumer tastes. *Journal of Consumer Research, 20*(2), 245–256. http://www.jstor.org/stable/2489272.

Holt, D. (2004). *How Brands Become Icons: The Principles of Cultural Branding*. Boston: Harvard Business School Press.

Holt, D. (2020). *Cultural Innovation*. Boston: Harvard Business Review.

Holt, D. and Cameron, D. (2010). *Cultural Strategy – Using Innovative Ideologies to Build Breakthrough Brands*. Oxford: Oxford Press.

Lin, J. D., Kim, N., Uduehi, E. and Keinan, A. (2023). Culture for Sale: unpacking consumer perceptions of cultural appropriation. *Journal of Consumer Research*. https://doi.org/10.1093/jcr/ucad076.

Millward, P., Widdop, P. and Halpin, M. (2017). A 'Different Class'? Homophily and heterophily in the social class networks of Britpop. *Cultural Sociology, 11*(3), 318–336. https://doi.org/10.1177/1749975517712045.

Stillerman, J. (2015). *The Sociology of Consumption: A Global Approach*. Bristol: Policy Press.

Warde, A. (2014). After taste: culture, consumption and theories of practice. *Journal of Consumer Culture, 14*(3), 279–303. https://doi.org/10.1177/1469540514547828.

Williams, R. (1976). *Keywords*. London: Fontana.

32

THE GREAT GAME OF FOOTBALL DIPLOMACY

Australia versus Wales

Stuart Murray and Gavin Price

Introduction

Football is more than a game. It is a global phenomenon with an estimated fanbase of around five billion people (FIFA, 2022). The ecosystem required to produce and support the game includes a wide range of stakeholders, from football associations, players, coaches, and officials to businesses, old and new media firms, non-governmental organisations (NGOs), and government ministries (FIFA, 2021). Football also generates billions in revenue from broadcasting rights, sponsorships, merchandise, and ticket sales. In Europe, for example, the UEFA Champions League boasts top-tier corporate sponsors such as Heineken, PlayStation, Turkish Airlines, Lay's, FedEx, and Mastercard and generated USD 606.3 million in sponsorship revenue for the 2022–2023 season, according to GlobalData (2023).

Football diplomacy can be defined as the strategic use of football by state and non-state actors to realise goals ranging from foreign policy to trade, branding and raising awareness of the importance of human security issues, for example. The activity involves a plural cast of stakeholders who co-opt the beautiful game to promote peace, social cohesion, and development, as well as – ideally – positive economic and political outcomes. As Postlethwaite and Price (2023) note, football diplomacy's activities can include "progressive or soft power agendas such as social inclusion, promoting culture and tourism or encouraging women and girls in sport and leadership through to more traditional diplomatic or hard power variables such as leveraging the sport as a platform to enhance international trade and security".

This chapter provides two case studies of football diplomacy on Australia and Wales, a devolved United Kingdom (UK) nation. It argues and

DOI: 10.4324/9781003473671-37

demonstrates that while the practice of football diplomacy is strong, scholarship is lacking.

Australian (Aussie) Football Diplomacy

Australia's football activities markedly increased in 2005, the year Football Federation Australia (FFA) left the Oceania Football Confederation (OFC) for the Asian Football Confederation (AFC). Australia's membership of the AFC created opportunities for engagement with Asian and Middle Eastern countries through various international-level tournaments and continental club-level competitions. The AFC Champions League, for example, provides staging posts for regular fixtures between Australian and Asian club teams, which the Department of Foreign Affairs and Trade (DFAT) leverages to build diplomatic, business, and cultural ties with seven of Australia's top ten trading partners, including China, Japan, and the Republic of Korea. Back in 2014, for example, the Australian government poured AUD $5.2 million into *Match Australia* (Austrade, 2014), an international sports business and networking platform connecting Australian businesses with regional partners through sporting events, especially leading up to Australia's successful hosting of the men's 2015 AFC Asian Cup Tournament.

Football fixtures also generate opportunities for informal yet vital dialogue with officials from estranged countries such as Iran, Iraq, Palestine, and Lebanon. Such informal avenues, venues, and forums often provide the only contact. Football, or footballers, thus act as mediators and representatives of sensitive human rights topics that governments fail to address. Shortly before the FIFA World Cup 2022 Qatar, for example, 16 players from the Australian Men's squad released "a collective statement of protest against Qatar's human rights record, calling for 'effective remedy' for migrant workers and the decriminalisation of same-sex relationships" (Rugari, 2022).

The Australian Government funds and supports the activities described above. This is because football also involves Australia's major migrant communities, such as the British, Croatians, Greeks, Irish, or Italians. Governments are increasingly seeking to connect with such diasporas at home and abroad. A good example came in the form of Australia and England's 2023 international double header in London, where both the women's and men's senior football teams played. Off the pitch, British and Australian diplomats, businessfolk, and influential figures from the arts, culture, and music industries built relationships, advanced mutual interests, and enjoyed a glass of wine while watching some good football. The fixtures also served as a reminder that the UK and Australia are close partners on matters of trade, tourism, shared values, and geo-strategic issues such as AUKUS, a trilateral security partnership for the Indo-Pacific region between Australia, the UK, and the USA.

Strength in sports diplomacy also comes in the ability to bid for, win, and host mega sports events. Such ability can be evidenced in the "Green and Gold Decade", a term that describes ten years of international sports events ranging from the 2022 FIBA Women's World Cup (held in Sydney) to BMX (2026), Rugby Union (2027, men; 2029, women), Netball (2015 and 2027), T20 (2028), and the 2032 Olympic and Paralympic Games Brisbane. More recently, Australia co-hosted the 2023 FIFA Women's World Cup 2023 (FWWC23) with New Zealand, where the Matildas secured a fourth-place finish and attracted record crowds and widespread, global media attention.

With billions tuning in all over the world, the FWWC23 allowed the government to promote Australia as an outward-focused, culturally diverse, inclusive, and progressive sporting nation. It also generated opportunities to use football as a diplomatic tool for promoting social inclusion, gender empowerment, and cultural relations activities. Akin to the Men's team's use of social media, the Matildas' squad also realised a video that argued for human rights and equal pay, while reminding the new army of fans of the arduous employment issues that past and present players fought for. In addition, the players called on FIFA to ensure that the tournament promoted gender empowerment, inclusion, and equity in sports and urged FIFA to leave a positive legacy of social inclusion after the tournament (Guardian Australia, 2023).

The tournament also broke new ground. For the first time, FIFA agreed to display the Aboriginal, Torres Strait Islander, and Māori flags during matches. The sight of the flags fluttering generated "enormous pride" and "pure jubilation" in the words of Karen Menzies, the first Indigenous woman to don a Matilda's shirt (The Washington Post, 2023). This move represented a step forward for Australia in reconciling with its First Nations people and Australian football. Furthermore, each of the nine host cities in the FWWC23 was referred to by both their English and indigenous names in all forms of communication, including signage, broadcasts, stadiums, and online material. This provided formal recognition of the indigenous languages of Australia and New Zealand and a mark of respect to the local cultures of First Nations Peoples as traditional landowners. Some examples include Tāmaki Makaurau/Auckland, Sydney/Gadigal Melbourne/Naarm, and Perth/Borloo.

The Matildas achieved a historic fourth-place finish at FWWC23, garnering support across national, regional, and international audiences. This success was personified by star players such as Sam Kerr, Mary Fowler, and Caitlin Foord, who proved to be excellent ambassadors for Australia's brand, diplomacy, and gender equity in international sports. Tim Harcourt, a former Chief Economist at Austrade, went so far as to propose that the team become official ambassadors for Australia. He argued that if Matthew Hayden and Lisa Sthalekar (cricket) can be ambassadors for Australian education in cricket-mad India, the Matildas could do the same in countries that follow football, the world's most popular sport (Harcourt, 2023). Such an argument was validated by Sam Kerr, who led Australia's representatives at King Charles' coronation in 2023 as the official flagbearer.

While this case study provides a helpful introduction, it only scratches the topic's surface. Other important areas of football diplomacy, such as the role of high-profile, former sports people like Tim Cahill, Harry Kewell, Moya Dodd, or Craig Foster play in promoting Australia's brand, foreign policy and diplomacy would prove worthy. Such individuals are major players in the realm of football diplomacy, working either on behalf of the Australian Government or other key Australian or global business and civil society stakeholders. Foster's work integrating football with human rights and social advocacy causes could easily warrant a stand-alone case study.

Wales-Cymru

Wales, also known as Cymru in the Welsh language, is a small country with a large football diplomacy footprint. The country has gained sports diplomacy and international cultural relations recognition due to its collaborative approach which, over the years, is encapsulated in the term "Team Wales". The partnership model brings together the Welsh Government, businesses, academia, the sports sector, and civil society organisations to deliver a range of activities involving football, diplomacy, and the arts (Murray and Price, 2020).

The Football Association of Wales (FAW) is one of the most prominent players in Team Wales. As the custodian of a rich football heritage closely linked to Wales' unique culture, language, and identity, the FAW oversees the Welsh national football team. It is recognised by both FIFA and UEFA, the international and European governing bodies for football, which confers the regime absolute football sovereignty, and equal status to powerful federations in France, Germany, or Spain, as well as in influential football governance forums such as UEFA's Executive Committee (UEFA ExCo). For example, the FAW's Professor Laura McAllister currently holds the influential position of Vice-President within UEFA's ExCo. For a small country, Wales enhances its global profile by ensuring Welsh football administrators operate at the top table of the world game.

Such activity also shows that Wales' limited political sovereignty within the UK system does not hold it back when it comes to football diplomacy. As a strong indicator of how the FAW and wider Team Wales partners have embraced the nation's status as an independent football and sporting nation, Cymru's appearance at the FIFA World Cup 2022 Finals offers a good example. The first time Cymru had qualified for football's international showpiece event since 1958, the tournament provided a rare, golden opportunity to showcase Wales to the world through a targeted programme of football diplomacy activities.

Taking Wales to the World during the 2022 FIFA World Cup

To promote Cymru at the Qatar 2022 FIFA World Cup Finals (FWC2022), the Welsh Government distributed a Partnership Support Fund (PSF) worth £1.8 million to support Team Wales activities. The fund supported 19 projects that involved over 320,000 people participating in or attending more than 2,200 cultural relations, business and diplomatic events and activities, reaching an audience of more than 5 million (Welsh Government, 2023). To deliver, the Welsh Government partnered with various Team Wales organisations with international reach and clout; renowned institutions such as Amgueddfa Cymru (Museums Wales), Urdd Gobaith Cymru (one of Europe's largest youth organisations), Welsh Arts International, Global Welsh (a diaspora organisation), and the FAW, among numerous others.

However, what made Welsh football diplomacy at FWC22 different was the innovative fusion of sport with culture, music, arts, language, history, and landscapes alongside more traditional activities such as trade and tourism. In preparation for the FWC22 Finals in Qatar, for example, the world's first football culture festival, Expo'r Wal Goch (Red Wall Festival), took place in Wrexham. The festival showcased Welsh domestic and international films, books, fashion, music, memorabilia, and included panel discussions on themes including football diplomacy, homophobia and sport, social inclusion in football and many other things. The innovative festival demonstrates that Welsh football diplomacy is not only driven by government or formal institutions but also organically by fans and broader civil society. Welsh football diplomacy is truly a whole-of-nation endeavour.

The Lleisiau Cymru (Voices Wales) World Cup Ambassadors programme was another success. The programme funded, trained, and supported four Welsh football and cultural diplomats. It sought to raise Wales' global profile, create long-lasting positive perceptions of the country, and reinforce relationships with key global partners. Four iconic Welsh figures were nominated as ambassadors: Professor Laura McAllister, a former Welsh international footballer, Olympic silver hurdling medallist and World Champion Colin Jackson CBE, London-based DJ and presenter Katie Owen, and renowned Chef Bryn Williams.

A third example from FIFA World Cup 2022 Qatar involved the FAW and the Arts Council of Wales, who joined forces to create the innovative Gŵyl Cymru Festival. The festival celebrated Welsh football and culture, from grassroots to international competitions. During the FWC22, over 300 events were held worldwide in more than 200 locations, featuring more than 500 artists (Gŵyl Cymru Festival, 2023). The FOCUS Wales music festival, for example, hosted gigs in New York and Montreal, featuring Welsh urban acts such as Lemfreck and Mace the Great. Meanwhile, the Red Wall's official brass band, The Barry Horns, performed fan favourites in Dubai. Every event was delivered in conjunction with formal diplomatic engagements or trade delegations in the host countries, demonstrating Cymru's unique fusion of football diplomacy, national interests, and cultural relations with the world.

Finally, Wales' brand in Qatar was amply supported by its friendly and very vocal fans. During the build-up to FWC22, the iconic 1960s protest song, "Yma o Hyd" (Still here), was selected as the official anthem for Wales' participation at FWC22. The song's lyrics express a sense of Welsh culture, linguistic pride, and determination in the face of adversity. This song has since become an important symbol of Welsh identity. The official music video featured 70,000 members of the Red Wall of Cymru National Football Supporters Club singing along with Dafydd Iwan, the legendary Welsh language activist and politician who wrote the song. Through music, passion, camaraderie, and respect for other nations, the Red Wall regard themselves as informal Ambassadors for Cymru at international fixtures. This has led to the term "diplomats in bucket hats" organically being applied to Welsh fans due to their iconic red, yellow, and green headwear when attending games overseas. At EURO 2016 in France, for example, the Red Wall won the UEFA award for the "outstanding contribution" of their fans, along with Iceland, the Republic of Ireland, and Northern Ireland.

This case study provides a glimpse into the diversity and scope of Welsh football diplomacy. However, numerous other themes merit further investigation. For instance, Hollywood actors Ryan Reynold's and Rob McElhenney's involvement with Wrexham Football Club in North Wales is a fascinating mixture of celebrity, football, and international relations. The club has received significant international attention through the highly acclaimed documentary series "Welcome to Wrexham", which offers an inside look at the club's operations and the people, culture, language and landscapes of the Wrexham region and wider Wales. Further research might also consider the FAW's numerous progressive programmes that focus on developing women's and girl's (female) football in Wales and broader social inclusion activities such as "PAWB Football for All", a programme aimed at making football accessible to all members of the community, regardless of their background, ability, or gender.

Additionally, the FAW boasts a world-leading coach education programme that has attracted retired elite players such as Thierry Henry (France), Tim Cahill (Australia), and Freddie Ljungberg (Sweden) to choose Cymru as their preferred destination for gaining professional accreditation and licenses. This serves as further proof that Cymru is a small nation with a large and fast-growing footballing footprint.

Conclusion

This chapter highlighted how Australia and Wales strategically co-opted football as a diplomatic tool that presents both nations as progressive, diverse, and inclusive destinations open to international business, tourism, cultural exchange, and engagement. The cases provided examples of how football diplomacy can lead to positive economic, cultural, and political outcomes, while creating whole-of-nation teams involving people from government, academe, football, commerce, and human rights.

The point of this chapter was to establish football diplomacy as a more recognised field of study. Although this has been achieved through the cases of Australia and Wales, the focus here has been primarily on football diplomacy at the national level. Future research might want to focus on the role of other stakeholders in developing this field, such as clubs, players, fans, media, and various civil society and NGOs.

To date, some scholarly attention has been paid to bilateral football diplomacy between nations, regions, cities, football federations, or significant clubs. Most of the work, however, focuses on Turkish-Armenian relations in the 1990s or the decision by Japan and Republic of Korea to co-host the 2002 FIFA World Cup jointly. This limited historical focus is strange, given that modern football diplomacy offers a constantly rich seam of case studies, sources, and evidence.

Future scholarly attention should focus on (at least) two aspects. First, how individual state and non-state actors employ the game of football to realise a broad range of diplomatic, business, and social ends. The unique diplomacy of FIFA, how Didier Drogba and the Cote D'Ivoire team stopped a Civil War in 2005, or how the game might be strategically co-opted to consider progressive feminist agendas and end results are good examples of fertile topics. The same might be said of, second, the interaction between footballers, sporting regimes, and governments, that is, the massive, complex, and barely understood network required to provide the 24/7/365 smorgasbord of the World Game. Paraphrasing the diplomacy scholar Raymond Cohen (1998, p. 1), football diplomacy truly is the "engine room" that drives every aspect of the game; as magnificent as it is misunderstood.

References

Austrade (2014). Match Australia – International Business Sports Program. https://singapore.embassy.gov.au/sing/ahcsg_140409_article_matchaustralia.html

Cohen, R. (1998). *Putting Diplomatic Studies on the Map. Diplomatic Studies Program Newsletter*. Leicester: Leicester University.

FIFA (2021). The Football Landscape. https://publications.fifa.com/en/vision-report-2021/the-football-landscape/.

FIFA (2022). One Month On: 5 billion engaged with the FIFA World Cup Qatar 2022. https://www.fifa.com/tournaments/mens/worldcup/qatar2022/news/one-month-on-5-billion-engaged-with-the-fifa-world-cup-qatar-2022-tm.

GlobalData (2023). UEFA Champions League generates $606.3 million sponsorship revenue for the 2023 season, reveals GlobalData. https://www.globaldata.com/media/sport/uefa-champions-league-generates-606-3-million-sponsorship-revenue-2023-season-reveals-globaldata/.

Guardian Australia (2023). Matildas take aim at Fifa over prize money in video released days before World Cup kickoff. https://www.youtube.com/watch?v=bmczaehpdto.

Gŵyl Cymru Festival (2023). Cymru. Football, Creativity. https://www.wales.com/visit/sport/gwyl-cymru-creative-festival-biggest-cities-and-smallest-villages

Harcourt, T. (2023). Can the Matildas waltz onto the world stage for Australia's sport diplomacy? Lowy Institute Interpreter. https://www.lowyinstitute.org/the-interpreter/can-matildas-waltz-world-stage-australia-s-sport-diplomacy.

Murray, S. and Price, G. (2020). Towards a Welsh sports diplomacy strategy. https://wales.britishcouncil.org/en/creating-sports-diplomacy-strateg y-wales.

Postlethwaite, V. and Price, G. (2023). FIFA Women's World Cup 2023 and sports diplomacy at a confederation level. In A. Beissel, V. Postlethwaite, A. Grainger and J. E. Brice (Eds.), *The 2023 FIFA Women's World Cup: Politics, Representation, and Management* (1st ed.) (pp. 113–126). Abingdon: Routledge.

Rugari, V. (2022). Socceroos, Football Australia speak out on Qatar's human rights record. *The Sydney Morning Herald*. https://www.smh.com.au/sport/soccer/socceroos-football-australia-speak-out-on-qatar-s-human-rights-record-20221025-p5bsph.html.

Washington Post (2023). You might notice some new flags at the World Cup. Here's why it's a big deal. https://www.washingtonpost.com/sports/2023/07/20/world-cup-soccer-indigenous-flags/.

Welsh Government (2023). Press release – Welsh Government strategy to promote Wales to the World during 2022 FIFA World Cup hailed as success. https://www.gov.wales/welsh-government-strategy-promote-wales-world-during-2022-fifa-world-cup-hailed-success-report.

33

FOOTBALL, GEOPOLITICS, AND DIGITAL TECHNOLOGIES

A Dynamic Nexus Shaping Global Dynamics

Samir Ceric and Sanchit Mehra

Introduction

Football, often heralded as a "beautiful game," transcends its role as a mere sport to become a mirror reflecting the geopolitical and technological currents of the 21st century. The dynamic of football is changing, deviating from conventional as the game itself changes. Football's growing attractiveness on a global scale, players moving across continents, and the substantial financial influx are the three main drivers of this change. It compels us to consider whether we are at the threshold of a new age, heralding the death of European and South American domination.

In this chapter, we embark on a comprehensive exploration of the intricate interplay between football, geopolitics, and digital technologies, examining the intricate relationships between these three components and how they interact to affect things globally. Football is getting a digital makeover, but it's not just about the game anymore. It's also about how it relates to global events and the newest technological developments. From historical perspectives to contemporary developments and future implications, we navigate the multifaceted dimensions that define this complex relationship.

The story of football is being profoundly rewritten as players travel the world, the beautiful game becomes ever more popular, and large sums of money are being invested. It's more than just a change of scenery; it's a re-evaluation of power structures and standards for what constitutes great football (Poli, 2010).

DOI: 10.4324/9781003473671-38

Historical Foundations: Football as a Geopolitical Battleground

The historical roots of the intersection between football and geopolitics run deep. In the early 20th century, football emerged as a tool for national expression, its matches serving as symbolic battlegrounds for political ideologies. Given the abundance of points of contact and shared features between the two universes, football's reflection in geopolitics can be thought of as a maze that leads into a complex system of parallels (Scutti and Wendt, 2016). Football has a geopolitical element similar to that of war. The "Match of the Century" during the 1970 World Cup, where West Germany and Italy faced off, is a poignant example of Cold War rivalries echoing on the pitch. Drawing from sources like David Goldblatt's "The Ball is Round," we explore how football has historically mirrored and sometimes intensified geopolitical tensions (Giulianotti, 1999).

In the rich tapestry of football's past development, the fields have functioned as more than just places for skill. Rather, they serve as platforms for the development of geopolitical stories that have a lasting impact on the international scene. Beyond just being a competitive event, Russia's hosting of the 2018 World Cup gave the country a rare chance to break through longstanding barriers and preconceptions and reveal a new side amidst changing political tides. In a similar vein, the event that took place in Qatar in 2023 offered an opportunity to overcome cultural barriers between the Islamic and Western worlds, going beyond a simple football match. These occurrences reflect a narrative of transformation, where football's impact extends beyond the pitch, echoing bigger developments in global power relations (Haghirian and Robles-Gil, 2021; Reiche, 2018).

Globalisation and Football: A Symbiotic Relationship

Football has become more than just a sport; it becomes a captivating arena where countries compete for dominance and power. Football serves as a mirror for how the forces of globalisation are reshaping our planet. Leagues, which were formerly restricted by national boundaries, are now seen as worldwide spectacles, indicating a significant change. This section explores the complex relationship between football and geopolitical influences in our globalised world, drawing on concepts from "Globalisation and Football." Football's story unfolds as a monument to its symbiotic relationship with the forces of globalisation, from changing ownership structures and spikes in foreign investments to the growing international fans. Away from the pitch, Fédération Internationale de Football Association's (FIFA's) expansion reflects a striving for both athletic excellence and the development of a unique political identity in the international sphere.

Football has evolved beyond its modest beginnings and now has a governing body, organisational structure, and set of rules. This shift has endowed football with qualities evocative of a particular geopolitical framework (Giulianotti and Robertson, 2007). Exceptional football teams' economic transformation into multinational businesses is a striking example of the complex interplay between regional origins and external influences. This merger offers the potential not just to democratise international governance but also to transform the financial landscape of the game, as expressed by Horne (2012). Tiesler and Coelho's investigation of globalisation's influence on football goes into cross-border economic movements, international migration, and the intriguing marriage of tradition and modernity (Tiesler and Coelho, 2007).

The Digital Revolution in Football Fan Engagement

The advent of digital technologies has revolutionised how football is experienced and consumed. Social media platforms like Twitter, Facebook, and Instagram have become the agora for global football discourse. Analysing works like Stefan Lawrence's "Digital Football Cultures," we delve into the transformative impact of social media on fan engagement, exploring how it has democratised the conversation, empowered fans, and brought supporters from disparate corners of the world together. These platforms have changed the nature of football fandom by democratising dialogue, empowering fans, and bringing supporters together across vast geographic distances. However, this digital revolution comes with its challenges, navigating corporate and media interests while leveraging digital channels for advocacy, communication, and community building, showcasing the digital revolution in football fan engagement, shedding light on both its transformative potential and the hurdles it presents (Fenton et al., 2019; Numerato, 2016).

Even with all of its promise, ongoing control, censorship, and surveillance make it difficult to create the perfect speech environment that is necessary for fan empowerment and increasing club involvement. Supporters are divided along lines firmly ingrained in the ownership and culture of their local teams due to the substantial barriers built by corporate interests and media manipulation. Through a detailed analysis of both its benefits and drawbacks in this dynamic setting, this research explores the complex dynamics of technology's impact on football fan participation (McLean and Wainwright, 2009). This study sheds light on the complex landscape of technological impact on the fandom and unveils the complexity of the digital revolution in football fan engagement. It does this by balancing promise and obstacle.

Technological Innovations on the Pitch: Data Analytics and Wearables

Football is a dynamic sport that reveals a rich tapestry of technical and artistic variation. A symphony of many playing styles is created as several teams, regions, and countries provide their interpretations of the beautiful game.

However, the game's very fabric is woven with the technological revolution, which has an impact that goes beyond the fan experience. This investigation explores the revolutionary effects of wearables, data analytics, and video analysis on football management, drawing on insights from Chris Anderson and David Sally's "The Numbers Game." These developments have evolved into essential elements that have altered player performance, injury avoidance, and tactical approaches, changing the fundamental dynamics of the game. Simultaneously, the worldwide embrace of football works as a unifying force, eliminating distinctions between local games and supporting the formation of a unified global football culture (Giulianotti and Robertson, 2007). This study presents a thorough narrative that portrays both diversity and unity in the beautiful game by dissecting the complex interactions between technical advancements on the pitch and the changing football scenario.

With promises of affordability, accessibility, and user-friendliness, technological innovations have positioned themselves as clubs' crucial allies. These instruments, nearly viewed as trusted companions, have not only been accepted but heartily welcomed into the fabric of the sport, propelled by their strong marketing assertions. Due to their widespread use, there is a parallel search for software solutions as a means of converting the vast amounts of data produced by wearable technology into useful performance metrics. This method illuminates the precise paths of each player on the pitch and is similar to the painting of elaborate portraits (Gamble et al., 2020). Entering the world of wearables and data analytics on the pitch, this investigation reveals a story of integration, dependability, and calculated choices, revealing the complex relationship between football and these game-changing technologies.

Geopolitical Forces in Football Club Ownership

FIFA has always preferred the interests of its well-established European and South American constituencies in the complex realm of football governance. But a deeper look at the ownership arrangements of football teams reveals a complex web of geopolitical effects. Several foreign investors strategically buy shares in elite European and international clubs, frequently on behalf of their home countries. A thorough examination guided by scholarly understanding reveals the complex relationships between these ownership arrangements. Outside of the football pitch, they impact and reflect geopolitical alignments, adding to the soft power dynamics of countries. Examining the intricate relationship between geopolitical factors and football club ownership paves the way for understanding the intersections of global politics and sport, as well as the varied facets of influence in the beautiful game.

A complicated ballet of geopolitical factors is orchestrated inside the intricate fabric of football club ownership, with each force pulling in a different direction. With a focus on the complex interplay of corporate, political, and commercial pressures inside the enormous spectacle of the FIFA World Cup, Cornelissen's views offer a startling light into this complicated ballet (Cornelissen, 2010). Delving deeper into the governance of football clubs, Hassan's research reveals the complex effects of commercialisation. In this landscape, certain clubs adeptly tread the tightrope, masterfully balancing financial interests with the eternal nature of the sport (Hassan and Hamil, 2011).

In the thriving European football club investment market, ownership is a key factor that significantly impacts the complex structure of the game. The introduction of both domestic and foreign private investors represents a transformative age, as ownership decisions resoundingly alter the football scene (Holt, 2007). The story of ownership complexities that emerge from these combined studies shows how social, political, and economic factors interact to shape football clubs' futures. It develops as a human drama on the great stage of the beautiful game, transcending simple business (Rohde and Breuer, 2018). This investigation reveals the many facets that add to the drama that is developing in the world of football ownership as it untangles the compelling tale of geopolitical forces at work in football club ownership.

Political Boycotts, Protests, and Football Tournaments

Football competitions have become venues for political protest and expression in recent years, as seen by players using their platforms for activism and diplomatic boycotts of important games. This examination, which draws on scholarly analyses and current cases, addresses the moral conundrums that football's regulatory bodies are facing in the face of political protests. It draws attention to the precarious balance that exists between international politics and sports. A more nuanced perspective is added to the discussion by Lewis's analogy of the World Cup to the Olympics, which highlights historical political innocence. Together, these points highlight the complex nature of political boycotts and protests and their effects on the football tournament landscape (Wren-Lewis and Clarke, 1983).

Darby's historical analysis takes us back to the 1966 World Cup when off-field incidents had a lasting impact on both the competition and football worldwide. The deliberate decision made by African countries to boycott the qualifying stages in protest of what they saw as an unfair distribution of World Cup Finals spots was a crucial but frequently disregarded element. This diplomatic position of the Confédération Africaine de Football (CAF) in reaction to an 'outrageously unfair' chance reflected a complex and emotional response (Darby, 2019). Turning now to the 2010 FIFA World Cup in South Africa, Cornelissen's research reveals an engrossing story of how massive gatherings become more than just passive spectacles; they become active forums for political conversation. This research into political boycotts, protests, and football tournaments gives a gripping account of how these events transcend mere sport, becoming significant spaces for political expression and societal participation (Cornelissen, 2012).

E-Sports and Virtual Football: Redefining the Playing Field

A new dimension of football has evolved in the vast expanse of the digital era: virtual football and e-sports. Through an analysis of Andy Miah's "E-Sports and the Changing Context of Football," this investigation reveals how competitive gaming has a profoundly transforming effect. It has not only attracted a new type of fan base, but it has also made it more difficult to distinguish between virtual and real worlds. The forays into e-sports by football clubs highlight even more how digital technology has been woven into the fundamental fabric of the game (Miah, 2017). Virtual sports contests have become more professional because of eSports' development, especially in the FIFA football game series, and many players now recognise eSports as real sports (Zagała and Strzelecki, 2019).

The merger of sports and digital cultures, especially the rise of competitive computer game playing, is explored as a rethinking of the social mandate of sports. In addition to using their eyes, players assess the playing field by feeling the wind, manipulating the ball, touching the grass, and pressing their fingers and studs into the ground. The 2010 FIFA World Cup saw football players display this act of haptic exercise. Because of the unpredictable nature of this technology on the field of play, players changed their practice routines using the Adidas Jabulani, the official match ball (Mazza and Russo, 2023).

Challenges and Controversies: The Dark Side of the Digital Era

The benefits of football's digital age are matched by daunting difficulties in a constantly changing field. Digital communication's instantaneous nature has made problems like disinformation, online abuse, and the political exploitation of sports more prominent. Using a variety of sources, this research critically looks at the less positive aspects of football's digital age, exploring how stakeholders deal with responsibility and moral dilemmas in the face of this quick change. David and Milward (2012) warn us that cheaper alternative channels in football pose an immediate threat to traditional TV rights, as noted by eminent scholars; McLean and Wainwright (2009) examine the entry of big businesses and media into football, highlighting their potential to limit and isolate the fan base. When taken as a whole, these studies highlight the urgent need for a thorough investigation of how digital changes affect the dynamics of television, the active fan base, and the larger leisure and sports environment. Unveiling the not-so-bright side of the digital era in football, this research endeavours to identify and appreciate the difficulties and controversies that are defining the present sports environment (David and Milward, 2012; McLean and Wainwright, 2009).

The Future Landscape: Extended Reality, Blockchain, and Beyond

With an eye towards the future, we investigate possible paths at the nexus of digital technology, geopolitics, and football. New technologies have the potential to completely change the fan experience, especially in extended reality, where they can be used to combine virtual and augmented reality. On the other hand, the use of blockchain technology holds promise for transforming transparency in domains such as tickets, goods verification, and player transfers, providing insight into the game's revolutionary development. This speculative project, which draws from state-of-the-art works and professional perspectives, envisages and muses over the potential shapes of the football landscape and offers insights into the anticipated dynamic shifts in the years to come.

Conclusion

Covering the interwoven fields of geopolitics, digital technologies, and football, this thorough investigation presents a colourful tapestry that reflects the dynamics of the world today. Disclosing a story that goes beyond the echoes of history, negotiates changes in the present, and muses about potential futures, the connection between these components goes much beyond the football pitch. Capturing the essence of our interconnected society, it is a dynamic tale that reflects the complex dance of power, influence, and technological advancement. Along the way, the combination of digital technologies, geopolitics, and football becomes clear as a profound representation of the intricate interconnectivity that shapes our world today.

References

Cornelissen, S. (2010). 'Football's tsars: Proprietorship, corporatism and politics in the 2010', 13 January 2024, accessed via https://www.tandfonline.com/doi/full/10.1080/14660970903331458.

Cornelissen, S. (2012). 'Our struggles are bigger than the World Cup: Civic Activism, state', 13 January 2024, accessed via https://onlinelibrary.wiley.com/doi/10.1111/j.1468-4446.2012.01412.x.

Darby, D. P. (2019). 'Politics, resistance and patronage: The African boycott of the 1966', 13 January 2024, accessed via https://www.tandfonline.com/doi/full/10.1080/14660970.2019.1680494.

David, M. and Millward, P. (2012). 'Football's coming home?: Digital Reterritorialization, contradictions', 13 January 2024, accessed via https://onlinelibrary.wiley.com/doi/10.1111/j.1468-4446.2012.01413.x.

Fenton, A., Cooper-Ryan, A. M. and Vasilica, C. M. (2019). Smartphone fitness apps and football fans. In *Football as Medicine* (1st edition). Routledge. https://doi.org/10.4324/9780429284892-15

Gamble, P., Chia, L. and Allen, S. (2020). 'The illogic of being data-driven: Reasserting control and restoring', 13 January 2024, accessed via https://www.tandfonline.com/doi/full/10.1080/24733938.2020.1854842.

Giulianotti, R. (1999). 'Football. A sociology of the global game', 7 January 2024, accessed via https://hrcak.srce.hr/file/227468.

Giulianotti, R. and Robertson, R. (2007). 'Recovering the social: Globalization, football and transnationalism', 13 January 2024, accessed via https://onlinelibrary.wiley.com/doi/10.1111/j.1471-0374.2007.00163.x.

Haghirian, M. and Robles-Gil, P. (2021). 'Soft Power and the 2022 World Cup in Qatar: Learning from experiences of past mega-sporting event hosts', 11 January 2024, accessed via https://doi.org/10.29117/tis.2021.0074.

Hassan, D. and Hamil, S. (2011). 'Who owns football?', 13 January 2024, accessed via https://www.gbv.de/dms/zbw/563224339.pdf.

Holt, M. (2007). 'The ownership and control of elite club competition in European', 7 January 2024, accessed via https://www.tandfonline.com/doi/full/10.1080/14660970600989491.

Horne, J. (2012). 'Globalization and Football', 13 January 2024, accessed via https://www.tandfonline.com/doi/full/10.1080/02614367.2011.589216.

Mazza, B. and Russo, G. (2023). 'The value of esports football: Towards new models of consumption and', 13 January 2024, accessed via https://www.tandfonline.com/doi/full/10.1080/21582041.2023.2172204.

McLean, R. and Wainwright, D. W. (2009). Social networks, football fans, fantasy and reality: how corporate and media interests are invading our lifeworld. *Journal of Information, Communication and Ethics in Society*, 7 January 2024, accessed via https://doi.org/10.1108/14779960910938098.

Miah, A. (2017). Sport 2.0: Transforming Sports for a Digital World. The MIT Press. https://direct.mit.edu/books/monograph/3648/Sport-2-0Transforming-Sports-for-a-Digital-World

Numerato, D. (2016). Behind the digital curtain: Ethnography, football fan activism and social change. *Qualitative Research*, 16(5), 575–591. https://doi.org/10.1177/1468794115611207.

Poli, R. (2010). 'Understanding globalization through football: The new international', 13 January 2024, accessed via https://journals.sagepub.com/doi/10.1177/1012690210370640.

Reiche, D. (2018). 'Issues around the FIFA World Cup 2018 in Russia: A showcase of how sports and politics mix', 11 January 2024, accessed via https://www.degruyter.com/document/doi/10.1515/sug-2018-0013/html.

Rohde, M. and Breuer, C. (2018). 'Competing by investments or efficiency? Exploring financial and sporting efficiency of club ownership structures in European football', 13 January 2024, accessed via https://www.tandfonline.com/doi/full/10.1016/j.smr.2018.01.001.

Scutti, G. and Wendt, J. (2016). 'Football and geopolitics', 13 January 2024, accessed via http://geosport.uoradea.ro/2016_2/2016_12_GSS_Scutti_Wendt_16.05.05.021.pdf.

Tiesler, N. and Coelho, J. N. (2007), 'Globalized football at a lusocentric glance: Struggles with markets and migration, tradition and modernities, the loss and the beauty', 13 January 2024, accessed via https://www.tandfonline.com/doi/abs/10.1080/14660970701440675.

Wren-Lewis, J. and Clarke, A. (1983). 'The World Cup – a political football', 13 January 2024, accessed via https://journals.sagepub.com/doi/abs/10.1177/026327648300100310.

Zagała, K. and Strzelecki, A. (2019). 'Esports evolution in football game series', 13 January 2024, accessed via https://sciendo.com/article/10.2478/pcssr-2019-0020.

34

THE SUPRANATIONAL COMPETITIVE PROMISE OF THE THREE SEAS INITIATIVE IN CENTRAL EUROPE

Olivier Jarosz, Konstantin Kornakov, and Adam Metelski

Introduction

In recent years, there has been an increasing stratification in club football (Union of European Football Associations [UEFA], 2023). Wealthy clubs are becoming even wealthier, while smaller clubs from less populous and less affluent countries find it hard to keep up. Financial results indicate a gap between the clubs from the so-called Big Five leagues (England, Spain, Germany, Italy and France) and the rest of the clubs in Europe. It's worth noting that in 2021, the revenues of the richest football league in the world, the Premier League, amounted to €5549 million, followed by the second-ranked financial league, Spain's La Liga, with €3041 million, the third-ranked German Bundesliga with €2987 million, the fourth Italian Serie A with €2564 million, the fifth French Ligue 1 with €1575 million, and the sixth-ranked Russian league with only €777 million (UEFA, 2023). So there is a financial gap between the top Big Five and the next leagues. What's more, the English Premier League (EPL) definitely stands out from other countries (Iorwerth et al., 2018) in what can be termed as the "top-1". Some are beginning to wonder if such a situation is good for football (Adelugba, 2023). Thirty-one years after its launch, the Premier League is the template for all others for generating both the most wealth and the most excitement around the world in what can be described as a scale economy approach to sport business. There's not just one factor behind it, there are many such as heritage (the game was invented here), global language, a very pro-business environment that facilitates foreign investment, as well as excellent marketing and production (Marcotti, 2022). On top of all of the above, though, one particular factor serves as the enabler for the EPL model: demographics and specifically population size.

DOI: 10.4324/9781003473671-39

And the best example to demonstrate this is the growing disparity between the economies of the English and Scottish top divisions, which shows that, despite very similar heritages, languages, business environments and marketing methods, there seems to be a critical population volume factor at play that creates a multiplier effect for media rights. Table 34.1 presents the value of media rights in the top leagues in Europe, as well as Austria, Greece, Poland and Scotland.

A person may wonder whether there still is a chance for the emergence of some other strong leagues in Europe? Do the leagues from Central Europe have any chance to catch up with leagues from Big Five? The short answer, and especially considering the economic figures, seems to be "no", at least in the current development model. The chart (see Figure 34.1) shows how European football leagues have progressed in terms of revenues in the period from 2012 to 2021.

The EPL in the years 2012–2021 has developed the fastest – by 100%. The second league that recorded the greatest growth during this period was the Spanish La Liga. The smaller leagues in Europe were grouped together and it should be noted that in the analysed period, the slowest development was in those from places 6 to 10 in the UEFA ranking (9%), followed by those from places 11 to 20 in the UEFA ranking (28%). Evidently, if the smaller leagues are growing at a slower pace, they will never be able to catch up the front-runners, so an alternative model would be required to change this narrative.

In this chapter, we decided to refer to history and competitions that were played in Europe over 100 years ago, and we also addressed the topic of the

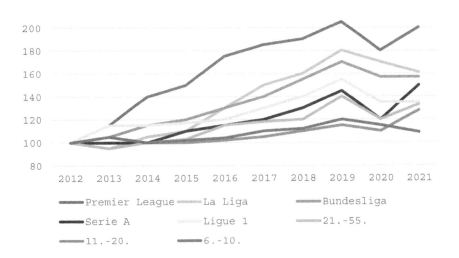

FIGURE 34.1 Revenue growth index of the top five leagues and the lower leagues grouped together

Source: Based on data from UEFA (2023).

TABLE 34.1 The value of media rights in the top five leagues in Europe and Austria, Greece and Poland

Country	League	Domestic media rights per year (€M)	Population (in million)	Media rights cost per capita (€)	Contract length	Broadcaster
England	Premier League	1,850	55.9	33.11	2022–2025	Sky Sports, BT Sport, Amazon Prime
Germany	Bundesliga 2. Bundesliga	1,100	83.2	13.22	2021–2025	Sky, DAZN, ProSieben
Spain	La Liga	870	47.35	18.37	2022–2027	Telefonica, DAZN
Italy	Serie A	927	59.55	15.57	2021–2024	Sky Sport, DAZN
France	Ligue 1 and Ligue 2	582	67.39	8.63	2021–2024	Amazon Prime, Canal+ Sport
Greece	Super League Greece	68	10.72	6.34	Rights are decentralised	Nova Sports, Cosmote TV
Poland	Ekstraklasa	66	37.95	1.73	2023–2027	Canal+, TVP Sport
Austria	Austrian Bundesliga	40	8.91	4.49	2022–2026	Sky Osterreich
Scotland	Premiership, Championship, SWPL	29	5.44	5.33	2020–2029	Sky Sports, BBC

Source: Based on data from LTT Sports (2022).

Three Seas Initiative. This is a forum of 13 countries in the European Union, and two partner-participants (Ukraine and Moldova), running along a north–south axis from the Baltic Sea to the Adriatic, Black and also the Mediterranean Seas, since Greece joined in 2023. The Three Seas Initiative is designed to promote cooperation in energy, transport, and digital sectors. Is there a way to leverage the demographic and economic potential of Central Europe in football? Our analyses indicate that the involved countries combined have immense potential, both in terms of demographics, economy, and football, with even a shared football heritage and innovative spirit. But only if they join forces.

The Formation of Football in Central Europe

When you look back at association football's origins and its initial spread around Europe and the world, there are not too many individual pivotal moments where you can say for certain that "without this particular event football would not have become the world's favourite team sport". It seems more like a groundswell of small circumstances, meetings, travels, decisions: someone studying in England bringing back a football, a British factory owner in a foreign land setting up a team for his employees, a tour by a football team or students choosing to set up their own team to play a new game. But one thing that is possible to identify within this timeline of different events is a particular significance of certain geographical areas to the growth of football's popularity and its development.

One of these areas, and probably the most impactful one in continental Europe in the early stages of the game's development, is the Danube basin, which now includes many of the countries that used to form part of what at the time was known as the Austrian Empire, the Habsburg Monarchy or Austro-Hungary (Judson, 2016). What is important to know is that the house of Habsburg had its origins in early mediaeval times, in the lands of what is now modern Switzerland. Over time, though, it came to dominate very significant parts of Western and Central Europe, with the main power base in Vienna, Austria. It was one of the major political, military and economic powers of Old Europe until defeat in World War I gave rise to the empire's dissolution and the creation of independent states in its place (Cook, 2018). How was it so significant in terms of football, if it was not the first continental area to play football outside of the British Isles, nor the first to organise clubs or football federations? Well, this is certainly the case, but they were nevertheless among the early adopters of the game, as the first clubs in Vienna were being set up in the early 1890s (First Vienna FC, 2023). Around the same time, football clubs also began to be set up in the imperial centres of Prague or Budapest, and a little later in such places as Croatia and the Habsburg Empire's Polish and Ukrainian lands. But this is not the most important contribution of the Danubians to global football: ultimately, football clubs were being set up in many parts of the world at this time. What was much more important was that from this area sprung a particular way of playing based on trickery and combinations, and a keen interest in tactical innovation, which spread through the Danubian basin and arguably influenced a lot of subsequent continental styles in major football powers like Italy and Spain, as well as more globally. So much so that some of the best coaches, players and teams of today can trace at least some of their footballing identity back to those lands, even if they never played or coached there themselves.

With an origin point in a British manager called Jim Hogan (Hyne, 2019), who worked in different Austro-Hungarian teams from before World War I, the timeline of famous coaches coming from this area is truly impressive. But this is not all, the Danubian football goldmine also produced such influential figures as Bela Guttman (Porter, 2021), who influenced football tactics and management styles in his Austro-Hungarian birthplace, but also in Italy and Portugal. Another one is Gusztav Sebes (Young, 2020), who coached the brilliant Magyars of the 1950s pioneering the 4-2-4 formation, the precursor to 4-4-2, and produced what was one of the seminal scorelines in football history, when Hungary beat England with a quite disrespectful 6-3 at Wembley in what was called the "match of the century". This result demonstrated the advances made by Continental European football in comparison with the archaic methods of the British pioneers, and the epicentre of these advances was the Danubian basin area.

If tactical advances and innovative management techniques are not enough by themselves to make the point, the Danubians were also instrumental in developing our whole modern approach to club and national team football competitions based on international tournaments. As early as 1897, clubs from different parts of the Austrian Empire had a competition called the Challenge Cup (Gottfried Fuchs, 2012), which was played until 1911. After World War I on the ruins of what was the Habsburg monarchy, the Mitropa Cup (Wojtaszyn, 2017) was founded in 1927 for participants from Austria, Hungary, Czechoslovakia and Yugoslavia, i.e. the newly independent states from what was Austro-Hungary before World War I. It was a cup-style knockout competition for professional teams to ensure high-level matches with potential for generating revenue and clearly is one of the reasons for our modern blueprint of what European club football should be like. At the time, these countries were pioneers of professionalisation in Europe, as professional leagues in round-robin format were launched in Austria in 1924, Hungary in 1925 and Czechoslovakia in 1926. Poland, which was not part of the Mitropa tournament, but whose football federation had its roots in the clubs and regional association formed in Austro-Hungarian Lviv in the early 1900s, also launched a professional league in 1927 (Miatkowski and

Owsiański, 2022). All of this was before similar leagues were launched in France (1932), Germany (1963), Italy (1929) or Spain (1928). The success of the Mitropa Cup was keenly observed around Europe and eventually gave rise to other similar competitions like the Copa Latina following World War II, which included clubs from France, Italy, Portugal and Spain. But more significantly, it was also one of the precursors to UEFA's club competition portfolio, as UEFA itself was not created until 1954, with the European Cup and the Inter-Cities Fairs Cup being launched from 1955. And even this is not all: in the same way as the Mitropa Cup was created to cater for professional clubs, the Danubian region was also instrumental in launching regular continental-level competitions for its national teams. The Central European International Cup (D'Avanzo, 2020) was also played from 1927 by the national teams of Austria, Czechoslovakia, Hungary, Italy, Switzerland and Yugoslavia, almost mirroring the original participants of the club competition, with Poland and Romania joining for the amateur part of the roster. UEFA's equivalent European Championship was only launched in 1958.

Three Seas Initiative in the 21st Century

Early success of football in the Danube region clearly had its roots in shared experiences and an enhanced sense of co-operation based on having until recently formed part of a common space. But this feeling can wear off as countries pursue their independence, and in the case of the Danubian states this was also exacerbated by the ravages of World War II, which steamrolled through these lands between 1939 and 1945, and the different post-war experiences, as the Iron Curtain divided territories and communities for many decades thereafter. So, has that post-Habsburg collaborative spirit felt previously in the coffee houses of Budapest and Vienna, and the beer halls of Prague, and which gave rise to so many football innovations in the 1920s and 1930s, completely fallen by the wayside with the passage of time, or can we still talk about a space that can rekindle this former spirit of cooperation, leveraging a set of common experiences and shared roots? There certainly seem to be a lot of common base conditions that could make shared development possible: starting from the size of countries in the Danube basin as being small to medium-sized, to plenty of similar experiences from history such as war devastation and Soviet/Communist dictate, and the Danube River itself, flowing from the South-Western corner of Germany to the Black Sea.

In 2015, the shared potential for development was identified through the emergence of the Three Seas Initiative (3 Seas 1 Opportunity, 2023), which includes most of the modern countries that back in 1919 were fully or partially within the Habsburg monarchy prior to its collapse. All together this initiative encompasses 13 European Union nations, spanning across a north-south axis from the Baltic Sea to the Adriatic, Black and Mediterranean Seas.

In an era marked by profound shifts in the global power dynamics, driven by the escalating influence of Asian and Middle Eastern nations, particularly China and Saudi Arabia, coupled with Russia's as-yet-unresolved imperial ambitions, and the ongoing instability in the Middle East and Africa leading to migration challenges, along with the pressing issue of advancing climate change, the collective hurdles confronting the members of the Initiative extend well beyond economic considerations. Therefore, the concept of enhancing collaboration among the Three Seas Initiative countries must also factor in the multifaceted threats to the security and stability of Central and Eastern European nations, which have a substantial impact on the viability of realising the core economic principles of the Initiative. The Three Seas Initiative member states granted Ukraine participating partner status at a summit in Riga in 2022. Interestingly, in 2023, more countries such as Greece (member) and Moldova (partner-participant) also joined the Three Seas initiative (Mihai, 2023). This shows that the initiative is seen positively by countries in this part of Europe.

The Three Seas project is primarily focused on building and upgrading transport and energy links between the Baltic, Black, Adriatic and Mediterranean seas, but it could also become a fascinating location for imagining some sort of common approach to building a new football powerhouse for the middle of the 21st century. This would address some of the major challenges presented to the modern football industry by the very same transformative processes, which meant that prominence was wrestled away from medium-sized innovative nations in favour of the big leagues in populous

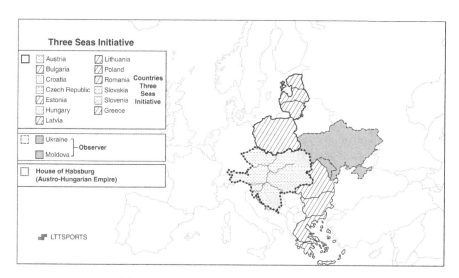

FIGURE 34.2   Map of the countries included in the Three Seas Initiative

Source: Based on LTT Sports (2023).

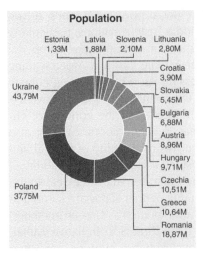 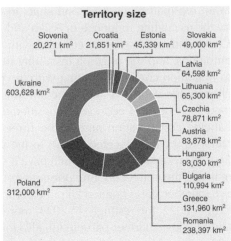

FIGURE 34.3 (a) Population and (b) territory size of the countries included in the Three Seas initiative and Ukraine

Source: Based on LTT Sports (2023).

and rich countries. With a market of about 160 million people, if also counting Ukraine, and a combined gross domestic product (GDP) of well over €2.5 trillion and set to continue growing, the economic and demographic bases are certainly there for an economy of scale approach to football business, similar to the EPL model. At the same time, arguably, apart from Poland, the countries comprising this region are not large enough individually to create the necessary conditions for significant long-term sporting and economic success, which makes a collaborative approach the obvious solution (Figure 34.2).

The chart (see Figure 34.3) displays the populations of individual countries that are members of the Three Seas Initiative and Ukraine. Ukraine (a partner-participant) and Poland have by far the largest populations, with Romania, Czech Republic and Greece also having over 10 million citizens. Similarly, in terms of territory, Ukraine and Poland are the largest. When considering all the countries, it must be acknowledged that both in terms of population and territory, this constitutes a very significant part of Europe, with a substantial demographic potential.

In Table 34.2, data regarding various economic indicators of the countries participating in the Three Seas Initiative has been compiled. Nominal GDP, GDP in terms of purchasing power parity (PPP) as well as these two indicators per capita have been presented. The highest nominal GDP can be found in Poland and Austria. If we take into account the per capita calculation of this indicator, Austria can be clearly identified as the wealthiest country, followed by Slovenia with an almost two times smaller nominal GDP per capita than Austria. Once again, summarising, it must be stated that all the countries collectively possess a

TABLE 34.2 Various GDP indicators of the countries included in the Three Seas Initiative

GDP in USD (2022)	Austria	Bulgaria	Croatia	Czechia	Estonia	Greece	Hungary	Latvia	Lithuania	Poland	Romania	Slovakia	Slovenia
GDP Nominal	471.40B	89.04B	70.96B	290.92B	38.10B	219.06B	178.79B	41.15B	70.33B	688.18B	301.26B	115.47B	62.18B
GDP PPP	614.31B	217.11B	155.62B	525.73B	62.80B	389.22B	405.80B	75.25B	137.11B	1625.23B	794.05B	203.47B	105.50B
GDP Nominal per capita	52.13K	13.77K	18.41K	27.64K	28.33K	20.73K	18.46K	21.85K	24.83K	18.32K	15.89K	21.26K	29.48K
GDP PPP per capita	67.93K	33.58K	40.38K	49.94K	46.70K	36.83K	41.91K	39.96K	48.40K	43.29K	41.89K	37.50K	50.03K

Source: Based on data from World Bank (2023).

substantial economic potential, which would be more than capable of supporting a top-quality football competition on the scale of the top-5 countries.

Additionally, we examined factors indicating the potential of football in the countries that are part of the Three Seas Initiative. Detailed data is presented in Table 34.3. We paid attention to when the national federation was established and when the first league season was played. It's worth noting that currently, only the Austrian Bundesliga is in the top 10 UEFA ranking, but a total of 13 clubs are in the top 100 UEFA rankings, not counting the ones from Ukraine or Moldova (another 3). Interestingly, the combined value of all players participating in the top leagues of Three Seas Initiative countries is €2.622 billion, while the combined value of players in the EPL is €11.040 billion (Transfermarkt, 2023). These numbers illustrate the gap between the best league in Europe and the other leagues, when they are operating individually.

How Could a Joint Competition Emerge?

Can a new Mitropa Initiative in parallel with the Three Seas solve the long-term challenges and open up a new period when football in Mittel Europa is once again at the forefront of the global game? Could, to some extent, a return to history and the creation of a joint competition among the countries of the Three Seas Initiative help in competing with the so-called Big Five leagues in Europe? The EPL has significantly widened the gap from other leagues in recent years, and currently, it seems that leagues in individual countries, especially those smaller in population and less affluent, have relatively small chances of competing in club football with the best in Europe. Despite the obvious advantages and potential, creating a transnational competition of this nature and size would, of course, come with very significant challenges, not least on the football governance level. In this case, there would be a need to engage with 13 separate football associations plus their respective leagues (in some cases), the continental governing body UEFA and the international governing body FIFA, as well as important stakeholders such as player unions and supporter groups.

The key to unlocking this opportunity will be in demonstrating to the respective national associations that sanctioning such a competition would bring them more benefits in the short, medium and long term than not sanctioning it, which would require a robust solidarity and redistribution mechanism to be put in place, in line with the European model of sport approach endorsed by the EU authorities. Having a pre-existing political and economic platform that brings all these countries together, in the shape of the Three Seas Initiative, could serve as a short cut to engaging the political leadership of the countries, if they would be willing to add sport development into the roadmap of the organisation.

TABLE 34.3 Various club football indicators of the countries included in the Three Seas initiative

	Austria	Bulgaria	Croatia	Czechia	Estonia	Greece	Hungary	Latvia	Lithuania	Poland	Romania	Slovakia	Slovenia
FA first year	1904	1923	1912	1901	1921	1926	1901	1921	1922	1919	1909	1928	1920
League first year	1911	1924	1992	1925	1992	1927	1901	1927	1991	1927	1909	1993	1991
No. of top league clubs	12	16	10	16	10	14	12	10	10	18	16	12	10
UEFA league ranking	10	27	18	15	47	19	25	35	38	24	26	28	31
Clubs in UEFA top-100 10-year ranking	3	1	1	2	0	2	1	0	0	1	1	1	0
Combined squad value in top league (€)	418.83	158.10	241.26	225.49	23.84	419.20	139.83	40.52	41.05	255.03	223.79	75.89	60.75
Average player value in top league (€)	1.20M	386K	847K	511K	99K	993K	416K	150K	159K	461K	437K	246K	234K

Source: Based on data from LTT Sports (2023).

Conclusion

The Three Seas Initiative, spanning from the Baltic to the Adriatic, Black and from 2023 also to the Mediterranean Seas, offers a platform for collaboration that could be extended to cover the sport industry. This initiative, comprising 13 European Union nations, carries to some extent the legacy of the former Habsburg monarchy, pivoting on its Danube spine. Ukraine's participation as a partner in 2022, and subsequent additions like Greece and Moldova, reflect growing interest and potential for a collective approach. While primarily focused on building and upgrading transport and energy links, the Three Seas Initiative also holds the potential to catalyse a common approach towards building a new football powerhouse in Central Europe, overcoming the problem of being comprised mostly of smaller markets, which individually do not have the capacity to compete with the best leagues. With a market of approximately 160 million people and a combined GDP exceeding €2.5 trillion, the economic and demographic foundation is solid. However, individual countries and their football ecosystems may need to align together to create the conditions for sustained sporting and economic success. While challenges persist, the Three Seas Initiative presents a promising opportunity to rekindle the spirit of cooperation. By leveraging shared experiences and resources, this region could emerge as a formidable player in both economic development and football on the global stage. The potential is substantial, and with concerted effort, Mittel Europa may once again lead the way in the beautiful game.

References

3 Seas 1 Opportunity (2023). *Three Seas*. Available at: https://3s1o.org/en/conference/three-seas [Accessed 30 October 2023].

Adelugba, R. (2023). *Is the Premier League Too Powerful — And If So, Why?* Available at: https://breakingthelines.com/opinion/is-the-premier-league-too-powerful-and-if-so-why/ [Accessed 31 October 2023].

Cook, W. (2018). *A century on from the collapse of the Habsburg empire, could Austria be on the brink once more?* Available at: https://www.independent.co.uk/news/long_reads/vienna-habsburg-empire-collapse-1918-europe-2018-eurozone-eu-a8398646.html [Accessed 31 October 2023].

D'Avanzo, M. (2020). *History of the European International Cup 1927–1960*. Available at: https://sportsmemories.be/Book.aspx?id=24781.

First Vienna FC (2023). *Club History | First Vienna FC 1894*. Available at: https://www.firstviennafc.at/vereinsgeschichte.html?lang=en [Accessed 31 October 2023].

Gottfried Fuchs (2012). *Before The 'D'…Association Football around the world, 1863–1937: Austria/Habsburg Monarchy – Challenge Cup 1897–98*. Available at: https://gottfriedfuchs.blogspot.com/2012/08/austriahabsburg-monarchy-challenge-cup.html [Accessed 31 October 2023].

Hyne, A. (2019). *Jimmy Hogan : The Greatest Football Coach Ever?* La Vergne: Lightning Source.

Iorwerth, H., Tomkins, P. and Riley, G. (2018). Financial doping in the English Premier League. *Sport, Ethics and Philosophy, 12*(3), 272–291. https://doi.org/10.1080/175 11321.2017.1351484.

Judson, P. M. (2016) *The Habsburg Empire, The Habsburg Empire*. Harvard University Press. https://doi.org/10.2307/J.CTVJSF5RQ.

LTT Sports (2022). *Pitchside Monitor: Recognising Player Values, and Interview with Eric Abidal*. Available at: https://www.linkedin.com/pulse/what-do-you-think-biggest-unrealised-resource-football-industry-/ [Accessed 12 November 2023].

LTT Sports (2023). *Pitchside Monitor: Habsburg Empire and Football: A Story for the Ages*. Available at: https://www.linkedin.com/pulse/can-new-mitropa-initiative-parallel-three-seas-bring-football/ [Accessed 12 November 2023].

Marcotti, G. (2022). *Why the Premier League's success goes deeper than its star power, competitiveness or upsets*. Available at: https://www.espn.com/soccer/story/_/id/37632203/why-premier-league-success-goes-deeper-star-power-competitiveness-upsets [Accessed 31 October 2023].

Miatkowski, J. and Owsiański, J. (2022). *1927. Ten pierwszy sezon ligowy*. Poznań: Bogucki.

Mihai, C. (2023). *Three Seas Initiative to enlarge with Greece says Romanian president –EURACTIV.com*. Available at: https://www.euractiv.com/section/politics/news/three-seas-initiative-to-enlarge-with-greece-says-romanian-president/ [Accessed 30 October 2023].

Porter, J. (2021). *Bela Guttmann and the European Curse That Could Last a Century for Benfica*. Available at: https://www.thesportsman.com/features/bela-guttmann-and-the-european-curse-that-could-last-a-century-for-benfica [Accessed 31 October 2023].

Transfermarkt (2023). *Premier League*. Available at: https://www.transfermarkt.pl/premier-league/startseite/wettbewerb/GB1 [Accessed 31 October 2023].

UEFA (2023). *The European Club Footballing Landscape*. Available at: https://editorial.uefa.com/resources/027e-174740f39cc6-d205dd2e86bf-1000/ecfl_bm_report_2022_high_resolution_.pdf.

Wojtaszyn, D. (2017). Mitropa-Cup. Kreowanie koncepcji politycznej poprzez sport. *Przegląd Zachodni, 4*(365), 187–196.

World Bank (2023). *GDP*. Available at: https://data.worldbank.org/indicator/NY.GDP.PCAP.PP.CD [Accessed 30 October 2023].

Young, A. (2020). *Gusztáv Sebes' Hungary 1953 Magical Magyars*. Available at: https://www.passion4fm.com/gusztav-sebes-hungary-1953-magical-magyars-football-manager-tactics/ [Accessed 31 October 2023].

35

FOOTBALL AND FORCED MIGRATION

Sicily and the Central Mediterranean Route

Alessio Norrito

Introduction

We are on the 65th minute of Bologna vs Atalanta (20 March 2022, Serie A, season 2021/2022), when the coach of the team from Bergamo decides to make a substitution. Luis Muriel out, Moustapha Cissé in. It does not take long for the match to change, as on the 82nd minute the youngster scores the winning goal for Atalanta. The next day, the newspapers highlight the fairytale goal of Cissé, and his unexpected winning debut. We don't have to go so far back in time to understand why this is a fairytale. In January of the same year, two months before his scoring debut, Cissé was playing in the 8th tier of Italian football. If we go back to September 2019, we see more nuances of this fairytale, where a 16-year-old Cisse' arrives on a makeshift boat in Sicily, after having crossed the desert and the Mediterranean Sea. After the death of his father, he decided to leave Conakry and embark on the deadly journey to Europe to rebuild his life.

Cisse' is one of more than 2.4 million people who have crossed the Mediterranean Sea on makeshift boats to reach Europe since 2015 (UNHCR, 2023). His situation of escaping persecution or life-threatening poverty is shared by many asylum-seekers, who see themselves as holding a brighter future in Europe (McMahon and Sigona, 2018). It is fair to say that football has changed the life of Moustapha, a fairytale narrative that is often associated with the transformative power of sport (Reid, 2017). Nonetheless, a critical outlook of the transformative power of sport is to also look at those who may have been left behind while the game develops in its social, economic, political, and overall global prowess (Giulianotti, 2011; Giulianotti and Robertson, 2012). Since 2013, more than 28,000 people have died in the Central Mediterranean

DOI: 10.4324/9781003473671-40

Route (UNHCR ODP, 2023). This number reports the confirmed deaths at sea and is expected to be a significant undercount, due to the difficulty of counting and fully accounting for the dynamics of boat accidents and drowning (IOM, 2023). This chapter will focus on the harsh realities that are found on the other side of the coin, in relation to the transformative and aspirational power of global football. Specifically, it looks at how the geopolitical expansion of football can contribute to the decision-making processes of asylum-seekers crossing the Mediterranean and the dangers that the attractiveness of European football produces in a global context.

This chapter is elaborated from a larger research project conducted from 2020 to 2023. The study was informed by a process of data collection consisting of interviews and focus groups involving 29 male refugees and 5 non-refugee experts, as well as several site visits across Sicily with further informal conversations and qualitative observations. Through the format of an instrumental case study (Stake, 1995), the project sought to understand the value of football for the resettlement of refugees. In this chapter, I will draw from the diary entries written as part of the site visits and related qualitative observations, as these were written with the aim of pursuing tacit knowledge, and best account for the contextual of the research. Particularly, diary entries were taken to include knowledge and observations on the geopolitical macrosystems that would influence the value of football for refugee resettlement. Through a purposeful thematic analysis driven by the data collected and the existing theorization of football as a force for good (Fereday and Muir-Cochrane, 2006), I have sought to link individual experiences with geopolitical forces in the Mediterranean. The following paragraphs present these two themes, before drawing conclusions on their interconnectedness.

Chasing Global Fairytales

It is perhaps in Lampedusa where this narration should start, the southern-most Sicilian island where most makeshift boats attempt to land. The refugee camp of Lampedusa is an island within an island, a secluded building within a small plot of land in the middle of the Mediterranean Sea, that is also a popular tourist destination (Melotti et al., 2018). The purpose of its refugee camp is that of a temporary location for people that have just disembarked from the Mediterranean crossing, a place where to wait while their fate is decided by a regulated allocation (or expulsion) process (Garelli and Tazzioli, 2016). Within this secluded, highly liminal space, football makes its presence felt. People tend to disembark with Italian football shirts, or with scarves and apparel from their country of origin. In a journey where they cannot bring much along, they choose football to represent themselves (Norrito and Mason, 2023). Some shirt choices are representative of the geopolitical distortion that football creates. A social worker explained that once they saw a person disembark with a S.S. Lazio shirt, a team that is infamous for holding a neo-fascist faction of supporters among their ranks (Testa and Armstrong, 2010). I thought of it as an important contradiction, of someone who knows football so much to choose Lazio as the way to present himself, and yet does not know of the ties that some supporters have with discriminatory ideologies.

I would have found an answer to this question later on, reflecting on a series of interview that I had in a refugee camp in mainland Sicily. The more I spoke with participants, the more I realized that it is about the man that is wearing the shirt, and not the shirt itself. Darby et al. (2022) talk about football idols and how young people try to emulate these idols that share the same aspirational masculine characteristic. They also want to be role models and become heroes in the community, emulating the success of fellow black players such as Didier Drogba and Samuel Eto'o (Giardina, 2013; Künzler and Poli, 2013). In this research, however, more contemporary idols have been presented as examples. Some reported idols replicated the physicality often stereotyped to black players (Kilvington, 2021; McCarthy et al., 2003), yet presented European examples. In this sense, Sergio Ramos was a very popular idol. Others would find idols for both the inside and the outside of the pitch, such as Sadio Mané or Marcus Rashford, expressing how they would like to replicate their success and give back to their community. There was no on-field relation, just the direct belief that the footballer status can bring change. That of the footballer status is an important point of reflection in relation to the power of football. The belief is that footballers bring change, not necessarily football. And they do so through their game-changing fairytales.

The issue with fairytales is that, as the term suggests, these are unlikely to happen and are sometimes a work of fantasy. When the power of football is pushed as a fairytale maker, there is the concrete risk of evangelistic and mythopoeic claims (Coalter, 2013). Similarly, as shown, it is within these fairytales that individuals find hope in sport (Stone, 2018). The purpose of this chapter is not to discuss the tension between the power of hope for change but to report on its existence as an important premise to fully consider what drives people to cross a deadly sea with a football shirt on. This is a phenomenon that the regulating forces of the global game are aware of Gianni Infantino, head of FIFA, suggested at a Parliamentary Assembly of the Council of Europe that "we need to find ways to include the whole world to give hope to Africans so that they don't need to cross the Mediterranean in order to find maybe a better life but, more probably, death in the sea" (MacInnes, 2022). The controversial use of a humanitarian tragedy by FIFA was later revisited, with Infantino justifying that his words were taken out of context and were not directly related to football. Nonetheless, it still shows that the issue has reached the highest peaks of the sport.

Young male asylum-seekers do not leave their countries because of football, but rather because of the differing, complex, and life-threatening conditions that they are found within (Idemudia and Boehnke, 2020). However, once they make the decision to leave their country of origin, they may make the decision of choosing where to go. The data shows that the attractiveness of football represents one of the reasons why asylum-seekers could choose Europe over other destinations (Norrito et al., 2023). The attractiveness of football has reached also the most deprived settings of the world, showing its truly global nature in the case of refugees who end up being in Sicily. But just like Sicily becomes more global through the bottom-up arrival of refugees and asylum-seekers (Melotti et al., 2018), the island is also experiencing a top-down globalization that is currently happening through football.

Global from the Top, Harmful at the Bottom?

Indeed, football teams in Sicily have started entering the radar of global football corporations and, as a result, they are losing local ownership in favour of global players. Palermo F.C. is now part of Emirates and Chinese-owned City Football Group (CFG), while Catania FC is owned by the Italian-Australian entrepreneur Ross Pelligra. Both groups support a multi-club ownership model, meaning that Palermo and Catania are part of a wider portfolio of teams owned by the same group. While possessing an already global following, also as a result of many years of Sicilian emigration (Casati, 2018; Reeder, 2001), this is the very first time that Sicilian teams have belonged to truly global entities. CFG owns several teams across the World, with Manchester City being their flagship team and one of the most successful clubs in contemporary times. Palermo F.C. is the very first club the group owns in Italy. In the case of Catania FC, Pelligra took over after the old team was declared bankrupt and therefore rebuilt the team from the fourth division. While not with the same magnitude and public interest of CFG, Pelligra was also on the verge of acquiring Adelaide FC, has submitted a bid to acquire Perth Glory in the summer of 2023, and has investments in basketball and golf in Australia. The case for CFG and Pelligra to be included in this analysis is to show that this attractiveness does not come only from a bottom-up approach, where fairytales are made by the story of successful asylum-seekers. Instead, the "fairylands" of global football are expanding and moving geographically closer to contexts that are affected by forced migration. This result is a direct effect of politics of expansion that are occurring not only at multinational club levels but also from an overall governmental approach.

One of the statutory objective of FIFA is to "improve the game constantly and promote it globally". A second one is to "make football work for society". The vision for 2023, and what can be considered a mission statement of FIFA, is that of "making football truly global". Therefore, it would be unfair and uninformed to leave the burden of making sense of football for change just to refugees and asylum-seekers. There is an underlying geopolitical strategy of expansion at both organizational and club level that ultimately influences the attractiveness of football. The more football becomes attractive, the more it will attract people to its epicentres. And when the promise of football is that of change, it is only natural that the sport will attract those that most desperately need change in their lives, and see themselves as part of the game.

This chapter has shown the connection between football and forced migration, showing how the ongoing attractiveness and globalization of the sport may influence the decision-making of asylum-seekers and refugees in the Central Mediterranean. Football should have a more critical engagement in relation to its association with change, both at a regulatory and organizational level. Responsibility should be taken in making sure that the improvement of the game better aligns with necessities in society, by considering the mythopoeic perception that football creates. Particularly, it should be further emphasized that football players and individual fandom play a central role in shaping the perception of what transformational change through football looks like. In the case of refugees, this chapter shines a light on the fact that the attractiveness of football may play a role in the Mediterranean crossing. However, more research needs to be done to underpin the role of football as a driver for forced migration, particularly against other competing or complementary drivers. Further understanding is a necessary step to further harness and facilitate fairytales to happen over tragedies, and for football to find an appropriate, measured, and critical role in contributing to positive change in the context of forced migration.

I started this chapter with the story of Moustapha Cisse', a story that has eventually become a fairytale, an example of the *life* that football can give. Yet, to emphasize the necessity of understanding the interplay that football has with dangerous forms of migration, I will conclude with a story of *death* in relation to football. That is the story of Mory Karamoko, who gave his life so that his brother Cherif could make the journey to Italy. Cherif has written a book about their journey, titled "Salvati tu che hai un sogno" (2021). I brought the book with me often while doing fieldwork, as a detailed and emotional narrative of the Central Mediterranean Route and the people within. The title of the book can be roughly translated as "Save yourself, you have a dream", and it was the last sentence that Mory said to his younger brother, before disappearing between the waves and leaving him hanging on a floating piece of the makeshift boat that just failed them. That dream that his brother had was to become a footballer. And while Mory's memory lives thanks to the incredible activism of his brother, there are many other stories in the Mediterranean Sea that we will never get to hear.

References

Casati, N. (2018). How cities shape refugee centres: 'Deservingness' and 'good aid' in a Sicilian town. *Journal of Ethnic and Migration Studies, 44*(5), 792–808.

Coalter, F. (2013). *Sport for Development: What Game Are We Playing?* Abingdon: Routledge.

Darby, P., Esson, J. and Ungruhe, C. (2022). *African Football Migration: Aspirations, Experiences and Trajectories.* Manchester: Manchester University Press.

Fereday, J. and Muir-Cochrane, E. (2006). Demonstrating rigor using thematic analysis: a hybrid approach of inductive and deductive coding and theme development. *International Journal of Qualitative Methods, 5*(1), 80–92.

Garelli, G. and Tazzioli, M. (2016). The EU hotspot approach at Lampedusa. *Open Democracy, 26,* 2016.

Giardina, M. D. (2013). One day, one goal? PUMA, corporate philanthropy and the cultural politics of brand 'Africa'. In R. Field and B. Kidd (Eds.), *Forty Years of Sport and Social Change, 1968–2008* (pp. 130–142). Abingdon: Routledge.

Giulianotti, R. (2011). The sport, development and peace sector: a model of four social policy domains. *Journal of Social Policy, 40*(4), 757–776.

Giulianotti, R. and Robertson, R. (2012). Mapping the global football field: a sociological model of transnational forces within the world game. *The British Journal of Sociology, 63*(2), 216–240.

Idemudia, E. and Boehnke, K. (2020). *Psychosocial Experiences of African Migrants in Six European Countries: A Mixed Method Study* (p. 237). Springer Nature.

IOM (2023). Mediterranean | Missing Migrants Project. Retrieved 26 October 2023, from https://missingmigrants.iom.int/region/mediterranean.

Karamoko, C. (2021). *Salvati tu che hai un sogno.* Milan: Mondadori.

Kilvington, D. (2021). 'He needs pulling down a peg or two': assessing online fan responses to racialized discourse in sports broadcasting. *Northern Lights: Film & Media Studies Yearbook, 19*(1), 25–41.

Künzler, D. and Poli, R. (2013). The African footballer as visual object and figure of success: Didier Drogba and social meaning. In S. Baller, G. Miescher and C. Rassool (Eds.), *Global Perspectives on Football in Africa* (pp. 69–83). Abingdon: Routledge.

MacInnes, P. (2022). Fifa president: more World Cups could save African migrants from death in the sea. *The Guardian Online.* Retrieved 26 October 2023, from https://www.theguardian.com/football/2022/jan/26/fifa-gianni-infantino-biennial-world-cup-could-save-african-migrants-from-death-in-the-sea.

McCarthy, D., Jones, R. L. and Potrac, P. (2003). Constructing images and interpreting realities: the case of the black soccer player on television. *International Review for the Sociology of Sport, 38*(2), 217–238.

McMahon, S. and Sigona, N. (2018). Navigating the Central Mediterranean in a time of 'crisis': disentangling migration governance and migrant journeys. *Sociology, 52*(3), 497–514.

Melotti, M., Ruspini, E. and Marra, E. (2018). Migration, tourism and peace: Lampedusa as a social laboratory. *Anatolia, 29*(2), 215–224.

Norrito, A. and Mason, C. (2023). Lampedusa, football and COVID-19: transitions at the border and the role of sport. *Contemporary Social Science, 18*(1), 26–40.

Norrito, A., Michelini, E., Giulianotti, R. and Mason, C. (2023). 'Refugee footballers': a socioecological exploration of forced migrants in the Italian and German elite football system. *International Review for the Sociology of Sport, 59*(1), 119–138.

Reeder, L. (2001). Conflict across the Atlantic: women, family and mass male migration in Sicily, 1880–1920. *International Review of Social History, 46*(3), 371–391.

Reid, G. (2017). A fairytale narrative for community sport? Exploring the politics of sport social enterprise. *International Journal of Sport Policy and Politics, 9*(4), 597–611.

Stake, R. E. (1995). *The Art of Case Study Research*. Thousand Oaks: Sage.

Stone, C. (2018). Utopian community football? Sport, hope and belongingness in the lives of refugees and asylum seekers. *Leisure Studies*, *37*(2), 171–183.

Testa, A. and Armstrong, G. (2010). *Football, Fascism and Fandom: The Ultras of Italian Football*. London: A&C Black.

UNHCR (2023). Mediterranean Situation – Italy. Retrieved 26 October 2023, from https://data2.unhcr.org/en/situations/mediterranean/location/5205.

UNHCR Operational Data Portal (ODP) (2023). Retrieved 26 October 2023, from https://data.unhcr.org/en/dataviz/95?sv=0&geo=0#_ga=2.240583043.1604276434.1657720311-1466244015.1602252904.

INDEX

Note: – *Italicized* page references refer to figures, **bold** references refer to tables, and page references with "n" refer to endnotes.

Printed and bound by CPI Group (UK) Ltd, Croydon, CR0 4YY

03/12/2024

01799555-0016